THE
ESSENTIAL GARDENER

STEFAN BUCZACKI

The
ESSENTIAL
GARDENER

WITH PHOTOGRAPHS

BY

ANDREW LAWSON

Grange
BOOKS

THIS EDITION PRODUCED BY CARLTON BOOKS

This edition published 1993 by Grange Books
An Imprint of Grange Books PLC
The Grange
Grange Yard
LONDON
SE1 3AG

First published in Great Britain in 1991 by
Sidgwick & Jackson Limited

Copyright © Dr Stefan Buczacki 1991
including photographs on pages 50, 64, 75, 78, 79, 80, 139, 173

All other photographs © Andrew Lawson 1991

Illustrations © Rob Dalton 1991

ISBN 1 85627 491 8

Printed in Singapore

CONTENTS

PART THREE: STOCKING YOUR GARDEN

INTRODUCTION

THIS is a personal book. It contains only facts and information that I have been able to verify from my own experience. This alone will set it apart from many other gardening books, but rather greater justification than this is required if yet another horticultural volume is to be offered to a public already faced with dozens more each year. It is a general gardening book in that it covers most of the vast spectrum of subjects that the word gardening embraces. But this too has been attempted countless times before. Where I am sure this volume differs is that, unlike any other general gardening book, it contains only the information that I believe the average gardener of today actually requires.

In a sense, therefore, it is as easy to describe the book by what it does not contain as by what it does. I have assumed that the reader will be a gardener who is keen on his or her hobby and has a moderate amount of leisure time, but also has no wish to spend all that time actually doing gardening tasks. Enjoying the garden is at least as important as creating it. You will not, therefore, find details of how to mix your own composts or create a bridge graft. Nor will you find an assumption that you wish to raise all of your own plants from seed, want to feed a family of ten from the results of your labours or desire a lawn to rival that of the local bowling club. Conversely, you *will* be told where to place your herb bed, how to hide your washing line, how important are organic fertilisers and relatively how unimportant most pesticides. Above all, my purpose is to show you how to enjoy your garden. I believe that the book contains everything that 80 per cent of gardeners will ever need to know; and 80 per cent of everything that all gardeners ever need to know.

PART ONE

Creating Your Garden

Living with your garden

ONE of the most difficult in-built attitudes to overcome when discussing garden planning is the one that considers the garden as something wholly separate and distinct in place, form and function from the house. The house is your home; the garden is something that you glimpse through the windows. Although it may provide you with vegetables and fruit for the kitchen and cut flowers for the dining-room table, in no sense do you live in it. This is a peculiarly north temperate, and especially British, attitude, for in warmer parts of continental Europe, in the United States and in Australia, for instance, the garden is seen and used as an outdoor room or, if it is large enough, almost as an outdoor home. Admittedly, many of the most attractive and desirable features of the English garden style, such as the herbaceous or mixed border, do not lend themselves readily to having people wandering around within them, but they can nonetheless be admired and appreciated all the more if the people concerned have other reasons for being elsewhere in the garden. The real reason that the British do not live more in their gardens is the weather – only in regions where reasonably predictable warm weather occurs regularly will people think in any sense of actually living outdoors.

A well designed family garden, showing siting of the following elements: French windows leading to paved patio with small herb garden; patio paved with natural stone, containing formal pool; lawn with removable rotary washing line; removable swing on bark chippings, screened by climbers; compost boxes screened by rose-covered pergola; 'family' fruit trees; vegetable plot screened by strategically placed shrubs and climbers.

But a relatively short and unpredictable summer need not be a bar to at least some outdoor living, and there are several ways in which parts of the garden can be used to provide the wherewithal for this – on a grand scale, a swimming pool can be the lure, on a smaller one, a summerhouse and a barbecue. Appropriately positioned patios and pergolas have their part to play too, while garden lighting can be both enhancing and inviting. Even a conservatory will take you part way into the garden, although I consider this an extension to the house rather than a real garden feature.

Even in a large garden, a swimming pool can dominate through its colour and shape as well as its size. It will almost inevitably be positioned near the house and the most important design aspect to take into account when choosing one is to maintain a sense of scale with the remainder of the garden. In many gardens, a small plunge pool is the most realistic answer to make best use of space, although it may seem disproportionately costly.

Summerhouses, of course, must be placed where they will capture the maximum sunlight (although window blinds will be found useful too) and care will be needed to ensure that their presence doesn't conflict with the needs of sun-loving shrubs, vegetables, greenhouses or other warmth-requiring garden components. Most summerhouses appear very stark because there seems to be a general reluctance to plant climbers against them. My first action on purchasing a summerhouse is to clothe the structure with trellis and plant such perfumed climbers as roses, jasmine or even honeysuckle (although it is a little undisciplined) to scramble over it. Be sure to have a small paved area in front of the summerhouse on which to stand chairs and a table. Indeed, a paved area or patio, whether or not it is linked to a summerhouse, is a most important feature for outdoor living. It too should be placed where it will receive sun at the time of day it is most likely to be used and should preferably be close enough to the house so that carrying drinks and food to it will not be a chore. And it must be large enough; the area required to accommodate a table and surrounding chairs is almost inevitably greater than you imagine, for there must be room to draw the chairs back from the table without falling off the edge of the patio. Set out your furniture first before defining the limits of the area.

Barbecues are an essential adjunct to any form of outdoor life – and there is much to be said for cooking food outdoors on a barbecue even if the weather is too cold for it to be eaten there, and it must be returned to the house. My strong personal preference is for a portable barbecue. This may be of whatever type takes your fancy (although, for me, no gas or electrical appliance will ever compare with one using real charcoal, ignited in the traditional way). Having portable equipment means that no design constraints are imposed on your garden, although if your need is for something larger than can be readily transported and you must have a fixed barbecue site, this should be well away from overhanging trees. It can be decorated with plants in terracotta pots when not in use.

Garden lighting is perhaps the least appreciated of all the ways that can be used to enhance outdoor living. It can fill two quite separate roles. Placed alongside steps, at dark corners or close to pools, lighting can greatly improve garden safety. But it can also be used to bring a garden to life at night – carefully positioned and directed spotlights can give dramatic impact to trees, shrubs or other large plants and to statues and similar garden ornaments. Use a modern low voltage system with stick or umbrella pattern lamps, which are versatile and easy to install. Try several different positions before deciding on the best for your own garden.

Far too frequently, I hear the complaint, 'Of course, our garden will never be really attractive because . . .' and there then follows a list of excuses, such as the position of the fuel bunker, oil tank, washing line and sundry other unattractive necessities of life. Surprisingly few of these substantial objects cannot be moved – modern rotary clothes lines, of course, are easily stowed away after use; and because the previous owner installed the oil tank in precisely the spot where your sweet peas would best be situated is no reason for you to tolerate the same. Even when there is no possibility of moving them, unsightly fuel tanks and bunkers can be screened by erecting trellis around them – although be sure to leave a gap of 60–100 cm (2–3 ft) around oil tanks to permit the free flow of air and allow access for painting. Special rules may apply to the erection of screening around liquid petroleum gas containers which are usually the property of the gas supplying company.

Garden design and planning

MOST gardens appear as they do more by accident than design. There are two main reasons for this. First, a gardener taking over an established garden is generally loath to change the existing layout – or at least loath to change it very quickly or extensively. This may be because of lack of time, lack of inclination or simply lack of appreciation of how significantly his or her gardening life could be improved by relatively small but well thought-out design changes. And second, on a new site, the financial limitations consequent on having just purchased a house, or a belief that the task is just too daunting, prevent many new gardeners from planning their garden in its entirety. They are content to let things evolve piecemeal. (Interestingly, nonetheless, a new trend in some areas has been for builders or developers to offer a professionally planned garden as part of an overall house-purchase package. Even if you are given this opportunity, however, it is enormously helpful to be table to talk to the garden designer in his own language.)

I hope that I can persuade you that planning your garden is really a matter of applied commonsense. I find it useful to think of the key elements of garden design in the form of three questions: how do you make the most of what your garden site offers? How do you make your garden function effectively for your needs? And (something almost every owner wants) how do you make your garden appear larger than it really is?

First, therefore, what does your garden site offer you as a garden planner? Your soil will dictate to a greater or lesser extent the types of plant that you can grow – to a greater extent if it is markedly acid or alkaline; to a lesser extent if it is merely very sandy or clayey – but there are probably no actual garden features that any soil prevents you from having if you are prepared to compromise slightly on the choice of plants.

Whilst many gardens appear as they do more by accident than design, careful planning will ensure the most attractive and functional blend of formal and informal components; and will ensure that features with special site requirements, such as a pool, are placed in the best position.

The topography of the site – the humps, hollows and slopes – can influence the ease with which digging or lawn mowing can be performed, but should be considered positively too. A slope is always the best position for a rock garden; the top of a slope is the best place, in an overall sloping garden, for a fairly formal pool while the foot of a slope is best for an informal one, where natural spilling-over of water at the edges enables the margins to be softened with bog and waterside plants. The base of a hollow, or even the foot of a slope, is often a poor place for a fruit garden because dense, cold, frosty air accumulates there and will damage the blossom. Such a site is also no place for slightly tender or early flushing or blossoming ornamentals. Conversely, the top of a slope is often a windy place and this too will make for an unproductive fruit garden because pollinating insects are blown away.

The only existing plants that you should seriously consider keeping in your garden design are trees, for they are the only types of vegetation that cannot be moved or quickly replaced. Many very good gardens are largely designed around one or more mature trees, for these generally dictate where much of the light and shadow lies and, because they draw heavily on the food and water reserves of the soil, also dictate where you *cannot* place vegetable and fruit gardens or mixed borders. The presence of trees, especially deciduous trees, will also influence the positioning of the pools and the greenhouse – neither of which benefit from shade or falling leaves. But does your garden have special and unusual natural features? Among those that I consider valuable and important enough to justify reorganising other garden activities are a natural outcrop of rock that offers you the chance to have a *real* rock garden; and a stream, or even a wet ditch, around which you can plant a bog garden.

There are two aspects to making your garden function effectively for you. The first is to position features thoughtfully. A vegetable garden must have as

Not all garden design considerations are very obvious. One of the least appreciated aspects of pond positioning, for instance, is that when they are placed very close to planted areas, as here, care must be exercised to ensure that fertilizer is not sprayed or washed into the water.

much sun as possible, yet as it is not usually a particularly attractive feature (but see p. 113), it should be carefully screened to separate it visually from the rest of the garden, without the screen itself casting much shade. Positioning the vegetable plot on the southern or western boundaries of the garden is the easiest way to do this. Conversely, a herb garden is functional and attractive, and full advantage of both aspects can be taken by placing it as close to the kitchen as possible. When positioning purely ornamental beds and borders, be sure to place them where they can be appreciated at the time of year in which they will be at their best. This is most important for a shrubbery grown for winter colour – there is little point in placing it at the furthest point from the house where no one will venture in winter time.

The second way in which your garden can be made to function well is to ensure that it is designed for labour-saving maintenance. On p. 49 I discuss various ways in which the choice of plants and use of particular techniques can save you time and trouble but the basic design of the garden is significant too. The single most annoying and time-consuming gardening task is trying to mow twists and corners of a lawn that are too small for the mower and are therefore either left untidy or must be cut laboriously with shears. A gravel path adjoining a lawn is visually lovely, but you must be prepared occasionally to brush stones from the grass. A gravel path adjoining a vegetable plot, however, can be a nightmare as you walk from soil to gravel and pick up vast quantities of the path on your muddy footwear.

Creating an illusion of space is not difficult in most gardens, and very rewarding too. Give the impression that there are a great many plants in your garden whilst at the same time filling relatively little of the area with them. The simplest way to achieve this apparent conjuring trick is to keep the centre of the garden open (with lawn is the easiest way) and to confine most of your plants to the periphery. This also has the advantage of obscuring the boundary fences or wall, so making it impossible to see where your property ends. This effect can be improved still further if there is open space beyond your garden (fields or parkland for instance) that can be glimpsed through gaps in these border plantings. And make good use of curves in lawns, beds, borders and paths to suggest that there is something beyond what can actually being seen. Placing a focal point (for example an ornament or statue) so that it is glimpsed through an archway or a gap between two plantings also helps to take the eye a long way, and enhance the feeling of distance.

Once you have decided that your garden would benefit from a degree of design or re-design, how many of the changes must be worked out in detail beforehand? I have a suspicion that many would-be designers of their own gardens are put off by the detailed scale plans (often beautifully executed in watercolours) that they see in books and magazines. These are fine for professionals and theorists but I have never seen such a plan translated into practice without considerable modification. I find it much more effective simply to equip myself with several sheets of plain paper on which the outline of the garden is shown, place myself at a vantage point (usually a bedroom window) and start to sketch in the various features that I want to retain or introduce. The most important single feature is a focal point, but the precise positioning of this can only be decided from ground level when you look at the garden from the various possible viewpoints – windows, house doorways, gates or paths. In a large garden, you will probably require more than one focal point to provide visual satisfaction from different spots. It really does all boil down eventually to commonsense.

Colouring your garden

Whilst the combining of plant colours offers almost infinite variations, some almost invariably look right whilst some invariably do not. I am particularly attracted by blends of yellow and blue, as here, where the yellow and black of Rudbeckia fulgida deamii *is a perfect companion for the double blue flowers of the Michaelmas daisy* Aster novi-belgii *'Marie Ballard'.*

Y OU need only walk into other people's homes, let alone their gardens, to see that individuals' concepts of which colour combinations give us pleasure and satisfaction vary enormously. I once had to judge a garden in which the sum total of the plants used was around 4,000 African and French marigolds in all imaginable (and a few unimaginable) shades, across the vast spectrum from orange to yellow. I shall never again seek to tell people which flower colours they should choose. What I can do, nonetheless, is to give some suggestions that may not have occurred to you and also to indicate the colour blends that to most people have the effects of restfulness, assertiveness or other states of mind.

For reasons that have more, I think, to do with human psychology than gardening or art, we perceive reds and oranges as fiery, hot and aggressive, while blues, greens and whites are cool and restful. But the effects of different colour combinations can be demonstrated most clearly by looking at the spectral colours of white light (red, orange, yellow, green, blue, indigo, violet) arranged in circular form. Adjacent colours are then seen to harmonise,

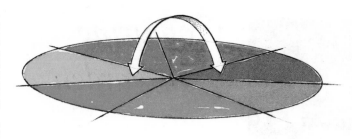
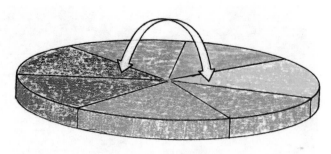

In this colour spectrum, it is evident that the colours immediately facing each other on opposite sides make the most striking clashes.

while colours on opposite sides of the circle make strong contrasts which some people will find unattractive. Seeing the juxtaposition of some shades of green with some violets or of some oranges with some blues, for instance, will immediately rule them out of many people's gardening (or home decorating) considerations.

It is also helpful to realise that certain colours are easier to achieve at some times of the year than at others. If you think of the early spring, for instance, you will realise that it is predominantly a time of yellows and oranges – crocuses, aconites and daffodils are among the most obvious flowers. The height of summer is very largely coloured by reds, pinks and whites while the autumn brings browns and oranges again, with a particular scarcity of blues. Largely, these seasonal trends reflect the differing seasonal frequencies of the pollinating insects that the flowers are seeking to attract, some insects being more attracted than others to certain colours (although of course some of the colours, tones and patterns that are 'seen' by insects are not visible to our eyes at all). But, in essence, it helps to follow nature's inclinations rather than fight them; if your desire, for instance, is for a blue autumn border, you will be creating an inordinate degree of frustration for yourself. Remember, too, that some colours are very much more readily seen from a distance than are others; even a large bed of dark blues and purple will vanish without trace when viewed from a house window some 30 metres (33 yards) distant.

There is an apparently limitless range of colours in a garden at the height of summer, and then the variety seems to drop as the number of plants in flower tails off towards winter. In fact, however, the range of flower colour available in the dead of winter is just as great; it simply requires rather more careful hunting through nursery catalogues and reference books to find representative flowers for each shade. But despite the huge range of flower colour overall, the types of coloured pigment that cause it fall into only two main groups. On the one hand are the anthocyanins that are responsible for blues and reds, and on the other the carotenoids that are revealed as creams, yellows and oranges, occasionally verging on red. Chemically, they are very distinct and this has a bearing on the appearance of the flowers containing them. The carotenoids are chemically stable and give rise to flowers of fairly uniform colour that change little in hue throughout their lives. Anthocyanins are much more 'fluid' and both red and blue flowers generally display some of the other colour and also change as they age – red flowers very often become bluish with the passage of time.

Colour can be used in your garden in two main ways. Either you group together plants predominantly of one colour, or you blend them. At its extreme, the single colour approach is exemplified by the white gardens, red gardens and large silver beds or golden borders so beloved of some of the great garden designers of the past. In many ways, these are easy to create, for it is fairly simple to browse through your plant catalogues and produce lists

of white or red varieties (remembering that foliage of appropriate colour can be as valuable as flowers) and then check their relative heights, spreads and flowering times. I prefer, however, when using the single-colour approach, not to try to employ that colour to the total exclusion of all others. Rather, I prefer to impose the white, red or yellow on a background of green, envisaging the garden or border as a green canvas on which spots or large blotches of the other colour are placed. Apart from considering this aesthetically more subtle, I find it avoids the difficulty – which you would have in all but a white border or garden – of blending together the innumerable different shades of the selected colour.

But in the more usual instance of creating a bed, border or garden of mixed colours my rule book can be no more than a collection of personal suggestions. With formal bedding, a striking contrast (call it a colour clash if you wish) between adjacent plants or groups of plants is often desirable. For the formal bed is a floral recreation of some clearly defined pattern which may range from a simple geometrical repeat to a complex and intricate picture. Attempting to be subtle here and create an equivalent of pastel watercolours is rarely successful – it is more akin to poster colours, and painting by numbers.

By contrast, in a mixed or herbaceous border, careful gradations are usually thought more effective. In offering guidelines here, I can do no better than turn to the advice of the mistress of the mixed border planting, Gertrude Jekyll. In the early part of this century, she experimented for many years at her home, Munstead Wood in Surrey, with borders in excess of 200 feet long and 14 feet deep and came to strong and, I believe, important and immensely valuable conclusions that are as valid for the small mixed borders of the modern garden as they were for her horticultural splendours. The basic

No one knew more or taught others more about combining plant colours and sizes than Gertrude Jekyll. The influence of her approach is very evident here in the graduated borders of 'The Priory' at Kemerton in Worcestershire.

foliage colour that Jekyll used was, of course, green, although towards the ends of borders she endeavoured to use grey or slightly silvery leaved plants. The flower colours in the centre were intensely strong and vibrant oranges and reds which then graded on either side through strong yellows, pinks and blues to paler yellows, cream, pinks and pale blues at the ends. However much the so-called riot of colour appeals to you, I am sure you will find that this style with graded colours is undeniably lovely and, I think, more restful to live with.

Especially in autumn and winter, bear in mind the value of coloured fruits and coloured bark on trees and shrubs to continue a chosen theme. Whilst information on flower colours is readily obtained from catalogues, that on fruit and bark colour is much less so, and I have therefore listed some widely available plants with those features in a range of colours.

Finally, when you select plants and colours for particular situations, do take account of the surrounding physical features of the garden too. Although neutral colours, such as those of concrete or most gravels, will blend readily with almost all plant colours, certain types of brick or coloured modern paving blocks will work much less satisfactorily in some combinations than others.

Rosa rugosa *'Alba' has fruits as fine as any rose of this type.*

Acer griseum, *the Chinese paper-bark maple, never fails to turn heads; sadly, demand for this plant in reasonable sizes almost always outstrips supply in nurseries.*

SOME EASY-TO-GROW TREES AND SHRUBS WITH ESPECIALLY STRIKING FRUIT OR BARK FOR WINTER COLOUR

PLANT	FEATURES
Acer griseum (paper bark maple)	Coppery, flaking bark
Betula jaquemontii (Himalayan birch)	Pure white bark
Celastrus orbiculatus (climber)	Red and gold fruits
Clematis tangutica (climber)	White, feathery fruits
Clerodendrum trichotomum	Red fruits in a purple calyx
Cornus stolonifera 'Flaviramea' (dogwood)	Yellow bark
Cornus alba elegantissima (dogwood)	Red bark
Cotoneaster spp.	Red or yellow fruits
Eucalyptus spp.	Smooth, bluish bark
Hippophae rhamnoides (sea buckthorn)	Orange fruits
Hydrangea villosa (climbing hydrangea)	Coppery, flaking bark
Ilex spp. (hollies)	Red or yellow fruits
Malus (some varieties) (crab apples)	Red, green or yellow fruits
Prunus serrula (Tibetan cherry)	Shining, coppery bark
Pyracantha spp. (firethorns)	Red, orange or yellow fruits
Rosa rugosa (some varieties)	Red or orange fruits
Rubus cockburnianus (white bramble)	White bark
Salix daphnoides (willow)	Purple bark with white bloom
Sorbus (some spp.) (mountain ashes)	Yellow, pink or white fruits
Symphoricarpos spp. (snowberries)	White fruits

I believe that in almost all situations, there is no better boundary for a garden than a hedge, and on pp. 154–159 I discuss the merits of the different types of hedging plant. But I realise that there are many gardens where a hedge is impracticable, because it would be too expensive, would look inappropriate or, most usually, because the owner requires a boundary more quickly than even the fastest growing hedge offers. The other possibilities therefore are a wall or a fence. Before considering their relative merits, however, it is important to appraise what is expected of any boundary, be it wall, fence or hedge. There is in practice often a legal requirement, that you may not be aware of, to fence (or less frequently to maintain a wall or hedge) to define the boundary. But in any event, a protective boundary is desirable if, for instance, you keep livestock in your garden (when you would be liable for any damage they cause when straying) or if you have some hazard such as a pool, into which a neighbour might fall. Aside from any prudent or obligatory legal requirements, a sound boundary will afford you privacy and, most importantly, shelter.

The shelter that both you and your garden benefit from most is shelter from the wind – seldom is shelter from the sun either necessary or desirable; in fact it is often an incidental *dis*advantage of windbreak shelter. The benefits that plants derive from shelter are enormous. The wind is a potent physical force which can actually uproot or break large trees; but this is a relatively infrequent occurrence. Much more significant is that it is a highly potent drying force that stunts plant growth. You will see evidence of this most clearly in a field of farm crops. Close to a boundary hedge, the height of the cereals or other plants is significantly greater than it is in the open (apart possibly from where, very close to the hedge, the hedgerow plants themselves actually compete with the crop). And on exposed cliffs or mountains,

Boundaries for the garden

A garden boundary can be very much more than merely a physical means of marking the limits of your property. Yew makes a magnificent hedge and, given time and patience, can become (as shown here at Hidcote) almost the most important garden feature of all.

the trees and shrubs are all noticeably stunted for the same reason – the wind dries moisture from the leaf surfaces faster than the plant is able to replace it from the soil and also causes the death of buds through drying them out.

So the strength of the wind must be diminished, but merely erecting a solid physical barrier is not the best way to achieve this. For a solid barrier serves merely to deflect the wind upwards, resulting in eddies on the lee side and, in consequence, the accumulation of leaves and other debris in your garden. And a solid barrier is subject to tremendous stresses and strains which demand a structure of enormous strength. Careful research, mainly on the types of protective barriers required around forest plantations and commercial fruit tree orchards, has revealed that the most efficient barrier for diminishing the wind strength (and at the same time, suffering as little stress as possible on itself) should be 50% permeable – in other words, one that has an equal area of gaps and of solid structure presented to the wind. The same research also revealed that the main benefits from the lessening of wind strength by such a barrier are apparent for a distance to leeward equal to about ten times its height – thus a 2-metre high barrier will provide good protection for about 20 metres, adequate for most gardens.

The choice then lies between the various types of walls and fences. Most traditional walls are solid structures, lacking the desirable 50% permeability and therefore prone to induce eddy formation; but robust enough nonetheless to withstand the full force of the wind. In many parts of the country, dry stone or other types of wall are integral parts of the landscape and they should always be used in areas where they are a traditional feature – provided it is possible still to find craftsmen able to build them. In many old town gardens, brick walls are important features of the urban landscape and whenever practicable should be repaired rather than replaced with fencing. But in modern gardens, modern materials are appropriate, and a large range of attractive building blocks is now available, many with gaps as part of their integral design. Unfortunately, the individual gaps in wall blocks tend to be much larger than those in fences and whilst having the same effect on the wind, are much less efficient at protecting your privacy.

The most popular modern fence is that built from panels of some form of overlapping softwood planks. But it is the most popular because it is the cheapest. It lacks both wind permeability and physical strength, so where financial constraints dictate that this must be the choice, ensure that every vertical post is braced by a diagonal. I prefer to sink the vertical posts at least 60 cm (2 ft) into the ground and to ram them in, rather than use concrete – they will thus be much simpler to replace in years to come. Don't be dragooned by a fencing contractor or salesman into accepting posts sunk only 45 cm (18 in) or, worse, 30 cm (12 in) simply because that is his standard practice. The life of softwood panelled fences can be increased by using soil boards at the base to protect the main structure from contact with the ground, and by treating them every three or four years with a colourless, non-toxic preservative. The somewhat drab effect of softwood panels can be relieved by having the posts 30 cm (12 in) taller than the fence and erecting trellis along the top. This will enable you to train roses, clematis or other climbers most attractively, but you should be aware that this will add to the structural instability, especially if you use evergreen climbers which will present a considerable surface area to strong winter gales.

Only a little more costly than softwood panels is a traditional rural alternative that has greater durability, permeability and a much more

attractive appearance. In several parts of the country it is now possible to buy hurdles, usually of interwoven hazel, constructed in various standard sizes. Indeed, the more enterprising fencing manufacturers are producing ranges of durable fencing in several different patterns that are well worth seeking before you commit yourself to a major capital outlay. Perhaps the ideal, for the gardener requiring instant shelter and privacy but with the vision to plan for the future of the garden, is to use fence panels of some sort but then to plant a hedge on the sunny side of them. When the hedge has matured, the panels can be removed (and, if they happen to be hazel hurdles, re-used to good effect as attractive objects elsewhere in the garden).

I wish that more gardeners would make use of traditional interwoven hazel hurdles as fencing. They are extremely attractive in their own right, can be used to support climbers, offer a high degree of wind permeability (and hence structural strength) and will outlive softwood fence panels.

Paths and paved areas

THERE is a great deal more to any garden than its plants. Indeed, I often think it is the non-living framework that is the more important conveyor of mood, style and purpose. Whilst in a large garden, the paths and other paved or unplanted parts *may* serve merely as routes from one bed or border to another, they can be as intrinsically valuable from a design standpoint as in a small courtyard where they comprise most of the area. You should, in fact, take at least as much care in your choice of the 'hard' parts of your garden as in your choice of plants, for mistakes made there will be very much more difficult to rectify; transplanting a paved terrace is no easy matter.

On pp. 10–11 and also on p. 14 I have described the way in which some of the non-planted areas of the garden play important roles in its overall design, and how the positioning of them should be influenced by the way in which your garden is intended to serve the needs of you and your family. Here, I shall concentrate purely on structural and constructional considerations.

Paths should provide the means for people to move easily from one part of the garden to another, and I include people pushing wheelbarrows or lawn-mowers. The width of the path and the sharpness of any corners must take account of this, and a path less than about 65 cm (26 in) wide will create problems. (Wheelchairs (see p. 51) necessitate special attention.) All the possible constructional materials have their advantages and their drawbacks so I will give brief comments on those you are most likely to be offered. Much of this information is of course equally applicable to paths and to larger areas such as courtyards, sun terraces or what I suppose I must (albeit reluctantly) in modern parlance call patios.

BRICK   Well-laid bricks, in an appropriate setting, can be splendid. As with other paving materials, they are generally most successful aesthetically when they reflect the construction of the house – think of the magnificent brick Tudor houses with matching paths and terraces. It is very important, however, to use bricks that can withstand the wear and tear of being walked on and, even more significantly, are tolerant of frost. Modern 'engineering' bricks are suitable, as are bricks specially made for the purpose and sometimes called paviors. Bricks may be laid in a great variety of patterns, the particular pattern chosen being important for it will dictate strongly the overall feel of the area.

CONCRETE   This is relatively inexpensive but should not be used for continuous areas of more than about 3 square metres (10 sq ft) because of problems consequent on its expansion and contraction. I find concrete visually dull (it takes a very long time to weather acceptably) and it can become slippery in wet conditions (although the surface appearance and grip can be improved by brushing the mixture with a stiff broom before it dries). Mixing more than a small volume by hand is very hard work, but the minimum quantities that can be purchased as a ready-mix are usually too great for most garden applications. Hiring a concrete mixer is a useful solution to the problem, but personally, I can find no use for concrete in the garden other than as an anchoring agent – for greenhouse or shed foundations for instance.

GRASS   Grass paths (in effect, narrow lawns) have a very limited use as links between two larger areas of turf, provided they are likely to suffer little

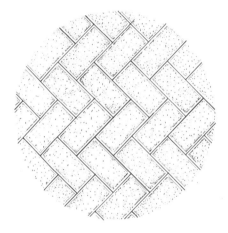

Bricks laid in a herringbone pattern.

Opposite: I am an unashamed advocate of the use of gravel in gardens. It makes attractively textured paths and courtyards, plants can be placed directly into it if necessary, it is simplicity itself to lay and it is very inexpensive.

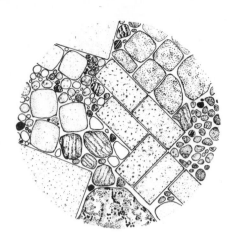

'Mosaic' of various reclaimed stones, bricks and pebbles.

more traffic than the passage of a lawnmower. As thoroughfares in winter, they will soon be reduced to quagmires. Where it is desirable or necessary to walk continually over a small area of turf, however, there are ways in which the damage to the grass can be minimised (see p. 152).

PEBBLES AND COBBLES These are naturally rounded water-worn stones, cobbles being the larger of the two types. If laid very carefully, set in mortar, they can be used to create a path but will always be difficult to walk on, and even harder to use wheeled vehicles over. Where they do have merit is if laid fairly irregularly (or even loosely piled) in discrete areas to break up the monotony of a large expanse of other material. Pebbles and cobbles of different colours and sizes can be bought pre-packed from garden centres or, sometimes, selected loose. They should never be collected from the sea-shore.

PRE-CAST AND NATURAL SLABS When the pre-cast slabs are of concrete, my dislike of the material is echoed here too, although I accept that in a very formal setting (the Italianate courtyard for instance), some of the better quality concrete slabs can create the appropriate feel. But there are many modern slabs of reconstituted or artificial stone that have much to commend them. Real stone (the fine quality millstone grit called York stone for instance) is prohibitively expensive and rightly so, for the sources from which it can be quarried are fast diminishing and I certainly do not condone any further depletion of our natural geology. Occasionally, you may be able to obtain second-hand stone slabs but otherwise I advise you to choose the artificial alternative. This is actually easier to lay, being of uniform thickness, but it is important to cut it, or have it cut for you, into individual slabs of differing sizes; only then will those types that mimic natural stone look acceptably 'authentic'.

Where a fairly large area must be laid with slabs (or where an area of concrete slabs has been 'inherited' with an established garden), the visual monotony can be much improved by removing some slabs and replacing them with another material – bricks or cobbles for instance.

SETTS AND SIMILAR ARTIFICIAL BLOCKS Setts are brick-like blocks of natural stone, often granite. They are expensive, but were much used at one time to form the surface of town streets and pavements and can sometimes be obtained second-hand when street excavations are being made by local authorities. Granite setts can be extremely attractive when used in small quantities and arranged in some geometric pattern, especially in combination with other paving materials. There are now many artificial sett-like blocks available in a range of colours and shapes. Like concrete slabs, however, they are only really suitable for a formal situation, especially for a town garden.

TARMAC If you finish reading this book having received any message at all, I hope that it will be to resolve never to use tarmac in your garden. This material is a splendid invention for roads and pavements but used in your garden it too will look like roads and pavements. No amount of planting or combination with other materials can ever, I believe, put right the mistake, once made.

Chipped bark is a useful alternative to gravel for the more rural parts of the garden, having all of gravel's advantages and yet presenting less of a problem by not adhering as annoyingly to muddy boots.

BARK In recent years, one other loose material has become widely available and although fairly expensive and in need of periodic topping up, it is both attractive and useful. This is shredded bark, which is obtainable in varying degrees of coarseness for different purposes. I discuss its use as mulch elsewhere (pp. 67, 90) but so-called ornamental grades are excellent for laying beneath climbing frames or swings (see p. 29) and for forming rustic paths through planted parts of the garden. For paths, bark should be laid approximately 4–5 cm (1½ to 2 in) deep and although the rapidity with which it degrades seems to vary between soils, in most gardens a topping-up of no more than about 1 cm (½ inch) depth should be needed annually.

WOOD Many gardening books, influenced by some garden designers, suggest that wood, either as planks or as cross-sections of rough-hewn tree trunks, makes a suitable material for paths or larger areas. It doesn't. Wood has several important disadvantages. If smooth, it becomes very dangerously slippery when wet, a problem enhanced as it ages and becomes covered with algal growth; if rough, it will have dangerous splinters; and at best, it can only have a fairly limited life. Wooden paths are among those many features that look splendid in gardens at the Chelsea Flower Show and similar showcases but which shouldn't be taken too seriously, for they bear no relationship at all to real gardening or real life.

GRAVEL Gravel (either real gravel, comprising small, naturally rounded particles, or an artificial gravel of crushed stone) is not only the cheapest material with which to cover a large area, I believe it is also one of the best. By careful choice of particle size and colour, you can effect a considerable influence on the overall feel of your garden – although in general, a crushed stone of the type that occurs naturally in your area often looks best and is certainly cheapest. Gravel almost flows into difficult corners and around irregular shapes, looks attractive in combination with almost all other materials and is very easy to plant into. There is, of course, a debit side. Gravel can be carried on footwear into the house and onto the lawn. It will be especially readily picked up when muddy boots trample across it. Periodic raking is necessary to maintain an attractive surface and, of course, just as plants can be planted into it, so weeds will grow through it too. Nonetheless, none of these factors has persuaded me that gravel is anything other than a very valuable, attractive and cheap garden surface. The provision of strategically placed boot scrapers, a narrow edging between gravel and grass, an underlying 'carpet' of permeable plastic sheet and/or a twice-yearly application of an appropriate weedkiller will help overcome the slight difficulties.

Whatever paving material is used, it must be adequately bedded – concrete slabs, bricks or setts on sand or mortar; concrete poured preferably onto firmed rubble; and gravel, chippings or bark onto well-firmed soil. The bedding materials should dictate the contour of the path – sloping from the centre to the sides for drainage. Take especial care when laying a path or other paved area alongside a house not to cover the damp-proof course in the house wall.

When planning a path or other hard area, you will need to decide not only on the material to be used for the surface but possibly that needed for an edging also. Loose materials such as gravel obviously must be confined, but it is worth bearing in mind that a combination of materials (stone slabs with a brick edging, for instance) can improve the overall appearance. Bricks laid on edge, tiles, concrete or other kerbs can all be used, but all, of course, can add appreciably to your costs. For confining gravel or bark on paths, I have made extensive use of inexpensive half-round timber, as sold for farm fencing. This will usually have been pressure-treated with preservative but can be given an additional coat of water-based or other preservative if required. Such rails are usually sold in lengths of about 3–4 m (10–13 ft) which can readily be sawn as needed and anchored by sharpened hardwood pegs approximately 45 cm (18 in) long.

Gardening with and for children

Fast growing and big are the requirements for plants that most immediately appeal to children; and few plants come faster or bigger than Helianthus annuus.

SPEAK to almost anyone in the gardening business and they will tell you that one of the saddest features of the subject is the paucity of young people who attend gardening society meetings, exhibit at shows or buy gardening magazines. But we should distinguish between young people and children. For I can understand that in the teenage years and slightly after, there are many other attractions and demands on individuals' time; only when young adults first own a garden do they begin to take gardening seriously. But children are another matter, for most have access to some sort of family garden (even if it is only a window box) and encouragement given at this early stage of their lives will reap its reward when they have their own gardens later.

Do be careful with your 'don'ts' in any garden with children. Saying 'no' too frequently when they venture onto your own beds and borders will cause them to associate plants and gardening in general with something untouchable. Far better to explain carefully why it is not a good idea to walk through the newly emerging potatoes. Let them envisage things from the plants' point of view and to see them as living things – although please spare them the ridiculous notion that plants will be hurt if they are damaged.

Encouragement is the appropriate word with children, for most have relatively little patience and expect results both quickly and dramatically. I am convinced that setting aside a small area specially for children's use is the ideal way in which to stimulate their interest. But please don't be tempted to give them a spot in which you are unable to grow anything yourself; you should do quite the reverse. In the open garden, choose a place where the growing conditions are good, where the soil has already been well amended with organic matter, and where there is good exposure to sunshine. An area of about 3.5–4 square metres (37½–43 sq ft) will allow them plenty of scope, although in a small garden, of course, this may need to be scaled down. Choose an area that is close enough to a tap for the children not to have to carry cans of water long distances.

In a world increasingly aware of the damage that can so easily be caused to the natural environment, let us please set off our children on the right lines. Introduce them early to the importance of recycling – a compost bin of their own may be impractical but children must certainly be encouraged to contribute the debris from their own plot to the family bin. And, most importantly, explain to them how the thing works. Dissuade them from using any pesticides on their plants – there will be time enough later when they can be selective enough to make minimal use of the safer, less persistent substances on a few occasions. Whilst they are young enough to be impressionable, let their garden plot teach them the value of all animal and plant life (including the species that we call pests). But let it also serve to show them that life is a struggle – the plants they choose to grow will not survive if weeds too are allowed to flourish.

What are the types of plant most appealing to children? Hardy annuals raised from seed sown directly outside are almost always the most satisfactory, offering so much in return for so little. Vegetables are rewarding too, for they actually offer something edible; although I am uncertain if, having grown spinach themselves, easy as it is, children will necessarily eat it more readily. Radishes are the easiest vegetable of all, closely followed by lettuce (the small varieties such as 'Little Gem'), salad onions, carrots (especially the quick growing, early, spherical-rooted types), runner beans (which produce more dramatic results more quickly than almost any other vegetable) and courgettes. But almost all vegetables are worthwhile and only available space need be the limiting factor. Among flowers, the list is longer still. Sunflowers are almost essential because of their astonishing size but candytuft, calendulas (pot marigolds), nasturtiums (remember that you can eat the flowers), pansies, poppies, schizanthus, and ten-week stocks are all rewarding. When choosing seeds, however, either from a mail order catalogue or from a garden centre display, do allow your children some choice. There may be items that appeal to them from the pictures on the packets, and only by trying them will they discover if they are easy or frustratingly difficult. It may also be worthwhile buying a few plants – partly to give the children encouragement while their seeds germinate but also to demonstrate that some garden plants can only be propagated by cuttings. Actually allowing them to take cuttings themselves will of course prove a tremendous fillip in due course.

Teach your children the value of their garden tools (remember that some manufacturers produce ranges of good quality small tools that the children can have solely for their own use). Show them that they should wipe over the tools and put them away at the end of their gardening activities. (I am not naive enough to expect your children to be inherently any better than mine at tidying away but in the garden, at least, they can always (I hope) follow a parental example.) And teach them garden hygiene also – always to wash their hands after gardening.

So much for gardening *for* children. It is also important to consider gardening *with* children, especially those too young to understand even the basics of horticulture. The most important rule here must be a don't – don't have a garden pool (and fill in any existing pool) while children are very young; a small child can drown in a very few centimetres of water. Children of course also expect swings, sand-pits, tree-houses, rope ladders and the like. But there is absolutely no reason why the entire garden should take on the appearance of a municipal playground. If the garden is large enough, set aside an area for play things – preferably an area visible from the house (or, at least, from the kitchen) without being too obtrusive. Alternatively, choose items that can be put away easily and simply and that are made from materials that blend with the environment. Children's garden equipment need not be of luridly coloured plastic; relatively inexpensive wood items are readily available. Nor need such features as sand-pits be planned as permanent garden features – they can be constructed in such a way as to be capable of being changed later into rock gardens, or even into pools.

Sweet peas are indispensable in any garden. Children especially will enjoy their bounteous growth and also the pleasure of being able to produce something that their parents will appreciate as picked flowers for the house.

The greenhouse – its use and management

A recent survey suggested that a greenhouse headed most people's list of gardening desiderata. And I am quite sure that everyone who has ever had a greenhouse could not manage again without. It is almost certainly the largest single gardening purchase that any gardener is likely to make, yet very often the selection of size and type of structure is done ill-advisedly and still far too frequently I see greenhouses that are not being used in the most efficient manner. With a little planning and forethought you can ensure that your greenhouse provides you with numerous options – a facility for raising hardy and half-hardy plants for transplanting outdoors; space for over-wintering tender plants either in a dormant or an actively growing state; an unrivalled opportunity to produce both summer and winter salad crops; protection for a grapevine, peach or other marginally hardy fruit plant; scope for raising and maintaining house plants; even, if you wish, an area that can be converted into a tropical forest for tender orchids and other delights. Of course a single greenhouse, even a large one, cannot be all things to all gardeners, so I shall take the course that I believe will be of greatest value to most and base my greenhouse advice on the systems that many years of trial and error have proved to be most useful to me. Details of the ways in which individual types of plant can be grown in greenhouses are given elsewhere in the book.

After deciding that they can afford a greenhouse, most people's next concern is where it should be put. Few of us have a site that satisfies all the desirable criteria, but ideally it should be as close as possible to mains electricity and water supplies, in a level, open yet sheltered position, away from trees (especially deciduous trees) and large enough for the greenhouse to be orientated with its long axis east-west, for the most uniform illumination.

Although unusual greenhouses of visually appealing shape are available (including domes, which are very efficient at sunlight capture), they are generally inconvenient in operation and extremely expensive per unit of usable floor area; I do not recommend them. There are merits and dis-advantages in both of the most commonly seen, practical, free-standing greenhouse forms; these are the 'glass to ground' pattern, usually with slightly sloping sides, and the older style, with walls that are solid below staging level. The former generally have aluminium frames, the latter almost invariably wooden. I prefer the latter, partly because of the merits of wood (see below) but also because of the smaller heat loss through the solid side walls and the greater ease with which use can be made of the entire floor area. And I have never found any disadvantages arising from the use of solid lower walls, even with plants that are growing from floor level. The same arguments apply, of course, to a lean-to greenhouse which is, in effect, half of a free-standing structure and has considerable merits, particularly in a small garden. It utilises some of the warmth from the adjoining wall and makes good use of ground area that would otherwise probably be neglected for gardening activity. A lean-to is only really effective, however, against a south-facing wall and even then it is highly desirable for the vertical inner wall to be painted white to reflect as much light as possible into the structure.

Most modern greenhouse frames are aluminium although wooden ones (either deal or the much more durable softwood, red cedar) are still available. A wooden frame requires more maintenance – deal should be painted or treated with preservative annually and even red cedar should be treated every two or three years. Whilst aluminium will therefore be the most popular option, I must point out the advantages that a wooden greenhouse confers.

Less heat is lost through a wooden frame, the fixing of insulation and other attachments inside is usually easier, the structure is generally more resilient to gales, and, most significantly I believe, in many gardens, especially of old houses, a wooden building blends in a way that an aluminium one never can.

Whatever the constructional material, every greenhouse should be firmly anchored to the ground and preferably erected on 20 cm (8 inch) deep concrete foundations. Easily the best floor for a greenhouse is gravel over firmed soil. This permits water to drain away freely, and an annual treatment with a garden disinfectant will eliminate any pests, disease organisms or weeds.

Although most conventional greenhouses utilise glass held in frames, much cheaper structures are available which use one or other form of clear plastic. Though they provide useful additional space for protecting plants, they have several drawbacks and cannot really be considered a substitute for a glazed greenhouse. All plastic sheet has a limited life and will need replacing after two or three years as it becomes torn by the wind, attracts dirt by static electricity and is rendered more or less brittle by the ultra-violet radiation in sunlight. Moreover, whilst plastic transmits heat more readily than glass, this is a two-edged attribute for it will cool down more quickly too.

The most popular size of garden greenhouse for many years was 1.8m × 2.4m (6ft × 8ft) but more recently the 3m × 2.4m (10ft × 8ft) has gained greater favour, and this is the approximate size that I recommend for general garden use. Although offering 66% greater floor area, the purchase price per square metre is less, and the winter heating costs only about 25% higher. Ideally, a glazed, or even a heavy-duty plastic sheet, partition should be erected inside to divide the greenhouse into two equal compartments and

Greenhouse positioning requires careful thought. This is less because they are unsightly objects (indeed, wooden ones can be most attractive) than because they must be allowed maximum exposure to the sun whilst not being too obtrusive.

31

increase its functional flexibility. This allows for a greenhouse management system that I believe offers the most widespread appeal.

Most gardeners will wish to use their greenhouse for raising tomatoes during the summer months and, as most families require about six plants, a 1.8m × 2.4m (6ft × 8ft) structure will be almost fully occupied by them from April until September, leaving no room for raising seedlings in the spring and no room for cuttings in late summer. But with the subdivided larger greenhouse, one compartment (the outer one) may be used to accommodate the six tomato plants (three down each side), with room on the floor in front of and between them for peppers and aubergines. (Alternatively, one of the tomatoes could give way to a cucumber plant although I have more to say about the growing of cucumbers in greenhouses on p. 119.) After these summer crops have been removed, the same compartment can provide sheltered frost-free space for overwintering fairly hardy plants such as fuchsias, or for raising winter lettuce (its capacity increased, if necessary, by installing movable staging for the winter only). The second (inner) compartment contains permanent staging (including a small, heated sand bench or other propagator system) and the greenhouse heating source and is used for overwintering more tender subjects such as pelargoniums and for facilitating early- and late-season plant raising. In very cold spells in the winter, or when you might want to accommodate more than the usual number of tender plants, you can open the internal partition and heat the whole of the house. Between the removal of the summer crops and the preparation of the greenhouse for the winter, the whole interior should be cleared of plants and other materials, scrubbed inside with a garden disinfectant, washed down with clean water and fumigated with a fungicide and insecticide 'smoke'.

A greenhouse with no artificial heat supply (generally referred to as a

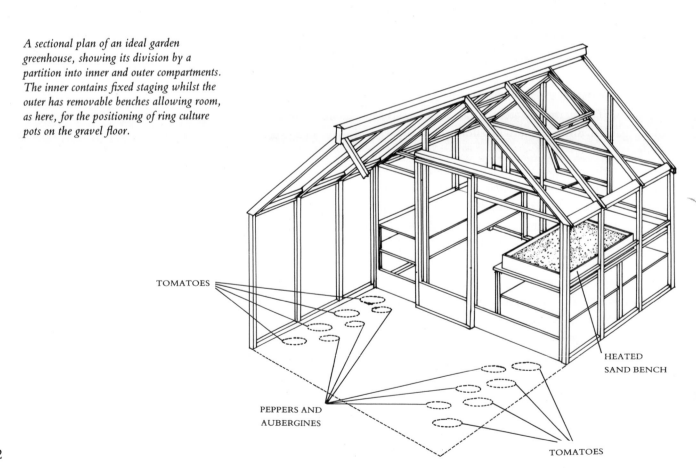

A sectional plan of an ideal garden greenhouse, showing its division by a partition into inner and outer compartments. The inner contains fixed staging whilst the outer has removable benches allowing room, as here, for the positioning of ring culture pots on the gravel floor.

TOMATOES

HEATED
SAND BENCH

PEPPERS AND
AUBERGINES

TOMATOES

cold greenhouse) will offer only a small proportion of its real potential. Even with insulation, it will probably not be frost-free in many winters. By far the simplest and most easily regulated heating system is a thermostatically controlled electric fan heater, operated most economically and advantageously if it is set to maintain a minimum of 7°C (44.6°F). At this temperature, well above freezing point, tender plants can be overwintered safely, some plants such as winter lettuce will continue to grow well, and by the time that seedlings have been pricked on from the propagator in the spring, the daytime temperature will be elevated by the sun to enable them to grow satisfactorily. Below 7°C, you will have plant survival but not much growth, whilst above it, you will be wasting money – every 2.8°C (5°F) rise in temperature approximately doubles the amount of heat required and hence the running cost. Of course, such a system requires a mains electricity supply which will be expensive to install if the greenhouse is at some distance from the house. Where mains voltage cannot be provided, a paraffin heater is a poor alternative for space heating; a low-voltage electric propagator or heating mat (on which seed trays may be stood) can be arranged very simply by running a low voltage wire from a transformer connected to the nearest main. Complete kits including the transformer are available.

Every greenhouse, artificially heated or not, should have insulation added inside for the winter. The most easily erected and efficient material is double-skin bubble polythene film, which will cut down heat loss by about 40%. But such are the vagaries of climate that soon after it is removed in spring, you will need to apply some shading to the outside of the glass to prevent the greenhouse from overheating. The most popular shade 'paint' is unaffected by rain but can be wiped off with a dry cloth in the autumn. It will lower the transmission of light and heating infra-red radiation by 20–30%.

Even the best shading paint, in the coolest of summers, will not fully prevent a greenhouse from overheating. To aid the cooling, and to permit a free flow of air into and out of the house, good ventilation is essential too. Vents should be fitted both in the sides (as low down as practicable) and in the roof of the greenhouse, and are much more easily provided for when the greenhouse is first ordered than added later. The total area of opening vents should be at least 15% of the greenhouse floor area. Automatic vents that operate on an expansion principle are very useful if you cannot attend to the greenhouse during the daytime.

I have never found it necessary to install artificial lighting for plant raising in a garden greenhouse. Generally, the benefits derived from artificial lighting in prolonging plants' growing seasons are only realised when the greenhouse is also heated to an unrealistically high level during the winter.

Watering in a greenhouse is a perpetual headache, especially during the height of summer when tomatoes and other crops are consuming it in vast quantities. I have discussed the various ways of growing these plants elsewhere in the book but from a watering standpoint alone, I believe that the ring culture system leaves all others standing. All that is required is a trench approximately 30–35 cm (12–14 in) deep and 35–40 cm (14–16 in) wide, running along the side(s) of the greenhouse. This should be fully lined with heavy-gauge plastic sheet and filled with pea gravel which is watered copiously; once a week during the summer is generally sufficient. The bottomless pots containing the plants stand on this gravel and whilst liquid fertiliser is applied to the compost in the pot, the plant's water supply comes via the second root system that develops in the gravel bed.

For most gardeners, the principal reason for owning a greenhouse is to produce their own tomatoes. They are certainly rewarding crops and, most importantly, they allow you to grow well flavoured varieties that may be difficult to obtain in shops. Nonetheless, they do require fairly constant attention to feeding, watering, side-shooting, tying-in and pest control if they are to give of their best.

For watering smaller plants in pots on the bench, there is no wholly satisfactory technique and most gardeners will probably be content to rely on the watering can. Capillary matting has its uses, but is only really effective when all pots are of the same size and it generally works more satisfactorily with clay than plastic pots for these make better contact with the mat. The water-absorbent mat itself must be laid in a tray or similar receptacle on top of the staging, and is linked via a short wick to a reservoir of water. Capillary mats must be washed and disinfected at least annually. Several more or less automated trickle and mist (overhead) watering systems are becoming available for garden greenhouses but all have their shortcomings. They are often very fiddly to assemble, commonly suffer from nozzle blockages from algae growing on any liquid fertiliser that splashes on to them, and are dependent for really effective use on a nearby mains water supply. And of course, the use of overhead watering in a greenhouse with mains electricity is potentially very dangerous. Nonetheless, however inconvenient it may be to transport mains water, I would urge you not to use water from a rainwater butt or barrel in the greenhouse. It is fine for the open garden but inevitably accumulates pests and disease-causing organisms that will proliferate in the warmth.

FOR as long as there have been gardeners, plants have been grown in containers, and I believe that every gardener's activities can be enhanced by at least a few tubs, troughs, window boxes, hanging baskets or even growing bags. There are two aspects to container gardening. On the one hand it can provide almost an entire garden for those with very confined space, and on the other, it can be used instantly to change the appearance of a much larger area. Nonetheless, the choice and handling of the containers is the same in each case. Some of the principles of container gardening are also applicable to small raised beds, table beds and peat beds, which I discuss in detail in my account of alpine plants (p. 237).

Container gardening

A visit to any garden centre will reveal a huge array of containers, varying in size and shape and manufactured from a wide range of materials including various plastics, terracotta, wood, concrete and reconstituted stone. Aesthetic considerations and cost will play a major part in dictating your choice but there are certain other features that are important, depending on the purpose to which you intend to put the container. First, therefore, I shall consider free-standing containers and suggest some of the features that you should take into account when making your choice.

A cubic metre of potting compost weighs approximately 1 tonne. If you plan to move full containers therefore (and on p. 38 I shall make some suggestions as to why you might wish to do this) the size of the container and the volume of compost it will contain become very important considerations. I find that a terracotta tub about 40 cm (16 in) tall and 36 cm (14½ in) in diameter is the maximum that can be moved comfortably, when full, by an average man. Concrete containers of the same size will of course be proportionately heavier. Conversely, many containers, although superfi-

Growing plants in containers offers instant versatility. Not only can dull corners be quickly enlivened but a container with one type of plant can be replaced with another as soon as its attractiveness declines.

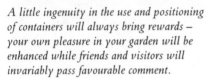

A little ingenuity in the use and positioning of containers will always bring rewards – your own pleasure in your garden will be enhanced while friends and visitors will invariably pass favourable comment.

cially attractive, are too small or so shaped that they contain too small a volume of compost to be functionally effective. They fail partly because they require watering unrealistically often and also because there is insufficient space for the roots of a plant that has large enough leaf and flower growth to be attractive. Some concrete containers, for instance, appear fairly large externally but have very thick walls and a very limited internal space shaped like an inverted pyramid. (Some of the containers sold for attaching to walls also contain very small volumes; I shall discuss the special situation of hanging baskets shortly but flat-backed wall pots are in my experience particularly troublesome.) As a rule of thumb, I would advise you against choosing any container that has an internal volume less than that of a conventional plant pot 20 cm (8 in) in diameter.

Stability of free-standing pots is another important consideration and is actually a function of several features – height, the ratio of height to diameter, volume of compost, type of compost (a soil-based compost is very much heavier than the equivalent volume of a peat-based one), size of plant and relative exposure and windiness of the site. From my own experience I believe that it is most important, for stability, to avoid containers that taper sharply downwards and have a basal diameter less than about two-thirds that of the top; the taller the container, the more important this ratio becomes.

I would never for preference choose a plastic container. They will always look like plastic containers and thus inferior; they are easily damaged if moved when full; many types discolour and become more brittle with age; and they suffer from the important drawback of being impermeable to water and air, thus plants in them are likely to suffer from waterlogging and consequent root damage. They do, of course, have the advantage of being relatively cheap and you can certainly buy a large number and so immediately colour a new garden at a time when there will certainly be more pressing demands on your funds. I suggest therefore that if you must begin your container gardening life with plastic pots (or even with really make-do vessels such as old paint cans), you should gradually replace them, one or two per year, with more attractive and traditional types.

The unglazed earthenware called terracotta has been used to make plant containers for centuries and is undeniably lovely, if expensive. But choose carefully – there are some very attractive Italian and Spanish pots that cannot tolerate even a slight degree of frost without flaking or cracking. These must therefore be taken under cover in the winter. The frost tolerance of terracotta depends on the nature of the clay used and the way that it is fired. Some manufacturers are now so confident of their materials that they offer a ten-year guarantee of frost resistance, so their pots can safely be planted with perennials and left outdoors permanently. For efficiency, use your non-hardy terracotta pots for plants such as specimen fuchsias, that must themselves be taken into the protection of greenhouse or conservatory in the winter.

Troughs or other containers hewn from natural stone are beautiful but now extremely scarce and prohibitively expensive. Their place has been taken by moulded concrete and reconstituted stone vessels, some of which are very difficult to distinguish from the originals. Check that such containers too are frost-tolerant and check also that they do not contain a chemical setting or hardening agent that is toxic to plants until really well weathered. The easiest way to encourage the growth of lichen and algae, and so simulate more closely a genuine old stone container, is occasionally to paint the concrete with milk or liquid cow manure.

Wooden half barrels offer easily the cheapest way of obtaining really large containers but should be painted inside and out with a non-toxic preservative before use – and remember to drill several drainage holes in the bottom before the barrel is filled with compost. It is very difficult to move a half barrel when full of compost but if it must be done, try using three rollers cut from lengths of old scaffolding pipe – few other materials readily available are sufficiently strong.

Window boxes are a special delight in inner city gardens, provided they are out of reach of vandals, and for apartment dwellers. Much the best system is to invest in wooden boxes, which may have to be made specially, of the size and shape of your own window ledge, with drainage holes. These should be treated with preservative inside and lined with plastic sheet. Within this wooden frame, you may then place plastic troughs and pots containing the plants. This arrangement permits you to plant up the containers and allows the plants to mature before placing them on view. It also gives you the flexibility of replacing individual pots or troughs during the summer.

Hanging baskets present special difficulties. Their weight when full and wet is considerable and support brackets must be strongly anchored. For reasons of weight, if none other, peat-based compost is much to be preferred. Drainage should be free but not so liberal that the basket requires watering more than once each day. Some restrictive liner is necessary, and whilst the natural sponginess of *Sphagnum* moss is ideal, it is now difficult or costly to obtain; the easiest method nowadays is to buy fibre liners shaped to the basket. Nonetheless, it is essential to cut holes in the liner through which the plants are placed and from which they can grow. Many modern baskets are too shallow to be effective and the compost inevitably dries out very rapidly; a basket should preferably be at least 30 cm (12 inches) in diameter and at leat 18 cm (7¼ inches) deep.

The choice of compost for containers is relatively straightforward. If the plants are to be grown at least semi-perenially, by which I mean for more than one season, use a soil-based potting compost such as John Innes No. 3 (or a more gritty mixture for alpines [see p. 237]). If they are to be grown as annuals for one season only, use a soil-less potting compost. Always remember that the nutrient reserves in a soil-less compost are less than in a

The window box is among the commonest of plant containers but its versatility will be increased if it is used as the holder for individual, smaller vessels that can be added or removed as the flowers within them come into or fade from bloom.

Large containers such as this wooden half-barrel are invaluable for raising dwarf fruit trees. This crab apple on the dwarfing rootstock M.27 gives excellent yields and a similar system could be used to provide apples – even in a garden with no open soil beds at all.

soil-based type and that liquid feeding, which is essential for all plants in containers, should begin for them after about three weeks, whereas a soil-based compost should not need supplementing for twice this long. Once the plants are established, bear in mind that, with no water reserves to tap at depth, they will need watering at least once and preferably twice a week (with a feed once a week) if in tubs, and once a day, with twice weekly feeding, in hanging baskets.

Growing bags are discussed again under the subject of vegetables (p. 127) but although popular for this purpose, and to some extent for annual ornamentals too, they have serious limitations. In a greenhouse, I much prefer the ring-culture system (p. 33) of raising tomatoes and similar plants and urge all greenhouse tomato growers to consider this very seriously. Growing bags are useful for growing tomatoes, cucumbers and similar crops outdoors on paved areas where there is no access to bare soil, and there are now several ways of overcoming the difficulty of providing support for plants raised in this way, but the plastic growing bag has a major drawback in that watering is very hard to regulate. It is impossible to see if the compost is wet or dry, and plants can easily suffer from both extremes. Certainly the growing bag is no system for anyone who is likely to be away from home for several days at a time, unless they wish to indulge themselves with an automated water system (p. 34).

I have mentioned that container gardening offers flexibility and this is its great merit, combined with the fact that an arrangement of a few containers can instantly transform any garden area. Among particular uses of containers that you might wish to consider are: using pots at the sides of garden steps to break the hardness of the edge; planting a small group of containers and moving them every two weeks or so into and out of a shaded area in order to provide colour in a way that would be impossible with a permanent planting in such a spot; growing a fruit tree on a dwarfing rootstock (see p. 142) in a large tub to obtain fruit even from a courtyard garden; using tubs for growing bulbs (either, as with lilies, in the form of a permanent planting or, as with daffodils and tulips, to provide colour before summer annuals take over); planting a small selection of pots with herbs to be positioned close to the kitchen.

Containers are often used very effectively to conceal unsightly features but remember that if you use one to disguise a drain or man-hole cover, it is wise to support the tub on wooden battens placed either side of the offending object. It will then be easier to move and less likely to damage the cover. Finally, a word of caution for those who container-garden in high-rise city apartments. Do ascertain the weight restrictions imposed on your floor; remember that statistic – a cubic metre of compost weighs 1 tonne.

Wild flowers
in the garden

TO most older gardeners, wild flowers in gardens are synonymous with weeds. In short, they have no place in an environment that, by definition, is one for cultivated vegetation. Today, the thinking is radically different and many people not only conserve wild flowers where they find them naturally but actually sow or plant them in their gardens. Some companies now specialise in the sale of native plant seed, displays composed entirely of wild flowers are granted awards at major horticultural shows, and gardening competitions include categories for the 'best wild flower or wild life garden'. This is a trend that has spread beyond the amateur gardening fraternity; whilst many local councils were (and in some places still are) vilified for spraying roadside verges with weedkiller, other authorities are buying native flower seeds at vast expense for the mass sowing of motorway embankments. What has happened?

I believe that a pedigree for wild flower gardening can be traced back to 1962 when the American writer Rachel Carson published her profoundly disturbing book, *Silent Spring*. Much of her concern centred on the widespread use of persistent pesticides which possess very damaging side-effects. But it is only a short step from noting the deaths of birds of prey from organochlorine insecticides to the posing of questions about almost every other human interference with the natural environment. So it came to be recognised that the increasing scarcity of many once-familiar wild flowers (the corncockle is an obvious example) was attributable to an increase in the use of herbicides by farmers and others and to the destruction of more and more of their natural habitats, partly by agricultural and forestry activity but also because of the encroachment of urban areas and motorways into what had once been countryside.

Many of the much loved 'cottage garden' plants such as these foxgloves are little changed from wild species, and, like them, have the habit of self-seeding with abandon – a mixed blessing, underlining the fact that this type of garden cannot be a euphemism for neglect but requires careful management.

Gradually, it was realised that it is hard, and in many cases impossible, to turn back the clock and replace what has disappeared, so some gardeners felt that they could play a helpful part by growing wild flowers in their gardens. I have to be honest and say that I don't think that the growing of rare wild flowers in gardens is likely to make a very great environmental impact. They will still be rare in the wild, and none of us is likely to grow species that would otherwise become extinct. Nonetheless, some native plants are very attractive and of course they also have value as food for other forms of wildlife, so here some more positive contribution towards conservation's ends may be achieved. But anyone who begins to cultivate native plants, especially in a small garden, will soon discover that many present problems – the very problems that have caused horticulturists in the past to reject them or selectively breed from them to produce plants more appropriate for gardening. First, most native plants have fairly short flowering seasons, and in a small area it is difficult to grow a large enough range to provide interest all year round. Second, many native plants are remarkably invasive, especially when grown in a garden, away from their natural competitors. I am astonished to see that seeds of ground elder, bindweed and hairy bittercress, for instance, are offered for sale with no warning of their potential. A plot of native plants requires very careful management – if you leave it to its own devices, you will have, not a wild garden, but a wilderness, and it is essential to remove the more aggressive plants if the others are to survive.

Some of the loveliest native plants, these snake's head fritillaries among them, may be difficult to establish and require careful tending in the early stages. Once they are established, however, they will give continuing pleasure for years to come.

There are three principal ways in which native plants might be used in a garden: in a partial imitation of a semi-wild habitat (a woodland, hedge, stream or pond-side for instance); in a reconstruction of what is generally called a wild-flower meadow – the type of cultivated grassland used for hay production before the advent of hybrid grasses and selective herbicides; or as individuals, more or less integrated with cultivated types. Please don't be tempted to try the first unless you have the natural habitat upon which you can capitalise, nor the second, unless you really have the space. For although the self-perpetuating wild-flower meadow is perhaps the most appealing way of growing wild flowers, it will look extremely untidy for much of the year and in a small, urban garden will render you most unpopular with neighbours who may not share your fondness for arable farming in miniature.

Given a small garden, therefore, I would urge you to be selective and not try to save the nation's wildlife single-handed. I have listed native plants that I believe are valuable in a small area, and I have included a small number that are especially attractive and fairly long-lasting in their own right, together with a few that are important food plants for valuable and increasingly rare wildlife – butterflies especially. (It is one thing to *attract* butterflies to your garden – a buddleia, an ice plant and a clump of Michaelmas daisies will achieve that, but this will do nothing to help them perpetuate. For this, you must supply their larval food plant.)

The plants that I have listed may be used in the shrubbery, herbaceous or mixed border, rock or trough garden, pool or other appropriate garden feature in exactly the same way as you would use more conventional garden plants. None of the species I have chosen is invasive, but conversely care may be needed to ensure that some of them are not swamped by particularly vigorous or large cultivated plants – once again, I must emphasise that growing native plants in a garden requires constant management. They may be raised from seed using either the hardy annual or the tree and shrub raising techniques (pp. 99 and 103). Alternatively, if you have neither room nor inclination to raise your own plants, most are readily obtainable either from large garden centres or by mail order from specialist nurseries. You should never, of course, collect them from their natural habitats. Every wild plant,

The so-called wildflower meadow such as this one containing naturalised dog tooth violet Erythronium dens-canis *and the exquisite miniature daffodil* Narcissus bulbocodium *(neither in fact true British natives) is one of the hardest types of wildflower planting to achieve successfully. Care is needed in the early stages to prevent the flowers from being swamped by the grass.*

no matter how common, is protected by law and may only be uprooted with the specific consent of the owner of the land on which it grows. Some rare species may not be uprooted or disturbed under any circumstances.

The larger-scale use of native plants requires a rather different approach but offers rather greater scope. If you have a small wooded area, a large hedge composed of native plants or a large pool (not one with a hard, artificial courtyard surround), you have the opportunity to plant and encourage other native species. In fact, it is perfectly possible to create a representation of a natural pool and on p. 246 I explain how this can be done, although you will be a patient woodland wild-flower gardener if you first have to plant your

SOME NATIVE PLANTS SUITABLE FOR INTRODUCING TO A LARGE GARDEN WOODLAND HABITAT

Bluebell [*Hyacinthoides non-scripta*] (P)

Dog's mercury [*Mercurialis perennis*] (P)

Foxglove [*Digitalis purpurea*] (P)

Ivy [*Hedera helix*] (P)

Lesser celandine [*Ranunculus ficaria*] (P)

Lily-of-the-valley [*Convallaria majalis*] (P)

Primrose [*Primula vulgaris*] (P)

Solomon's seal [*Polygonatum multiflorum*] (P)

Stinking hellebore [*Helleborus foetidus*] (P)

White dead nettle [*Lamium album*] (P)

Wild strawberry [*Fragaria versca*] (P)

Wood anemone [*Anemone nemorosa*] (P)

Wood cranesbill [*Geranium sylvaticum*] (P)

A = annual B = biennial P = perennial

wood. It is possible to buy so-called wild-flower seed mixtures for sowing directly in each of these habitats, but my advice is very firmly not to do so. Even if you are extremely fortunate and all of your seed mixture germinates, it is important to remember that it is a mixture – a complete jumble of plants that naturally may grow in the same general habitat but actually do so in fairly discrete groups where they are not in direct competition with each other. It is very much better to choose a range of species and sow these either directly into separate areas within the habitat, or, better still, to raise them in pots and then plant them so they can spread naturally. In the lists, I have suggested species for woodland, hedgerow and wet habitats that I have found particularly easy, rewarding and environmentally useful.

For many people, the ideal wild-flower garden feature is the one that is in fact not a natural habitat at all but a replica of an old cultivated meadow. It is sometimes suggested that this can be created by 'leaving your lawn un-weeded and unmown for a few weeks in summer' but whilst this may produce a lovely thing for the summer, it will be a mud-bath in winter when the durable, hard-wearing grasses have been competed out. A wild-flower meadow must be sown directly, using a meadow seed mixture (and even then you will almost certainly need to introduce a few pot-raised species later).

One of the biggest difficulties with establishing such a meadow, even where your garden contains a large enough area (and I believe that about 100 square metres (1076 sq ft) is the minimum), is the nutrient content of the soil. For where a soil has previously been used as a conventional garden (especially where it has been used for vegetable growing), the chances are that it will have a high nitrogen content. The consequence of this is that grasses and some of the clovers and vetches present in your meadow mixture of wildflower seeds will proliferate at the expense of the others. It is very useful first, therefore, to lower the nitrogen content of the soil and/or suppress the growth of these vigorous plants. There are various ways of doing this but easily the most effective that I have seen is to augment the seed mixture with hemi-parasitic plants (yellow rattle, *Rhinanthus*, is the most readily obtained) which will depress the vigour of some of the more aggressive species. If you are prepared to spend a season growing a nitrogen-demanding crop, so much the better; closely planted cabbages are ideal (but remember, no fertiliser).

Prepare the area for sowing the meadow exactly as I describe for a lawn (p. 148), using the same seeding rate, but omit the fertiliser, of course. I find that autumn is the best time for doing this. Management is probably more important with a meadow than with any other native plant feature. Many gardeners have a good display of flowers in the early stages but few thereafter because they have cut the meadow before the plants have had time to set, mature and shed their seed. The best plan is to use a rotary mower with a grass collector in the first season. Set the blades high (about 7.5 cm [3 in]) and cut the new meadow throughout the first summer. Thereafter, leave the cutting until as late in the summer as you can (exactly as if you were haymaking commercially). You will probably find that the rotary mower cannot then cope so you must use either a traditional scythe (traditionally hard) or a modern cord trimmer and use a lawn or hay rake to remove the cut grass after a few days.

SOME NATIVE (OR NATURALISED) PLANTS SUITABLE FOR GROWING IN SMALL GARDENS

PLANT	SUITABLE FOR
Bloody crane's bill [*Geranium sanguineum*] (P)	Herbaceous/mixed border
Bugle [*Ajuga reptans*] (P)	Shady border
Cheddar pink [*Dianthus gratianopolitanus*] (P)	Rock Garden
Common dog violet [*Viola riviniana*] (P)	Front of border, shady border
Common figwort [*Scrophularia nodosa*] (P)	Herbaceous/mixed border
Common toadflax [*Linaria vulgaris*] (P)	Herbaceous/mixed border
Corncockle [*Agrostemma githago*] (A)	Front of border
Cornflower [*Centaurea cyanus*] (A)	Front of border
Corn marigold [*Chrysanthemum segetum*] (P)	Herbaceous/mixed border
Cowslip [*Primula veris*] (P)	Front of border, rock garden
Dusky cranesbill [*Geranium phaeum*] (P)	Shady border
Field scabious [*Knaughtia arvensis*] (P)	Front of border
Foxglove [*Digitalis purpurea*] (B/P)	Herbaceous/mixed/shady border
Great bellflower [*Campanula latifolia*] (P)	Herbaceous/mixed border
Greater celandine [*Chelidonium majus*] (P)	Herbaceous/mixed border
Greater knapweed [*Centaurea scabiosa*] (P)	Herbaceous/mixed border
Green hellebore [*Helleborus viridis*] (P)	Herbaceous/mixed/shady border
Heartsease [*Viola tricolor*] (A/B)	Front of border, among paving
Hemp agrimony [*Empatorium cannabinum*] (p)	Herbaceous/mixed border
Herb Robert [*Geranium robertianum*] (A/B)	Rock garden
Lady's mantle [*Alchemilla mollis*] (P)	Herbaceous/mixed/shady border
Lawn chamomile [*Chamaemelum nobile*] (P)	Herb garden
Marsh marigold [*Caltha palustris*] (P)	Damp border
Masterwort [*Astrantia major*] (P)	Herbaceous/mixed border
Meadow cranesbill [*Geranium pratense*] (P)	Herbaceous/mixed border
Night-flowering catchfly [*Silene noctiflora*] (P)	Herbaceous/mixed border
Ox-eye daisy [*Leucanthemum vulgare*] (P)	Herbaceous/mixed border
Pheasant's eye [*Adonis annua*] (A)	Herbaceous/mixed border
Primrose [*Primula vulgaris*] (P)	Rock garden, front of border
Purple loosestrife [*Lythrum salicaria*] (P)	Damp border
Red valerian [*Centranthus ruber*] (P)	Herbaceous/mixed border
Sea campion [*Silene maritima*] (P)	Rock garden
Small scabious [*Scabiosa columbaria*] (P)	Front of border
Sneezewort [*Achillea ptarmica*] (P)	Herbaceous/mixed border
Stinking hellebore [*Helleborus foetidus*] (P)	Herbaceous/mixed/shady border
Teasel [*Dipsacus fullonum*] (P)	Herbaceous/mixed border
Thrift [*Armeria maritima*] (P)	Rock garden
Wallflower [*Cheiranthus cheiri*] (B)	Herbaceous/mixed border
White campion [*Silene dioica*] (P)	Herbaceous/mixed border
Wild thyme [*Thymus vulgaris*] (P)	Herb garden, among paving
Wood anemone [*Anemone nemorosa*] (P)	Underplanting in shrubbery
Wood cranesbill [*Geranium sylvaticum*] (P)	Shady border
Yellow loosestrife [*Lysimachia vulgaris*] (P)	Herbaceous/mixed border

A = annual   B = biennial   P = perennial

SOME NATIVE PLANTS SUITABLE FOR INTRODUCING TO A LARGE GARDEN WATERSIDE HABITAT

Brooklime [*Veronica beccabunga*] (P)

Bugle [*Ajuga reptans*] (P)

Creeping Jenny [*Lysimachia nummularia*] (P)

Hemp agrimony [*Eupatorium cannabinum*] (P)

Lesser spearwort [*Ranunculus flammula*] (P)

Marsh marigold [*Caltha palustris*] (P)

Marsh woundwort [*Stachys palustris*] (P)

Meadowsweet [*Filipendula ulmaria*] (P)

Purple loosestrife [*Lythrum salicaria*] (P)

Yellow iris [*Iris pseudacorus*] (P)

Water figwort [*Scrophularia aquatica*] (P)

Water forget-me-not [*Myosotis scorpioides*] (P)

Water mint [*Mentha aquatica*] (P)

Water plantain [*Alisma plantago-aquatica*] (P)

A = annual   B = biennial   P = perennial

SOME NATIVE PLANTS SUITABLE FOR PLANTING ALONGSIDE HEDGES

Many of the above species will grow well alongside hedges (although some are fairly invasive and may spread into the remainder of the garden) but the following are especially characteristic of this habitat:

Common dog violet [*Viola riviniana*] (P)

Cow parsley [*Anthriscus sylvestris*] (P)

Hedge woundwort [*Stachys sylvatica*]

Jack-by-the-hedge [*Alliaria petiolata*] (B)

Lords and ladies [*Arum maculatum*] (P)

Primrose [*Primula vulgaris*] (P)

Snowdrop [*Galanthus nivalis*] (P)

Stinging nettle [*Urtica dioica*] (P)

White bryony [*Bryonia cretica*] (P)

A = annual B = biennial P = perennial

The compost heap and 'organic gardening'

I am very fond of my compost bin; in many ways it represents the nerve centre of the garden. A double bin such as this one is very much easier to manage than a single structure.

THE expression 'organic gardening' is a fairly recent arrival in gardeners' everyday vocabulary. Yet, perhaps without actually giving themselves this rather mysterious title, all good gardeners have always been organic in their methods. Admittedly, today, the expression includes a range of rather different and unrelated features so first I must clarify it and at least define what the subject means to me.

If you look for a dictionary definition of organic, the word will appear in several guises. Of these, the one most relevant to gardening is 'derived from or characteristic of plants and animals'. Taken in relation to manures and composts, this is fairly understandable and this is the subject that I shall consider in detail here. In relation to pesticides and fertilisers, the matter is much less straightforward, partly because some pesticides and fertilisers derived from plants or animals are functionally identical to others of artificial or mineral origin, and also because some plant and animal products are actually highly toxic and environmentally damaging (a 'natural' or organic origin for these substances therefore is no guarantee of safety). I shall consider the relative merits of organic and other pesticides and fertilisers in detail later (pp. 79 and 62), but first I must return to composts and manures, their uses and origins.

At the outset, I shall dispel a common myth. Composts and/or manures are of vital importance in every garden – this is my reason for saying that all good gardeners are 'organic' gardeners – but their importance is not primarily as a source of plant food. The nutrient content of all composts and manures is very small, and whilst many of them can form a useful addition to a plant feeding programme, it is fertilisers that really play this role. I have listed the common types of manure and compost that you are likely to encounter and have indicated their approximate nutrient contents (in terms of the three major nutrients, nitrogen, phosphate and potash). But perhaps I should also illustrate exactly what these figures mean in practice. Old cow manure (not manure from old cows) contains on average 0.4% by weight of nitrogen. A crop of summer cabbage plants requires about 25 g of nitrogen per square metre during its life. If you intend to supply all of this as well-rotted cow manure, you will need to cover every square metre of your brassica plot with over 6 kg of manure. Even then, the plants will be short of phosphate and potash. You can supply these nutrients much more readily with a handful of general balanced fertiliser. Whilst manures and composts are of limited value as plant foods, as aids to improving soil structure, however, they are quite indispensable.

On p. 58 I explain how to add humus to the soil and why it improves the soil's structure. Humus is a general word that includes composts, manures and other forms of what are also sometimes called organic matter. Which should you choose and from where should you obtain them? Technically, there is little to choose between any of these materials as improvers of soil structure. There are, however, a few other considerations. Peat and pulverised bark contain almost no nutrients; the remainder, as I have already suggested, a very small but nonetheless welcome amount. Both fresh bark and sawdust should always be composted before being added to the soil for they may contain toxic substances that a few months of rain and weathering will safely remove. (Because of its very fine nature, sawdust, in practice, is perhaps the least useful of all the common forms of organic matter.) Fresh bark always carries the slight risk of being contaminated with honey fungus although bagged, proprietary branded bark from a reputable manufacturer should be perfectly safe to use without composting. I shall have more to say later about this substance in its role as a moisture-retaining and weed-suppressing mulch.

Any fresh animal manure or fresh plant material such as bracken or seaweed will begin to decompose as soon as it is added to the soil. The bacteria that effect this decomposition will remove some nitrogen from the soil as their own nutrient. For this reason, fresh organic matter should not be dug into the garden at a time of year when plants will soon be in need of that nitrogen. In practice, this means in the spring. Thus, fresh manures and other matter should only be applied directly to the soil in the autumn. Otherwise, they should be composted first.

From my references to composting it will perhaps be apparent by now why I consider a well made and well maintained compost heap to be the core of any well managed garden. It embodies so much of the essence of what organic gardening means to me. In the compost heap, fresh organic matter can be allowed to undergo its first stages of decomposition without depleting the soil of valuable nitrogen. But there is more to it than this, for the compost heap enables all waste organic matter from the garden to be converted into a form that can again be useful. There are few more depressing sights for a gardener than the dustbin full of plant waste, the municipal skip piled high with lawn mowings or the smoke of an autumn bonfire curling upwards as valuable leaves are oxidised into the atmosphere and on to the neighbours' washing.

The stages in compost heap management are shown in the diagrams, but some additional points should be made. As will be apparent from the illustrations, heap is really a misnomer for the structure that I advocate. At its best this is a well-aerated bin. Aeration is the key to good compost-making and although some gardeners claim to have made good compost in almost completely enclosed vessels and even plastic bags, I am not among them. Small, plastic, barrel-style containers with plenty of holes in the sides are fairly effective and can be useful for the smaller garden. But wherever space permits, I recommend strongly that you use a slatted wooden bin of about 1.2 m^3. Best of all is a double bin; one side can be filled while the other matures.

Construction of a compost heap. Boxes with slatted fronts allow easy access so that contents can be turned. Note small wooden blocks fixed to the undersides of the removable slats to aerate the compost heap. Plastic mesh on top holds the compost in position.

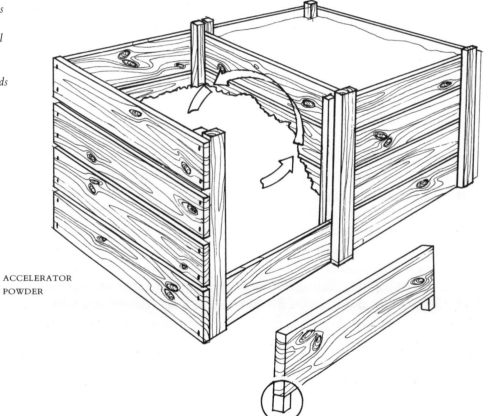

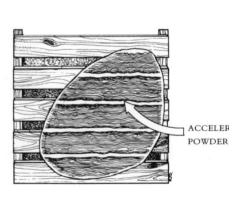

ACCELERATOR
POWDER

Between layers of organic waste is a scattering of compost accelerator.

After air, the most important additional ingredients for successful compost-making are a source of nitrogen, to encourage bacterial action, and water. The nitrogen is applied most readily with a proprietary compost 'accelerator' powder which should be sprinkled over the organic matter after every 15–20 cm (6–8 in) of depth has been filled. If the bin is carefully sited, natural rainfall will keep it moist, and additional watering should only be needed in the driest weather. Almost inevitably, the bin will be positioned in a corner of the garden, and a fence or overhanging branch may provide sufficient shelter to prevent waterlogging. If not, then a coarse plastic net over the top will be helpful.

It is quite unnecessary to add soil to a compost bin. The only conceivable reason for doing so would be to supply bacteria, but there will be plenty of them on and around the waste plant material. Many gardeners and gardening books suggest that lime should be added to compost. I can only say that I have never found this necessary. Ideally, the compost in the bin should be turned at least once. This will ensure that all the debris experiences the highest temperatures, which will occur in the centre. In practice, it is easiest to turn material about three weeks after it has been added – turning the contents of an entire bin is physically almost impossible. Compost should be ready to use after about six months, although the upper quarter or so of the contents may be inadequately decomposed by that time and so should be transferred to a second bin or used to start a new batch in the first one.

I have been quoted as saying that anything can be added to a compost bin. This is not quite correct; anything can be added, but not all of it will decompose and a very few items may actually be detrimental. It is perhaps easiest to list the substances that I would not add to my compost bin. Any plastic, metallic or mineral matter will not break down. Animal remains such as chicken carcasses will gradually decompose but may attract vermin before they do so. Newspaper will certainly decompose but if it is not shredded, it will very effectively block the passage of air and water through the compost. Glossy paper as used for magazines rarely decomposes quickly, even when finely chopped. Leaves decompose much more slowly than most other forms of organic matter and are best excluded from the compost bin and stacked separately in a simple cage made from posts and chicken wire. If thoroughly wetted and compressed as they are added (children will enjoy jumping on them), they will be converted in about twelve months to leaf mould, an excellent and attractive mulching material. (Always remember that any organic mulch, although laid on the surface, will gradually become incorporated into the body of the soil through the action of earthworms.)

Woody material from prunings and from the cutting back of herbaceous plants in autumn provides a very useful coarse-textured material to complement softer, leafy matter, but must be shredded first to increase its surface area. An electric or petrol powered shredder is one of the most useful (and satisfying) garden appliances that you can buy. Lawn mowings provide the bulk of most gardeners' compostable matter during the summer months and if the bin is well aerated, they should not become slimy in the way that some people complain of. Nonetheless, every opportunity should be taken, even during the summer, to augment them with other material and a stack of shredded woody matter could perhaps be set aside for this purpose. Mowings from lawns on which selective weedkillers have been used are perfectly safe provided at least six months elapse (as will usually be the case) before the compost is added to the soil. Anyone with large old apple trees will have a good supply of surplus windfall fruit to dispose of in the autumn. These can certainly be placed on the compost bin but are best sliced with a spade as they are added to break their resilient skins; they should be blended with fibrous matter too.

The compost bin is an ideal repository for almost all garden weeds and provided it is well-managed, I believe (and have proved to myself) that no residual problems are likely to remain. I discuss this in more detail in relation to garden weed control in general (p. 92).

A compost shredder has joined my list of gardening indispensables and means that nearly all debris can be recycled. It is always wise to buy the most powerful shredder that you can afford as small models can clog frustratingly often. And do wear safety goggles and gloves.

SOME COMMON TYPES OF MANURE AND COMPOST

MANURES	Approximate % contents of main nutrients*			FEATURES OF SPECIAL INTEREST
	N	P	K	
Fresh farmyard	1.2	0.4	0.5	Add to the soil in autumn or compost it first
Rotted farmyard	0.4	0.2	0.6	Safe to apply to the soil in spring
Stable	0.7	0.5	0.6	Lower moisture content than farmyard; easier to handle
Pig	0.6	0.6	0.4	Strong smell a disadvantage especially in urban areas
Sheep	0.8	0.5	0.4	Low in moisture; easy to handle but rarely available in large amounts
Rabbit	0.5	1.2	0.5	Fairly high phosphate content but rarely available in large amounts
Chicken	2.0	1.8	1.0	Relatively high in all nutrients but can cause an imbalance between nitrogen and potash; compost before using
Pigeon	3.4	1.4	1.2	Very high in nitrogen in relation to potash but rarely available in large quantities; compost before using
Dog	0.4	0.2	0.1	Almost useless as no fibre content; always compost kennel waste before use for health reasons
COMPOSTS				
Bracken	2.0	0.2	0.5	Always compost before use
Garden compost	0.7	0.4	0.4	Care needed to avoid weed problems if inefficiently made
Leaf mould	0.4	0.2	0.3	Rots very slowly; better made separately from compost for mulching
Mushroom compost	0.6	0.5	0.9	High lime content; can give problems from the insecticide residues it may contain
Sawdust	0.2	0.1	0.1	Not recommended, except for blueberries; rots very slowly and may be toxic to some plants
Seaweed	0.6	0.3	1.0	Attracts flies when fresh and best composted first
Silage waste	0.2	0.1	0.6	Can be added directly to soil; nutritionally has a fairly high potash content
Soot	3.6	0.1	0.1	Compost first to avoid severe nutrient imbalance; possible toxic residues
Spent hops	1.1	0.3	0.1	Compost first; care is needed to avoid an imbalance between nitrogen and potash
Straw	0.5	0.2	0.9	Always compost before use

*N = nitrogen
P = phosphate
K = potash

Remember that the characteristics of manures will vary with the types of bedding used for the animals and with other differences in the conditions in which they have been kept. The nutrient contents will also generally decline with increasing age of the material and storage in the open.

WHILST there is every shade of attitude amongst gardeners from the besotted to the careless, very, very few people actually seek to make their gardening a full-time pursuit. Even those who do are unlikely to prefer the routine, maintenance aspects of the subject to planning and preparing new features. In effect, therefore, almost everyone has an interest in labour-saving techniques but there is one group of gardeners that has greater concern in this than most. Being elderly, infirm or handicapped need not mean an end to gardening activity, but it does mean that labour-saving methods, and those suitable for people with manipulative problems, become all important.

Labour-saving gardening

The simplest way to devise a labour-saving garden is to consider those aspects of gardening that occupy most time; and eliminate them. Of course, the larger the garden, the more it is likely to be time-consuming to manage. I believe that around half an acre is the most that any gardener with a full-time occupation and no paid gardening help can cope with effectively. But if you have no choice in the size of your garden, the simplest way to manage a large area is by grassing it; although not with a lawn. Confine close mowing to a small area near to the house and treat the remainder as rough grass. This requires much less frequent mowing and can be used as the basis of an attractive planting with native flowers (which themselves benefit of course from being left unmown until late in the summer); perhaps under an orchard of fruit trees. Bulbs, especially daffodils and narcissi, allowed to naturalise in the grass, will provide delightful spring colour with almost no requirement for routine maintenance. Indeed, any types of bulb that do not require annual lifting are well worthwhile.

Whilst I would certainly not advocate what I term 'hard gardening' – covering a garden with paving, gravel or similar non-plant surface – over a

Although annual plants are fairly labour intensive if raised from seed, the effort required can be cut down considerably if they are bought as transplants. Growing them in a raised bed enables infirm gardeners to tend them with relative ease.

With careful planning and forethought few types of gardening activity can be ruled out, even for disabled gardeners. Here, a small garden pool has been constructed on the raised bed principle.

large area, it can be valuable in small gardens where a lawn would soon be reduced to a quagmire in the winter. Plants may be grown in large containers on such a surface and provide a most attractive appearance, as countless thousands of inner city courtyard gardens testify.

Ornamental trees and shrubs for the most part need little attention, even in containers; the majority will thrive perfectly well with little or no pruning and even roses will be practical if the choice is limited to the shrub varieties (although roses in general make poor container plants). Climbing plants present slightly more difficulty for there are very few that will provide good colour and cover without at least some pruning. Nonetheless, in less formal positions, where they may be allowed freer rein, some types of clematis for instance will be effective (see p. 184).

All plants grown as annuals are labour-intensive in some way. The work involved in raising them yourself from seed can of course be avoided by buying trays of young plants from a garden centre, but you will still be faced with the chore of hardening them off, planting them out and then of watering and liquid feeding them regularly throughout the summer. Set against this is the undeniable appeal of the almost instant colour that bedding plants provide. But if time or enthusiasm are in short supply, use them in small areas close to the house; and if watering will present problems, limit your choice to the slightly more robust types such as pelargoniums, fibrous rooted begonias and busy lizzies. Sweet peas and petunias look attractive and appealing but both must be picked or dead-headed continually if they are not to set seed and so decline very dramatically in new flower production. Growing bedding plants in containers is appealing and seemingly offers a great deal of colour for very little garden room. But containers too are labour-intensive (see p. 35) and on a hot courtyard or balcony, daily attention to watering must be given throughout the summer.

Much of what I have said about bedding plants applies to vegetables too. They will not thrive without constant watering and you will also have the additional work involved in weeding between the rows and in the beds. Among the least labour-intensive vegetable crops are the root vegetables such as carrots and parsnips, but they are also among the most difficult to grow, requiring very careful soil preparation. It is perfectly possible to grow satisfactory crops of French and dwarf runner beans, radishes, lettuces and other small leafy crops such as spinach with once-a-week attention to watering. But peas, climbing runner beans and most of the larger crop plants such as potatoes, cauliflowers, broccoli and Brussels sprouts all require additional attention in the form of staking or some other special cultural technique, and are best avoided by anyone with limited time.

Although I have stressed the importance of feeding your plants constantly throughout the summer, even this can be minimised if slow-release fertilisers such as bone meal are incorporated into beds and borders before planting. In larger containers, use soil-based composts, which have an inherently greater reservoir of available nutrient.

After watering and feeding, the gardening operation most consuming of time is weeding. I have already mentioned the part that weeding plays in adding to the work of maintaining a vegetable garden, but if you adopt more permanent plantings of herbaceous perennials or trees and shrubs, weed control can be all but eliminated. I know, for I have proved it myself; and the knowledge that weeds are not usurping your property can give a great deal of peace of mind if you are constantly having to work away from home. The

The Oregon grape, Mahonia aquifolium, is not only a very robust shrub that will survive in the poorest of conditions, but it also offers attractively perfumed yellow flowers in the early, dark days of the year.

answer lies quite simply in mulching, the finest weed suppressing technique of all (p. 90). If your garden has an entrenched population of perennial weeds which mulching will not suppress, I concede that a season or two of concerted effort with a systemic weedkiller will be required first. Thereafter, a thick organic mulch will be your greatest ally – and will, of course, minimise your watering effort too (p. 67).

The special problems attendant on gardening with some form of handicap have fortunately become much more widely recognised in recent years and several organisations exist to cater especially for such needs. There are two aspects to the subject – the design of the garden itself, and the tools and techniques used for gardening activity. Unfortunately, I have no scope to discuss every disability and the problems it presents, so perhaps my purpose is best served by pointing out some of the commonest situations. Wheelchairs will not readily go up and down steps nor through narrow gates. A person confined to a wheelchair cannot readily reach – they require long-handled tools, or the garden itself must be brought up to their level by means of raised beds. Long-handled tools must be lightweight and should, if possible, incorporate some lever or other principle by which work can be achieved for less effort; many wheelchair gardeners have not only impaired mobility but impaired strength too.

I appreciate that raised beds are easier and cheaper to describe than construct, but it may be possible to enlist the help of a charitable organisation to help defray the initial cost. A small raised bed with brick surrounds need not be very expensive, and even a single bed can give immense joy and satisfaction to someone who otherwise would be unable to garden at all.

Blind or partially-sighted gardeners will of course derive delight from selections of plants that are perfumed but there are other considerations too. The sense of touch is especially important and plants that are pleasing to handle, perhaps through their silky foliage, will be appreciated, especially if handling them releases a perfume too. Conversely, it is important to avoid sticky, prickly or otherwise unpleasant types of vegetation in a garden for those with visual defects.

SOME PLANTS WITH PARTICULARLY STRONG FLOWER OR FOLIAGE SCENT

Buddleia alternifolia (shrub)
Cheiranthus (wallflower) (biennial)
Chimonanthus praecox (winter sweet) (shrub)
Daphne (most species) (shrub)
Hyacinthus (hyacinth) (perennial bulb)
Jasminum officinale (summer jasmine) (shrub)
Lavandula (lavender) (shrub)
Lonicera (honeysuckle) (climber)
Lily (many forms are highly scented, but *Lilium regale* especially so) (perennial bulb)
Mahonia (most species) (shrub)
Mentha (all species) (mints) (perennial)
Mignonette (annual)
Myrtus (myrtle) (shrub)
Nicotiana (ornamental tobacco) (annual)
Philadelphus (most forms) (mock orange) (shrub)
Rosmarinus (rosemary) (shrub)
Roses (many forms – but less appealing because of their thorns)
Thymus (thyme) (shrub)
Viburnum × bodnantense (shrub)
Viburnum fragrans (shrub)

PART TWO

Maintaining Your Garden

Garden tools

WHILST green fingers may well be very valuable attributes in the garden, you will not be a horticulturist for long before you realise that a rather more extensive set of tools is needed for successful gardening. For centuries, of course, gardeners have managed solely with hand tools, but the effectiveness and relatively low cost of modern power tools mean that they now have a crucial part to play in taking out much of the chore from routine and tedious tasks. In all except the very small garden, therefore, I rank some power tools as almost indispensable.

It is an oft-repeated maxim that the more you pay, the better the product and, by and large, this is true of garden tools. But remember that you are not buying some disposable merchandise, you are acquiring the wherewithal to enjoy your gardening for many years, if not a lifetime, so buy the best that you can afford. Gardening tools are very personal items, however, and I would advise you most strongly never to buy any that you have not handled. If possible, you should actually borrow tools of different types and brands from gardening friends and neighbours in order to find those that suit you – there is an enormous range in weight and ease of operation. For hand tools, I am wedded to stainless steel, though they are considerably more expensive than basic carbon steel models. But once you have dug or hoed with stainless steel tools, I honestly believe that you will never be satisfied again with less. They move more easily through the soil, they remain sharp for longer and they require the minimum of maintenance (a mere wipe with a cloth after use). If your finances for buying garden tools are strictly limited, however, your priorities among stainless steel tools should be those that most benefit from the smooth finish – a spade and trowel and a push hoe.

And so to my shortlist of essential cultivating tools for every gardener with open soil to till: a spade and fork (of small border varieties rather than full-sized; these can come later if you progress to large-scale vegetable growing); a hand trowel and hand fork; a push hoe and a spring-tine rake (sometimes called a lawn rake; this is much more versatile than a normal garden rake with rigid teeth). You can save money by opting for detachable head cultivators (those where one handle enables you to change from hoe to rake or other long-handled appliance), although personally I find the inconvenience outweighs the benefits. In any event, lightweight, aluminium handles are to be preferred for cultivators while slightly pliable wood is best for spades and forks (where ash is the norm for long handled versions and beech for the small, hand tools).

Secateurs are the most important cutting tool, and here the choice lies principally between scissor action or by-pass tools, with two blades, and the anvil action models with one. The former deal more gently with soft stems, while the latter are valuable for cutting hard, woody tissue without themselves being harmed. I am still unsure which of these I would opt for if I could have only one, but in inexperienced hands, I think it would be the anvil pattern. Even more than with cultivating tools, quality pays in cutting-edge tools, and if cheap, poorly made secateurs are frustrating, then cheap shears are even more so. Nonetheless, after a powered lawnmower, powered hedge trimmers would be my next labour-saving purchase, so it may be that except for the smallest gardens, the days of the short-handled garden shears are numbered. The modern single-handed shears are nonetheless very useful for trimming into difficult corners and for dead-heading or cutting back such bushy plants as heathers. And for lawn edging, no power cutter in the world can give anything remotely like the finish of a long-handled

Over the years I have accumulated tools for most garden purposes. Not everyone will need quite as extensive a range as this but I hope that my ordered nature shows through and that you will provide each of your tools with a peg on which to hang it.

Opposite: Only a few minutes' effort is needed at the end of a day's gardening activity to clean tools before they are put away but this attention will be repaid many times over in the added life that it gives them.

lawn edge shear; laborious they may be to use, but the end result is splendid.

The half-moon lawn edging knife is relatively inexpensive but gives a straight edge at the start of the season such as no spade ever will, so I consider it well worth the investment. Lawnmowers themselves now come in an astonishing array of types but there remain two basic principles of lawn mowing – that based on a cylinder of rotating blades and that based on some form of slasher, which these days is more likely to be of nylon than metal. After many years of evaluating a large number of machines, my preferences lie with large petrol-engined wheeled rotary, petrol-engined cylinder and electric cylinder mowers (all with grass collectors) and small electric hover rotary machines. If I had one small lawn, I would use the electric cylinder. As it is, I have fairly large lawns of fairly good turf, so have the other three, using the big rotary (which is really at home on rougher, tougher grass) early in the season while the surface is slightly uneven, wet and still littered with the debris of winter, the big cylinder during the summer to give a smooth finish and attractive stripes, and the small hover to reach beneath over-hanging shrubs and into difficult corners. The latter is, I admit, a luxury, but I hope these various uses will indicate which machine you will find the most useful for your garden.

Whilst I have suggested a lawn rake as your only garden rake, it will be of little use for one particularly laborious task – the periodic removal of moss from the lawn – and it is here that electric lawn rakes are invaluable. Their collectors, however, are uselessly small. Much the best plan is to use the machine without the collector, and rake the moss and 'thatch' into heaps afterwards.

The only remaining power tool that I now place among my gardening indispensables is a compost shredder. I say this for two reasons, the first being that my garden, as everyone else's, benefits from as much compost as I can provide; and shredding enables me to compost a great deal more coarse material, and to compost a great deal more quickly and efficiently than otherwise I could. And the second is that in enabling me to compost so much more material, I am spared the problem of transporting it elsewhere as rubbish. But I must be cautious here in my recommendation, for whilst the debris from a small garden can be coped with by a small electric shredder of around 1000 watts, larger gardens really will only be served by large electric, or better still, petrol-engined, machines costing several hundreds of pounds.

Soil care and management

THE soil is your most precious gardening asset. It must be cared for and respected. These remarks will appear curious to anyone who is possessed of a light, free-draining sand that seems more appropriate for deckchairs than plants; or, worse still, with a soil so heavy that a dinner service could be fashioned from it. But it is as true, nonetheless, as my next statement – that every soil can be improved and every soil is potentially fertile.

The soil is an important and very complex medium, although only a basic understanding of what it is and what it does is needed to ensure that your gardening activities are productive. I shall introduce you therefore to the two important characteristics of soil, its texture and its structure. A soil's texture is an expression of the relative amounts it contains of three types of mineral particles. In decreasing size, these are sand, silt and clay. It is quite easy to see these proportions by shaking up a small sample of soil with water in a bottle and then allowing the sediment to settle – the dense sand settles first at the bottom, the less dense silt next and the clay (often after a long time) on top. Rubbed between moistened fingers, a very sandy soil feels gritty, a very clayey soil, greasy.

A clay soil is hard to cultivate, poorly draining and very slow to warm up in spring. However, the minute clay particles do have the ability to hold plant nutrients very effectively. A sandy soil, by contrast, is easy to dig and quick to warm up but drains freely, losing both water and nutrients as it does so. Whilst some plants thrive in a heavy clay soil and others in a light sand, the ideal soil for most gardening activities is a loam, a general term for a soil that contains a readily workable blend of sand, silt and clay. Actually altering texture by adjusting the natural proportions of the three types of mineral matter in your soil is not practicable. But what can be done is to alter the structure of the soil – the balance of mineral and other matter, water and air that is expressed in how well the soil is formed into crumbs. If you carry out the experiment with soil in a bottle of water, you will find that, in addition to the settled sediment, there will also be some material floating on top of the water. This is the key to improving the structure. It is organic matter or humus, the dead remains of plants in a state of partial decomposition through the activity of soil fungi and bacteria.

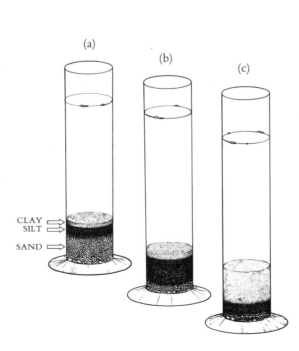

CLAY
SILT
SAND

(a)

(b)

(c)

SOIL ANALYSIS.
(a) sandy soil.
(b) loamy soil.
(c) clayey soil.

Humus is important, for it has sponge-like properties that improve the moisture retentiveness of a sandy soil, yet it also contains natural glues that help to bind the mineral matter into crumbs, between which are spaces. This process operates in heavy clays too so, paradoxically, the same material can improve both free-draining and waterlogged soils. If you regularly add organic matter to your soil, your gardening will inevitably improve. On p. 62 and p. 67 I explain in more detail the value of organic matter of different types in aiding the supply both of water and food to plants. But the basic maxim is so important that I make no excuse for repeating it – the only way to improve either a clayey or a sandy soil is by regularly incorporating organic matter. If the garden is large, then do a little thoroughly at a time, rather than spreading both organic matter and effort thinly over all.

The soil in any garden plot or bed should be dug when plants are removed from it and this is the time when organic matter is most easily incorporated. With a normal vegetable plot or annual flower bed, this will generally be every year, in the autumn. With a deep vegetable bed (see p. 114) it will be every five or six years. With a herbaceous border or soft fruit garden, it might be every seven or ten years. With a shrubbery, it could be only a couple of times in a gardening life – although the soil must be dug locally whenever an individual tree or shrub is removed. The reason for digging is to correct the accumulated structural damage; a vegetable plot will have been walked on, the soil compressed and the crumb structure and drainage impaired. Even if you seldom walk through your ornamental beds and borders, the natural beating activity of rain will fairly effectively compress the soil over a period of time.

Digging, to most people, simply entails turning over the soil with spade or fork, preferably in a systematic fashion from one side of the plot to the other. If it is done in autumn, the clods can be left fairly large, for the action of winter rain and frost will break them down further. (On p. 99 I outline the final preparations, which will usually be done in spring, needed to make the soil ready for plants or seeds.) As the soil is turned, so organic matter in the shape of compost or manure can be roughly forked in. The activity of worms during the winter will ensure that it is dragged down and more thoroughly mixed into the soil. This type of digging, called single digging, is generally satisfactory for a plot that is dug annually. However, the accumulated effects of several years without cultivation necessitates a more thorough operation. This is called double digging and it is hard but valuable work.

To double dig, you should work from side to side of the area as before, but the soil should be removed to two spades' depth, in effect, to produce a trench about 40 cm (16 inches) deep each time you cross the plot. Organic matter should be laid in the bottom of trench and forked in thoroughly. Then more organic matter should be forked in as the trench is filled.

After texture and structure, the third important soil feature of which you should be aware is its relative acidity or alkalinity, for this in part dictates how well your plants will grow. Unlike texture and structure, however, acidity and alkalinity can be quantified relatively easily on a scale called pH. The pH of soil ranges from about 3 for a very acidic peat to about 8.5 for a very thin soil overlying chalk. (The full chemical pH scale actually spans from 0 to 14 and the mid-point, 7, is called neutral.) Most types of plant have difficulty in taking up essential mineral nutrients from an alkaline soil for the nutrients become combined chemically *in situ*. On p. 64 I suggest some ways of ensuring that plants can receive their required nutrients under such conditions, but for most types of plant (and certainly for most fruit and vegetables) a soil that is slightly acidic (with a pH of about 6.5) will give the best results. How can you discover how close your soil is to this ideal and what can be done to alter it? Quite the easiest way of roughly gauging the pH of your soil is to look at the vegetation growing naturally or in neighbouring gardens in your area. If there are rhododendrons and azaleas to be found, then the soil will be highly acidic, whereas if raspberries display markedly yellowed leaves with dark green veins, the chances are that it is alkaline. Having established this crude guideline, however, it is important to determine the pH rather more precisely before attempting to make any adjustment. Garden centres sell small so-called pH testing meters but I do not find them satisfactory. They do not in fact measure pH at all (chemically, this is a very complex operation) and the system they employ can at best give only a crude approximation. I recommend instead that you use one of the small kits that rely on the colour change of an indicator dye.

After determining your soil pH, you may wish to effect an adjustment. To raise the pH of an acidic soil, you must add lime. The best time to do this is in the autumn, using ground limestone or 'garden lime'. If at all possible, use a rotary cultivator to incorporate it thoroughly into the soil. Because the amount to add will vary depending both on the initial pH of your soil and on its texture, most manufacturers of test kits supply a graph or chart to show the correct dose in different conditions. Check the pH again after about nine months to determine if a further liming is necessary. Never add lime to soil as a simple routine. Even on light soils with a low organic content from which lime disappears most readily, an application about once every four or five years should be adequate. If you over-lime, you may encounter the problems with nutrient uptake that I mentioned earlier, and you may also predispose some plants to disease problems – potatoes to scab for example. Only with the special problems of brassicas and clubroot disease is very heavy liming justified but I say more about this on p. 82. And never apply lime within one month of applying animal manure to the soil, for the two will react together and liberate harmful ammonia.

If your soil is naturally very alkaline – especially if the pH reading is above 7.5 – it is much harder to alter matters. On a small scale, it is possible to bring about a slight reduction by adding sulphur, which is sold at garden centres for the purpose. This is converted in the soil to dilute sulphuric acid and will go some way towards neutralising the alkalinity but the results will never be as effective as those that lime brings about in the opposite direction. Applying fertilisers that contain ammonium sulphate as a nitrogen source (see p. 65) will also help to lower pH to some extent. Whenever you grow any plants on alkaline soils that are not specially adapted to such conditions, you should take additional precautions to ensure they receive essential nutrients by using sequestrene as I describe on p. 64.

Of course, there will be instances when it is impracticable or prohibitively expensive to alter the pH of a garden soil other than on a very small scale. Your priority and effort then should be expended on adjusting the soil in the vegetable plot and choosing your ornamental plants carefully. Easily the bigger problems attach to alkaline soils, for most ornamentals will at least tolerate acid conditions. I have listed some common ornamental plants, therefore, that are particularly unsuitable for conditions of high alkalinity and which will inevitably give poor results there. But if you have an alkaline soil yet really hanker for dwarf rhododendrons and similar acid-loving species, you will derive much pleasure and satisfaction from constructing a small peat bed (see p. 237).

SOME ORNAMENTAL PLANTS UNSUITABLE FOR ALKALINE SOILS

Chilean firebush [*Embothrium*]	*Kalmia*
Enkianthus	Lilies [many]
Eucryphia	*Lithospermum*
Fothergilla	*Magnolia* [some]
Gaultheria	*Meconopsis*
Gentians [except *Gentiana acaulis* and	*Pernettya*
G. septemfida]	*Pieris*
Gum trees [*Eucalyptus*]	*Rhododendron*
Heaths [*Erica* species except *E. carnea*]	Summer-flowering heather [*Calluna*]
Camellia	*Vaccinium*
Irish heath [*Daboecia*]	

Finally, a mention of the ways to ensure that your plants derive the optimum benefit from soil nutrients. It is impossible to garden successfully unless you replace with fertilisers the nutrients that plants remove, and on p. 65 I give some guidelines for fertiliser choice and use. You may be tempted to buy one of the small test kits sold for assessing the nutrient status of your soil. Resist this temptation. Such kits are unreliable, partly because the methods they employ are inefficient but also because the levels of some nutrients in the soil change extremely quickly, especially after rainfall. If your plants are seriously short of any particular nutrient, they will soon tell you, and on p. 64 I explain how to recognise their symptoms. But in fact, plants should rarely be short of nutrient if you follow my fertiliser guidelines and if, in the vegetable garden, where the greatest demands are being placed on the soil's nutrient reserves, you practise crop rotation.

A crop rotation such as is practised in vegetable gardens is simply a management scheme to ensure that the same type of crop is not grown on the same area of soil more than once every three years. The reasoning behind it is two-fold. Different plants require differing proportions of each soil nutrient and thus the whole spectrum of nutrients will be utilised. It is also widely claimed that rotation will allow pests and diseases present in the soil to die away between crops (each problem is often specific to certain types of crop). This second notion is fine for commercial growers, where the distance between the plots in a rotation may be a kilometre or more, but it has little advantage in a garden where pests can fly or crawl the few metres necessary and disease-contaminated soil will be carried on boots and tools.

An ideal three-year vegetable crop rotation requires each crop to occupy a similar area of land for similar periods. Clearly this would be impossible in a modern sized garden, but in the scheme that I offer, I have grouped together plants with similar fertiliser needs and have kept separate from the rotation those plants that can or should be grown on the same area for longer than one season. I believe that my scheme will offer approximate self-sufficiency in vegetables for a family of four, but obviously individual gardeners may well wish to make adjustments to meet their own likes and dislikes. Nonetheless, as far as possible, the overall types of plant in each of the three groups should remain the same.

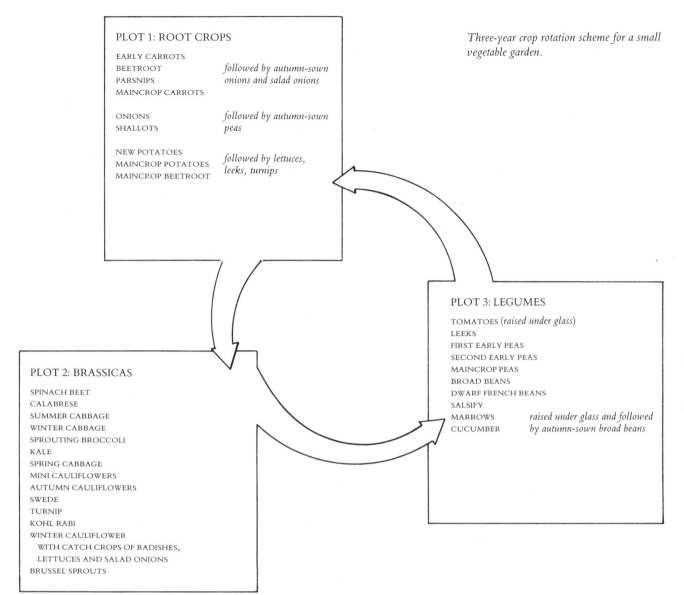

PLOT 1: ROOT CROPS

EARLY CARROTS
BEETROOT
PARSNIPS
MAINCROP CARROTS

*followed by autumn-sown
onions and salad onions*

ONIONS
SHALLOTS

*followed by autumn-sown
peas*

NEW POTATOES
MAINCROP POTATOES
MAINCROP BEETROOT

*followed by lettuces,
leeks, turnips*

*Three-year crop rotation scheme for a small
vegetable garden.*

PLOT 3: LEGUMES

TOMATOES (*raised under glass*)
LEEKS
FIRST EARLY PEAS
SECOND EARLY PEAS
MAINCROP PEAS
BROAD BEANS
DWARF FRENCH BEANS
SALSIFY
MARROWS
CUCUMBER

*raised under glass and followed
by autumn-sown broad beans*

PLOT 2: BRASSICAS

SPINACH BEET
CALABRESE
SUMMER CABBAGE
WINTER CABBAGE
SPROUTING BROCCOLI
KALE
SPRING CABBAGE
MINI CAULIFLOWERS
AUTUMN CAULIFLOWERS
SWEDE
TURNIP
KOHL RABI
WINTER CAULIFLOWER
   WITH CATCH CROPS OF RADISHES,
   LETTUCES AND SALAD ONIONS
BRUSSEL SPROUTS

Plant feeding

IF through choice or accident, you do not give your garden plants any fertiliser, they will still survive. Presumably, therefore, like wild plants, they already have a supply of nutrient, so what merit is there in spending money and effort to give them more? A logical question, but one with an equally logical, if slightly complicated, answer. Yes, your plants, in common with wild plants, do have a supply of food already – the soil provides them with minerals from which their roots can take up such essential elements as nitrogen, phosphorus and potassium in solution. And the air that surrounds them also provides water and, most importantly, carbon dioxide. These two compounds are combined together, using sunlight as an energy source, to form carbohydrates, the process taking place in green tissues with the aid of the energy-trapping green pigment chlorophyll.

No gardener can actually influence the composition of the air, although when you confine plants in greenhouses and frames, it is worth remembering that among the roles of good ventilation is the supplying of at least part of the plants' nutrient source. But the soil is a different matter. Naturally, almost all of our soils contain sufficient nutrients for plants to grow, flower, set and shed their seed and so perpetuate the species – hence the wild world. But we, as gardeners, have come to expect rather more of our plants than their wild hedgerow relatives produce. We expect bigger, showier flowers, larger fruit and, in the case of vegetables, plump succulent leaves. So we must on the one hand give them more than nature's food alone, to enable them to produce this; but we must also replace annually the nutrient that is lost when we harvest our crops or dispose of our spent ornamentals – nature simply lets the remains rot where they fall.

Plant feeding can be as simple or complicated as you care to make it. My experience is that most gardens can manage with a modest range of fertilisers and I have listed those that I consider the most important, together with their uses in the garden. But having offered you my selection of fertilisers, I must add that there are other considerations too, some of which you will need to know, some of which you are entitled to know.

In my discussion of the organic manures and composts that are added to soil, I made reference to the distinction between organic and non-organic fertilisers. It is important that I should now say more about this because the subject has become one of widespread interest and arouses some degree of emotion. Organic fertilisers, using the definition that I gave on p. 44, are derived from a once-living organism. This is generally obvious from their names – dried blood, hoof and horn, bonemeal, seaweed extract and so on. Non-organic fertilisers may be manufactured in a chemical factory (ammonium sulphate, for instance) or be obtained by greater or lesser amounts of purification of some mineral rock (rock phosphate is the best-known example). I believe it is important to understand that plants cannot distinguish between different sources of their nutrients: they absorb them in very simple chemical form, and whether their nitrogen came originally from ammonium sulphate or from dried blood is immaterial. It is often claimed that vegetables grown with organic fertilisers taste better than those grown with artificial types. This may be so. I have never proved it to my own satisfaction and I cannot imagine how such a difference could arise, but there it is. I feel we need to look for slightly more tangible reasons when making our choices.

Environmental contamination is something definitely to be avoided and there is certainly considerable evidence that the widespread commercial use of artificial nitrogen-containing fertilisers has caused such problems. In gardens, of course, both quantities and impact will be very much less but it may well be that this is a matter that you wish to have no part in at all. But there can be despoiling of the environment in the manufacture and extraction of fertilisers too, and no one who has visited a slaughterhouse, a bonemeal factory or a blood drying plant will imagine again that unpleasantness is limited to non-organic products. Ultimately, I feel that one of the best reasons for choosing organic or organically-based products is that of their mode of action – how, and how quickly, are the nutrients released into the soil?

Rapidity of action is important in choosing any fertiliser. A slow-release product such as bonemeal, which breaks down in the soil over a long period of time to release phosphate, is ideal when planting perennials. Fairly finely ground bonemeal, together with dried blood, fish meal and finely ground sulphate of potash, in the form of the mixture called blood, fish and bone, provides a somewhat quicker acting, all-round blend for the start of the growing season. But for really quick results, you need the gardening equivalent of the soluble aspirin – the liquid fertiliser that really comes into its own during the height of summer when crops in general, and the fast growers like tomatoes in particular, are putting on new leaves, flowers and fruits at a prodigious rate. At these times of fast growth, it is often useful to be able to apply such liquid fertilisers as foliar feeds; sprayed onto the leaves, they can be absorbed directly, although not in such large quantities as pass in through the more normal pathway of the roots. Almost all liquid fertilisers are non-organic, and this underlines my feeling that you should choose according to your needs. If the best and cheapest slow-release form of phosphate, for instance, happens to be organic, you should select it. But there

One of the most useful innovations of recent years has been the hose-end diluter, a device that renders plant feeding a much simpler task. The reservoir is filled with concentrated soluble fertiliser and the flow of water through the hose-pipe draws out sufficient to provide a correctly diluted fertiliser spray.

Your own plants will tell you when they are in need of feeding. This raspberry leaf, for instance, betrays the classic symptoms of iron deficiency.

is no intrinsic reason why any fertiliser should or should not be better, simply because it is or is not organic in origin.

How are fertilisers best applied to your plants? A liquid fertiliser applied to the roots will obviously be delivered most simply from a watering can, and one applied to the leaves through a sprayer. At least one fertiliser manufacturer offers a so-called hose-end dilutor, a device that attaches to a watering-can spout and draws concentrate from the can as water from a hose pipe passes through it. This is very useful for applying liquid to a large area such as a lawn. Somewhat similar hose-end contrivances operate on a spray-gun principle and necessitate inserting a fertiliser pellet into a hand-held hose-end appliance, or adding a soluble solid fertiliser to a small volume of water to produce a concentrate.

Solid fertilisers such as bonemeal or blood, fish and bone are most conveniently applied by the handful (preferably wearing a thin rubber glove) but hands vary considerably in size and the same handful of dried blood will contain much less weight than the same of basic slag. In all of my guidelines for plant feeding, I express fertiliser doses by weight, therefore, but I suggest that you spend half an hour with a set of scales to determine the approximate weight contained by your own handfuls of each of the solid fertilisers that you use. Write these values on a card to be kept in your shed, garage or other store. The best general rule when applying solid fertiliser to the soil around plants is to scatter it uniformly over an area approximating to the spread of the above-ground parts – this will usually be the same as the area to which the roots extend below. When applying solid fertiliser to a lawn, it is all but impossible to spread it uniformly enough by hand to prevent a mosaic of light and dark patches of grass appearing. An inexpensive wheeled spreader is an excellent investment therefore.

In accounts of fertilisers, you will often read of trace elements and their deficiencies. As their name implies, trace elements are those nutrients required by plants in very small amounts. Despite what you may be told elsewhere, almost no garden soil is naturally deficient in any of them and there will hardly ever be occasions when problems arise. Soil-less growing composts are a different matter but all fertilisers formulated for use in such conditions have adequate trace elements added. One important element which I refer to as a minor nutrient (in other words, one required in less amounts than the major nutrients, nitrogen, phosphorus and potassium, but more than the trace substances) is iron. And iron, almost alone among non-major nutrients, is often deficient – not because it is actually in short supply (after all, it is iron that is largely responsible for the overall red-brown colour of soil) but because, in alkaline conditions, it reacts with other substances so that plants are unable to absorb it. A shortage of iron in plant tissues results in the leaves becoming yellowed (although with conspicuous dark green veins), with consequent poor overall growth. If your garden soil is alkaline, therefore, it is wise to supply additional iron in a form called sequestrene (which can be absorbed easily) to those species most prone to the deficiency. Hydrangeas, raspberries, roses and strawberries are the most important among them, although it is sensible to apply sequestrene also to plants being grown in a peat bed (p. 237) constructed over naturally alkaline soil.

1. *A balanced general purpose solid fertiliser*

The commonest artificial blend available in Britain is the granular mixture called Growmore which contains 7% of each of the major nutrients, nitrogen (N), phosphate (P) and potash (K) (it is thus commonly expressed in shorthand as a 7:7:7 fertiliser). Different levels tend to be set in different countries and in the United States the most widely used artificial mixture is a 5:10:10.

The principal organically *based* compound fertiliser is blood, fish and bone, a blend of dried blood, fish meal, finely ground bonemeal and sulphate of potash (not, of course, organic). Like all organically based fertilisers, it is of more variable composition but is approximately 5.1:5:6.5. The nitrogen from the dried blood tends to be available slightly more slowly than that from the ammonium sulphate in artificial mixtures, and the phosphorus is released more slowly from the bone-meal component.

These general purpose compound fertilisers are particularly valuable for use among vegetables and other plants at, or just before, the start of the growing season. I have expressed the approximate solid fertiliser requirements of vegetables and other plants elsewhere in the book in terms of a product (such as these) that contains around 6% of nitrogen.

2. *A general purpose liquid fertiliser, relatively high in potassium*

Bearing in mind the usefulness of a liquid feed during rapid summer growth, and also the value of potassium for flower and fruit development, a fertiliser of this type should be the mainstay of most gardeners' fertiliser usage during the height of the season. There are several branded liquid products of this nature, varying in their relative nutrient contents and most containing additional minor and trace elements – an advantage since they tend to be used extensively for plants growing in peat-based composts as well as for those in soil. The concentrated liquid tomato fertilisers, for instance, generally with a composition of around 5:5:9 derived from inorganic components, are of this type. Most of the liquid fertilisers purchased in the form of soluble powders or crystals also fall into this category, having nutrient ratios of about 15:5:20.

3. *Bonemeal (organic) or superphosphate (artificial)*

I believe there is little difference between these alternatives for the slow release of phosphorus to aid the establishment of perennials. They should be used routinely at the rate of about 175 g/square metre (5½ oz/sq yd) in the planting of trees, shrubs, herbaceous perennials and bulbs therefore.

4. *Two lawn fertilisers*

Lawns should generally be fed twice a year, in spring and in autumn, but the plants' nutrient requirements are different at these times. I discuss lawn feeding and lawn management in some detail on p. 153, but two powder-formulated lawn fertilisers should be among your plant food stocks – one with a relatively high nitrogen content for spring and summer use and one relatively lower in nitrogen for autumn and winter application. The latter is also the type of fertiliser that I recommend for application before seeding or turfing.

5. *John Innes Base*

Most gardens contain at least some pots or other containers for summer flowers, bulbs, wallflowers and other ornamentals. Whilst I advise you to replace the peat or loam-based compost in small pots and window boxes every season, this is scarcely practicable with larger tubs and half-barrel sized containers. Nonetheless, if these are filled initially with a good quality loam-based potting compost such as John Innes No. 3, they can serve reliably for several years without being refilled if the top few centimetres of old compost are removed and replaced with a mixture of peat and a fertiliser called John Innes Base at about 70 g/square metre (2½ oz/sq yd) at each replanting.

6. *Rose fertiliser*

The demands imposed by gardeners on their roses and the demands that the plants in turn impose on the soil's nutrient reserves are high. Fertilisers have been formulated specifically for the purpose of feeding roses, therefore, and these contain a blend of the major nutrients with special emphasis on the potassium to encourage flower development. Most branded products also contain additional magnesium, for roses are rather unusually prone to deficiency of this element. In general, I apply rose fertilisers at the rate of about 35 g/square metre (1 oz/sq yd) following the spring pruning and again after the first flush of summer flowers in late June. Although formulated specifically for roses, such fertilisers provide an ideal balanced feed for other flowering shrubs also and I feed them all at the same time.

Plant watering

Garden watering systems now come in a vast array of patterns, suitable for every size and shape of garden and every type of plant. Some can be as entrancingly lovely as ornamental fountains too as they paint constantly changing water patterns in the sunlight.

FROM the very beginning of our horticultural experience, we gardeners learn that plants require food and water. But whilst most of us can readily accept and understand that plant feeding requires a degree of logic and commonsense, this is certainly less true of watering. I am fairly sure that until recently only those gardeners who live in very dry areas, where use of hose-pipes is restricted almost every summer, have given more than a passing thought to the subject of meaningful water usage. This has now changed and is likely to change even more for one simple reason. Almost all of us, even those in areas with high rainfall and large water reserves, will be charged for the volume of water that we use; it will no longer be available *ad lib* for a fixed sum. How can we ensure, therefore, that we obtain the best value for our money; or, to put it another way, how should our gardens be watered in order that the plants obtain the greatest benefit?

It will come as no surprise to learn that with plant watering, as with other aspects of plant husbandry, commercial growers have thought about the matter in some detail. Indeed, the optimal use of water for commercial field vegetable crops has come from the results of very careful research. It is of course quite impractical to expect you, as gardeners, precisely to relate watering to rainfall and soil moisture content, or even to make very significant adjustments between different parts of the garden in the time and quantity of their watering. But without too much difficulty, you can, I hope, differentiate spatially between lawns, vegetable plots, fruit gardens and ornamental beds and borders when using a sprinkler; and can very readily arrange to give more or less water, more or less often to individual types of plant when using a watering can. And we can all, I hope, understand enough about rainfall and soil to ensure that the water that is delivered naturally and free of charge from the clouds stays long enough in our gardens to achieve some use.

First, therefore, the ways to make best use of rainfall. In my account of soil management (p. 58), I stressed the value of digging in organic matter for its improvement of soil structure and explained how this will help maintain a balance between too much of the rainfall draining uselessly away and too much being retained to cause waterlogging. During the summer, whatever the soil type, it is essential to limit the amount of water that is lost through evaporation from the soil surface. And the way to achieve this is with one of my most valued gardening practices – mulching. Apply a mulch of about 5 cm (2 inch) thickness, preferably of garden compost or well rotted manure, and you will not only achieve the benefits of weed control (p. 90) but moisture loss through the soil surface will be kept to a minimum. A mulch for soil moisture retention should of course be applied during the spring, but only do so while the soil is full of moisture. The covering, like any blanket, will only keep the soil in its existing condition. A dry soil, therefore, will remain dry.

Water is not only lost through the soil surface but also through leaf surfaces, so by having fewer leaves more water will be retained. To a gardener, the notion of growing fewer plants must sound a trifle ludicrous but in a dry area, in a hot summer, that extra superfluous row of cabbages could well be denying valuable moisture to their lettuce neighbours. Never forget that weeds are plants, too, and they also lose water through their leaves. Keeping down weed growth, therefore, can also, in drought conditions, help retain the soil's moisture reserves.

Rainwater can and should be stored whenever possible. Every greenhouse, shed or other garden outbuilding can very usefully have a rainwater butt adjoining it, but from experience I have always been wary of using such stored rainwater in the greenhouse. Almost unavoidably, insect larvae, algae and other organisms (including some pests and diseases) will proliferate in the stored water and whilst these will generally be of no consequence for crops growing in beds and borders, the warm, cossetting conditions of the greenhouse can cause them to flourish, to the detriment of plants in pots or growing bags.

But given that rainwater alone will seldom be adequate, we return to the matter of garden watering. First, let me knock on the head any suggestion that tap water is likely to cause harm to plants, no matter how revolting some tap water tastes to us. Chlorine or other purifying agents will not affect plant life, and all tap water may be used for all plants, although lime-hating rhododendrons and azaleas grown in pots may suffer some yellowing when watered with hard water. I have watered rhododendrons growing outdoors in garden beds with very hard water for many years and have never found them to experience any problems. But if water is to be used meaningfully, it should only be applied to plants at the time they most need it; for despite what I have said about plants' water requirements, it is only at certain stages of growth that their demands become really critical and (unless prolonged drought conditions prevail) supplementary watering should not be needed constantly. The best rule of thumb is to water plants as the parts that are the reason for their cultivation begin to mature. This applies especially to annuals, such as bedding plants and vegetables, and to fairly shallowly rooted perennials such as soft fruit and most herbaceous ornamentals. It does not, however, apply to lawns which, despite being shallow rooted, have quite remarkable powers of recovery (never, in time of water shortage, waste time, effort, money and water on your lawn). The logic means, therefore, that cabbages require water as their heads fill, lettuces as they begin to heart, potatoes as the tubers start to swell (around flowering time), raspberries as their fruit begin to expand and, of course, flowers as the buds burst. It also means that whereas for many plants, use of valuable water can be localised to a relatively few weeks, plants such as bedding annuals, with buds bursting and flowers opening continuously, will need constant attention. Hence my comment (p. 50) that these are not plants for the gardener who cannot be more or less permanently present with watering can or hose pipe.

During periods of water restriction, domestic waste water from washing up and baths will be perfectly usable in the garden. Only when it is contaminated with bleach or chemical disinfectants is damage to plants likely to ensue. And in general, watering late in the evening is beneficial because the water then has chance to soak into the soil surrounding the roots before the sun's heat evaporates it into the atmosphere.

The equipment available for garden watering has changed beyond recognition in recent years and the manufacturers' catalogues now contain whole armouries of hose-end sprayers, hose-pipes, hose reels and associated devices. Whilst requirements will obviously vary somewhat with the size of garden, my shortlist of important watering equipment is as follows: an appropriate length of double-wall knitted hose; a through-flow hose reel; a hose-end sprayer of lance pattern (for long reach) that incorporates a valve to shut off the water at the delivery end; and an adjustable oscillating or (for large areas) a gyrating sprinkler. You will, of course, also benefit enormously from having an outside tap with a screw thread, and will be aided by a metering device that attaches to the tap and switches off the water after a predetermined volume has been delivered. My advice strongly is to choose snap fit connectors, and also to opt for one only of the major manufacturers; quite frequently, leaking or unsatisfactory connections come from a watering system of mixed manufacture.

PRUNING is perhaps the least immediately accessible of gardening's skills. It is a technique from which many gardeners shy away and even those who practise it routinely are often blissfully unaware of the reasoning behind their actions – or even that any real reasoning exists. This is unfortunate, first because pruning is neither complicated nor illogical, second because it can be immensely satisfying and third because, done properly, it may make the difference between having plants that are rewarding and efficient and those that truly are neither use nor ornament.

Moreover, whilst pruning is generally imagined to be an operation performed only on trees and shrubs, any removal of shoots, branches, flowers or other parts from a growing plant is a type of pruning and subject therefore to the same underlying principles. The continual pruning of a

Pruning

(a)

Training a fruit tree in fan form

(a) Early in the first summer after planting a well-feathered maiden (a young tree with several side branches), cut out the main shoot at a point just above a pair of strong side branches (or arms) about 30 cm (1 ft) above soil level. Tie these arms onto diagonal canes attached to the main support wires.

(b)

(b) In the next spring, cut back each of the two arms to points above a bud about 30 cm (1 ft) from the main stem. Cut back shoots arising from the arms to three or four buds from their bases.

(c)

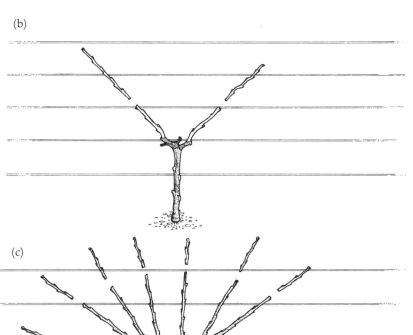

(c) By the following spring, further shoots will have elongated from the arms. Two should be selected above and two below each of the initial shoots, tied in and shortened as before. Other superfluous shoots should be cut back to their bases. On a large wall, this operation can be repeated in the following year, creating more arms, but should be stopped once the allotted space is covered with well-spaced arm branches in a fan pattern. Thereafter, follow the annual pruning routine outlined on p. 146, the 'side-shoots' referred to there being those arising from the main framework arms.

69

Long-handled pruners make a useful addition to your armoury if you have established fruit trees. And using them is safer than climbing. Right: Tie in selected young shoots to form cordons as early as possible.

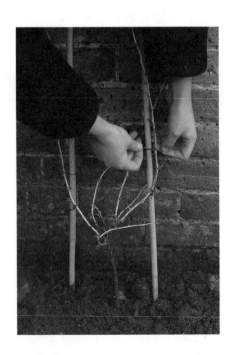

When pruning blackcurrants, cut back as close to the base as possible.

young plant will dictate its overall shape as it matures, an operation called training. As well as rendering a plant of convenient form for a particular site in the garden, the training method can also have a considerable bearing on the plant's effectiveness and productivity. Cordon- or fan-trained fruit trees grown against walls are good examples of this and on p. 69 I have shown the formative training of a fan suitable for plums, peaches, apricots or cherries. Training a plant into a chosen shape is therefore the first objective of pruning. The second is to increase its production of leafy shoots (part of the reason for pruning or clipping hedges), or of flowers and fruits (the usual reason with ornamental and fruit plants). A further purpose of pruning is to encourage overall vigorous growth by permitting the access of light and air to all parts of the plant through the removal of overcrowded shoots and branches. And finally, pruning can be used to improve the health of a plant by removing either diseased parts or those redundant or moribund tissues (dead flowers for instance) that are likely to provide disease-causing fungi and bacteria with a foothold. Regular dead-heading of roses and of summer-flowering herbaceous and bedding plants, therefore, has both aesthetic and important practical features.

The way in which pruning dictates the shape, form and productivity of a plant is not simply a negative one. In other words, shaping is not merely achieved through the removal of certain shoots. It is achieved more specifically because taking off the end of a shoot, with its associated buds, actually stimulates the buds lower down to burst into life. This is why regular clipping of a hedge will thicken its overall growth. A similar effect results when a shoot is merely bent downwards approximately to the horizontal, rather than actually cut off, a technique especially valuable when the lower parts of a wall are to be clothed with a climbing rose and when some fruit trees are producing excessively long shoots but few accessible fruit. This important principle of pruning and training is based on disrupting the phenomenon called apical dominance – the growing buds at and close to the tip (apex) of a shoot produce chemicals that actually inhibit the growth of those below them.

Although finger and thumb are valuable tools for pinching out soft shoot tips or the branches of non-woody plants (tomatoes for instance), something

Pinching out a shoot.

more robust is necessary for most pruning tasks. Pruning with a knife is a very difficult and potentially amputational technique and I do not recommend it. Details of the merits of the various other types of pruning tool are given on p. 55 but for most tasks, a pair of secateurs (sometimes called pruners) will be adequate. For thicker, tougher stems, loppers and a pruning saw are necessary. Hedge clipping is achieved either with hand shears or powered trimmers; their respective merits are considered on p. 55. Many gardeners with substantial tree lopping to undertake (see below) are tempted to buy a chain-saw. Whilst these are astonishingly efficient appliances in experienced hands, they are also potentially the most dangerous of all gardening tools and so in the table below I have listed some essential rules that all chain saw users should follow.

SAFETY RULES FOR USING A CHAIN SAW

1. Have the saw regularly serviced and sharpened by a qualified agent – do not do it yourself.
2. Never saw downwards onto soil.
3. Always wear approved safety goggles.
4. Always wear approved safety gloves.
5. Never allow children near a chain saw.
6. Do not leave the start key with the saw when children are around.
7. Never support wood to be sawn with your foot or have anyone else hold it – wedge it into a sawing horse or other support.
8. Always check the chain oil before beginning to saw.
9. Never use the saw when you are tired.
10. Never use the saw with one hand, or carry it with the chain moving.
11. Never climb a tree to use the saw unless you are very experienced and know how to support yourself safely, and never lift the saw above head height.
12. Never use the saw when wearing loose or very lightweight clothing or shoes such as a loose tie, shorts or sandals.

Varied as different plant tissues are in thickness, robustness and position, certain general pruning principles apply to all. Always make pruning cuts

Correct pruning cut, above a bud and sloping away from it.

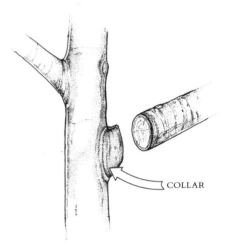

Removing a branch from a tree, avoiding damage to the collar.

COLLAR

immediately above a bud, leaf, flower, branch division or other actively growing structure – never in the middle of a length of shoot. This will ensure that natural healing of the cut surface takes place swiftly and that the cut shoot does not simply wither and allow decay organisms to become established and threaten the remainder of the plant. Always slope the cut away from the bud or other organ and not so close as to damage it. Approximately 5 mm (¼ inch) above is generally satisfactory. Particular care is needed when removing large branches from trees, especially from the main trunk. Never allow the saw cut to damage the swollen base or collar of the branch; for within this zone are the tissues that promote healing, and if their function is impaired, wood-rotting fungi can easily gain access to the main body of the tree, with serious and possibly fatal consequences for the plant. Never apply wound-sealing compounds to the surfaces of pruning cuts. They were once widely recommended but have now been shown not to be beneficial. Sometimes they are actually detrimental because they impair natural healing processes, asphyxiate the tissues and encourage conditions in which decay organisms can establish.

Probably the most puzzling aspects of pruning are those relating to the severity of the operation and the time of year when it is performed – in other words, how much to cut off and when to do it. I have listed each plant's specific pruning requirements under the individual plant descriptions elsewhere in the book, but if you examine these guidelines closely, you will see that some general principles apply to all. The severity of pruning all woody flowering and fruiting plants is dictated by plant vigour, whereas the season in which the pruning should be performed is closely influenced by flowering time. Let's first consider vigour.

I mentioned earlier that the removal of apical buds stimulates others (usually called lateral or side-buds) to grow. So long as the base of the plant is not damaged, the more of the main shoot that is removed, the greater will be the stimulation of the side shoot growth. And the greater the severity with which these, in turn, are cut back, the greater will be the proliferation of shoot growth overall. The practical consequence is that severe (or, as it is usually called, hard) pruning should be used in order to encourage more growth from a plant that is growing feebly or is inherently of weak constitution. Conversely, a very strongly growing plant should in general be pruned lightly in order to contain its vigour. These differences apply as much to individual plant varieties as they do to species – a strongly growing and very vigorous cluster-flowered (floribunda) rose such as 'Queen Elizabeth', for instance, should be pruned very much more lightly than a weaker growing variety such as 'Korresia'.

The timing of pruning is also governed by basically simple considerations. Flowering shrubs bear their flowers in one of two ways – either on the shoots produced during the current year or on those produced in the previous or earlier years. Generally, plants that flower in the first half of the year do so on the previous year's growth; those that flower in the second half do so on the current season's shoots. In order not to cut away the new flower buds, therefore, early flowering shrubs should be pruned immediately after they have flowered; and generally they require light pruning. Those plants that flower later in the season should be pruned sometime between the end of flowering and the beginning of the next year's growth, in early spring. Proportionately more of the later flowering plants benefit from hard pruning. Plants that are only marginally hardy in many areas (hydrangeas and outdoor fuchsias for example), are best not pruned until the spring, so that the old shoots can give added protection to the crown of the plants against the damaging effects of winter cold.

Most of what I have said so far relates to the pruning of the above-ground parts of plants, but there will be a few occasions when root pruning is desirable. Usually the necessity for root pruning established trees and shrubs arises only when an inappropriate choice has been made of a plant for a particular site and for various reasons it is undesirable completely to remove and replace the individual. Root pruning is most commonly used with apple, pear or a few types of ornamental trees but should never be done on plums or other *Prunus* species, willows or poplars, as they will respond by excessive production of suckers. Root pruning is achieved by carefully digging a circular trench, in autumn, approximately 45 cm (18 in deep) and at a radius from the trunk determined by allowing about 12 cm (5 in) for every 1 cm (½ in) of trunk diameter. The fine roots should be left intact and the thickest roots severed. After the completion of the operation and refilling of the trench, the plant will almost certainly require the added support of a stake. There is one other use of root pruning: quite commonly, new plants benefit from some trimming of their roots before planting to stimulate the increased production of nutrient-absorbing fine rootlets; details of these are given, where appropriate, under the individual plant descriptions.

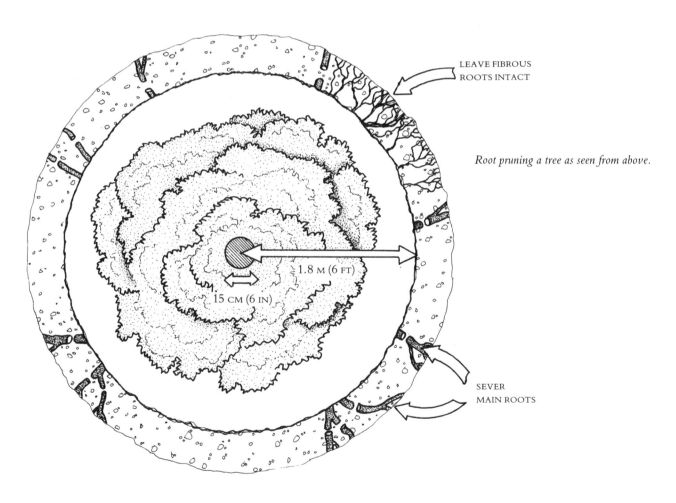

LEAVE FIBROUS
ROOTS INTACT

1.8 M (6 FT)

15 CM (6 IN)

SEVER
MAIN ROOTS

Root pruning a tree as seen from above.

Whilst trees in gardens (other than fruit trees) almost never require routine pruning of any sort, it will sometimes be necessary to remove entire branches that have been damaged by gales or are obstructing paths or other access. Whilst the cutting off of individual branches can be fairly straightforward, there will be many instances when the branch overhangs buildings or other obstacles. For the removal of such branches, and for the wholesale reduction in size of trees that have grown too large for their site, I urge you to employ a tree surgeon, affiliated to a recognised professional body. Not only will he have the practical experience which is undeniably important but he will also have full insurance protection in the event of any mishaps. Above all, I must emphasise, it is extremely dangerous to saw through the trunks or branches of trees that have been blown down by a storm and which have come to rest in a position where the timber is under strain.

The total removal of unwanted trees is also generally a matter for the professional. Apart from the difficulty and danger of felling the tree itself, and despite advertisers' claims, there is no simple (and certainly no chemical) method of removing stumps. They must be dug up, ground down or winched out, the latter two, especially, being operations that require large and expensive equipment for which ready access must be available.

I mentioned sucker production in relation to root pruning, but this development of shoots directly from the roots rather than the main stem or trunk is a common feature of many garden trees and shrubs, where the chosen variety has been grafted onto a different rootstock. Such grafting is commonly performed by nurserymen when a variety grows slowly or feebly on its own roots or where (as with apple trees especially) an appropriate choice of rootstock can dictate the vigour and ultimate size of the tree. Among very common instances of sucker production among ornamental shrubs are those that arise when rhododendron hybrids are grafted onto *Rhododendron ponticum*, or roses are grafted onto briar or other wild species rootstock. Suckers should always be removed, for they will invariably draw nutrient away from the grafted variety and should be pulled, not cut, away if the result is not merely to be the stimulation of yet more suckers.

Pulling out a sucker.

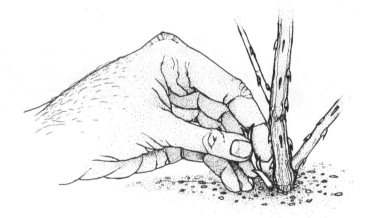

In general, my advice on pruning is only to prune when you have checked and made quite sure that it is necessary, but conversely not to neglect pruning those plants that must always have some annual attention to give of their best. Remember that care in choosing varieties of trees and shrubs, and simple routine attention (such as rubbing off buds or leaf clusters that arise on the bark of standard specimens) will very often obviate the necessity for any remedial pruning later.

THE thought that their plants will almost inevitably fall prey to some foul affliction causes consternation to many novice gardeners. Many are swayed by advertisements and promotional literature to arm themselves with a small arsenal of sprays, puffer packs, granules and other types of chemical hardware in the belief that without them, their gardening efforts will be as nought. Increasingly, in the modern garden, they are matched by those who will having nothing of such things, and who convince themselves that their gardens will stay healthy without any need for human intervention, citing the ancient maxim of the balance of nature as their most trustworthy ally. I believe that neither is correct. Evidence against the former is provided by the many attractive and productive gardens (mine included) where chemical use is kept to a minimum. And the case against nature always being one's ally was summed up rather graphically in a letter that I received recently which comprised the single line question – 'Why don't slugs eat the weeds?'

Plant diseases are caused by fungi, by bacteria or by viruses. Those caused by microscopic fungi are easily the most numerous in gardens. Lacking the ability to photosynthesise, fungi feed on other organisms. Most are content to feed on dead material, and among them are many species that play an important part in breaking down humus in the soil or the compost heap. But others feed on living tissues and thus cause disease in the organisms they attack – mildews, rusts and canker fungi are among familiar examples. A few important garden fungi can live with equal facility on dead or living matter – the familiar grey mould fungus *Botrytis* is among them – and are able to survive on old plant debris and use it as a springboard from which to launch their spores and spread to living plants.

Bacteria are of little significance in bringing about garden diseases but viruses, sub-microscopic and unseen, are insidious trouble-makers. For they can only exist within the cells of another organism and they permeate the

'Know your enemy' is a useful maxim in gardening. Whilst wasps, for instance, can cause some damage to fruit and can be extremely annoying, this must be counterbalanced by their valuable role in catching and killing many other insect pests.

entire tissues of plants, sapping their strength and resulting in poor, enfeebled individuals. Whilst fungi are spread, through the medium of their spores, by rain, wind or in contaminated soil, viruses are usually dispersed by aphids or other creatures that suck the sap. They are also spread from parent plant to offspring whenever plants are multiplied vegetatively – by cuttings for instance. Small wonder, therefore, that potatoes, dahlias, carnations, fruit trees and others that are normally propagated in this way are especially prone to virus problems.

Pests all belong to the animal kingdom and almost every group of animals has some representatives that we would define as troublesome. They do not cause diseases, but bring about problems because they number our garden plants among their food supplies. Although they are so diverse in size and form, I find it useful to think of pests in two big categories – the chewers and the suckers. Chewing pests range from deer, hares and rabbits at the large end of the spectrum to slugs, caterpillars and maggots at the other. Although they can cause tremendous damage, most chewing pests do not usually multiply *in situ* on the plant or in the garden bed, so at least the increase in damage is not exponential. By contrast, the sucking pests comprise a limited but very important group of insects, including aphids, whiteflies and scale insects. They cause damage by a gradual process of weakening, as they insert their hypodermic-like feeding apparatus to dine on the cells' contents. And they *do* multiply on affected plants and in warm summer weather can do so with astonishing rapidity, with the result that leaves and shoots soon become seething masses of gorging insect life, and the plants themselves begin a rapid and certain downhill path.

Given that every garden will be at least slightly improved if pests and diseases don't take their toll, there are various approaches to minimising the damage they cause. The first falls under the heading of 'prevention is better than cure' and here I would direct you to take particular care over the new plants that you bring into your garden. When buying transplant-sized herbaceous perennials, crowns, rootstocks or young trees and shrubs, always inspect them carefully and cut away any obviously damaged or diseased parts. Some diseases can be carried on seeds, although they will rarely be obvious from the seed itself. If you buy packeted seed from a reputable supplier, it is improbable that it will be contaminated. If you save seed from your own plants, however, it is most important that you do so only from those individuals that are themselves healthy and vigorous.

Perhaps the commonest source of problems among planting stock lies with bulbs of ornamentals. Whilst the best suppliers take great trouble to raise and sell only high quality, healthy material, inferior job lots are, regrettably, still to be found. If you examine these closely, you will find that they are generally undersized and often bear surface lesions, the signs of some pest or disease attack. Planting these in your garden may result in poor plants with few or small flowers, but more importantly, it may introduce into your garden some new problem, and many diseases, once established in the soil, will stay there for a very long time.

From what I have said about viruses, it will be obvious that the importance of buying new stock carries a special implication, for the symptoms of disease will almost always be invisible externally. Only when the plants grow and reveal themselves as feeble, misshapen or poor-yielding will the contamination become apparent. It is therefore extremely important only to buy new stocks of plants that are vulnerable to virus problems from

reputable suppliers and, in many instances (fruit trees and bushes and potatoes most notably), only to buy those that are certified in some manner as virus free. Remember, moreover, that once such potatoes, strawberries or other virus-free stocks are planted in your garden, they will inevitably become contaminated as aphids and other agents introduce viruses into them. It is a false economy to save from the stock for propagation therefore; buy fresh each time you plant.

Aphids have a dual importance as pests for they not only cause direct damage through their sap-sucking activities but also commonly inject viruses into the plant.

Accepting that the use of disease- and pest-free planting stock is important in keeping a garden healthy, is there any realistic way that a garden can be managed to help maintain this health? Can the oft-quoted balance of nature really be made to work in our favour? I mentioned earlier my correspondent's question concerning why slugs only attack garden plants, not weeds: herein lies an unavoidable truth – lettuces are more attractive to slugs and to other pests than are most wild plants or weeds, for the very same reason that they are more attractive to us. Garden vegetables are soft and succulent; they have been bred and selected precisely for this reason. Garden flowers similarly are larger, their tissues softer than those of their wild relatives. So in setting aside an area of our gardens (or giving them over entirely) to native vegetation, far from creating an environment within which pests might prefer to feed, we are doing just the opposite. We are providing them with cover and shelter within which to hide and breed, while nearby supplying food of a succulence beyond their wildest dreams. Of course, every garden, be it wild or domestic, contains predators as well as pests, and microscopic fungi and other organisms that may limit the impact of disease-causing species. But by the very act of cultivating, we have tipped the balance towards the opposition.

Before describing some of the direct ways that pests and diseases may be combatted, however, I have one more maxim that may help a little: a tidy garden is generally a healthy garden. Pests require hiding places; many disease-causing fungi have the annoying ability to survive on plant remains, from there to attack our growing crops, so the clearing away of garden rubbish is essential. The pile of pots or old seed trays behind the greenhouse will provide an ideal hiding place for slugs during the daytime, and the mound of rotten pea sticks left for several years in the corner of the vegetable plot is an irresistible temptation to woodlice – they didn't after all acquire the prefix wood for nothing.

The familiar but erratically occurring symptoms of leaf-cutter bee activity on rose leaves are a good example of where gardeners must be tolerant. There can be no justification in spraying the plants with chemical insecticide on the off-chance that a leaf-cutter bee may appear.

Even so, when prevention and cleanliness have played their part, there will come a time for direct assault. I don't dismiss the so-called traditional remedies – such as home-made herbal decoctions or the use of companion planting – in attempting to control pest and disease problems. If they work for you (or even if you think they do), all to the good; but you must turn to the specialist literature describing such procedures for I have been unable to convince myself that their effectiveness justifies my giving them space here. There is, in practice, another reason for leaving home-produced brews out of consideration. Legislation, at least in Britain, has outlawed their use. Now, only 'approved products' may be used for pest and disease control. I cannot believe that outlawing the use of water to spray greenfly from rose bushes is precisely what the legislators had in mind when they drew up their rule book; but there it is. Legally, you must use a proprietary approved product. But in using a proprietary substance to control a pest or disease problem, it is important to understand that each type of product has a specific function.

Insecticides are chemicals intended to kill insects, whereas fungicides kill fungi. But not all pests are insects and not all diseases have a fungal cause and in practice, most insecticides have some effect on other living creatures – including mammals, which is why we must take precautions when handling them. Some insecticides will have some controlling effect on woodlice and millepedes but almost none will control mites, eelworms, slugs or snails. For the latter, however, specific molluscicides are available. Some fungicides will control bacteria but none will control viruses, although the impact of viruses can be diminished by controlling the aphids which so often introduce them into plant tissues.

If you enter a garden centre or shop, the array of two hundred or more products on offer for pest and disease control is bewildering. It is important first, however, to appreciate that the actual number of different chemical ingredients is perhaps only a quarter of this total, for the same substances are sold under different brand names. It is the name of the chemical ingredient that is generally used in published gardening advice, and I have followed this policy in the detailed recommendations that I give for specific problems on specific plants. These ingredient names are always on the product label, although they may be in small print.

You should appreciate, too, that not all insecticides and fungicides control every problem with equal efficiency, and not all are appropriate or safe on all types of plant. One important distinction is that of systemic and contact chemicals. By analogy with translocated and contact weedkillers (p. 91), the former are absorbed into plants and moved within their tissues. Thus they may eradicate established fungal infection or seek out concealed pests. Being absorbed into the sap means, moreover, that they will be taken up by sucking pests and be especially effective in controlling them. By contrast, contact substances are effective only where they land – any parts of the plant missed will remain unprotected. Being sprayed onto the surface means, too, that contact chemicals are at the mercy of the weather; if they are applied shortly before heavy rain, their effectiveness will be short-lived. Because of this, therefore, contact chemicals must be used more frequently, although you should realise that systemic substances do not maintain their effectiveness forever; they may slowly be inactivated within the plant's tissues and, of course, as the plant grows, their concentration and hence their usefulness will be diluted.

There is another most important consideration with edible crops. Because systemic substances are absorbed into the tissues, they will be present when we harvest and eat the plants. For this reason, for all chemicals, there is a minimum period that must elapse after spraying before edible crops are considered safe to eat. In practice, because there is always the slight possibility of the produce being tainted and because I am anxious not to eat pesticides in any quantity, I never use systemic insecticides on edible crops. Generally, fungicides are rather safer and there may be occasions when a systemic fungicide treatment on a fruit or vegetable seems justified.

Increasingly, however, gardeners will be confronted with advice only to use 'organic' or 'natural' chemicals. These are substances of plant, animal or, in some instances, mineral origin. Although refined or otherwise processed in a factory, they are not wholly of artificial origin. There has grown up a belief that these are all inherently safer in some way than purely artificial chemicals, although I am uncertain why this should be. There is no logical reason why a plant-derived substance such as derris or rotenone (pyrethrum) which happens to be used as a pesticide should be any safer than other plant-

Coral spot disease exemplifies the need for garden hygiene. It occurs most commonly on dead twigs, old prunings and pea sticks, but if not cleared away can spread into living shoots and cause serious die-back of many types of trees and shrubs.

Clubroot disease, which affects members of the cabbage family, is both devastating and ineradicable. Prevention is essential if your garden soil is uncontaminated and is best achieved by raising brassica and wall flower plants from seed instead of buying plants.

derived substances such as strychnine, cocaine or digitalis. Nor, indeed, is there logical reason why they should be safer than, say, permethrin or pirimicarb, which happen to have been synthesised artificially. Pirimicarb, in fact, has the considerable merit of being selective for aphids and will cause little or no harm to their natural predators such as ladybirds and hover flies, and that certainly can't be said of any organic insecticide. Nor is there any reason to suppose that because a substance occurs naturally in the environment, it will do no harm when re-applied to it. Derris, for example, is used as an insecticide at many thousand times its naturally occurring concentration; and it is, incidentally, highly poisonous to fish.

Everyone sees some brown rot disease on their fruit every year but it too is an example of a problem that cannot be controlled by chemicals and must be tolerated.

To help you make a choice from the many chemical insecticides and fungicides available to gardeners, I have listed the salient features of each. For use in the average garden, however, one fungicide spray, one insecticide spray and one insecticide dust, together with tar oil winter wash and a slug killer will be adequate. In a separate Table, I have itemised the major types of pest and disease problem with the appropriate treatment to adopt for each. (In the specific plant categories, of course, I have indicated the major pest and disease problems of each type of plant so by cross referring it will be possible to decide on the appropriate course of action in each case.) And, finally, I have provided a key to help you identify the commonest problems on plants.

You will have gathered from what I have said that whilst gardening by its very actions disturbs the balance of nature, we should take whatever steps we can to ensure that natural predators and parasites are able to play their part in keeping down pest and disease numbers. There are, however, a few instances where it has proved possible to use one organism quite deliberately to help control another. Such techniques have become known as biological control and on p. 87 I have listed those biological control methods available to gardeners, with the strengths and limitations of each.

SYSTEMIC AND CONTACT FUNGICIDES AND INSECTICIDES AND OTHER PESTICIDAL CHEMICALS AVAILABLE TO GARDENERS

SYSTEMIC FUNGICIDES
Benomyl
Carbendazim
Myclobutanil
Propiconazole
Thiophanate-methyl
Triforine

CONTACT FUNGICIDES
Bordeaux mixture and other inorganic
  copper salt mixtures
Captan
Dinocap
Mancozeb
Mercurous chloride
Sulphur
Thiram
Tecnazene

CONTACT INSECTICIDES
Borax
Bromophos
Carbaryl
Derris
Diazinon
Fenitrothion
Gamma-HCH
Malathion
Permethrin
Phoxim
Pirimicarb
Pirimiphos methyl
Pyrethrum
Resmethrin
Tar oil

SYSTEMIC INSECTICIDES
Dimethoate
Formothion

BIRD REPELLENTS
Aluminium ammonium sulphate

RODENTICIDES
Coumatetryl
Difenacoum

MOLLUSCICIDES
Methiocarb
Metaldehyde

WORM KILLERS
Chlordane

Some of these chemicals are only available in particular formulations, or in combination with certain other chemicals. Some may also be marketed for specific pest or disease problems only. In every case, you *must* read the label directions carefully to be sure that the product is being used for the purpose and in the manner for which it is intended. The names given above are those of the active chemical ingredients. These will not be the same as the product names but will be found printed on the product label.

SYMPTOMS OF COMMON PROBLEMS

Symptoms on leaves

PROBLEM	DETAIL	PROBABLE CAUSE
1. Wilting	General	Short of water Root pest or disease Wilt disease
2. Holed	Generally ragged	Small pests (millepedes, flea beetles, woodlice) Capsid bugs
	Elongated holes; usually with slime present	Slugs or snails
	Fairly large holes over entire leaf or confined to edges	Caterpillars Beetles
	Semi-circular pieces taken from edges	Leaf-cutter bees
3. Discoloured	Black	Sooty mould
	Predominantly red	Short of water
	More or less bleached	Nutrient deficiency Short of water Too much water
	Silvery (plums)	Silver leaf disease
	Irregular yellowish patterns	Virus
	Irregular tunnels	Leaf miner
	Surface flecking	Leafhopper
	Brown (scorched) in spring	Frost

Symptoms on leaves continued

PROBLEM	DETAIL	PROBABLE CAUSE
4. Spotted	Brownish, angular, with mould beneath	Downy mildew
	Brownish, irregular, no mould	Leaf spot
	Dark brown or black, crusty	Scab
	Small, dusty, brown, black or bright coloured	Rust
5. Mouldy	Black	Sooty mould
	Grey, fluffy	Grey mould
	White (or rarely brown), velvety	Mildew
	Brown (tomatoes)	Leaf mould
	White, beneath leaves (potatoes)	Blight
6. Infested with insects	White, moth-like, tiny	Whiteflies
	Green, grey, black or other colour	Aphids
	White, woolly (indoors)	Mealy bug
	Flat, encrusted, like limpets	Scale insects
	Large, six legs, worm-like	Caterpillars
7. Curling	Insects present also	See 6
	Tightly rolled (roses)	Sawfly
	Puckered, reddish (almonds, peaches)	Peach leaf curl
	Puckered, yellowish (pears)	Pear leaf blister mite
8. Cobwebs present	Plant wilting	Red spider mite

Symptoms on fruit

PROBLEM	DETAIL	PROBABLE CAUSE
1. Pieces eaten away	Fruit close to ground	Slugs
		Mice, voles
	Tree fruits	Birds
		Wasps
2. Distorted	With rounded bumps (apples)	Capsid bugs
	Black powder within (sweet corn)	Smut
	Ribbon-like scars (apple)	Sawfly
	Split (tomatoes)	Short of water
3. Discoloured	Uneven ripening (tomatoes)	Virus
		Nutrient deficiency
4. Mouldy	While on plant (tomato)	Grey mould
	While on plant (tree fruit)	Brown rot
	In store	Fungal decay
5. Spotted	Tree fruit	Scab
	Tomato	Ghost spot
6. Maggoty	Tree fruit	Caterpillars (codling moth)
	Peas	Caterpillars (pea moth)
	Raspberries	Beetle
7. Dropping prematurely	Pears	Pear midge
	Apples (in summer)	June drop (normal occurrence on healthy trees)

Symptoms on flowers

PROBLEM	DETAIL	PROBABLE CAUSE
1. Drooping	General	Short of water End of flowering period
2. Tattered	Masses of tiny holes	Caterpillars
	Large pieces torn away	Birds
3. Removed entirely	Usually discarded nearby	Birds
4. Distorted	Usually only a few plants affected in a bed	Virus
5. Discoloured	Powdery white covering	Mildew
6. Mouldy	Fluffy grey mould	Grey mould

Symptoms on roots and bulbs

PROBLEM	DETAIL	PROBABLE CAUSE
1. Decayed	General	Decay fungi
2. Parts eaten away	General	Small soil pests (millepedes, wireworms, leatherjackets)
	Corms and bulbs	Vine weevil
3. With irregular swellings	Brassicas and wallflowers	Clubroot
	Potatoes	Eelworm
	Peas and Beans	Root nodules
4. Maggoty	General	Fly larvae
5. With warty spots	Root vegetables	Scab
6. Irregularly distorted	Root vegetables	See individual entries for each vegetable

Symptoms on stems or branches

PROBLEM	DETAIL	PROBABLE CAUSE
1. Eaten through	On young plants	Slugs or snails
	On older plants	Mice, voles, rabbits
	On young trees	Rabbits, hares, deer
2. Infested with insects	Green, grey, black or other colour	Aphids
	White, woolly, on tree bark	Woolly aphid
	Flat, encrusted, like limpets	Scale insects
	Large, six legs, worm-like	Caterpillars
3. Rotten, toadstools or bracket fungi may be present	At base, young plants	Stem and foot rot
	On trees or shrubs	Decay fungus
4. Blister on tree bark	More or less spherical	Gall
	Target-like	Canker
5. Dying back	General	Short of water Canker or coral spot Root pest or disease

PROBLEM	DETAIL	PROBABLE CAUSE
6. Abnormal growth	Like bird's nest	Witches' broom
	Leafy plant	Mistletoe
	Buds swollen (blackcurrant)	Big bud

TREATMENTS FOR COMMON PEST AND DISEASE PROBLEMS

PROBLEM	TREATMENT
Aphids	Use any proprietary contact insecticide; pick off affected shoots by hand or wash off insects with hose.
Beetles	Normally, treatment is not necessary or justified but in cases of extensive attack use any proprietary contact insecticide.
Big Bud	Pick off the affected buds and make plans for replacing the affected bushes within about twelve months.
Birds	Erect netting or other protection; in really severe cases, erect bird scarers but remember that all birds enjoy legal protection and may not be harmed.
Blight	In wet seasons, apply a protective spray in early July to potatoes and outdoor tomatoes with a fungicide containing mancozeb.
Brown rot	No treatment is practicable but at the end of the season remove and destroy any shrivelled fruit still hanging on the tree or lying on the ground.
Canker	Cut out and destroy affected branches; no chemical treatment is possible.
Capsid bugs	The insects are too unpredictable and erratic in occurrence to make any treatment feasible.
Caterpillars	Pick off by hand if the caterpillars can be found and are present in small numbers. If masses of insects occur, pick off and destroy entire affected leaves or use any proprietary contact insecticide.
Clubroot	Remove and destroy affected plants (do not compost them). Try to avoid growing brassicas on the same land for as long as possible, apply lime and then, when susceptible plants are to be grown on the site once more, raise each plant in an individual pot and plant it out complete with the pot ball of compost.
Codling moth	No treatment is feasible; a proportion of the apples will always be affected.
Coral spot	Cut away and destroy affected branches or twigs, cutting well into the healthy wood. On valuable ornamental plants, then spray the surrounding branches with a systemic fungicide.
Decay fungus (including honey fungus)	Where honey fungus is suspected, call in expert assistance – the advice may well be to have the tree removed, the stump ground out and the soil drenched with a

PROBLEM	TREATMENT
	special fungicide. For other types of decay fungi felling is rarely necessary, but with decay in the main trunk you should be aware that the tree will be inherently unstable.
Deer	The only protection is that afforded by a stout fence at least 2 m (6½ ft) high.
Downy mildew	Normally no treatment is justified but with lettuces in wet seasons, spray with mancozeb according to manufacturer's instructions. If the disease is persistently troublesome, try growing the variety 'Avondefiance'.
Eelworm	No treatment is feasible but it is important to avoid growing susceptible plants (or, at least, plants of the same type) on the area for as long as possible; in the case of potatoes, at least five years.
Flea beetles	Clear away any plant debris as soon as crops have been harvested; dust derris around seedlings if attacks are severe and persistent in dry seasons.
Fly larvae	In most instances, no control is feasible but for cabbage root fly control on leafy brassicas, use brassica collars on the soil around the stem bases to dissuade the female flies from egg laying. To protect carrots from carrot fly, keep thinning and other disturbance of the foliage to a minimum and, if attacks are severe and persistent, try erecting a 60 cm (2 ft) high 'fence' of plastic sheet around the carrot bed; the low-flying insects are deterred by this.
Fungal decay	Destroy affected parts; no other treatment is feasible.
Gall	Normally no treatment is justified but cut out if severely disfiguring.
Ghost spot	No treatment is feasible but check fruit carefully for, in cool conditions, the symptoms can lead to grey mould outbreaks.
Grey mould	Destroy affected parts; spray with systemic fungicide, improve ventilation in greenhouses and, if possible, provide some heat at the end of the season.
Hares	The only protection is that afforded by tree protectors and wire netting.
Leaf-cutter bees	The insects are too erratic and unpredictable to make any treatment practicable.

TREATMENTS FOR COMMON PEST AND DISEASE PROBLEMS

PROBLEM	TREATMENT	PROBLEM	TREATMENT
Leaf hopper	The insects are too erratic and unpredictable to make any treatment practicable.		attacks. In greenhouses, destroy severely affected plants and mist the house regularly.
Leaf miner	Remove and destroy affected leaves on herbaceous plants; no treatment is feasible on trees.	*Root pest*	Normally, no treatment is feasible but with severe and persistent attacks, dust around affected plants with derris or other soil insecticide.
Leaf mould	Remove severely affected leaves and spray the plants with systemic fungicide.	*Root disease*	Destroy severely affected plants and try to avoid growing the same type of plant in the area for at least three years.
Leaf spot	In most instances no treatment is necessary for leaf spot diseases are rarely severe. Where attacks appear to be related to general poor growth, however, spray with systemic fungicide according to manufacturer's instructions, taking particular care not to use on edible plants for which approval is not given. Roses should be sprayed with a proprietary fungicide mixture to control blackspot, routinely from early May.	*Root nodules*	No treatment needed; a normal and important feature of leguminous plants.
		Rust	Spray ornamental plants with propiconazole or, with roses, myclobutanil fungicide. Copper-containing fungicides or mancozeb may give some control on edible plants if used according to the manufacturer's directions.
Leatherjackets	No chemical treatments are feasible for most plants but cultivate affected soil regularly in order to bring the larvae to the surface where birds will feed on them. On lawns, try watering the affected area with a proprietary lawn pest killer.	*Sawfly*	No treatment is feasible.
		Scab	Although scab can be controlled in gardens, I am not convinced that it is worth attempting other than on young apple trees. Then, a systemic fungicide should be sprayed according to the manufacturer's instructions.
Mealy bug	Use small paint brush dipped in methylated spirits to treat each insect colony.		
Mice	Set traps or use proprietary poison baits.	*Scale insects*	On ornamental plants, spray or drench with systemic insecticide; on edible plants no treatment is feasible.
Mildew (powdery mildew)	Ensure that plants are not allowed to become too dry and apply systemic fungicide or sulphur.	*Silver leaf disease*	Cut off any badly affected branches, then wait to see if the rest of the tree recovers. If it does not, and especially if silvering appears on the leaves of suckers, the tree will not recover and should be cut down.
Millepedes	Destroy affected plants or plant parts and dust affected area with derris.		
Mistletoe	No treatment needed but if severely disfiguring, affected parts may be cut out.		
Nutrient deficiency	See p. 64.	*Slugs*	Use proprietary slug pellets or liquid controls or home-made remedies such as traps baited with beer. Surround valuable plants such as lettuce beds with fine powders such as ash or soot or a low barrier of finely spiny twigs such as gorse.
Pea moth	No chemical treatment is feasible but if attacks persist for more than one season, try sowing some seeds earlier and some later to try and avoid having too many plants in flower during June and July when egg laying takes place.		
		Snails	If serious, use methods recommended for slugs but generally they are less of a problem and fewer in number and can be combatted by collecting them by hand and by locating and eradicating them from their hiding places.
Peach leaf curl	Spraying with copper-containing fungicide as the leaves unfold in spring, and again just after leaf fall in autumn, may give some protection but is seldom entirely satisfactory.		
		Smut	Too infrequent in occurrence to justify control measures but destroy affected plants when found.
Pear leaf blister mite	No treatment is feasible.	*Sooty mould*	Wash off mould with water or destroy badly affected leaves and then identify and treat the insect pest responsible for the honeydew on which the mould grows.
Pear midge	Collect and destroy affected fruitlets; no other treatment is feasible.		
Rabbits	The only sure protection is by using a wire netting fence with the lower edge buried at least 30 cm (12 ins) in the soil.	*Stem and foot rot*	Avoid growing plants of the type affected on the same site for about three years and take steps to improve drainage of the affected area.
Red spider mite	Outdoors, no treatment is feasible, although keeping plants well watered and mulched will help limit the impact of		

TREATMENTS FOR COMMON PEST AND DISEASE PROBLEMS

PROBLEM	TREATMENT	PROBLEM	TREATMENT
Vine weevil	Treat the root area of affected plants by dusting with a proprietary soil insecticide. Check carefully for the signs of larvae when repotting plants.		with contact insecticide as soon as pests are seen and repeat the treatment every few days. Destroy any plants that do not show signs of recovery.
Virus	If effects are severe, destroy affected plants and replace with fresh (using virus-free stock if appropriate). If effects are mild, no treatment is necessary.	Wilt disease	Destroy severely affected plants and try to avoid growing the same type of plant on the area for at least three years. With clematis, cut back hard and wait to see if plant recovers. Plant new clematis 15 cm (6 in) deeper than normal where wilt is a problem.
Voles	Set mouse traps or use proprietary poison baits.		
Wasps	No treatment is necessary unless nests are very close to houses when they should be destroyed using proprietary chemical products.	Witches' broom	Normally no treatment is justified but cut out if severely disfiguring.
Whiteflies	Outdoors, no treatment is feasible. In greenhouses, be absolutely vigilant in checking plants for signs of attack. Spray	Woodlice	Dust around plants with proprietary soil insecticide and locate and eradicate them from their hiding places.

EFFECTIVE BIOLOGICAL CONTROL MEASURES AVAILABLE TO GARDENERS

PROBLEM	TREATMENT
Greenhouse white fly control	Use the parasitic wasp-like insect *Encarsia formosa*. Cultures should be purchased in the form of leaf pieces bearing immature whitefly parasitised by the wasp, which lays its eggs in them. The colony will establish itself in the greenhouse provided the temperature does not normally fall below about 15°C (59°F) at night nor below about 18°C (64°F) in the daytime.
Greenhouse red spider mite control	Use the red spider mite predatory mite *Phytoseiulus persimilis*. Cultures of the predators should be purchased and spread around the greenhouse where they will feed on the pests. The predator is unlikely to be effective if the temperature in the daytime falls much below about 18°C (64°F).
Caterpillar control	Use a culture of the bacterium *Bacillus thuringiensis* which should be sprayed onto the insects much as any other contact spray. It will not affect any other garden insects.

Weeds and weed control

The distinction between a wild-flower garden and a weedy garden may be merely a matter of terminology but weed seeds can spread from wilder to 'tamer' areas. And the presence of a pool presents the need for special care in pest control for several garden chemicals are highly poisonous to fish.

YOU will not garden for very long before you discover that your chosen plants are not the only ones to have a claim to your soil. The native vegetation will be all too keen to win back its birthright, and whilst native plants growing in the fields and hedgerows are admired, protected and called wild flowers, a rather different attitude, and the name weed, tend to prevail in gardens. If you don't exercise some form of weed control, your garden will inevitably suffer for, as natives, weeds are better adapted to your local climatic and other conditions. By virtue of their greater hardiness, faster reproductive rate or other reasons, they are, quite simply, more efficient competitors for light, water and the available nutrients.

Many different plant species can be considered significant as garden weeds – perhaps fifty or sixty are of major importance in Britain. Their relative effects on your gardening activities will vary depending on features such as the area in which you live and the type of soil in your garden. Nonetheless, it is possible to group weed species into two major categories on the basis of the way they grow and reproduce, and these groupings largely dictate their efficiency as competitors and the control measures that are likely to be effective against them.

Most numerous, in terms of species, are annual weeds. Common garden examples include groundsel, shepherd's purse, hairy bittercress and chickweed. Like all other annual plants, they pass their entire life cycle from seed to seed within the course of one season, the seeds themselves ensuring their survival through the unfavourable winter period to the next spring. In practice, many species are even more efficient than this, for their seeds can germinate almost immediately after being shed. When this is combined with very rapid growth, more than one generation (with consequent vast multiplication in numbers) can occur within a single year. Moreover, once they are in the soil, by no means all of the seeds germinate at the same time – a residue remains that continues to give rise to fresh seedlings over a period of years. Although some seeds (of perennials as well as annuals) can survive in the soil for thirty years or more, there is considerable truth in the old adage of 'one year's seeding leads to seven year's weeding', for after about seven years, an initial population of seeds, shed from its parent plant, will usually have been reduced to a fairly insignificant level. But I must stress that weed growth, like all other aspects of gardening activity, is dynamic, not static. For *each* fresh batch of seeds that germinates during those seven years will, in turn, shed its own offspring and these too will persist for a lengthy period. The message I hope is becoming clear – the key to staying on top of annual weed control is to use some method that eliminates the weeds before they have had a chance to set and disperse their seeds.

The second great group of garden weeds consists of the perennials. There are a few, shallowly rooted, perennial weeds such as daisies that behave, in beds and borders, in much the same way as annuals, although in lawns and paths they assume a rather different status that I shall come to in due course. For the present, however, my concern is a much more important group that, for simplicity, I call persistent perennials. All perennials differ from annuals, of course, in that each individual lives for longer than one season (although not, in a literal sense, forever). Whilst they too produce seeds, sometimes in large numbers, their importance as garden weeds derives much more from their vegetative methods of spreading. The precise method each weed species employs will dictate how difficult it is to control. Deeply growing or widely creeping roots, far spreading rhizomes, creeping stems and tiny bulb-like bodies called bulbils are the most important among these vegetative methods. Physically, a large amount of root or rhizome growth creates problems in that it is difficult to locate and difficult to dig out, but this problem pales into insignificance alongside the fact that these plants can regenerate from small pieces broken off from the parent. Sometimes, as with the deep roots of docks, regeneration can only occur from the top few centimetres, whereas with dandelions it can do so from any root fragment. When, as with couch grass, regeneration can take place from a tiny fragment of a huge rhizome system that is inherently very brittle, the difficulties are compounded further. Perhaps the most intractable of all perennial weeds are those that produce bulbils, for these are so small that they are impossible to eradicate physically and, moreover, in the case of the notorious pink-flowered *Oxalis*, are produced by a plant that is unaffected by all available weedkillers.

So much for the problems; what of their treatment? I confess that I would find it hard to garden without recourse to some weedkillers, and

I imagine that most other gardeners will discover the same. But a major aspect, in fact the front line of weed control, should be purely physical methods. The most straightforward means of controlling annual or shallowly rooted perennial weeds are by digging or pulling them up or by cutting them down. Your hands and a weeding fork are the tools for the former and a Dutch or similar type of hoe for the latter. You can dig or pull up weeds at almost any time of year, but hoeing should only be done if the weather is warm and dry, when the plants will shrivel quickly. If you hoe in wet weather, there is a good chance that many weeds will not actually be severed, merely jostled and transplanted, and there are indeed some species, such as groundsel, that can regenerate roots in moist soil even when their stems have been cut through and they can actually continue to mature their seeds when the entire plant has been sliced into fragments.

The purely physical approach is of much less value with persistent perennial weeds, principally because of the near impossibility of removing every fragment of root and rhizome and also because of the plants' abilities to regenerate from the pieces left behind. Nonetheless, when clearing a new area of land, especially on a light soil, I have many times proved that it is perfectly possible to eradicate couch grass, nettles, thistles and several other types of perennial weed by regular digging, with a fork, not a spade (and certainly not with a powered rotary cultivator). I doubt if the extremely far-reaching weeds such as bindweed or ground elder can ever be cleared totally in this way, although it is sometimes claimed that repeatedly (by which I mean at least weekly) hoeing off the above-ground growth will so weaken the plants that they will gradually degenerate. On lawns, it is often possible to remove small numbers of daisies, dandelions and other rosette forming perennials by means of a small, two-pronged digging tool generally called a daisy grubber. Even so, it is all too easy to snap off a long tap root from which re-growth may occur.

Hoeing and digging are, at best, only curative methods of annual weed control; how much better it would be, surely, if we could prevent them from emerging at all. In my account of seed sowing, I have mentioned the importance of placing the seeds at the correct depth in the soil, for if they are buried too deeply their food reserves will be inadequate for the young seedling to reach the light at the soil surface. Exactly the same principle can be employed to control annual weeds. Whilst naturally their seeds lie on the soil surface where they were shed or are washed down by rain a few millimetres below the surface, we can simulate much greater burial by laying additional material on top of the soil. Much the simplest way to do this is with an organic mulch such as compost, leaf mould, well rotted manure, bark. All are satisfactory and, in my experience, a thickness of about 5 cm (2 inches) will prevent most annual weed seedlings from reaching the surface. In time, of course, the organic matter will become incorporated into the body of the soil through the action of earthworms and other organisms and will need topping up. I adopt a routine of mulching in the autumn (when the covering has the added advantage of giving frost protection to plants' crowns) and again in the spring, while the soil is still moist. Of the materials I have mentioned, bark is rotted down and incorporated most slowly (which is fortunate as it is easily the most expensive) but the equivalent of perhaps 50% of the initial thickness will need to be added anew each year. In fact, because bark is so expensive, but also very attractive, it is generally best used for the most important beds and borders close to the house.

The simplest and most effective method of annual weed control is with a mulch. Black plastic is certainly efficient although scarcely pleasing to the eye. In more ornamental areas of the garden an organic mulch would be a better choice.

An alternative to an organic mulch for weed control is opaque plastic sheet. Laying such sheet over the soil surface has other gardening uses – to warm the soil before sowing (p. 100), for moisture conservation (p. 67) and as a simple method of growing potatoes. It is certainly effective too as a weed suppressor, but is scarcely pretty to behold, and its main use therefore is likely to be in the vegetable rather than the ornamental garden.

It is almost impossible to eradicate perennial weeds by mulching; or at least, by organic mulching. Unlike a seed, an established root or rhizome system offers to a plant a massive food reserve that is well able to support the growth of light-seeking shoots through many centimetres or even metres of soil and mulch. For similar reasons, growth from bulbils or from tubers such as those of lesser celandine will also not be suppressed by mulching – I have traced a celandine shoot vertically for 45 cm (18 in) through the soil from a small, buried tuber fragment. It may be possible to eliminate some perennial weeds by using a plastic mulch for a long period of time and so deny them light even when they reach the soil surface. I am certain, however, that this technique would only be effective if the plastic could be left in place continuously for at least two seasons.

On lawns and paths it is virtually impossible to control all weed growth physically, and there will also be occasions when it is difficult to keep on top of an annual weed problem in this way. It is, for instance, not always practicable to mulch all parts of the garden – soil being prepared for seed sowing for example – and in the spring especially, with weed seedlings emerging at a prodigious rate and the land too wet for hoeing, even annual weed growth can soon become out of hand. Hence my reason for saying that I would be surprised if many gardeners could manage totally without resorting to a weedkiller. But choice of an appropriate weedkiller is critically important. Using the wrong weedkiller can have disastrous consequences, worse than with any other type of garden chemical. We need to consider five principle types of product although, as will be apparent, these categories are not all mutually exclusive.

It is important to remember first that only you know the difference between a weed and a garden plant – in other words, it is you as a gardener who must play a major part in deciding how effective and safe a weedkiller is to be by directing it to the right place. *Total* weedkillers kill all vegetation with which they come into contact. By contrast, *selective* weedkillers only kill certain types of plant, and the most important subdivision of this group is into those that kill only broad-leaved weeds and can therefore be used safely on lawns, and those few (only one of which is available to gardeners) that kill only grasses and are therefore safe almost everywhere *except* on a lawn. Some other weedkillers are selective in the sense that they can only kill seedlings and are safe to use, therefore, among established plants, but would be devastating in a seedbed. Some weedkillers work by *contact*, killing green tissues more or less through surface action; others are absorbed and then *translocated* within the plant, and these are obviously of special value for deep-rooted persistent perennial weeds. *Residual* weedkillers (which are also usually total weedkillers) persist in the soil for some weeks or months to kill seeds or freshly germinated seedlings. Clearly, a residual total weedkiller will render an area bereft of plant life for some time – even a season or more. Thus such a product should only be used on paths or other unplanted areas. Non-residual total weedkillers kill all existing vegetation but are rendered inactive in the soil and replanting or sowing can therefore proceed very soon afterwards.

I have listed the weedkillers that are currently available to gardeners and indicated their modes of action and garden uses. It will be apparent from the list that many are sold in proprietary mixtures for particular purposes but it is very important that you do not attempt to make up such mixtures yourself – two incompatible chemicals could produce a very harmful cocktail. Weedkillers are usually applied as a diluted liquid (made up from a powder or liquid concentrate) by watering can (especially on lawns or paths) or by sprayer. Never spray in windy weather and take especial care to ensure that the chemical is applied only to the target plants. Always wash out cans and sprayers thoroughly after use and as an added precaution, never use weedkiller containers for applying any other type of garden chemical.

Occasionally, weedkillers are applied as granules or as powders (some powdered lawn fertiliser mixtures, for instance, very usefully have a selective weedkiller incorporated with them) and at least one translocated weedkiller is available as a gel formulation for painting onto individual plants. I have never found this gel to be very effective, however, and prefer to obtain localised activity by using a liquid formulation in a small sprayer and shielding nearby plants. When spraying, remember that, in general, the finer the droplets, the more effective the coverage. And remember, too, that more than with any other type of garden chemical, weedkiller effectiveness is closely allied to climatic conditions. Warm dry weather, combined with a moist soil, is ideal, although the special conditions necessary for each product should be checked carefully from the label; the very useful translocated weedkiller glyphosate, for example, requires six hours without rain after application if it is to be fully absorbed into the plants' tissues.

When weeds are controlled with a weedkiller, the dead plants tend to shrivel away. When weeds are controlled physically, however, by hoeing or digging out, there is the question of how the remains should be treated. Almost all weeds can safely be disposed of in a properly functioning compost bin. The temperature in the bin should attain at least 70°C (158°F) and this will be adequate to kill almost all seeds. In practice, I can say that I have never known weed seeds of any type to survive my own compost heap; at least, no seedlings have ever emerged from compost subsequently spread as a soil mulch. My only reservation is with rhizomes of couch grass. I do not know the temperature necessary nor the period over which it must be maintained to kill these rhizomes, and as the consequences of spreading couch further are so serious, I feel that the rhizomes are better bagged up and removed to a public refuse tip.

CHEMICAL WEEDKILLERS AVAILABLE TO GARDENERS

CHEMICAL NAME	ACTIVITY	GARDEN USE/PLANTS KILLED
Alloxydim-sodium	translocated	selective (perennial grasses)
Aminotriazole/amitrole	translocated	total*
Atrazine	contact/residual	total*
Chloroxuron	residual	selective (principally moss)*
2,4 – D	translocated	selective (broad-leaved plants)*
Dalapon	translocated	selective (grasses)
Dicamba	translocated	selective (broad-leaved plants)*
Dichlobenil	residual	selective (seedlings and young plants)
Dichlorophen	contact	selective (principally moss)
Dichlorprop	translocated	selective (broad-leaved plants)*
Diquat	contact	total*
Diuron	residual	total*
Ferric sulphate	contact	selective (principally moss)*
Ferrous sulphate	contact	selective (principally moss)*
Glyphosate	translocated	total
MCPA	translocated	selective (broad-leaved plants)*
Mecoprop	contact	selective (broad-leaved plants)*
Paraquat	contact	total*
Propham	residual	selective (seeds/seedlings)
Simazine	residual	total**
Sodium chlorate	residual	total

* only available in proprietary mixture with other weedkillers
** available alone or in proprietary mixture with other weedkillers

SEEDS for your garden plants may be sown with some form of indoor protection or directly outdoors into the garden soil (either in the positions in which the plants are to grow or into a seed-bed from which they will later be transplanted). In this section, I shall concentrate on the first of these methods and on the procedures to follow with most types of seed. Some seeds do, nonetheless, require a little more coercion and on p. 103 I explain some of the techniques that can be used to persuade more difficult types to germinate.

Naturally, of course, all plants shed their seeds outdoors and it is there that they germinate, often following a period of dormancy or rest. So if the outdoors is good enough for nature to sow her seeds, why is it not good enough for us? There are two principal answers. The first relates to some of those types of plant that are naturally hardy enough to survive outdoors in our climate. By sowing their seeds indoors, in the warmth, we are effectively advancing the spring and thus giving them a head start by the time they are later moved outdoors. This in turn means that their flowering or cropping season is extended. Cauliflowers and bedding alyssum are typical of the hardy plants that benefit from such an indoor start. The second, and more important, answer is that many garden plants are native to climates warmer than ours. If they were to be sown directly outdoors, they would not experience a long enough period of adequate warmth to enable them to germinate, mature, flower and/or fruit before low temperatures at the end of the season slowed them down or frost finished them off. Tomatoes, cucumbers, bedding lobelia and pelargoniums are familiar examples in this group. In a few instances, warm-climate plants that grow very quickly (runner beans for example) can be cropped well from an outdoor sowing but give a longer productive season if the seed is sown indoors and the plants are moved outside later.

Seed sowing indoors and the half-hardy annual technique

It is essential to prick out young seedlings to give them space for further rapid growth. If they are left in the seedbox as originally planted (left), their cramped conditions will result in weak and spindly growth.

Plants that originate in warmer climates but can thrive perfectly well outdoors in our summers, although not our winters, are called half-hardy. Some of them (ageratum and nemesias for example) are naturally annuals but most (tomatoes, lobelias and pelargoniums for instance) are actually perennials. When grown in our gardens for one season only, in the way I have described, they nonetheless tend all to be called half-hardy annuals. And the technique of sowing seeds in indoor warmth before moving the plants outdoors once the danger of frost has passed is called the half-hardy annual technique, and I use this expression in my summaries of individual plants' growing conditions later in the book.

Sowing seeds and raising seedlings on the greenhouse bench or even on the kitchen window ledge is not only easy, it is also immensely satisfying. And whilst very few of us have either time or inclination to raise all of our garden plants in this way, your gardening will attain a new dimension in satisfaction if you can manage to produce at least some of your own plants from seeds that you have sown.

Almost invariably, your seeds will be bought fresh, packeted and branded from a reputable supplier, although on p. 102 I have given a few hints about storing seeds and saving seed from your own plants. Apart from the seed itself, you require certain other essentials for indoor plant-raising – a compost in which to sow the seeds, a propagator in which to put it, water, in some instances light (although in others, an absence of it) and some means of supplying an adequate temperature. The compost should be a proprietary peat-based or other soil-less mix, either of a type branded specifically for seed sowing or one of the universal types that are also suitable for the early growth of the young plant. Always use fresh compost for each batch of seeds. There are many types of propagator available and of course, at its simplest, a propagator need be no more than a plant pot. I believe the most versatile propagator, however, is one based on a standard-sized plastic seed tray (in Britain, these are generally manufactured with dimensions of approximately 35 cm × 24 cm × 5 cm deep (14 in × 9½ in × 2 in), a smaller tray of 18 cm × 24 cm × 5 cm deep (7 in × 9½ in × 2 in) being known as a half tray). A seed tray on its own, however, does not constitute a propagator because there is no means of keeping the compost moist. Traditionally, gardeners placed a sheet of glass over the seed tray for this purpose, but there are problems because of the small head height that this offers the young emerged seedling, and the care needed to raise the glass to permit ventilation. A plastic bag supported on four sticks will suffice in an emergency, but much the easiest and most versatile system is to use a purpose-made rigid plastic cover, approximately 14 cm (5½ in) tall, with adjustable vents. These can be purchased complete with the seed tray base but if you have an additional stock of trays, the same cover can be used again and again, as each batch of seedlings reaches the stage where it no longer requires a wholly moist atmosphere. But whatever equipment you adopt, ensure that it is disinfected and washed before being used again.

Generally, seeds require a slightly higher temperature in order to germinate than the resultant plants ever require again. Moreover, within fairly well defined limits for each type of seed, the higher the temperature, the more rapid and uniform the germination. Provision of an adequate and appropriate temperature is thus very important, but I see no merit in confusing you by listing temperatures far more precisely than you can ever hope to maintain them. In the specific descriptions of plants later in the book, therefore, I have defined plants' germination requirements within three broad temperature ranges: Low (less than 15.5°C [60°F]), Medium (15.5° – 21.5°C [60° – 70°F]) and High (above 21°C [70°F]). But how are the necessary temperatures to be achieved? The proverbial kitchen window ledge can suffice for seeds requiring what I have called a *medium* temperature, although always bear in mind that the temperature in the space between the window pane and drawn curtains will plummet at night. Ideally, the propagator should be moved further into the room in the evening therefore. Seeds that require a *high* temperature in order to germinate can usually be stimulated to do so by a brief spell in the airing cupboard. But because they will be in the dark, it is essential that the propagators are checked daily and moved into the light as soon as most of the seedlings have emerged.

Because of the inevitable fluctuations in temperature that occur in these makeshift conditions, germination and seedling emergence can be inconveniently erratic. Some form of heated propagator is a very sensible contrivance, therefore, at least for some types of seed. It is possible to buy versions of the basic seed-tray propagator with thermostatically controlled heating elements in the base but their major drawback is that the equipment is tied up until the seedlings are large enough to transplant. Much better is a system that permits individual seed trays to be removed from the heat source once the seedlings have emerged. These can be used either on a domestic window ledge or the greenhouse bench. Where there is no mains electricity supply to the greenhouse, low voltage heating mats on which the trays are placed are especially useful. A small transformer is plugged into a convenient mains socket in the house and a low-voltage wire run to the greenhouse.

My ideal system, however, for the greenhouse that does have mains electricity, is a heated sand bench – a large box filled with sand within which a thermostatically controlled heating cable is buried. These can be bought in ready-to-assemble form, and can also be made very easily from plywood to accommodate a heating cable and its associated thermostat. Take care to follow the manufacturer's instructions regarding the area of bench needed for particular lengths of cable, and take especial care to lay it in the pattern recommended and to avoid any cross-overs. If you are installing such a facility, remember also that when filled with sand, it will be very heavy and your greenhouse staging must be strong enough to bear it.

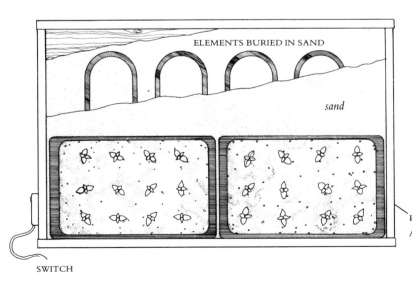

ELEMENTS BURIED IN SAND

sand

SWITCH

PLYWOOD BOX FRAME
APPROXIMATELY 12.5–15 CM (5–6 IN) DEEP

Plan of a heated sand bench showing looped heating cable buried beneath sand and with two seed trays on the surface.

Some seeds require light to germinate, and of course young seedlings must have adequate light in order to grow. I have never found artificial lighting to be necessary, however, when raising garden plants in either the house or the greenhouse.

The commonest mistakes made when sowing seeds are that the compost is too loose, too wet or too dry, or that the seeds are sown at the incorrect depth. Any of these features can lead to disappointment in poor or, at best, erratic germination. To ensure the compost is of the right consistency and moisture content, therefore, always buy a reputable brand and store it in a sealed bag to prevent the peat from drying out; it is very difficult to re-wet uniformly. Fill the propagator tray with loose compost, level with the top and then firm this down evenly (a small block of wood about 5 cm × 10 cm (2 in × 4 in) makes this very easy) so that its surface is approximately 1 cm (½ in) below the lip. Water the compost gently – I find that a child's watering can with a fine rose is ideal. A full-sized seed tray filled with fresh compost will require about 0.25 l (8 fl oz) of water. Leave the tray for about 1 hour to drain before sowing the seeds.

There are several methods of sowing, dictated principally by seed size. Very small seeds sold loose in packets (lobelia or fibrous-rooted begonia for instance) are best mixed with a small amount of inert coloured 'filler' such as fine brick dust and scattered over the surface of the compost. (Because of the difficulties of sowing these tiny seeds evenly, seed companies have tried various devices such as supplying them in small, pencil-like tubes in order to make the task easier.) Most tiny seeds such as these should not be covered with compost because their food reserves are inadequate for the emerged seedling to reach the surface. A few medium-sized seeds such as primulas must be sown on the surface and left uncovered, too, because darkness inhibits their germination. I believe that all other medium-sized seeds are better sown by gently sprinkling them from the corner of the packet along shallow rows rather than by scattering. Rows can be made with the edge of a plastic label or other convenient tool to the depth indicated for the individual seeds. Almost invariably, you will be advised to 'sow thinly' and in general this means that the space between individual seeds should be between 0.5 and 1 cm (¼ and ½ in), although you may well need to thin out the seedlings slightly after they emerge. The distance between rows should be 2–3 cm (¾–1½ in). After sowing, carefully push the compost back over the row and firm it with the wooden block as before.

Work out roughly how many plants of each type you require and don't sow more than twice this number of seeds (you can only make a rough estimate of the number, of course, with the very tiny ones). It will soon be apparent that often two or more types of seed can be sown in each tray, provided you remember to label them – small plastic labels and a waterproof marker are essential items of the seed raiser's equipment.

Seeds such as sweet peas that are large enough to be picked up with forceps (a very useful item of gardening equipment) are best sown individually by pushing them into the compost to appropriate depth. With most very large seeds (the pea and bean family offers many examples), the resulting seedlings are also large and the seeds are actually better sown directly into small pots of compost. Several 8.75 cm (3½ in) diameter pots can be stood in a seed tray under the propagator cover, and this technique is also valuable with plants such as cauliflowers or aubergines that resent the disturbance brought about by pricking on. Sow two seeds in each pot and, if both emerge, pull out the weaker. Increasingly, manufacturers are offering individual 'cellular' inserts comprising several small pot-like chambers to be filled with compost and placed within a seed tray, partly for the plants that resent upheaval but also to cut down the work involved in pricking on generally.

Most common types of seed germinate fairly uniformly (that is, all seedlings emerge at around the same time). Once most are showing their green cotyledons (seed leaves) above the compost, open the propagator vents half-way (or otherwise allow some ventilation on more simple propagators). As the seedlings stand upright and elongate, the vents should be opened fully, and when the first true leaves have expanded, the cover should be removed. It is very important to attend to watering carefully at this stage (using the small watering can) and to ensure that the seedlings are not exposed to direct hot sun. If at any time you must be away from home and unable to attend to the plants for more than a couple of days, no matter how tall the seedlings, put back the cover (with vents open) temporarily to retain moisture. It is easiest if the next stage, pricking on, can be performed for all seedlings in a tray at the same time, although with those types that germinate erratically (among common seeds, primulas, for instance, are notorious at germinating over many weeks), it will be necessary to prick on each seedling as it emerges.

Very small and relatively slow growing seedlings, especially of plants such as most bedding ornamentals that are grown in large numbers, should be pricked on to a second seed tray, prepared as the first. Space them approximately 3 cm (1¼ in) apart each way. More robust seedlings are better pricked on individually to 8.75 cm (3½ in) diameter pots. Lever the seedling from the compost with a small kitchen fork or similar tool. Although the customary advice is to hold the seedling by the cotyledons, rather than the stem, this can be difficult. The stems of many seedlings are robust enough to withstand injury, if held gently, but placing your thumb and forefinger around the mass of compost surrounding the upper roots is also effective. With a little practice, most gardeners will work out their own system. Very small seedlings such as lobelias, especially when they have been sown by scattering the seed, should be picked up in a small clump for pricking on; don't try to separate them individually.

Replant the seedlings to the same depth as before and press the compost around them gently – too firmly and you will damage the young roots; too loosely and the plant will re-establish with difficulty. A universal or potting compost should be used for pricking on and should be watered before and after the seedlings have been pricked into it.

Perhaps the most critical stage of all in the half-hardy annual technique is hardening off. Raised indoors in warmth, your seedlings will have large, thin-walled cells that will be very susceptible to damage from the widely fluctuating temperatures that occur outdoors, even in early summer. Hardening off is the process through which they are encouraged gradually to produce smaller-celled, more resilient tissue. The place to harden them off is the cold frame, into which the trays of seedlings are placed. I always allow at least two weeks for hardening off before planting out. In the first week, the frame cover is left half open in the day-time but closed at night. In the second week, it is left fully open in the daytime and half open at night. If you have no cold frame, trays or pots of seedlings may be put outside in the daytime and taken under cover at night, although this is a laborious task and an

After young seedlings have been raised in the warmth of the greenhouse, or other protected area, it is essential that they are placed in a cold frame for hardening off.

inexpensive cold frame makes a very worthwhile investment. As with a greenhouse, always buy the largest that you can afford – hardening-off space is very valuable in spring. I prefer the frames with wooden sides and glazed top. Those aluminium frames with glazed sides are more or less adequate for the hardening-off process, but are inefficient at performing the additional role of providing protection for relatively hardy plants, cuttings and seedlings through the winter. I have more to say about this use of cold frames on p. 107, whilst on p. 122 I describe their value for the more efficient cropping of such relatively tender plants as melons.

FOR many garden plants, following nature's system and sowing them directly outdoors into the garden soil (the hardy annual technique) makes more sense than using the half-hardy annual method that I described earlier. This is because many of those annuals that originated in climates similar to our own will grow quickly enough to flower or crop satisfactorily within the season of sowing. Valuable greenhouse space would be wasted on them. This is particularly true of plants that are required in very large numbers. Many annual vegetables (of which several are actually biennial in the wild) fall into this category, and this group also includes some of those plants (carrots and parsnips for example) that have long tap roots and cannot be transplanted very successfully. They too are better sown into the garden soil in the positions where they will grow. A few types of plant are sown outdoors but closely together into a seed bed from which they will be transplanted, rather than directly into their final growing positions. Some of the large leafy brassicas and the few biennial ornamentals such as wallflowers and sweet williams fall into this group – they grow fairly slowly and would thus occupy valuable growing space for a long, unproductive period. The procedure that I refer to elsewhere in the book as the biennial technique therefore simply means sowing the seeds outdoors in a seed bed and then moving the young plants when they are about 8 cm (3 in) tall to a transplant bed, spaced at about 5 cm (2 in) apart. They are finally transplanted to their growing positions in mid-autumn. Nonetheless, without exception, *all* plants that are sown directly outdoors in spring will benefit from some method of warming the soil to speed up or produce more uniform seed germination. But even before this comes the all-important matter of soil preparation.

Gardeners talk of obtaining a good tilth before sowing seeds. Tilth is a curious, almost indefinable quality that I can perhaps best sum up as the soil condition in which seeds will germinate and seedlings grow most satisfactorily. If that hasn't told you very much either, it means in practice that the soil crumbs must be broken down finely enough for the tiny roots to be able to make fairly unimpeded progress whilst at the same time there must be enough pores between the crumbs to ensure that the roots are well furnished with water and air. The soil must also be uniform in structure, all of these attributes combining to ensure that it warms up evenly and quickly.

Whether seeds are to be sown directly into their final growing positions or into a seedbed from which they will be transplanted, the soil preparation is the same, and we often talk of this as making a seedbed tilth. Hardly ever will you wish or need to convert a previously undug soil at the end of one cropping season directly into one with a seedbed tilth. The area should usually be roughly dug and organic matter incorporated in the autumn (see p. 58) and then left with fairly large clods over winter By the spring, the winter rains and frost will have broken these down, but the soil will still be in a lumpy and uneven state, almost certainly with some weed growth. It should then be dug again, using a fork rather than a spade, the weeds should be removed and the large lumps broken down with the back of the fork. This operation can be performed as soon as the soil begins to dry out in the spring – the precise timing will obviously vary with the part of the country in which you live and with the nature of your soil; as I mentioned on p. 57, a sandy soil will be in a workable condition much sooner than a clay. About one week before sowing, the area should be raked to remove any remaining large clods and at the same time an appropriate fertiliser should be scattered

Seed sowing outdoors and the hardy annual technique

over the soil and so incorporated into the upper few centimetres. (The fertilisers needed for different types of plant will be found with the individual plant details later in the book.) Rake alternately in directions at 90° to each other to obtain a level surface.

For sowings in the spring, some soil warming is greatly to be commended. There are two easy ways in which to do this. The first is to use cloches, and to arrange these over the positions in which the seeds will be sown (obviously, this is easiest if your seeds are to be sown in rows). The cloches should be replaced after sowing to aid early growth of the young plants. The second method is to lay plastic sheet over the soil surface, anchoring it at the edges by digging it into a shallow trench. This method is of greatest benefit when seeds are to be broadcast sown. Don't use clear plastic, for this will encourage weed growth, but there is little to choose between black and white.

In most instances, and certainly for all vegetables, the seeds are sown in rows. The spacing between the rows varies with the type of seed (see individual plant details), as does the depth to which the seed drill should be made, although the principle is the same in each case. You will certainly need a garden line to keep the row straight; although various drill-making devices are offered for sale, I have always found the simplest method to be the best. A bamboo cane, or the edge of a draw hoe, will make a perfectly adequate seed drill. As when using seed trays indoors, sowing thinly is the maxim to follow. Large seeds such as peas are most readily sown from the hand, but small ones should be tapped gently from the corner of the packet. After

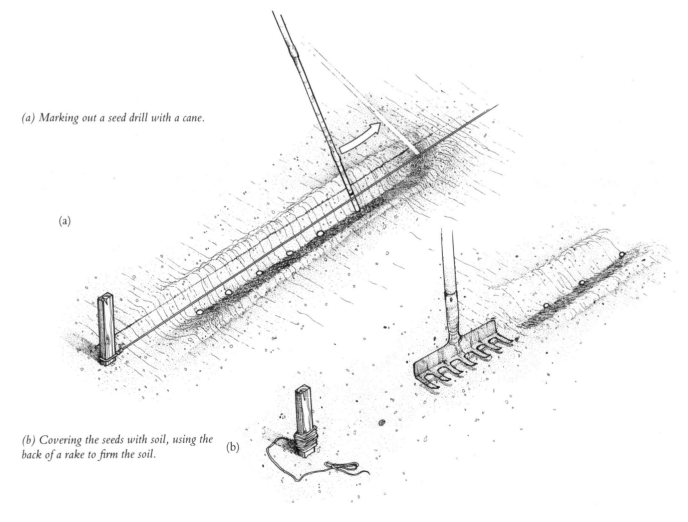

(a) Marking out a seed drill with a cane.

(a)

(b) Covering the seeds with soil, using the back of a rake to firm the soil.

(b)

sowing, carefully push back the soil over the drill with the back of the rake, taking care not to push the seeds out of the drill. It is then most important to firm the soil. Some gardeners do this by walking gently along the covered drill but this can compact clayey soils and my own preference is to use the more controlled method of tamping with the back of the rake.

Sometimes it is necessary for seeds to be broadcast sown. Summer flowering annuals, for instance, will be needed in groups rather than straight lines and discrete areas within beds and borders should be prepared for them, the soil being carefully raked away for sowing and then raked back again afterwards. The most important use of broadcast sowing is for a new lawn and I discuss this in detail with other aspects of lawn preparation on p. 151.

In the spring, it is most unlikely that the soil will dry out to the extent of delaying the germination of the seeds and emergence of the seedlings but sowings made later in the season will almost certainly require some additional watering. I describe watering systems in detail on p. 68 but for seedbeds it is most important to use a very fine sprinkler in order not to wash away the soil. You should not irrigate for more than about half an hour at a time to stop water from accumulating on the soil surface and, either directly or by causing capping, prevent the seeds from germinating.

The technique of transplanting your seedlings is basically the same whether the plants are to be put into containers of compost or into the open ground, although in the latter case the soil should be prepared carefully in essentially the same manner as that used in the preparation of a seedbed. Similarly, too, the soil may be pre-warmed before transplanting. This is especially beneficial with tomatoes which will invariably suffer a serious growth check when planted into cold soil or compost. Even in greenhouses, it is advisable to place growing bags or compost pots in position a week or more before planting.

I prefer to use two tools for transplanting – a hand fork, to remove the plants without damaging their roots, and a trowel to prepare the planting hole. When transplanting large numbers, you may find it useful to develop a technique of inserting the trowel, moving it back and then forwards in the soil and inserting the plant behind the blade. But for firming in the young plant afterwards, there is absolutely nothing better than a pair of hands. In general, it is safest to transplant to the depth at which the plant was growing previously; although most of the cabbage family benefit from slightly deeper planting, many young plants are killed or stunted through being planted too deeply. With such plants as cauliflowers, that have been raised individually in pots to lessen the check to growth, take care not to undo the good work by breaking up the ball of compost as it is knocked from the pot. For all plants, however, transplanting is a shock and inevitably some root damage will ensue. To help them regenerate new tissues rapidly, therefore, apply a dose of liquid fertiliser immediately afterwards, rather than merely watering them in as so often recommended.

More about seeds

SEEDS are so important in gardening that I make no apology for devoting a third part of the book to aspects of their use. Here, I shall cover two topics; first the advantages and disadvantages of saving seeds from your own garden plants, and second, an introduction to some of the ways in which the more obstinate seeds might be persuaded to germinate.

There are advantages in collecting seed from plants in your own garden. You will of course save money but, more importantly to my mind, you will gain immensely in satisfaction. With rare or unusual plants, obtained perhaps as gifts from a friend, it may be impossible to obtain seed commercially and, if the plant happens to be an annual, saving the seed provides you with the only way of perpetuating your stock. Many of the gardeners most successful at horticultural shows routinely save seed from strains of their particular vegetable specialities that they have kept season by season. But against all of this there must be set some disadvantages. Many of today's garden plants are F_1 hybrids and, strictly as plants, these have many merits. Generally, they are vigorous, large and strong growing, and they ripen uniformly (the latter, however, being an arguable virtue in the vegetable garden, where you may prefer your cabbages and Brussels sprouts to mature gradually over a period of weeks). They are also expensive because of the labour-intensive method by which they are produced – a cross between parental plants must be made afresh each year. Seed saved from F_1 hybrid cultivars, however, is useless, for the resulting offspring will be a complete and unpredictable hotchpotch.

Even with cultivars that are not F_1 hybrids, there is not always a guarantee that the seedlings you obtain will be identical to their parents. Plants such as peas that naturally are self-pollinating will almost invariably, in gardening parlance, 'come true' – there is no chance that stray pollen from another plant will interfere to affect the purity. But those types that naturally cross-pollinate may well have been fertilised by pollen from related cultivars growing nearby, although this in itself can offer the exciting prospect of something new and worthwhile turning up. Only among vegetables may this gamble prove a disappointment if the yield falls short of what you expect.

Given all these 'ifs' and 'buts', however, I find that there is no satisfaction in plant raising to match that of bringing to maturity plants that originate with seed that you have collected. It is important to make preparations to collect the seed just before it ripens and spills onto the ground. Cut off the heads of plants such as lupins, poppies, peas and beans, that produce dry seeds, and hang them upside down in a fairly warm but well ventilated and dry place with a paper bag tied over them. The seeds should then fall naturally into the bag. Seeds such as those of marrows and tomatoes, that are produced within soft and fleshy fruits, should be separated from the surrounding tissues and then washed thoroughly to remove any germination-inhibiting chemicals that may be present. Spread them to dry at room temperature before storing them in small paper envelopes.

Both for seeds that you have collected yourself and for commercial packeted seed (once the metal foil packet has been opened), storage conditions are important if the viability is to be retained for more than one season. The two factors that diminish the life of seeds are high temperature and high humidity. The ideal storage conditions, therefore, are provided by placing your seed packets inside a screw-top glass jar together with a small sachet of silica gel drying agent (which you should be able to buy from a chemist). The jar itself should then be placed in a refrigerator. Of course, even stored in this way, seeds will not last for ever, but in general, small and fairly hard seeds such as those of brassicas, tomatoes or poppies will maintain their viability for several years. Larger and more fleshy seeds such as peas and beans may only last for two years at the most.

Most packeted seed, certainly of the common garden cultivars, will usually germinate readily if the instructions on the seed packet (or listed in the plant descriptions at the end of the book) are followed. Where slightly unusual conditions are required, most seed companies are helpful in providing the necessary details. But when you have collected seeds from wild plants or from unusual types in your own garden, problems may arise, generally because the seed has some inbuilt dormancy mechanism that must be overcome. Largely by trial and error, however, a fund of expertise has built up about many of these plants and I have given the details where appropriate in the plant descriptions. In general, nonetheless, I always advocate dividing any newly acquired batch of seeds into two lots. Place the first lot in a refrigerator as I have described and then sow a few of these seeds after about one month, using the half-hardy annual technique. As well as providing good storage conditions, the refrigerator temperature may provide the conditions that simulate winter and thus break the dormancy mechanism of seeds that normally would lie on the ground until the spring. The second lot of seeds I sow immediately, my logic here being that in some types of seed (primulas are a good example), the natural dormancy does not set in until some time after the seed has been shed.

Some of the commonest problems arise when gardeners try to germinate the seeds of trees and shrubs. 'They *will* not germinate' is the cry from all sides. Usually this is because that great gardening virtue of patience has not been exercised to the full. Tree and shrub seeds generally take a long time to germinate and before they can do so, a hard seed coat or some other dormancy mechanism must be eroded. Much the easiest way to do this is by the operation called stratification. Simply place the ripe seeds (or small fruits) in shallow pans of coarse sand, burying the seeds about 2 cm (¾ in) below the surface. Then leave the pans outdoors in a sheltered place over winter. In the spring, place the pans in the slightly warmer conditions of a cold frame and germination should then begin, slowly and erratically, but surely. In some instances, root emergence takes place first, unseen, and you may have to wait a further year before the shoot arises.

There remains, however, a number of other common types of seed with which gardeners frequently experience problems. I have listed these below, together with the conditions that I have proved from my experience to be fairly reliable at persuading them to co-operate. In some instances, I have advocated using fresh seeds. Ideally, these should be freshly collected from the parent plant, but for most gardeners it will mean from a freshly opened foil packet.

Alstroemeria: Sow seeds 65mm (2½ in) deep, then keep them for 7 days at 21°C (70°F), then for 21 days in a refrigerator, then return them to 21°C (70°F).

Begonia: Sow seeds on the surface of the compost and keep them at a minimum temperature of 21°C (70°F) with good light.

Canna: Abrade the seed coat carefully, soak the seeds in water for 48 hours and then keep them at a minimum temperature of 21°C (70°F).

Cyclamen: Soak the seeds for 24 hours in water at 40°C (104°F), then sow them 2mm (1/10 in) deep and keep them at a temperature of 15–19°C (59–66°F) in the dark.

Impatiens: Sow the seeds on the surface of the compost and keep them at a minimum temperature of 21°C (70°F).

Meconopsis: Keep the seeds for 21 days in a refrigerator and then, after sowing, at a maximum temperature of 24°C (75°F).

Viola (incl. pansy): Sow the seeds 3mm (1/8 in) deep and keep them at a minimum temperature of 21°C (70°F) in the dark.

Primula: Sow fresh seeds on the surface of the compost and keep them at a maximum temperature of 20°C (68°F).

Sweet pea: Chip dark-seeded cultivars on the side of the seed opposite the 'eye'; keep them at a maximum temperature of 20°C (68°F).

Chipping hard seeds such as sweet peas with a knife point.

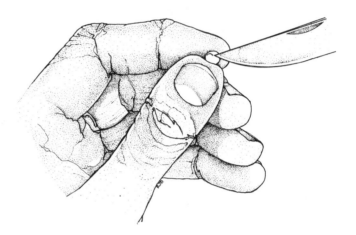

Thumbergia: Sow fresh seeds 3mm (1/8 in) deep and keep them at a temperature of 21–24°C (70–75°F).

Finally, I should mention a technique called fluid sowing. This is a valuable although fiddling procedure for seeds like parsnip that germinate very erratically. In essence, the seeds are pre-germinated onto damp paper, then washed into a gel (which protects the young shoot). The gel is squeezed out into the seed drill. Complete kits including the gel, with full instructions, may be purchased at garden centres.

Fluid sowing, showing germinated seeds being squeezed from plastic bag in a gel.

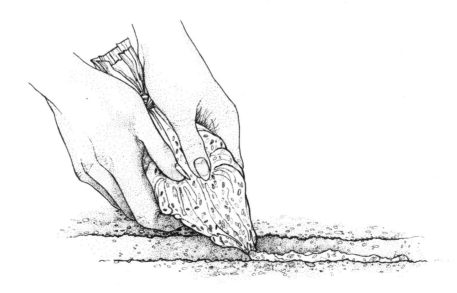

AMONG the greatest pleasures of gardening is that you can add, year by year, to your range of plants. You can do this of course by buying packeted seed (or even by saving your own), and sowing it either indoors or out, as I have described already. But beginning with a plant rather than with seed can provide you with a head start, so here I shall discuss some of the advantages and disadvantages of this approach and outline the ways in which you can multiply those plants you have already and provide some spares to give to friends and neighbours.

Buying plants from garden centres or nurseries rather than raising your own from seed offers you two main advantages. First, with annual bedding plants and vegetables especially, you will have been spared the time, trouble and expense involved in the sowing, germinating, pricking on and hardening off of a large number of plants (although, to be honest, not all plants offered for sale have in fact been adequately hardened off). You will also be unlikely to be able to devote as much time to the task as the professional plant raiser can, and you will be unlikely to have such good glasshouse or other facilities for the purpose. The counter to this is that you will pay proportionately very much more to off-set the nursery's own costs and provide them with a profit. But on balance, unless you are very enthusiastic and have a great deal of time to spare, I am sure that buying the common bedding plants that are required in relatively large numbers makes a good deal of sense for many gardeners. For those plants required in small numbers and for uncommon types that are less likely to be stocked at garden centres, raising them from seeds represents a better, if not the only, option.

The situation with vegetables is rather different, for most are sown directly outdoors. And in general those few types that are better raised for transplanting (runner beans for instance) are required in small numbers that should be within most gardeners' production capabilities – they tend to be fairly quick growing and in consequence to be sown later when the artificial heat required is unlikely to be prohibitively expensive. A major exception lies with the brassicas – cabbages, cauliflowers, Brussels sprouts and their kin which can be sown directly but are generally better transplanted. All of this group of plants are susceptible to the soil-borne disease clubroot (p. 82). Once present in your garden soil, clubroot is ineradicable and will impose very serious limitations on your vegetable brassica production, more or less indefinitely. Clubroot is often introduced into otherwise uncontaminated gardens through being present, invisibly, in the roots or in the soil adhering to the roots of transplants. And because there can be no guarantee that transplants you buy are free from the disease, I would urge all gardeners to raise their own brassica plants if at all possible.

The second big advantage in buying plants is of special importance with perennials. Here of course the value of the 'head-start' is much greater (you will be a patient gardener indeed if you opt to raise your own trees or even bulb-forming plants from seed), but the choice in varieties is of even bigger significance. Many of the best types of herbaceous perennials and shrubs (including almost all desirable rose varieties) do not produce seeds – having double flowers (and hence no stamens), they have lost the ability to do so. Even those with single or semi-double flowers are generally complex hybrids and bear seeds that give rise to a hotch-potch of plants, decidedly inferior to the parent – the offspring are said not to 'come true'. Thus, all of these types must be propagated by vegetative means, generally by cuttings, and so buying a plant is your only way of obtaining them.

Multiplying your plants

But once you have bought a plant or even raised one from seed to maturity, vegetative methods can be used to multiply it further. All of these techniques make use of plants' natural abilities to regenerate roots or shoots, although some of the methods of taking cuttings are rather far removed from events that happen routinely in nature. The simplest method of multiplication is by division – an old gardening adage but a true one. Large clumps of almost all types of herbaceous perennials (but not woody plants) can physically be pulled apart and the smaller pieces replanted. It is impossible to generalise regarding the age at which they should be divided, for it depends on their rate of growth, but in most instances, once the crown reaches 12 or 15 cm (5 or 6 in) in diameter, it can be divided (or, as it is often described, split). The best times of year to do this are autumn or early spring, the latter being preferable for plants that are less hardy or that, like paeonies, have large, fleshy tubers or rhizomes. I have listed under the individual plant descriptions any special features of division relating, for instance, to the depth of replanting, but in general the procedure is straightforward enough. Dig up the mature clump with a fork and pull it first into two, then more pieces. If possible, do this by hand, but if not, insert two forks, back to back, and lever the clump apart. Never use a spade, for this will sever and damage the roots. From a clump of about 15 cm (6 in) diameter, it should be possible to obtain approximately ten new plants, but always tear off and discard those parts that lay in the centre of the original crown – these will be degenerate and never give rise to vigorous new growth. Divided perennials should be replanted in exactly the same way as I have described for planting generally (p. 101).

Dividing a clump of primulas by hand.

After division, the most important method of vegetative propagation is by taking cuttings and in one form or another, this technique can be used with almost every type of plant, ranging from tiny alpines to forest trees. Very few species cannot be induced fairly easily to form new root tissues (the essence of this method of multiplication, new stem tissues then following as a matter of course), most of the exceptions being slow-growing plants with very close grained wood (holly is a common example) or those that produce copious amounts of latex. I have illustrated the features of the most important types of cuttings, but there are several important general considerations.

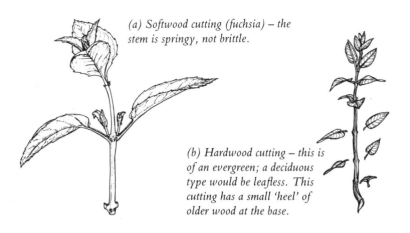

(a) Softwood cutting (fuchsia) – the stem is springy, not brittle.

(b) Hardwood cutting – this is of an evergreen; a deciduous type would be leafless. This cutting has a small 'heel' of older wood at the base.

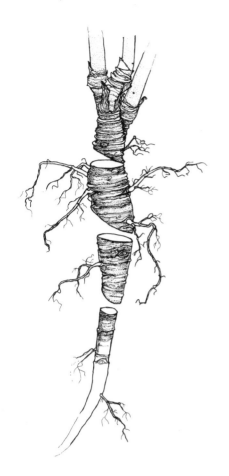

(c) Root cutting (sea-holly). These cuttings are treated rather differently – the root is trimmed into short lengths with a sloping cut at one end and a straight one at the other. Push them into pots of compost so that the tops of the cuttings just protrude.

Whilst rooting powder containing growth-promoting hormones is not essential for all types of cutting, used correctly it never does any harm. And because the powder also generally contains a fungicide to prevent rotting, it is sensible to use it routinely. Moisten the freshly cut end of the cutting, dip it in the powder (always buy fresh each season) and then knock off the excess. With the exception of hardwood cuttings, all should be rooted (or 'struck') in a covered chamber, either a propagator as used for seed sowing (p. 94) or a covered cold frame. It is very important to maintain a moist atmosphere around the cuttings for they will otherwise lose water through their leaves at a time when, lacking roots, they are unable to replace it from below. Even with a covered propagator, therefore, you should pay careful attention to the moisture content of the rooting medium and use a hand sprayer to mist over the cuttings regularly. The cold frame can also be used for hardwood cuttings although I prefer to root these in a sheltered spot in the open garden, inserting the shoots in a narrow 'V'-shaped trench in which sand has been layered. The essence of inducing new roots to form on any type of cutting is to provide good aeration in the rooting medium. For this reason, a pure peat-based compost is generally unsatisfactory and many different mixtures have been suggested. I almost always use a two-layered system, half-filling the propagator tray or pot with firmed peat-based potting compost and then topping up with a layer of horticultural sand. (For leaf cuttings, the layer of sand may need to be shallower than the peat). Each cutting is pushed into the sand until its lower end is at the sand-peat junction. Thus, when the new roots form, they immediately have available a good supply of nutrient-rich growing medium.

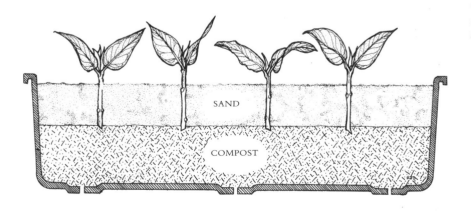

SAND

COMPOST

Cross-section of seed tray, showing cuttings inserted through a layer of sand so that their tips just penetrate the underlying compost.

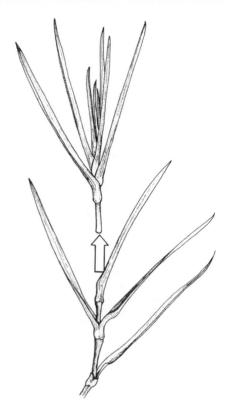

Pipings (pinks) – the shoot tip is pulled out.

Removing scales from a lily bulb.

OFF-SETS *(globe artichokes).*

(a) Remove strong shoots with a piece of root attached in April or November.
(b) Shoots taken in April can be planted out in their permanent positions immediately. Those taken in November should be potted in potting compost and overwintered in a cold frame.

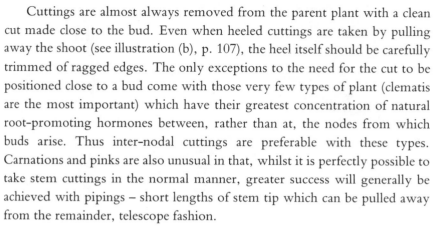

Cuttings are almost always removed from the parent plant with a clean cut made close to the bud. Even when heeled cuttings are taken by pulling away the shoot (see illustration (b), p. 107), the heel itself should be carefully trimmed of ragged edges. The only exceptions to the need for the cut to be positioned close to a bud come with those very few types of plant (clematis are the most important) which have their greatest concentration of natural root-promoting hormones between, rather than at, the nodes from which buds arise. Thus inter-nodal cuttings are preferable with these types. Carnations and pinks are also unusual in that, whilst it is perfectly possible to take stem cuttings in the normal manner, greater success will generally be achieved with pipings – short lengths of stem tip which can be pulled away from the remainder, telescope fashion.

Superficially rather different from cuttings, but in reality based on the same principle, is a useful method of multiplying lilies that enables several young plants to be obtained from one expensive bulb. Carefully pull away up to six of the fleshy outer scales (which are actually swollen leaves), place them in a plastic bag of peat-based potting compost, close the bag and hang it up in a warm place such as an airing cupboard. Within about three weeks, roots will form on the scales and they may then be potted up in individual pots of compost. Such plants should flower within two or three years.

Sometimes, the process of obtaining new plants can be speeded up by making use of the 'ready-made' offspring that some plants produce. The most important among these are runners (baby plants produced on long, wiry shoots), which are especially significant on strawberries; but I must emphasise that any method of multiplying *crop* plants by vegetative methods will sooner or later become self-defeating through the build-up of virus contamination in the plants and new, virus-free stock must be obtained periodically. The second common type of ready-made plant is the off-set. These are familiar on many species of *Agave*, *Aloe* and other succulents. When removing off-sets from parent plants, I find it preferable first to sever the connection between parent and offspring and then allow the young plant some weeks of independent existence to build up its own root system *in situ* before it is transplanted.

(a)

(b)

I have already mentioned that plants such as holly, with close-grained hard wood, root unpredictably or scarcely at all from cuttings. Many

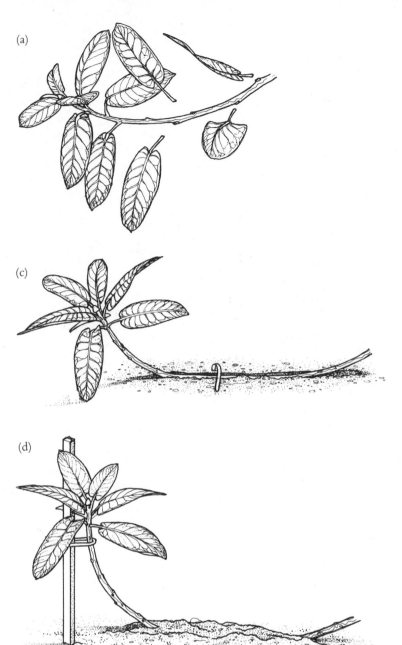

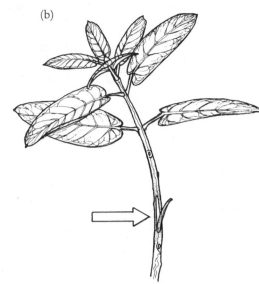

LAYERING RHODODENDRONS.

(a) Strip off leaves from branch, starting about 22.5cm (9in) from tip.

(b) Cut a shallow nick in the underside.

(c) Pin branch down into shallow trench half-filled with soil.

(d) Stake tip upright and cover branch with more soil. If the branch is very springy, you may need to weight it down with a rock or brick.

evergreens can also present problems, for even when cuttings are taken during their dormant season in the conventional hardwood manner, the continuing presence of leaves means that water will still be lost through them. What better technique therefore than one that ensures the 'cutting' has roots even before it is cut from its parent? Such a technique is called layering and is shown in the illustrations. The major virtues required for successful layering are those of patience (rooting can take two years) and a good memory, for over this time it is easy to forget where you have made the layer – a small cane inserted close by will help. Air layering is a rather similar and useful if unsightly technique, of particular value with large-leaved evergreen pot plants that lack both low-hanging branches and an area of soil in which to peg them.

PART THREE
Stocking Your Garden

IT saddens me that the vegetable garden is too often thought of as the poor relation of gardening as a whole. The very name generally accorded it, the vegetable plot, smacks of something less dignified than a border or a bed. Vegetables, moreover, are usually grown out of sight of the house, a situation reinforced by the allotment, which is usually well out of sight of everything except other allotments. Now whilst I am the first to admit that there are more eye-gladdening horticultural sights than serried ranks of Brussels sprouts or frost hardened leeks, the vegetable or kitchen garden, well planned and well managed, can be a most attractive feature. The fresh leaves of salad crops can be at least as appealing as many a bedding annual; and of course, there is no reason at all why unashamedly ornamental plants shouldn't be mixed with the edible. Visitors are both amazed and entranced by the dark blue lobelia 'Crystal Palace' that edges my lettuces and baby beetroot.

With few exceptions, vegetables are annual or biennial crops rather than perennials. This attribute is a mixed blessing however. As with any short-lived plants, they require a considerable degree of care and attention in respect of soil preparation, feeding, and especially of watering. In return, they offer you the matchless delight of fresh-grown produce, quite unlike anything that you will ever buy over a shop counter. And, of course, they provide you with the regular opportunity, each year, to learn from the previous season's successes and failures and to experiment anew.

The ideal site and the soil preparation for a vegetable garden are simply stated but not always as easily satisfied. The soil should be a moisture-retentive yet friable loam, preferably free from large stones and with a pH of around 6.5. The site should be as sunny as possible. But this is the ideal; countless vegetable gardens fall short of these standards yet still yield acceptable produce. Where conditions stray very far from these standards nonetheless, it may prove impossible to grow particular types of vegetable, and I have indicated these constraints in the individual descriptions.

In pondering the area required for a vegetable garden, consideration must inevitably be given to personal preferences; no one will wish to grow any crop that they don't actually enjoy. But there are other important considerations. Some vegetables give a very much greater yield per unit area than others, and in order to help you assess the numbers of plants to grow, I have listed approximate yields within the individual descriptions. More-over, some vegetables are much faster growing than others and more than one crop per season is the norm. You should try and ensure that the same vegetables (or at least, the same general types of vegetable) are not grown on the same land for two years in succession. This is the principle embodied in the practice of crop rotation but, as I indicated on p. 60, I do not believe that strict adherence to the traditional textbook notion of rotation is either necessary or, in smaller gardens, practicable. In addition, it may well be difficult to have even approximately similar areas for the three major vegetable types – root crops, peas and beans, and brassicas. In a small kitchen garden, there may in fact be no large leafy brassicas or potatoes at all, and the bulk of the area will be occupied by such plants as lettuce, radish and spring onions, the catch crops that are merely fitted in amongst other plants in a conventional rotation. And in any event, the few perennial vegetables such as rhubarb, and those like runner beans that have rather special site or soil preparation requirements, are best left outside any rotation scheme.

Whilst I have misgivings about the value of rigid rotations, I am

The vegetable garden

convinced by the usefulness of growing vegetables on the bed system wherever feasible. A vegetable bed is an area of soil approximately 1.2 m (4 ft) wide and as long as site conditions allow. Within this bed, the soil is double dug initially but should not then need to be dug again for four, five or even six seasons. The reason is simply that the main purpose of digging is to break up soil that has become compacted. Soil in the vegetable garden becomes compacted primarily because we have walked over it, but with a 1.2 m wide bed there is no need to walk on the cultivated area at all. All operations can be conducted from the sides although if transplanting or thinning are difficult, a plank bridge may be laid across, supported on two bricks. The bed system can be used even in a very small garden, for even the width is not sacrosanct, and narrower beds or even beds of irregular shape can be fitted in as appropriate.

All vegetable crops benefit from feeding: indeed, yields of many will be pitifully small without it, but the manner in which the feed is added is a highly personal choice. My preference is for the general purpose balanced, organically based, fertiliser blood, fish and bone but there is no reason why you should not use an entirely artificial product such as Growmore if you wish. And indeed, if there is a copious supply of farmyard manure, you could try to rely on this. In order to provide basic guidance on the very different fertiliser needs of the various types of vegetable, I have given, in the individual descriptions, the weights per square metre (and square yard) of blood, fish and bone that should be used. The best results will usually be obtained by applying half of this amount about one week before sowing or planting, and the remainder when the crop is half grown. Should you prefer to use Growmore, the weights should be reduced by about one quarter. Should you wish to try using farmyard manure or compost only, then the weights should be increased twenty times.

Watering is immensely important for vegetable crops but, as I have explained on p. 68, it should be used economically. As with fruit, apart from the moisture needed to ensure seed germination and seedling growth, my advice is to water when the particular objects of cultivation are maturing. Thus, you should water cabbages as the heads are swelling, cucumbers as the fruit fill out, potatoes as the tubers develop (roughly when the plants are in flower) and so forth.

Pests and diseases are inevitable on many vegetable crops but seldom should these cause real alarm. My advice, nonetheless, is never to use a systemic pesticide; in my experience, there is always the possibility of taint in the produce, and vegetable pests that can be controlled by a systemic product can almost invariably be controlled as effectively with a contact spray. Weed control too is important, but I control the weeds in my vegetable garden with a push hoe or a hand-weeding fork.

When choosing vegetable varieties, flavour should be the first criterion to adopt but remember too that some varieties are very much more suitable than others for freezing. Bear in mind that some varieties of lettuce or broccoli, for instance, are 'cut and come again' plants – you take a little each time and the plant regenerates. Such crops may be useful where space is limited.

In the following lists, my distances for spacing indicate that between the rows first, then that between the plants. The harvesting times are the numbers of weeks to elapse between sowing and the first harvest (generally, this is a range of the fastest and slowest growing varieties); and generally, the faster growing varieties are those for the early and very late parts of the season. I have indicated those varieties that are F_1 hybrids because of the advantages and disadvantages that these might offer over open-pollinated types. I have suggested in some instances where cloches might be useful, but remember that these will generally give very valuable protection at the beginning and end of the season.

Asparagus *Asparagus officinalis* Liliaceae

The most delicious of all the perennial vegetables, cropping for ten years or more, but at a price. The yield is low and the space that must be given over to the crop considerable. Although asparagus can be raised from seed, this is time-consuming and unreliable. For a crop that requires so high an investment of time, it is sensible to invest a little in the plants and buy one-year-old crowns, preferably frame rather than field raised, of a named variety.

PLANT: in spring; prepare a shallow planting trench, approximately 20 cm (8 in) deep and 30 cm (12 in) wide, mound soil approximately 8 cm (3 in) high in the base and spread the crowns on this. Then refill the trench.

FERTILISER: 200 g/square metre (6½ oz/sq yd).

SPACING: 30 cm × 30 cm (12 in × 12 in).

AFTER-CARE: apply liquid fertiliser after the end of cutting; cut down shoots in autumn and apply a thick mulch of manure or compost. Top dress with blood, fish and bone at above rate in early spring.

PEST, DISEASE OR OTHER PROBLEMS: asparagus beetle, rust, slugs.

HARVESTING: two years (do not harvest before the plants are three years old); then cut out young spears when they reach 10 cm (4 in) height, cutting 8 cm (3 in) below soil level. Do not cut after early June.

EXPECTED YIELD: 25 spears per plant per season once established.

STORING: freeze.

RECOMMENDED VARIETIES: 'Connovers Colossal'; 'Lorella'.

Aubergine *Solanum melongena* Solanaceae

A close relative of the potato and tomato but more tender. The elongated beautiful purple fruit cannot be eaten raw but are important ingredients of moussaka and ratatouille. Aubergines can be grown outside but are only reliably successful in mild areas and under tall barn cloches. My advice is always to grow them in a greenhouse.

SOW BY: half-hardy annual technique at medium temperature in early spring – a long growing season is needed. Sow into 9 cm (3½ in) diameter pots as they resent the disturbance brought about by pricking on.

PLANT: into growing bags, ring culture pots or, less satisfactorily, the soil of a greenhouse bed.

FERTILISER: as supplied in growing bag compost or use John Innes No. 3 potting compost in ring culture pot.

SPACING: three plants to a standard sized growing bag or 40 cm (16 in) between ring pots.

AFTER-CARE: feed as tomatoes (p. 127).

PEST, DISEASE OR OTHER PROBLEMS: red spider mite, white fly.

HARVESTING: 20 weeks; when fruit are approximately 15 cm (6 in) long and richly coloured.

EXPECTED YIELD: 5–6 fruits per plant.

STORING: not satisfactory.

RECOMMENDED VARIETIES: 'Bonica' (F_1); 'Rima' (F_1); 'Slice-Rite' (F_1).

Beetroot *Beta vulgaris* Chenopodiaceae

Probably the easiest of all the root crops for its roots stand well proud of the soil surface and are therefore less prone to suffer checks in rough or stony ground. Germination and early growth are frustratingly slow but thereafter, by sowing sequentially and choosing a range of varieties, it is possible to have crops maturing for nine months of the year, the only gap being approximately between March and June.

SOW BY: hardy annual technique directly into growing position and using cloches in the early part of the season.

FERTILISER: 375 g/square metre (12 oz/sq yd).

SPACING: 18 × 10 cm (7 × 4 in).

AFTER-CARE: keep well watered to avoid woodiness and lessen the chance of bolting in early varieties.

PEST, DISEASE OR OTHER PROBLEMS: leaf spot.

HARVESTING: 11–16 weeks when roots are no more than tennis-ball sized.

EXPECTED YIELD: 1.5–2.5 kg per metre (3–5lb per yard) of row.

STORING: in boxes of dry sand or peat – lift roots in October and *twist* off the leaves; or cover with at least 20 cm (8 in) of straw at beginning of December and leave in ground.

RECOMMENDED VARIETIES: *Early:* 'Avonearly', 'Boltardy'. *Maincrop and for storing:* 'Burpee's Golden' (yellow roots); 'Cheltenham Green Top' (elongated roots); 'Cylindra' (cylindrical roots); 'Detroit' (or 'Detroit' selections).

Broad bean *Vicia faba* Leguminosae

An invaluable and very hardy vegetable that offers the earliest crops of any of the bean family. In milder areas, sowing winter-hardy varieties in the autumn is worthwhile; in colder areas, you will be lucky in about three years out of five.

SOW BY: hardy annual technique in growing positions; sow winter-hardy varieties in November or other varieties from February onwards, using cloches in the early part of the season.

FERTILISER: 135 g/square metre (4½ oz/sq yd).

SPACING: 23 × 23 cm (9 × 9 in) (shorter varieties) or 45 × 30 cm (18 × 12 in) (taller varieties).

AFTER-CARE: use canes and string to support taller varieties; pinch out tops of stems as soon as first beans set to limit the impact of aphids and encourage earlier setting of other flowers.

PEST, DISEASE OR OTHER PROBLEMS: aphids (blackfly), grey mould, leaf spot, bumble bees and sparrows (remove flowers).

HARVESTING: 15 weeks (spring sowing) – 25 weeks (autumn

sowing), when pods reach approximately 8 cm (3 in).

EXPECTED YIELD: 3 kg per metre (6½ lb per yard) of row.

STORING: freeze.

RECOMMENDED VARIETIES: *Autumn sowing:* 'Aquadulce' (or 'Aquadulce' selections); 'The Sutton' (low growing). *Spring sowing:* 'Bonny Lad' (low growing), 'Hylon', 'Hysor', 'Meteor'.

Broccoli *Brassica oleracea botrytis* Cruciferae

These are the brassicas grown for their edible green and purple flower heads (although white winter cauliflower (p. 117) is also sometimes referred to as broccoli). They fall into two main groups, the winter- and spring-maturing, biennial, purple-sprouting types which occupy the ground for a very long time, and the autumn-maturing, annual, calabrese types. Additionally, there is a perennial variety that produces a very large plant but bears small green flower heads every spring. They are all valuable, however, in several ways: they are 'cut and come again' crops and so very useful in a small garden; they produce a crop that freezes very well; the flavour is mild; and they look attractive, which is more than you can say for most of their relatives.

SOW BY: hardy annual technique into a seed bed in April–May; transplant after six weeks into growing positions.

FERTILISER: 225 g/square metre (7½ oz/sq yd).

SPACING: 30 × 30 cm (12 × 12 in) (but 1 m × 1 m (39 × 39 in) for perennial broccoli).

AFTER-CARE: water regularly as the flower shoots (spears) begin to form.

PEST, DISEASE OR OTHER PROBLEMS: birds, cabbage root fly, caterpillars, clubroot.

HARVESTING: 40–45 weeks (purple sprouting) or 12 weeks (calabrese), when the flower heads are full and firm.

EXPECTED YIELD: 0.7 kg (1½ lb) per plant.

STORING: freeze.

RECOMMENDED VARIETIES: *Purple sprouting:* 'Christmas Purple Sprouting' (early); 'Early Purple Sprouting' (mid-season); 'Late Purple Sprouting' (late). *Calabrese:* 'Express Corona' (F₁) (early); 'Mercedes' (F₁) (early, compact habit); 'Green Comet' (F₁) (early- mid-season); 'Romanesco' (late). *Perennial:* 'Nine Star Perennial'.

Brussels sprouts *Brassica oleracea gemmifera* Cruciferae

The Brussels sprout can have no pretentions to being an attractive plant but as a winter vegetable it is invaluable. Traditionally, sprouts are said to require frosting before they acquire their best taste, but there is no evidence that this makes any difference. They are tall plants and must be firmed into the soil, and staked, too, in most areas. The Brussels sprout is a classic instance of the differing requirements of gardeners and commercial growers, for most modern varieties are F₁ hybrids on which the buttons mature simultaneously – ideal for mechanical harvesting machines, but less than ideal in the garden, where the old 'cut and come again' varieties have much to commend them.

SOW BY: hardy annual technique into a seed bed in March–April; transplant after six weeks into growing positions.

FERTILISER: 0.5 kg/square metre (1 lb/sq yd).

SPACING: 90 × 90 cm (36 × 36 in) for normal picking or 50 × 50 cm (20 × 20 in) with an F₁ hybrid variety to produce a crop

of small buttons for freezing.

AFTER-CARE: firm the soil after planting and, in exposed gardens, earth up around the bases and stake the plants; water as the buttons begin to swell.

PEST, DISEASE OR OTHER PROBLEMS: aphids, birds (netting may be needed to protect against wood pigeons in rural areas), cabbage root fly, caterpillars, clubroot.

HARVESTING: 27–36 weeks, when the buttons are hard.

EXPECTED YIELD: 1 kg (2 lb) per plant.

STORING: freeze.

RECOMMENDED VARIETIES: 'Achilles' (F₁) (mid-season); 'Bedford Fillbasket' (mid-season); 'Cambridge No.5' (mid-late-season); 'Citadel' (F₁) (mid- late-season); 'Peer Gynt' (F₁) (early- mid-season); 'Widgeon' (F₁) (mid-season).

Cabbage *Brassica oleracea capitata* Cruciferae

Brassica oleracea bullata – Savoy cabbage 'January King'

'The humble cabbage', as it has been described, is certainly an unsophisticated but a very useful plant, providing green vegetable all year round from its various varietal types. If carefully cooked, it can be quite delicious; the problem in the past has been that it suffers more than most from the British custom of boiling vegetables until they are quite unrecognisable. Cabbages are generally sub-divided on the basis of their maturing times into spring (including non-hearting spring greens), summer/autumn (including red cabbages) and winter (including the mainly crinkle-leaved types known as Savoys). Chinese cabbage is a quite different plant (p. 117).

SOW BY: hardy annual technique into a seed bed in July–August (spring cabbages), February–May (summer and autumn cabbage, using cloches for the earliest sowings) or April–May (winter cabbage). In each case, transplant to their growing positions after six weeks.

FERTILISER: 0.5 kg/square metre (1 lb/sq yd).

SPACING: 30 × 30 cm (12 × 12 in) (spring), 35 × 35 cm (14 × 14 in) (summer, autumn or winter).

AFTER-CARE: water as the heads begin to fill.

PEST, DISEASE OR OTHER PROBLEMS: aphids, cabbage root fly, caterpillars, clubroot.

HARVESTING: 20–35 weeks, once heads are hard.

EXPECTED YIELD: 0.3–1.25 kg (10 oz–2½ lb) per plant depending on variety.

STORING: not necessary, choose varieties with sequential maturing times.

RECOMMENDED VARIETIES: *Spring:* 'Pixie', 'Spring Hero' (F₁) (round-headed; other spring varieties have pointed heads). *Summer:* 'Derby Day', 'Hispi' (F₁) (very early), 'Primo' (also called 'Golden Acre'). *Autumn:* 'Minicole' (F₁), 'Red Drumhead' (red), 'Winningstadt'. *Winter*: 'Celtic' (F$_1$), 'Christmas Drumhead', 'January King' (Savoy).

Chinese cabbage *Brassica rapa chinensis* Cruciferae

This is perhaps the exotic vegetable that has been taken most successfully to the palates of the British. It is called a cabbage, looks like a cos lettuce, but is a close relative of the turnip and is cooked and eaten differently from all of them – the secret is to cook it very lightly by flash steaming. The problem with growing Chinese cabbage in the British climate is that the plants are very prone to bolt, because of the combination of long days and cool temperatures. The secret, therefore, is to wait until after mid-summer, choose a very fast growing variety, do not transplant, and never allow the soil to become dry.

SOW BY: hardy annual technique in growing position in July (although it is now claimed that some varieties are reliable when sown as early as April, I must confess myself sceptical).
FERTILISER: 175 g/square metre (5½ oz/sq yd).
SPACING: 25 × 25 cm (10 × 10 in).
AFTER-CARE: water carefully but constantly.
PEST, DISEASE OR OTHER PROBLEMS: cabbage root fly, clubroot.
HARVESTING: 9–10 weeks, when the heads are firm.
EXPECTED YIELD: 0.6–1 kg (1–2 lb) per plant.
STORING: not satisfactory.
RECOMMENDED VARIETIES: 'China Pride' (F$_1$), 'Kasumi' (F$_1$), 'Nagaoka' (F$_1$).

Capsicum or sweet pepper *Capsicum annuum* Solanaceae

These are the familiar green, red or yellow fruited peppers useful both in salads and in cooked dishes such as stuffed peppers; the very hot chili or cayenne peppers are of quite a different type. Closely related to tomatoes and aubergines, they are comparably hardy but, like aubergines, I suggest strongly that they are grown in a greenhouse.

SOW BY: half-hardy annual technique at medium temperature in early spring – a long growing season is needed. Sow into 9 cm (3½ in) diameter pots, as they resent the disturbance brought about by pricking on.
FERTILISER: as supplied in growing bag compost or use John Innes No.3 potting compost in ring culture pot.
SPACING: three plants to a standard sized growing bag, or 40 cm (16 in) between ring pots.
AFTER-CARE: feed as tomatoes (p. 127).
PEST, DISEASE OR OTHER PROBLEMS: red spider mite, white fly.
HARVESTING: 18 weeks; when fruit are firm; there is no difference in ripeness between differently coloured fruits.
EXPECTED YIELD: 6–8 fruits per plant.
STORING: not satisfactory.
RECOMMENDED VARIETIES: 'New Ace' (F$_1$) (green fruit); 'Canape' (F$_1$) (red fruit); 'Luteus' (F$_1$) (yellow fruit); 'Redskin' (F$_1$) (red fruit, only 35–40 cm (14–16 in) tall).

Carrot *Daucus carota* Umbelliferae

The most versatile and most attractive of all the root crops, carrots take up very little room. Moreover, their very attractive feathery foliage makes a useful aesthetic contribution to the ornamental kitchen garden. Unfortunately, they have two drawbacks. First, their roots will become irregular or fanged on a heavy or very stony soil, one where an impervious pan has been allowed to develop below the surface or one that has been amended with fresh manure. And second, they are prone to attack by the carrot fly, whose larvae tunnel into the roots.

SOW BY: hardy annual technique in growing positions sequentially (with appropriate early, mid-season or late varieties) from early March to July, using cloches for the earlier sowings. Sow as sparingly as possible to minimise the need for thinning as this disturbs the foliage and releases an aroma attractive to the carrot fly.
FERTILISER: 50 g/square metre (2 oz/sq yd).
SPACING: 15 × 6 cm (6 × 2½ in).
AFTER-CARE: disturb foliage as little as possible; water regularly as roots begin to swell – allowing the plants to dry out and then watering heavily causes them to split; draw up soil around crowns of large-rooted types to prevent greening.
PEST, DISEASE OR OTHER PROBLEMS: carrot fly, fanging, splitting.
HARVESTING: 12–16 weeks, when roots have reached desired size. Pull a few to sample first – it is a common mistake to allow them to become too large and woody.
EXPECTED YIELD: 1–1.5 kg per metre (2–3 lb per yard) of row.
STORING: in boxes of dry sand or peat – lift roots in October and cut off the leaves; or cover with at least 10 cm (4 in) of straw at beginning of December and leave in ground.
RECOMMENDED VARIETIES: *Early*: 'Early French Frame' (spherical), 'Early Nantes' (stump rooted). *Maincrop*: 'Autumn King' (stump rooted, excellent for storage), 'Chantenay Red Cored' (stump rooted), 'New Red Intermediate' (tapered, good for winter storage).

Cauliflower *Brassica oleracea botrytis* Cruciferae

The cauliflower classes score very highly at horticultural shows, a certain indication that they are difficult to grow. They are easily the most taxing of the brassicas and they are also big plants that are not really suitable for a small kitchen garden. But having said that, it is by the quality of his or her cauliflowers that the good vegetable gardener is judged. Perhaps the two most important aspects of their cultivation are that they are highly intolerant both of root disturbance and of being allowed to become dry. Cauliflowers fall into three main groups – the summer, autumn and winter varieties, although botanically winter cauliflowers are a form of broccoli and their name is misleading; they are winter hardy but do not mature until the spring.

SOW BY: hardy annual technique in March–May (depending on variety), providing cold frame or greenhouse protection for the earlier sowings, and transplant after six weeks. Always sow into 9 cm (3½ in) diameter pots to minimise the root disturbance when planting out.
FERTILISER: 375 g/square metre (12 oz/sq yd).
SPACING: 50 × 50 cm (20 × 20 in) (summer varieties) or 60 × 60 cm (24 × 24 in) (autumn and winter varieties).
AFTER-CARE: do not allow the soil to dry out. In hot seasons, tie some leaves of summer varieties over the curd to protect it.
PEST, DISEASE OR OTHER PROBLEMS: aphids, cabbage root fly, caterpillars, clubroot.
HARVESTING: 18–25 weeks (summer and autumn varieties), 40–50 weeks (winter varieties), when curds are full and white.

EXPECTED YIELD: 0.5–1 kg (1–2 lb) per plant.
STORING: freeze.
RECOMMENDED VARIETIES: *Summer or summer/autumn*: 'All-the-year-round', 'Dok', 'Snowball'. *Autumn*: 'Barrier Reef', 'Flora Blanca'. *Winter*: 'English Winter', 'St Agnes' (not frost hardy, for mild areas only), 'Walcheren Winter' (selections).

Celeriac or turnip-rooted celery *Apium graveolens rapaceum* Umbelliferae

Perhaps the least familiar among traditional vegetables, celeriac is a form of celery in which the swollen crowns are eaten. It is a crop that occupies a considerable amount of space and, like celery, it has one over-riding requirement – a rich, moisture-retentive soil.

SOW BY: half-hardy annual technique at medium temperature; raise plants in individual 9 cm (3½ in) diameter pots and plant out with minimal root disturbance after the danger of frost has passed.
FERTILISER: 175 g/square metre (5½ oz/sq yd).
SPACING: 30 × 30 cm (12 × 12 in).
AFTER-CARE: about two or three weeks after planting, begin regularly to pull away the lower leaves in order to expose the swelling crown. Then, in autumn, gradually hoe soil around the stem bases to cover them.
PEST, DISEASE OR OTHER PROBLEMS: slugs on young plants.
HARVESTING: 30 weeks; once swollen roots and stem base are 10–15 cm (4–6 in) in diameter.
EXPECTED YIELD: 1 kg per metre (2 lb per yard) of row.
STORING: in the ground; cover with straw in late autumn for protection.
RECOMMENDED VARIETIES: every seed company appears to have its own but I can find almost no difference between them.

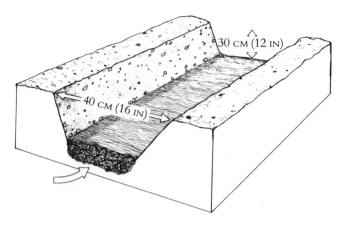

(a) Cross-section of a celery trench showing a layer of well-rotted organic matter in the base.

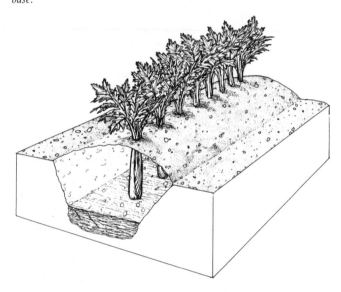

(b) Well-grown plants with the trench filled with soil and the stems buried for blanching.

Celery *Apium graveolens* Umbelliferae

Good celery is superb, poor celery, as exemplified by much of that imported for sale in supermarkets, is useless and tasteless. To a large degree, the differences are related to the two main celery types. The traditional, fine tasting stalks come from trenched celery; the useless pith from self-blanching. Certainly, it is possible to grow reasonably flavoured self-blanching celery but to my mind it will always be a second best. It is also not frost hardy and must be pulled before the autumn. But all celery varieties require a very rich, very moist soil; remember that its natural habitat is a marsh and you will understand why. For trenched celery, you will need to prepare a trench in spring, approximately 40 cm (16 in) wide and 30 cm (12 in) deep, with a layer of well compacted compost or well rotted manure in the base.
SOW BY: half-hardy annual technique at medium temperature. Raise plants in individual 9 cm (3½ in) diameter pots and plant out with minimal root disturbance after the danger of frost has passed. Trenched varieties are planted in the bottom of the trench which should then be filled with water.
FERTILISER: 175 g/square metre (5½ oz/sq yd).
SPACING: 20 × 20 cm (8 × 8 in) (self-blanching) or 20 cm (8 in) apart in the trench (trenched varieties).
AFTER-CARE: water all plants thoroughly; once trenched varieties are about 30 cm (12 in) tall, fill the trench with soil and continue to draw soil around them (eventually creating a ridge over the trench) so that only the tops of the plants show. To keep the stalks clean of soil, you may wrap newspaper or specially made celery collars around them, although these can encourage slugs to live within. You may prefer, as I do, not to protect the plants, but simply to tie the stalks loosely together, pile soil directly against them and accept that the outer stalks must be discarded.
PEST, DISEASE OR OTHER PROBLEMS: leaf spot (although this can be avoided by buying seed treated with hot water), splitting due to water shortage, slugs.
HARVESTING: 25 weeks (self-blanching) or 40 weeks (trenched), once the stalks are of acceptable size. Dig from one end of the trench and be sure not to expose the plants left in the ground.
EXPECTED YIELD: 2 kg per metre (4 lb per yard) of row.
STORING: not satisfactory.
RECOMMENDED VARIETIES: *Self-blanching*: 'Ivory Tower', 'Lathom Self-blanching'. *Trenched*: 'Giant White' (for use up to Christmas), 'Giant Pink' (hardy enough to stand into the New Year), 'Giant Red' (hardiest of all, will stand well into February).

Courgette (including vegetable marrow, pumpkin and squash) *Cucurbita pepo* Cucurbitaceae

Old gardening books described the cultivation of the marrow rather than the courgette, but this is a vegetable that has changed its appeal and is now much more usually eaten when very small. Pumpkins are almost entirely the preserve of those planning for Hallowe'en or an entry in the local giant vegetable contest. Squashes are similar in all respects to marrows, except that they have irregular shapes. The secrets for the successful cultivation of all of them are a rich soil and copious water. The easiest way to provide these conditions is to dig planting holes, approximately 30–40 cm (12–16 in) deep and of similar diameter and then refill them with a mixture of 3 parts by volume of compost or manure to 1 part of soil.

'Goldrush' courgette is a compact and most attractive addition to the kitchen garden.

SOW BY: half-hardy annual technique at medium temperature. Raise plants in individual 9 cm (3½ in) diameter pots, placing the seeds sideways into the compost; plant out after the danger of frost has passed.
FERTILISER: 15 g (½ oz) per planting position.
SPACING: 60 cm (24 in) (compact bush varieties), 120 cm (48 in) (trailing varieties).
AFTER-CARE: water copiously as soon as the fruits set.
PEST, DISEASE OR OTHER PROBLEMS: fruit rot (protect the fruits by laying straw beneath them), mildew, virus.
HARVESTING: 10–15 weeks, cut courgettes when approximately 10 cm (4 in) long; marrows when 25 cm (10 in) long and pumpkins as big as you wish.
EXPECTED YIELD: 15–20 courgettes per plant; 2–3 marrows or pumpkins per plant.
STORING: freeze courgettes; store marrows and pumpkins in a cool shed for about three months.
RECOMMENDED VARIETIES: *Trailing marrow varieties*: 'Long Green Trailing', 'Long White Trailing'. *Bush marrow varieties*: 'Green Bush'. *Courgette varieties (bush)*: 'Gold Rush' (golden), 'Zucchini' (green). *Pumpkin*: 'Mammoth'. *Summer squash*: 'Custard Yellow', 'Vegetable Spaghetti'.

Cucumber *Cucumis sativus* Cucurbitaceae

Cucumbers are closely related to courgettes, marrows, pumpkins and melons. They are plants of the humid sub-tropics, a good indication that they require moisture and warmth, although the improvements in hardiness that have come about through plant breeding mean that the outdoor cucumber is now a perfectly satisfactory plant for the British gardener. Although I have given details of greenhouse cucumber growing, therefore, I do believe that unless your wish is for a very early crop, the greenhouse space can better be given over to other things. Outdoors, prepare planting positions as for courgettes.

SOW BY: half-hardy annual technique at medium temperature, placing the seeds sideways into the compost. Raise plants in individual 9 cm (3½ in) diameter pots and plant out after the danger of frost has passed.
FERTILISER: growing bag compost (greenhouse varieties).
SPACING: two plants per growing bag or 45 cm (18 in) (outdoors).
AFTER-CARE: water copiously and feed greenhouse plants every two weeks with tomato fertiliser once the first fruits have set. Allow the plants to trail or train them up canes.
PEST, DISEASE OR OTHER PROBLEMS: mildew, virus.
HARVESTING: 12 weeks; when fruit are of acceptable size – remember that most outdoor cucumbers are of the inherently short, ridge type and will never look like shop-bought fruit.
EXPECTED YIELD: 20–25 per plant (greenhouse); 7–10 (outdoors).
STORING: not satisfactory.
RECOMMENDED VARIETIES: *Greenhouse*: 'Pepinex' (F_1), 'Petita' (F_1) (these are both all-female varieties so there is no need to remove male flowers to prevent pollination and a bitter taste, as with older types). *Outdoors*: 'Burpee Hybrid' (F_1), 'Hokus' (very short, gherkin variety for pickling), 'King of the Ridge', 'Tokyo Slicer' (F_1) (long fruit).

Endive *Cichorium endiva* Compositae

The endive is very evidently a relative of the lettuce but it has some important differences. It is hardier and can be cut during the winter. Against this is the fact that it takes much longer to grow and must be blanched to eliminate bitterness. There are both curled and plain-leaved varieties. All must have a sunny position, and rich moist soil.
SOW BY: hardy annual technique sequentially from April to September, but do not sow broad-leaved varieties before July.
FERTILISER: 175 g/square metre (5½ oz/sq yd).
SPACING: 20 × 10 cm (8 × 8 in).
AFTER-CARE: do not allow soil to dry out; cover plants when about 12 weeks old with crock pots with sealed holes, to blanch.
PEST, DISEASE OR OTHER PROBLEMS: slugs.
HARVESTING: 15 weeks (summer harvest) – 20 weeks (winter harvest).
EXPECTED YIELD: 4 plants per metre (yard) of row.
STORING: not satisfactory.
RECOMMENDED VARIETIES: *Broad-leaved*: 'Batavian', 'Golda'. *Curly leaved*: 'Green Curled', 'Ione'.

Florence Fennel *Foeniculum vulgare azoricum* Umbelliferae

Florence fennel is a form of the plant that is grown as a herb, but instead of the foliage and seeds, it is the swollen stem base that is the object of cultivation. It has a uniquely delightful aniseed flavour but has one drawback as a garden plant – it is big. It also requires a warm sunny position, a light soil and a good water supply to succeed.
SOW BY: hardy annual technique directly into growing positions from late April in succession until early July.
FERTILISER: 175 g/square metre (5½ oz/sq yd).

SPACING: 35 × 35 cm (14 × 14 in).

AFTER-CARE: do not allow the soil to become very dry; as soon as the bulb is about 2–3 cm (¾–1½ in) in diameter, draw soil around it with a hoe and continue to earth up for the remainder of the season as the bulb swells.

PEST, DISEASE OR OTHER PROBLEMS: none.

HARVESTING: 12–15 weeks, when the bulb is approximately 8 cm (3 in) in diameter.

EXPECTED YIELD: 3 bulbs per metre (yard) of row.

STORING: freeze.

RECOMMENDED VARIETIES: 'Perfection', 'Zefa Fino'.

French bean *Phaseolus vulgaris* Leguminosae

No matter what the continentals may say, the French bean is a second-class vegetable, serving usefully to tempt our palates until the runner bean crop is ready. It is nonetheless valuable, easy to grow and offers a considerable range of types, including some climbing forms which have the merit of giving a larger yield from a given area than the 60 cm (2 ft) tall bush varieties.

SOW BY: half-hardy annual technique in growing positions in April and May, using cloches for the first six weeks over the earlier sowings.

FERTILISER: 200 g/square metre (6½ oz/sq yd).

SPACING: 45 × 8 cm (18 × 3 in).

AFTER-CARE: use twigs or lightweight netting to support the plants as they develop.

PEST, DISEASE OR OTHER PROBLEMS: aphids.

HARVESTING: 8–13 weeks; when pods are full and brittle.

EXPECTED YIELD: 1 kg per metre (2 lb per yard) of row (bush varieties); 1.5 kg (3 lb) (climbing varieties).

STORING: freeze.

RECOMMENDED VARIETIES: *Bush*: 'Kinghorn Wax' (yellow, round or pencil podded), 'Pros Gitana' (round or pencil podded), 'The Prince' (flat podded). *Climbing*: 'Hunter' (flat podded).

Globe artichoke *Cynara scolymus* Compositae

Globe artichokes are just too big for their own good; it really is an enormous plant that is quite impossible to grow in a small garden. And the yield from one plant, even over the three or four years of its productive life, is not great. Even the amount of edible matter on one head (the heads are in fact unopened flowers) is minute; I sometimes wonder why we find them so delicious. Globe artichokes are plants of the sun and they require light, warm and well drained soil.

PLANT: off-sets in spring; remove new off-sets from the plants every few years to start afresh, and discard the old stock. Raising plants from seed is never as reliable.

FERTILISER: 175 g/square metre (5½ oz/sq yd).

SPACING: 1 m × 1 m (1 yd × 1 yd).

AFTER-CARE: cut down old foliage in autumn and mulch; treat the plants in much the same manner as herbaceous perennials (p. 202).

PEST, DISEASE OR OTHER PROBLEMS: aphids.

HARVESTING: 18 months, cut off terminal flower bud first, then remove others as they swell but before the flowers open.

EXPECTED YIELD: about 6 heads per plant per year for three or four years.

STORING: not satisfactory.

RECOMMENDED VARIETIES: 'Vert de Laon' – the variety usually sold as off-sets.

Hamburg parsley *Petroselenum crispum tuberosum* Umbelliferae

I have included this curious plant because I would like to see it grown more widely. It is a versatile thing, probably more shade tolerant than any other vegetable, very hardy, with the foliage of a broad-leaved parsley and roots like slender parsnips with a slight celery flavour. It will grow in any fairly well manured soil.

SOW BY: hardy annual technique in March (if cloches are available) or April.

FERTILISER: 135 g/square metre (4½ oz/sq yd).

SPACING: 30 × 30 cm (12 × 12 in).

AFTER-CARE: do not allow the soil to dry out.

PEST, DISEASE OR OTHER PROBLEMS: none.

HARVESTING: 30 × 35 weeks, when roots are approximately 20 cm (8 in) long.

EXPECTED YIELD: three roots per metre (yard) of row.

STORING: as parsnip.

RECOMMENDED VARIETIES: 'Omega'.

Jerusalem artichoke *Helianthus tuberosus* Compositae

The Jerusalem artichoke is closely related to the sunflower and is of similar size. It really is a gigantic plant, only of value in small gardens when planted along one side as a windbreak. They also take a very long time before the crop is mature but do have the advantage of growing in almost any soil. The tuberous roots are an acquired taste – my own preference is to boil them then serve them cold with a vinaigrette dressing.

PLANT: tubers.

FERTILISER: 50 g/square metre (2 oz/sq yd).

SPACING: 1 m × 50 cm (39 × 20 in).

AFTER-CARE: draw soil around the base of the plants when they are approximately 30 cm (12 in) tall. Provide stakes and wire supports as the plants develop, and pinch out flower buds as they form.

PEST, DISEASE OR OTHER PROBLEMS: none.

HARVESTING: 45–50 weeks, cut down stems in early autumn and lift as required during the winter.

EXPECTED YIELD: 1.5–2.5 kg (3–5 lb) per plant.

STORING: in ground where grown.

RECOMMENDED VARIETIES: 'Fuseau' – this has smooth tubers which are immeasurably easier to peel but can generally only be purchased from garden centres or specialist suppliers. You can use anonymous tubers from the supermarket but these are likely to be of knobbly varieties.

Kale *Brassica oleracea acephala* Cruciferae

This very useful vegetable is far too easily dismissed as cattle fodder. Yet it is extremely hardy and provides very appetising winter and early spring greens – provided the shoots are picked when young.

SOW BY: hardy annual technique in a seed bed in April or May (earlier for curly varieties); transplant into growing positions when plants are six weeks old.

FERTILISER: 500 g/square metre (1 lb/sq yd).

SPACING: 45 × 45 cm (18 × 18 in).

AFTER-CARE: stake during winter in windy areas.

PEST, DISEASE OR OTHER PROBLEMS: cabbage root fly, clubroot.

HARVESTING: 30–35 weeks, cut off shoots from top downwards but cut sparingly from each plant to allow more side-shoots to develop from below.

EXPECTED YIELD: 1 kg (2 lb) per plant.

STORING: freeze.

RECOMMENDED VARIETIES: 'Dwarf Green Curled', 'Frosty' (dwarf, curly leaved), 'Pentlandbrig' (a unique variety which additionally produces small, broccoli-like spears in spring), 'Tall Green Curled', 'Thousandhead' (plain leaved).

Kohl rabi *Brassica oleracea gongylodes* Cruciferae

In Britain, this is the least popular of all brassicas although in other parts of Europe it is among the most prized. It is a close relative of the cabbage and cauliflower rather than the turnip, although its appearance belies this. In fact, the swollen edible object is the stem base rather than the root and it suffers less than conventional root crops, therefore, from hard or stony soils. It is very important to grow kohl rabi with ample water for if it suffers checks to growth or is allowed to grow too slowly, it becomes tough and tasteless.

SOW BY: hardy annual technique in growing positions sequentially from April to August, although later sowings should be with purple varieties only.

FERTILISER: 200 g/square metre (6½ oz/sq yd).

SPACING: 30 × 15 cm (12 × 6 in).

AFTER-CARE: water regularly.

PEST, DISEASE OR OTHER PROBLEMS: cabbage root fly, clubroot.

HARVESTING: 8–12 weeks, when bulbs are approximately 6–7 cm (2–2½ in) in diameter.

EXPECTED YIELD: 6 bulbs per metre (yard) of row.

STORING: not satisfactory.

RECOMMENDED VARIETIES: 'Purple Vienna', 'Rowel' (F₁) (white), 'White Vienna'.

Leaf beet *Beta vulgaris cicla* Chenopodiaceae

Swiss chard

These are attractive (quite literally in some instances) plants to grow instead of spinach, which has the annoying habit of running to seed in dry summers. It must be said nonetheless that the flavour does tend to be rather stronger. The large leaved chards have very broad leaf mid-ribs which can be cut from the leaf blade and cooked separately; spinach beet (or perpetual spinach) is much more like the true spinach in appearance.

SOW BY: hardy annual technique in growing positions in April.

FERTILISER: 325 g/square metre (10½ oz/sq yd).

SPACING: 30 × 25 cm (12 × 10 in).

AFTER-CARE: do not allow soil to become very dry.

PEST, DISEASE OR OTHER PROBLEMS: none.

HARVESTING: 12 weeks, pull leaves as needed; the plants will continue to crop through the winter although in colder areas they are better with cloche protection (although very tall cloches will be needed).

EXPECTED YIELD: 1 kg per metre (2 lb per yard) of row.

STORING: not satisfactory.

RECOMMENDED VARIETIES: 'Rainbow Chard' (white, red and yellow stems), 'Ruby Chard' (red leaves), 'Spinach Beet', 'Swiss Chard' (also called sea-kale beet) (white midribs, green leaves).

Leek *Allium ampeloprasum* Liliaceae

Leeks are delicious when small and tender, dreadful when large and tough and miserable to look at at the best of times. They are not really plants for the ornamental kitchen garden, nor indeed the small one, for they must be grown in large quantities to be of any value. They are much less demanding than onions and do not require such a well manured, moisture retentive soil.

SOW BY: hardy annual technique into a seed bed in March or April and transplant in June when the plants are approximately 20 cm (8 in) tall. Trim the root and leaf tips before planting. Make holes 15 cm (6 in) deep, carefully drop the transplant in and then fill the hole with water.

FERTILISER: 300 g/square metre (10 oz/sq yd).

SPACING: 30 × 15 cm (12 × 16 in).

AFTER-CARE: once the plants have grown sufficiently to fill the holes, gradually draw soil around the stems to blanch them but do not earth up any more after the end of October.

PEST, DISEASE OR OTHER PROBLEMS: rust.

HARVESTING: 30–45 weeks; when stems are approximately 2 cm (¾ in) in diameter.

EXPECTED YIELD: 1.5 kg per metre (3 lb per yard) of row.

STORING: freeze.

RECOMMENDED VARIETIES: 'Giant Winter' (or one of the selections such as 'Catalina' or 'Wila') (late winter–spring); 'Musselburgh' (mid-winter).

Lettuce *Lactuca sativa* Compositae

The best, garden-fresh lettuce is close to the top of the kitchen garden's many virtues. It is also a compelling advertisement for growing your own because although the shop-bought product has improved in recent years, it is still no match for the genuine article. Lettuce is undemanding, to the extent that it will grow in most soils, although it is best in full sun. But the secret of good, tender lettuce is to grow it quickly – this means growing it in rich soil with plenty of water. It is possible, by careful choice of varieties, with careful husbandry and the availability of cloches and a frost-free greenhouse, to have fresh lettuce all the year round, although personally I prefer to switch to endive in the autumn. There are four main types of lettuce – the smooth-leaved butterhead or cabbage varieties, the curly-leaved crispheads, the upright, rather Chinese cabbage-like cos and the heartless loose-leaf varieties. There are also reddish- or purple-leaved forms of some of them.

SOW BY: hardy annual technique, but choose method appropriate to time of crop maturity:

○ for summer and early autumn crop, raise young plants

in greenhouse for transplanting outdoors in late March–April, and/or sow in growing positions from March to July, using cloches for the earliest sowings. For successional cropping in summer, sow a new row as the seedlings from the previous sowing emerge.

○ for early winter crop, sow in growing positions in August and cover with cloches from mid-September onwards.

○ for Christmas period and early New Year crop, sow or plant in growing positions in September in frost-free greenhouse (either in soil bed or growing bags) or outdoors under cloches.

○ for early spring crop, sow in growing positions in late August under cloches or in cold frame.

FERTILISER: 185 g/square metre (6 oz/sq yd).

SPACING: 30 × 30 cm (12 × 12 in) or 25 × 25 cm (10 × 10 in) (small varieties).

AFTER-CARE: water constantly and carefully.

PEST, DISEASE OR OTHER PROBLEMS: downy mildew, grey mould, root aphid, slugs.

HARVESTING: 6–15 weeks, when hearts are firm (except loose leaf varieties).

EXPECTED YIELD: 3–4 lettuces per metre (yard) of row.

STORING: not satisfactory.

RECOMMENDED VARIETIES: *Butterhead*: 'Kwiek' (winter crop), 'Tom Thumb' (summer-early autumn crop), 'Valdor' (late winter-spring crop). *Crisphead*: 'Avoncrisp' (later summer-autumn crop), 'Webb's Wonderful' (summer-early autumn crop). *Cos*: 'Little Gem' (summer-early autumn crop), 'Lobjoits Green' (summer-early autumn crop), 'Winter Density' (early spring crop). *Loose-leaf* (for summer-early autumn crop): 'Lollo Rossa' (green/red), 'Red Salad Bowl' (red), 'Salad Bowl'.

Melon *Cucumis melo* Cucurbitaceae

Botanically a fruit but, in common with many other fruits such as cucumbers and marrows, listed with the vegetables in most seed catalogues. Melons share many features with their close relative the cucumber; there are now many hardier varieties and their cultivation therefore is easier. They may similarly be grown in an unheated greenhouse but are never really successful outdoors and frame protection at least must be provided.

SOW BY: half-hardy annual technique at medium temperature, placing the seeds sideways into the compost. Raise plants in individual 9 cm (3½ in) diameter pots.

FERTILISER: growing bag compost (greenhouse varieties); in a frame, prepare planting positions as for courgettes.

SPACING: two plants per growing bag or 45 cm (18 in) (outdoors).

AFTER-CARE: water copiously and feed plants every two weeks with tomato fertiliser once the first fruits have set. Once the flowers are open, remove a male flower and use it to pollinate the females. The female flowers can readily be recognised for they have a small swelling (the young fruit) behind the petals. Train greenhouse plants up canes and along a system of horizontal support wires attached to the greenhouse roof. Nets will be needed to take the weight of the fruits. Outdoors, allow the plants to trail but support the fruit clear of the ground.

PEST, DISEASE OR OTHER PROBLEMS: mildew, virus.

HARVESTING: 12 weeks, when fruit are fully ripe – press gently on the end away from the stalk to check if it is slightly soft, indicating ripeness.

EXPECTED YIELD: 4–6 per plant (greenhouse); 3–4 (frames).

STORING: not satisfactory.

RECOMMENDED VARIETIES: 'Ogen' (yellow-green skin, green flesh), 'Sweetheart' (grey-green skin, orange flesh – the best overall for British conditions).

Onion, shallot and garlic *Allium cepa* Liliaceae

Onions must be left briefly to dry before storage.

Onions are absolutely essential in the kitchen, as any cook knows, but there are three different culinary ways in which onions are used. Those with large swollen bulbs are generally used for cooking, the young slender types are eaten raw as spring or salad onions, while certain varieties that form small, spherical bulbs are used for pickling. The growing conditions for all onions are similar in that they require a rich soil, well manured in the previous autumn – although this is much more important for the longer growing, bulbous types. Whilst salad onions are always grown from seed, bulb onions may be raised either from seed or from sets, which are small bulbs grown specially for planting. Starting the plants from sets obviously shortens the growing period and eliminates some of the uncertainty attached to raising them from seed – a clear advantage in colder areas. Shallots are rather strongly flavoured onions that produce clusters of small bulbs; they are always grown from sets. Garlic (*A. sativum*) is a close relative of the onion; it too is grown from sets, generally called cloves.

SOW BY: hardy annual technique in growing positions, sequentially from March to July and then again in August with winter-hardy varieties for a spring crop. Bulb onions may also be raised from seed sown in January in 9 cm (3½ in) diameter pots in the greenhouse for transplanting in April. Sets should be planted in March or April (or February for shallots) with their tips just protruding through the soil surface.

FERTILISER: 185 g/square metre (6 oz/sq yd).

SPACING: 25 × 10 cm (10 × 4 in) (bulb onions from seeds or sets), 25 × 15 cm (10 × 6 in) (shallots and garlic), 10 × 0.5 cm (4 × ¼ in) (spring onions).

AFTER-CARE: water carefully; do not hoe between the rows as this will damage the shallow roots.

PEST, DISEASE OR OTHER PROBLEMS: downy mildew, eelworm, neck rot, white rot.

HARVESTING: 18–22 weeks (spring sown or planted), up to 45 weeks (August sown); salad onions when bulbs are approximately 1 cm (½ in) in diameter; bulb onions, wait until about two weeks after the foliage yellows, then lift and allow them to dry in the sun.

EXPECTED YIELD: 1.5 kg per metre (3 lb per yard) of row.

STORING: dry, hung up in nets.

RECOMMENDED VARIETIES: *Bulb onions*: 'Ailsa Craig', 'Express Yellow O-X' (for August sowing), 'Rijnsburger',

'Sturon' (from sets). *Garlic*: buy unnamed cloves from shop or try to obtain the Isle of Wight strain from garden centres. *Salad onions*: 'White Lisbon' (for spring sowing), 'Winter Hardy White Lisbon' (for autumn sowing). *Shallot*: 'Hative de Niort', 'Santé'. *Pickling onion*: 'Paris Silverskin'.

Parsnip *Pastinaca sativa* Umbelliferae

The parsnip is an easy plant to grow, perhaps the easiest of all the root vegetables, but it is not to everyone's taste. Nonetheless, those who have savoured roast beef with roast parsnips will always find space in their garden for a row or two. Parsnips, at least the shorter-rooted varieties, are more readily grown than carrots in soil that is slightly rough and stony, although they are similarly intolerant of fresh manure.

SOW BY: hardy annual technique in March.
FERTILISER: 135 g/square metre (4½ oz/sq yd).
SPACING: 30 × 15 cm (12 × 6 in).
AFTER-CARE: little required; water only if very dry.
PEST, DISEASE OR OTHER PROBLEMS: canker (crown rot).
HARVESTING: 30–35 weeks; as leaves begin to die down in autumn.
EXPECTED YIELD: 1 kg per metre (2 lb per yard) of row.
STORING: in ground where grown.
RECOMMENDED VARIETIES: 'Avonresister' (canker resistant), 'Tender and True' (for better soils).

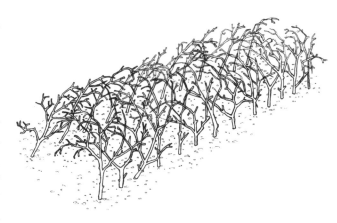

Supports for peas.

EXPECTED YIELD: 1.5 kg per metre (3 lb per yard) of row (in pods).
STORING: freeze.
RECOMMENDED VARIETIES: *Round seeded*: 'Feltham First', 'Meteor'. *Wrinkle seeded*: 'Kelvedon Wonder' (early); 'Onward' (second early), 'Senator' (maincrop), 'Hurst's Green Shaft' (maincrop). *Mangetout*: 'Oregon Sugar Pod', 'Sugar Snap' (up to 1.5 m tall but can be used both as mangetout and, later, as a normal pod pea). *Petit Pois*: 'Waverex'.

Pea *Pisum sativum* Leguminosae

It is particularly unfortunate that the fresh pea has declined in popularity in favour of the shop-bought frozen article, at a time when the range of types for home growing has never been more interesting. But it must be said that in some years, and on poor soils, the yield from a pea crop can be small. It is important therefore to ensure that the soil fertility is high (preferably by trenching it in the autumn) and that the plants are weaned carefully over their vulnerable seedling stage. There are several principal types of peas – round seeded for autumn or early spring sowing to give the earliest crops, wrinkled seeded types for later spring sowing (divided into early, second early and maincrop maturing times), mangetout varieties, in which the young pod is eaten whole, and petit pois varieties which produce very tiny peas even when mature. Within most of these groups there are tall and shorter growing types; for most garden purposes, I strongly recommend the latter.

SOW BY: half-hardy annual technique in October/November or February/March under cloches (round seeded varieties); sequentially from March to July (wrinkled seeded varieties); April/May (mangetout and petit pois varieties).
FERTILISER: none.
SPACING: in bands of three rows, 10 cm (4 in) apart, with 60 cm (24 in) between the central row of adjoining row triplets, and with plants 10 cm (4 in) apart within each row.
AFTER-CARE: erect twiggy sticks or proprietary pea netting to support the plants; use netting also to give protection from birds; maintain moisture in soil by mulching around young plants.
PEST, DISEASE OR OTHER PROBLEMS: birds, mice, mildew, root rot.
HARVESTING: 12–16 weeks; when pods are full (except mangetout which should be picked when about 8 cm (3 in) long); pick regularly from the bottom of the plants.

Potato *Solanum tuberosum* Solanaceae

Lift new potatoes a few at a time as they are needed.

The potato is the vegetable most taken for granted. It is gross, unattractive (except when in flower), relatively inexpensive to buy, something of a nuisance to grow, being only half hardy and prone to a hatful of problems. Yet if you cannot bring yourself to grow maincrop potatoes, surely you can find room for a few rows of earlies. For there really is no potato like a home-grown new one in the early summer. Although potatoes grow best on fairly well manured ground, they are very undemanding and are often used as the first crop to grow on previously uncropped land, where their extensive root system helps build up the soil structure and their dense canopy suppresses weeds.

PLANT: seed tubers in late March (early varieties) or mid-April (maincrop varieties). Always buy certified seed tubers and do not save tubers from your own crop for replanting. Tubers of early varieties must be bought in late January or February and first set out on trays in a warm, fairly light place to sprout.

FERTILISER: 375 g/square metre (12 oz/sq yd).

SPACING: 60 × 30 cm (24 × 12 in) (earlies) or 75 × 35 cm (30 × 14 in) (maincrop); 12 cm (5 in) deep.

AFTER-CARE: draw soil around the shoots as they emerge to protect them from frost; draw soil around the shoots again when they are about 20 cm (8 in) tall to prevent them from being exposed to the light and turning green. Water regularly when in flower.

PEST, DISEASE OR OTHER PROBLEMS: aphids, blight, slugs, tuber rots.

HARVESTING: 13 weeks (earlies)–22 weeks (maincrop); lift some earlies for inspection when flowers are fully open and harvest when tubers are 6–7 cm (2½–3 in) in diameter; with maincrop varieties, wait until about ten or fourteen days after shoots turn brown.

EXPECTED YIELD: 2 kg (4 lb) (earlies) to 3 kg (6 lb) (maincrop) per metre (yard) of row.

STORING: best for maincrop, in paper sacks in frost-free store.

RECOMMENDED VARIETIES: there are few areas of gardening in which there is more dispute than the relative merits of potato varieties. Partly this is due to variations in personal taste but also to the suitability of different varieties for particular methods of cooking, and their relative successes on different soils. The best way to discover varieties that at least grow well in your area is to ask experienced gardening neighbours. *Earlies*: 'Pentland Javelin' (white), 'Sharpe's Express' (white), 'Sutton's Foremost' (white). *Maincrop*: 'Desirée' (red skin, yellow flesh), 'King Edward' (pinkish skin, cream flesh).

Radish *Raphanus sativus* Cruciferae

The easiest of all vegetables to grow, radish will succeed in almost any soil and any situation, although in shade and denied water they will be tough and tasteless. They are quick growing plants and are ideal for filling in spaces between longer-term crops. There are two principal types of radish, the familiar spherical or cylindrically rooted summer salad varieties (more recently joined by long-rooted Japanese mooli types) and the much less widely grown spherical or cylindrical winter radishes. The commonest mistake made in radish growing is to sow the summer varieties after the end of June when, despite common advice to the contrary, it is very difficult indeed to prevent them from bolting.

SOW BY: hardy annual technique in growing positions from early March to June, using cloches for the earliest sowings.

FERTILISER: 50 g/square metre (2 oz/sq yd).

SPACING: 8 × 2–4 cm (3 × 1–1½ in) (summer varieties) or 15 × 15 cm (6 × 6 in) (winter varieties).

AFTER-CARE: do not allow plants to dry out.

PEST, DISEASE OR OTHER PROBLEMS: flea beetle.

HARVESTING: 3–6 weeks (summer varieties) or 9–12 weeks (winter varieties); when spherical and cylindrical summer types are approximately 2 cm (¾ in) in diameter; when winter types are approximately 5 cm (2 in) in diameter.

EXPECTED YIELD: 0.5 kg per metre (1 lb per yard) of row (summer varieties) or 1.5 kg per metre (3 lb per yard) of row (winter varieties).

STORING: winter varieties only, in boxes of dry sand or peat – lift roots in late October and cut off the leaves; or cover with at least 10 cm (4 in) of straw at beginning of December and leave in ground.

RECOMMENDED VARIETIES: *Summer varieties*: 'April Cross' (F₁) (long rooted Japanese), 'Cherry Belle' (spherical), 'French Breakfast' (cylindrical); *Winter varieties*: 'Black Spanish' (spherical, black), 'China Rose' (cylindrical, red).

Rhubarb *Rheum* × *cultorum* Polygonaceae

Rhubarb can very successfully and attractively be forced in an old chimney.

Rhubarb is rather too often treated as the joke of the vegetable garden; and in consequence is probably the most neglected vegetable crop plant. Although it will indeed crop very efficiently for year after year, it will nonetheless repay just a little care and attention. Choose your plant carefully, for the chances are that you will only ever buy one or two in a gardening lifetime.

Sticks should be pulled, not cut, from the plant.

PLANT: crowns in early spring on very well manured site; it is not worth growing from seed.

FERTILISER: 200 g/square metre (6½ oz/sq yd).

SPACING: one plant should suffice unless you intend to force some, but space at 1 m (1 yd) each way if more are needed.

AFTER-CARE: mulch heavily with well rotted manure or compost in early spring.

PEST, DISEASE OR OTHER PROBLEMS: none.

HARVESTING: pull (do not cut) sticks between March (in mild areas or seasons) and late July. Force plants by placing a large upturned pot over them in late winter; do not force the same plant again for at least two years.

EXPECTED YIELD: 2 kg (4 lb) per plant.

STORING: freeze.

RECOMMENDED VARIETIES: 'Hawke's Champagne', 'Timperley Early' (the best variety for forcing), 'Victoria' (late).

Runner bean *Phaseolus coccineus* Leguminosae

The archetypal English summer vegetable, runner beans have the enormous advantage of taking up very little room for the amount of crop obtained. They are attractive plants too – it is worth remembering that they were first brought to Europe from South America as ornamental climbers; by choosing varieties with different flower colours, a very appealing effect can be created. They can be grown on the same site for year after year until root rot troubles arise and force a move. The soil must be deep and well manured – although there is no need to go to the ridiculous lengths of making 1 m (1 yd) deep excavations as sometimes suggested. A 45 or 60 cm (18 or 24 in) deep trench, liberally dressed with manure when it is re-filled in autumn, is ideal. There are several ways to support the plants – a wigwam of canes or tall sticks (at least 2 m (6½ feet) tall) or, best, a ridge tent style arrangement with canes laid horizontally across the tops to support the ridge. Alternatively, to save on the cost of canes in the ridge tent system, one cane may be fixed horizontally close to soil level along each row of upright canes and some of the uprights replaced by strings tied to the lower and upper horizontal canes. There are two main types of runner bean – the traditional string beans, with a fibrous 'string' along the edge of the pod which must be pulled away before cooking, and the newer stringless types. Most of the string beans have better flavour. Additionally, there are a few dwarf, low growing varieties, but in limited space, French beans may be a better proposition.

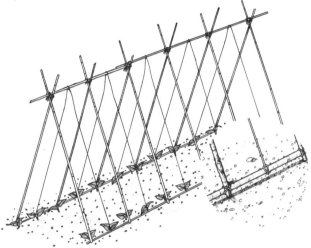

Support for runner beans, showing alternation of strings and canes. Inset shows method of attaching twine.

SOW BY: half-hardy annual technique in growing positions in mid–late May or, better, in 10 cm (4 in) diameter pots in a greenhouse, planting out as soon as the danger of frost has passed.

FERTILISER: 200 g/square metre (6½ oz/sq yd).

SPACING: 60 cm (24 in) between the two rows of canes and 15 cm (6 in) between adjacent canes (or strings) in the rows with one plant at the base of each cane.

AFTER-CARE: do not allow plants to dry out; difficulty is generally experienced in inducing the lowest flowers to set; this problem can be minimisd by mulching heavily once the plants are about 1 m (39 in) tall.

PEST, DISEASE OR OTHER PROBLEMS: bees and birds (removing or damaging flowers), leaf spot, root rot.

HARVESTING: 12 weeks; when pods are 15–20 cm (6–8 in) long (depending on variety); pick regularly to ensure continuing set of new pods.

EXPECTED YIELD: 8–19 kg per metre (16–20 lbs per yard) of double row.

STORING: freeze.

RECOMMENDED VARIETIES: 'Hammonds Dwarf Scarlet' (red flowers, string, the best of the dwarf varieties – only 40 cm (16 in) tall), 'Kelvedon Marvel' (red flowers, string, early), 'Painted Lady' (red and white bicoloured flowers, string), 'Polestar' (red flowers, stringless), 'White Emergo' (white flowers, string).

Salsify *Tragopogon porrifolius* and Scorzonera *Scorzonera hispanica* Compositae

Two similar, little grown but useful related root crops, requiring very similar treatment. They are grown much as parsnips and the roots may similarly be cooked in a variety of ways. In common with most other root crops, they succeed best in a light, free-draining soil free from stones or clods.

SOW BY: hardy annual technique in growing positions in April.
FERTILISER: 135 g/square metre (4½ oz/sq yd).
SPACING: 30 × 15 cm (12 × 6 in).
AFTER-CARE: little required; water in very dry weather.
PEST, DISEASE OR OTHER PROBLEMS: none.
HARVESTING: 24 weeks; judge maturity by timing from sowing.
EXPECTED YIELD: 0.5 kg per metre (1 lb per yard) of row.
STORING: in boxes of dry sand or peat – lift roots in late October and cut off the leaves.
RECOMMENDED VARIETIES: *Salsify*: 'Sandwich Island'. *Scorzonera*: 'Long John' (or 'Lange Jan').

Spinach *Spinacia oleracea* Chenopodiaceae

A delicious and much maligned vegetable, spinach is tastier than the substitutes such as Swiss chard although slightly tricky to grow as it is prone to run to seed if not sown in a rich moist soil and carefully tended. It must have a sunny situation if it is not to become tough and bitter.

SOW BY: hardy annual technique in growing position sequentially from March to the end of May.
FERTILISER: 135 g/square metre (4½ oz/sq yd).
SPACING: 25 × 15 cm (10 × 6 in).
AFTER-CARE: water carefully; do not allow plants to dry out.
PEST, DISEASE OR OTHER PROBLEMS: leaf spot.
HARVESTING: 8–15 weeks; when leaves are large enough to use, pull constantly, a little from each plant, to encourage more leaf production.
EXPECTED YIELD: 0.5–1 kg per metre (1–2 lbs per yard) of row.
STORING: freeze.
RECOMMENDED VARIETIES: 'Long Standing' (or selections such as 'Monarch Long Standing') (early but plants from later sowings may bolt), 'Norvak', 'Sigmaleaf'.

Swede *Brassica napus napobrassica* Cruciferae

Superficially one of the easiest and most undemanding of vegetables, in practice swedes are very difficult to grow well in a garden. Unless you have plenty of space, therefore, and are able to grow the plants in large numbers in blocks, much as farmers do, my advice is to give over the space to something more rewarding.

SOW BY: hardy annual technique in May or June.
FERTILISER: 135 g/square metre (4½ oz/sq yd).
SPACING: 30 × 20 cm (12 × 8 in).
AFTER-CARE: little needed.
PEST, DISEASE OR OTHER PROBLEMS: cabbage root fly, clubroot, flea beetle, mildew.
HARVESTING: 20 weeks; when roots are approximately 10 cm (4 in) in diameter.
EXPECTED YIELD: 4–5 kg per metre (8–10 lb per yard) of row.

STORING: in boxes of dry sand or peat – lift roots in late October and cut off the leaves.
RECOMMENDED VARIETIES: 'Marion'.

Sweet corn *Zea mays* Gramineae

Sweetcorn 'Kelvedon Glory'

The only grass crop grown as a garden vegetable, sweet corn is delicious but it is a plant for milder areas and large gardens – the yield per very large plant is depressingly small and in cold wet summers the whole exercise can be a disappointment. A sweet corn crop takes up room not only because each plant is big but because, being wind-pollinated, it is necessary to grow a fairly large block of plants to ensure success.

SOW BY: half-hardy annual technique at medium temperature, raising each plant individually in a 9 cm (3½ in) diameter pot and planting out after the danger of frost has passed.
FERTILISER: 135 g/square metre (4½ oz/sq yd).
SPACING: 45 × 45 cm (18 × 18 in).
AFTER-CARE: water carefully – do not allow soil to become very dry; earth up around stem bases when roots appear above the soil; shake the plants when the flowers (tassels) are fully open to help ensure pollination.
PEST, DISEASE OR OTHER PROBLEMS: frit fly.
HARVESTING: 13 weeks; when tassels turn brown, carefully peel back a little of the protective sheath over the cobs and press a few seeds with the thumbnail; when a runny but creamy liquid oozes out, they are ready.
EXPECTED YIELD: 2 cobs per plant (except on 'Minor' – see below).
STORING: freeze.

RECOMMENDED VARIETIES: 'Minor' (F_1) (miniature, 15 cm (6 in) long cobs, 4–6 per plant); 'Northern Belle' (F_1) (reliable in cooler areas), 'Sundance' (F_1), 'Sunrise' (F_1).

Tomato *Lycopersicon esculentum* Solanaceae

There are good reasons for considering the tomato to be the most important summer vegetable in most gardens. Certainly, more people have greenhouses to enable them to grow tomatoes than for any other reason. Despite the general improvement in flavour of commercial varieties in recent years, there is no doubt that the taste of the varieties available to gardeners offers a compelling argument in favour of the home-grown product. There are, in fact, two main ways of growing tomatoes – in a greenhouse or, in milder, more southerly areas, outside in the garden. Some varieties can be grown in both situations but the unstaked bush tomato is very much an outdoor plant. In the greenhouse, tomatoes may be grown in the soil of the greenhouse border, in pots or growing bags or, best of all, in ring culture beds (see p. 33).

SOW BY: half-hardy annual technique at medium temperature. Sow into 9 cm (3½ in) diameter pots approximately nine weeks before the plants are to be planted into their growing conditions. Outdoors, this planting time will be around the end of May when the danger of the last frost has passed. In the normal greenhouse, maintained at a minimum of about 7°C (44.5°F), it will be in mid-April.

FERTILISER: in greenhouse, use growing bag compost or, in ring culture beds, John Innes No. 3 soil-based compost. Outdoors, apply 200 g/square metre (6½ oz/sq yd).

SPACING: indoors, two plants per standard sized growing bag, or 45 cm (18 in) apart in bottomless ring culture pots or border soil. Outdoors, 75 × 45 cm (30 × 18 in).

AFTER-CARE: greenhouse and staked outdoor varieties must be tied in regularly to their supports and the side-shoots removed. Outdoor bush varieties should have straw placed beneath them to keep the fruit out of contact with the soil.

The good gardener is to be judged by how assiduously he ties in his tomatoes.

Water constantly; the soil or compost must not be allowed to dry out. Feed with a proprietary liquid tomato fertiliser from the time that the first fruit truss sets – twice a week for indoor and once a week for outdoor plants.

PEST, DISEASE OR OTHER PROBLEMS: aphids, blight (outdoors), blossom end rot, white fly, virus.

HARVESTING: 16 weeks (greenhouse), 20 weeks outdoors; when fruit are fully coloured. Green fruit may be collected at the end of the season and either used to make pickles or other preserves or ripened in warmth – it is warmth, not light, that brings about ripening.

EXPECTED YIELD: 3.5 kg (7 lb) per plant (greenhouse); 1.75 kg (3½ lbs) per plant (outdoors).

STORING: not satisfactory.

RECOMMENDED VARIETIES: *Greenhouse and outdoors*: 'Alicante', 'Gardener's Delight' (small fruit, matchless flavour), 'Yellow Perfection' (yellow fruit). *Greenhouse only*: 'Dombello' (large fruited, beefsteak type), 'Sweet 100' (F_1) (small fruit, almost as good a flavour as 'Gardener's Delight'). *Outdoors only*: 'The Amateur', 'Red Alert', 'Sleaford Abundance' (F_1).

Turnip *Brassica rapa rapifera* Cruciferae

The turnip is often dismissed as both boring to grow and boring to eat. But it is one of the vegetables that is most unexpectedly rewarding when home grown, closely spaced and eaten small. It is relatively easy to grow too, requiring none of the ideal soil conditions demanded by carrots.

SOW BY: hardy annual technique, in growing positions in succession from March to April (early varieties) or July to August (maincrop varieties).

FERTILISER: 135 g/square metre (4½ oz/sq yd).

SPACING: 20 × 10 cm (8 × 4 in) (early varieties) or 25 × 12 cm (10 × 5 in) (maincrop).

AFTER-CARE: do not allow soil to dry out.

PEST, DISEASE OR OTHER PROBLEMS: cabbage root fly, clubroot, flea beetle.

HARVESTING: 6–12 weeks; when 3–4 cm (1½–1¾ in) in diameter.

EXPECTED YIELD: 1–1.5 kg per metre (2–3 lb per yard) of row.

STORING: maincrop varieties only – in boxes of dry sand or peat – lift roots in late October and twist off the leaves; or cover with at least 10 cm (4 in) of straw at beginning of December and leave in ground.

RECOMMENDED VARIETIES: *Early varieties*: 'Purple Top Milan', 'Snowball'. *Maincrop varieties*: 'Golden Ball', 'Manchester Market'.

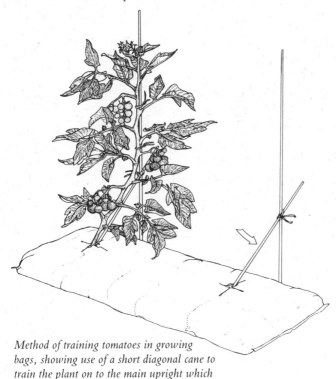

Method of training tomatoes in growing bags, showing use of a short diagonal cane to train the plant on to the main upright which is anchored behind the bag.

TO a horticulturist or botanist, the term herb is used for any plant lacking a woody structure but it has a quite different and not very strict meaning in the garden. A herb is simply any plant, woody or not, that is strongly aromatic and is used either for medicinal purposes or in cooking as a flavouring rather than as a food in its own right. Many herbs belong to the family Labiatiae and are characterised by markedly angled stems.

Most garden herbs originate from warm dry climates, the Mediterranean especially. They will generally succeed best therefore in the sunniest part of the garden and on a light, well-drained soil. Only mint, among common herbs, is really successful in partial shade. If your garden soil is naturally light or sandy, therefore, herbs will usually thrive without any major attention to the soil structure although on a clay soil it is essential to incorporate organic matter to lighten it. In practice, as herb gardens need only be fairly small (see below), constructing a raised bed for them is often the simplest answer on a really heavy, difficult site. As with vegetables, the soil for herbs should preferably be around neutral although the pH is not critical and even fairly strongly alkaline or acid conditions will still enable you to produce satisfactory results.

I believe that an area of about 4 square metres (4½ sq yds) is adequate for a good representative range of the important types of culinary herb, although if you plan to specialise and incorporate many of the medicinal species also, then a very much greater area will of course be needed. My own preference is to confine the herb garden itself largely to the culinary types and to use other herbs within other garden plantings – the mixed border, for instance, where their attractiveness and/or fragrance will be particularly valuable. It is most important, nonetheless, to position any dedicated herb garden close to the kitchen – herbs are always best freshly picked and any cook will rightly soon become frustrated at having to walk more than a few strides every time a dish is prepared.

The arrangement of the plants in a herb garden can be informal (simply placing the taller types at the back and the smaller to the front) although many gardeners find a formal style more attractive, mimicking the regimented herb gardens that have been used since mediaeval times. One popular version of the formal planting is to arrange the plants in a cartwheel pattern, using either a real cartwheel and planting the herbs between the spokes, or

The herb garden

A cartwheel herb garden.

Opposite: herb fennel.

constructing a facsimile wheel – from bricks, for instance. Whatever scheme is used, do bear in mind the need easily to reach all parts of the bed for picking the plants – stepping stones are very useful in a large area.

Herbs require relatively little feeding – a light top dressing of blood, fish and bone fertiliser (about 17 g per square metre/½ oz per sq yd) early in the spring will be satisfactory. And coming largely from dry climates, most herbs are tolerant of fairly long periods without water too, although of course their foliage will be softer and more tasty if they are not deliberately neglected.

Cooking, of course, does not stop with the end of the summer and there are several ways in which you can ensure a supply of herbs through the winter. The smaller types may be planted in pots and brought into the greenhouse or even placed on the kitchen window ledge, while larger ones may be protected outdoors with cloches. Almost all herbs can be dried but in almost every case the results bear little resemblance either in taste or appearance to the fresh material. When drying, it is best to use a fairly high temperature (about 25°C/77°F) for a short time; an airing cupboard is useful if the door is opened from time to time for ventilation. Most herbs should be tied in bunches and hung up to dry; the process will take from one to four days. Alternatively, many herbs dry well when simply covered with paper and placed in a microwave oven. But the easiest and best way to preserve herbs of almost all types is by freezing them. Pack them individually into plastic freezer bags; there is no need to blanch them first.

HERBS GROWN PREDOMINANTLY FOR CULINARY USE

Basil *Ocimum basilicum* Labiatae

One of the few important half-hardy herbs, and also one of the few herbs grown as an annual, although it is perennial in its native habitats. It probably originated in India where it has religious significance; in the kitchen, it is especially valuable chopped in salads – with tomatoes in particular. In temperate climates, it rarely exceeds 30–45 cm (12–18 in) and is a branched, light green plant with oval leaves and tiny whitish flowers.

PROPAGATE BY: Seed (normal basil) or stem cuttings (named forms).

SOW/PLANT BY: half-hardy annual technique in pots; medium temperature. Take cuttings in late summer.

TRANSPLANTING: avoid root disturbance by planting out in pot-ball.

SPACING: 20 cm (8 in); two or three plants should suffice.

AFTER-CARE: no special treatment.

PEST, DISEASE OR OTHER PROBLEMS: none.

HARVESTING: leaves, when young.

STORING: freeze or dry.

RECOMMENDED VARIETIES: the commonest culinary variety is not usually named but others sometimes seen are the purple-leaved 'Purpurascens', the lemon-scented 'Citriodorum', and the compact (20 cm/8 in) 'Minimum' (bush or Greek basil).

Basil

Bay (or sweet bay) *Laurus nobilis* Lauraceae

The largest important herb plant; a tall evergreen bush or small tree from the Mediterranean, reaching 6 m (20 feet) or more and having narrowly oval, rather leathery foliage. The leaves are used especially in soups and stews.

PROPAGATE BY: cuttings in late summer.

AFTER-CARE: may need protection from winter cold in some areas, although it regenerates well even when cut back hard by frost. Prune in summer to maintain shape; when grown in a large pot, trained as a standard and clipped with a ball-shaped head, the plants are especially prized.

PEST, DISEASE OR OTHER PROBLEMS: the bay sucker and scale insect are both sap-sucking pests that predispose the plant to sooty mould growth. Use contact insecticides in early summer and wash off mould from affected leaves.

HARVESTING: leaves, as needed.

STORING: dry.

RECOMMENDED VARIETIES: the normal species is used for culinary purposes but the golden-leaved 'Aurea', the willow-leaved 'Angustifolia' and the wavy-leaved 'Crispa' are useful ornamentals.

Chervil *Anthriscus cerefolium* Umbelliferae

White-flowered hardy European annual, resembling cow parsley but only about 60 cm (24 in) tall. Prefers more shade than most herbs and runs to seed quickly in full sun. Useful in salads and with fish, chicken and vegetable dishes.

PROPAGATE BY: seed.

SOW/PLANT BY: hardy annual technique, sowing where it is to be grown or in small pots.

TRANSPLANTING: only successful when planted out in pot ball.

SPACING: 20 cm (8 in); three or four plants will suffice.

AFTER-CARE: no special treatment.

PEST, DISEASE OR OTHER PROBLEMS: none.

HARVESTING: young leaves.

STORING: freeze or dry.

RECOMMENDED VARIETIES: species only available.

Chives *Allium schoenoprasum* Liliaceae

A clump-forming, non-bulbing perennial relative of the onion, approximately 25 cm (10 in) tall and with attractive red-purple flower heads. The chopped leaves are invaluable in salads.

PROPAGATE BY: seed or by division every three years.

SOW/PLANT BY: half-hardy annual technique.

SPACING: 25 cm (10 in) when used as edging; for culinary purposes, one plant should suffice.

AFTER-CARE: no special treatment.

PEST, DISEASE OR OTHER PROBLEMS: rust disease causes reddish-orange pustules on the leaves; difficult to control and affected plants should be replaced, planting the new stock on a fresh site.

HARVESTING: cut leaves as needed.

STORING: best fresh but can be frozen for winter use (leaves die down in autumn).

RECOMMENDED VARIETIES: species only available.

Coriander *Coriandrum sativum* Umbelliferae

Somewhat similar in many respects to chervil although not quite as hardy. Both leaves and seeds are useful – the former for stews and curries and the latter in salads, confectionery, chutneys. The stem and roots can also be used as a vegetable.

PROPAGATE BY: seed.

SOW/PLANT BY: hardy annual technique.

SPACING: 20–25 cm (8–10 in); three or four plants should suffice.

AFTER-CARE: no special treatment.

PEST, DISEASE OR OTHER PROBLEMS: none.

HARVESTING: pull young leaves as required; collect seeds as they ripen.

STORING: dry (seeds) or freeze (leaves).

RECOMMENDED VARIETIES: species only available.

Dill *Anethum graveolens* Umbelliferae

A tall (75–125 cm/30–50 in) annual, yellow-flowered umbellifer with very feathery foliage, similar to fennel to which it is closely related but slightly less hardy. Useful in pickles (seed and flower heads), in soups and with fish.

PROPAGATE BY: seed.

SOW/PLANT BY: hardy annual technique.

SPACING: 30 cm (12 in); two or three plants will suffice.

AFTER-CARE: no special treatment.

PEST, DISEASE OR OTHER PROBLEMS: none.

HARVESTING: cut young leaves or flower heads as required; collect seeds as they ripen.

STORING: dry (seeds), dry or freeze (leaves).

RECOMMENDED VARIETIES: species only available.

Fennel *Foeniculum vulgare* Umbelliferae

Very similar to dill but perennial and hardier. It has similar uses but with a stronger flavour although, unlike dill, the flower heads are not used. Although perennial, the plants soon become very large and fennel is best grown as an annual or biennial.

PROPAGATE BY: seed.

SOW/PLANT BY: hardy annual technique. Once established in a garden, fennel will self-seed very freely.

TRANSPLANTING: only when plants are very small; the long tap root is easily damaged.

SPACING: one plant will suffice.

AFTER-CARE: no special treatment although the large numbers of self-sown plants can become troublesome if not pulled out promptly.

PEST, DISEASE OR OTHER PROBLEMS: none.

HARVESTING: leaves as required; collect seeds as they ripen.

STORING: dry (seeds), freeze (leaves).

RECOMMENDED VARIETIES: bronze form has attractive, olive-green foliage but produces both green and bronze seedlings. A form with a swollen stem base is grown as a vegetable (p. 119).

Horseradish *Armoracia rusticana* Cruciferae

50–100 cm (20–40 in) tall with large elliptical, bright green and rather leathery leaves arising from a long, white tap root which is used, grated, to prepare horseradish sauce to accompany roast beef or smoked fish.

PROPAGATE BY: seed or root pieces.

SOW/PLANT BY: hardy annual technique; pieces of root will strike wherever they are placed in soil.

TRANSPLANTING: at any time.

SPACING: 30 cm (12 in).

AFTER-CARE: no special treatment but plants regenerate very easily and can become invasive if not dug up carefully and completely.

PEST, DISEASE OR OTHER PROBLEMS: none.

HARVESTING: dig up roots as required.

STORING: not generally worthwhile but can be preserved in wine vinegar.

RECOMMENDED VARIETIES: species only available.

Marjoram/oregano *Origanum* spp. Labiatae

Origanum vulgare 'Aureum'

Low-growing, clump-forming, slightly woody perennials with 60–80 cm (24–32 in) leafy stems arising annually from the base. Bear small, oval bright green leaves and masses of tiny pink-purple flowers. Have a wide range of uses in cooking and are valuable because the flavour is not too assertive.

PROPAGATE BY: seed or shoot cuttings taken in late summer.

SOW/PLANT BY: hardy annual technique or (for sweet mar-joram) half-hardy annual technique at medium temperature.

SPACING: 40 cm (16 in), but one plant of each type (see below) should suffice.

AFTER-CARE: cut back annual shoots to the base in autumn; divide every two or three years.

PEST, DISEASE OR OTHER PROBLEMS: none, although pale-leaved forms scorch in strong sun.

HARVESTING: young leaves as required.

STORING: dry or freeze.

RECOMMENDED VARIETIES: *O. vulgare* (oregano) – European varieties are more strongly flavoured than the wild British form. Pink- and white-flowered types occur but the golden-leaved form 'Aureum' (gold marjoram) is especially attractive. *O. majorana* (sweet marjoram) and *O. onites* (pot marjoram) are similar in their uses and occur in a range of varieties including an attractive crinkle leaved type of *O. onites*.

Mint *Mentha* spp. Labiatae

A large group of very strongly aromatic perennials, all with markedly angular stems and most with more or less oval leaves. Both tall growing (1 m/39 in) and creeping species occur. Their most important uses are in mint sauce and in teas and other drinks. Mints in general are more tolerant than other herbs of shade and wet soil.

PROPAGATE BY: root or stem cuttings, at any time from spring to autumn; the best forms do not come true from seed.

SPACING: one plant of each should suffice but almost all species are very invasive and are best confined by planting each in a 20 cm (8 in) diameter pot, sunk to its rim in the soil.

AFTER-CARE: cut down aerial shoots in autumn, lift the pot and trim away any emerging roots and runners. Renew from cuttings every three years.

PEST, DISEASE OR OTHER PROBLEMS: rust disease causes small, brownish lesions and distorts the plants. Destroy affected stock and plant new on a fresh site.

HARVESTING: leaves as required.

STORING: freeze; also pot up small parts of plants in autumn and bring indoors or into greenhouse for forcing.

RECOMMENDED VARIETIES: *M. gentilis* (ginger mint); *M. piperata* (black peppermint); *M. piperata* 'Crispa' (curly mint); *M. piperata* 'Citrata' (orange or eau de Cologne mint – not for culinary use, but exquisitely perfumed); *M. pulegium* (pennyroyal – a creeping peppermint that sends up tall shoots in summer); *M. spicata* (spearmint – the best for new potatoes); *M. suaveolens* (and variegated form 'Variegata') (apple mints – the best for mint sauce); *M. villosa* 'Alopecuroides' (Bowles' mint – also good for mint sauce).

Parsley *Petroselenum crispum* Umbelliferae

A densely leafy biennial, reaching approximately 40 cm (16 in) and producing tall umbels of greenish-yellow flowers in the second season. Invaluable for parsley sauce with meat and fish and as a garnish. Always succeeds best in a sunny position but with a moist, rich soil.

PROPAGATE BY: seed.

SOW/PLANT BY: hardy annual technique; parsley seed can prove difficult to germinate. Sow fresh batches in spring and autumn.

TRANSPLANTING: avoid root disturbance; either sow directly outdoors or in pots and then transplant in the pot ball.

SPACING: 15–20 cm (6–8 in) between plants.

AFTER-CARE: remove plants after twelve months and replace; use cloches for winter protection.

PEST, DISEASE OR OTHER PROBLEMS: carrot fly sometimes attacks the roots and causes the foliage to turn reddish. Destroy affected plants.

HARVESTING: leaves as required.

STORING: freeze (dried parsley is almost useless).

RECOMMENDED VARIETIES: 'Moss Curled'; 'Curlina' (a more compact form of the moss curled type); 'Plain Leaved' (*P. crispum* 'Neapolitanum') – a taller plant (60 cm/24 in) with flat, dark green leaves and a stronger flavour. 'Hamburg parsley' is a swollen rooted plant used as a vegetable (p. 120).

Rosemary *Rosmarinus officinalis* Labiatae

An evergreen bush, sometimes reaching 2 m (80 in) and with very woody stems from which soft lateral shoots bearing needle-like leaves and blue flowers arise. Most frequently used as a flavouring with lamb.

PROPAGATE BY: semi-hardwood cuttings with a heel in spring or late summer.

SPACING: one plant will suffice for culinary use but can also be used as a hedge (see p. 159).

AFTER-CARE: prune back each spring to maintain shape and vigour; left unpruned, plants soon become straggly and unkempt.

PEST, DISEASE OR OTHER PROBLEMS: none, although can be scorched or have shoots killed back in cold winters.

HARVESTING: sprigs as required.

STORING: can be dried but unnecessary as evergreen.

RECOMMENDED VARIETIES: several varieties exist with pink and white flowers as well as a range in the intensity of the blue. Ornamental forms also occur in a range of habits from more or less prostrate ('Prostratus' or 'Severn Sea') to upright ('Miss Jessop's Upright') but for culinary use, the normal species is satisfactory.

Sage *Salvia officinalis* Labiatae

A rather loose woody perennial, reaching approximately 60 cm (24 in) in height and with thick, leathery, oval leaves and small, purple or occasionally white (in form 'Alba') flowers. Strongly flavoured so used for stuffing and with other strong foods.

PROPAGATE BY: seed (normal species) or cuttings (selected forms) in late summer.

SOW/PLANT BY: hardy annual technique.

SPACING: one plant of each form should suffice.

AFTER-CARE: no special treatment but cut back shoots after flowering and replace with fresh plants after three years when it becomes very woody and straggly.

PEST, DISEASE OR OTHER PROBLEMS: none.

HARVESTING: leaves as required before flowering.

STORING: dry.

RECOMMENDED VARIETIES: in addition to the normal species, there are several attractive foliage variants, especially 'Purpurea' with purple leaves, 'Purpurea variegata' with variegated purple leaves and 'Icterina', a golden variegated form.

Sorrel *Rumex* spp. Polygonaceae

Sorrels are perennial herbs, related, and similar in appearance, to docks with large, rounded or oval leaves arising from a strong tap root. Very young leaves may be eaten in salads but sorrels are best used for making soups.

PROPAGATE BY: seed.

SOW/PLANT BY: hardy annual technique.

SPACING: 30 cm (12 in).

AFTER-CARE: divide plants after four or five years.

PEST, DISEASE OR OTHER PROBLEMS: none; leaf holes commonly caused by insect damage may be ignored.

HARVESTING: leaves as required.

STORING: not satisfactory.

RECOMMENDED VARIETIES: large, common or broad leaved sorrel (*R. acetosa*) has the largest leaves but is the least suitable as a herb. Much better are the smaller garden sorrel (*R. rugosus*) or French or buckler leaf sorrel, with more rounded leaves.

Tarragon *Artemisia dracunculus* Compositae

A herbaceous perennial with rather delicate upright shoots and soft, narrowly willow-like leaves. The flavour is subtly that of aniseed but quite distinct and distinctive. Because of its characteristic taste, tarragon should be used sparingly in salads but is especially valuable with chicken.

PROPAGATE BY: cuttings (take Irishman's cuttings with a small piece of root attached); does not produce seed.

SPACING: one plant will suffice.

AFTER-CARE: mound protective mulch around the crown in late autumn to protect from frost damage.

PEST, DISEASE OR OTHER PROBLEMS: none.

HARVESTING: leaves as required.

STORING: freeze.

RECOMMENDED VARIETIES: *A. dracunculus* is the true French tarragon (there are no named varieties) and with protection will grow almost everywhere. There is no justification therefore for using the larger, coarser but hardier Russian tarragon (*A. dracunculoides*) which is sometimes offered.

Thyme *Thymus* spp. Labiatae

Arguably the best known and most valuable of all herbs, thymes are woody perennials and generally form dwarf bushes although many types adopt a prostrate or creeping habit. Thymes are invaluable chopped in salads, in bouquets garnis, in stuffings and applied to many other culinary purposes.

PROPAGATE BY: cuttings, preferably with a heel of older wood. Although seed is widely offered, the best forms do not come true from seed.

SPACING: one plant of each type should suffice at a spacing of about 25 cm (10 in).

AFTER-CARE: trim back flowers as they fade and replace stock every three years.

PEST, DISEASE OR OTHER PROBLEMS: none.

HARVESTING: sprigs as needed.

STORING: dry.

RECOMMENDED VARIETIES: there are numerous varieties of several species, differing in overall habit, leaf colour and aroma. For culinary use, the most useful are: *T. citriodorus* 'Variegatus' (commonly called 'Silver Posie'), a small, bushy form with silver-edged leaves with the characteristic thyme flavour; *T.*

serpyllum 'Lemon Curd' for a lemon-scented type; and *T. herba-barona* for a caraway flavour. Among the most attractive of the ornamental and less strongly aromatic forms are *T. citriodorus* 'Aureus' with golden variegated leaves and *T. doefleri* 'Doone Valley', a creeping type with gold blotches on vivid green leaves.

HERBS GROWN PREDOMINANTLY FOR ORNAMENTAL, MEDICINAL OR OTHER NON-CULINARY USE

Bergamot (also called bee balm or Oswego tea) *Monarda didyma* Labiatae

A slender, herbaceous perennial reaching approximately 60–80 cm (24–32 in) and bearing a head of usually red, dead-nettle-like flowers at the top. Although bergamot has long been used for making aromatic teas and similar purposes, it is most often used today to add colour to the herb garden or as a valuable member of the herbaceous border.

PROPAGATE BY: cuttings or division; the best named forms do not come true from seed.

SPACING: 30 cm (12 in).

AFTER-CARE: as for ornamental herbaceous perennials (p. 202).

PEST, DISEASE OR OTHER PROBLEMS: none.

RECOMMENDED VARIETIES: 'Cambridge Scarlet' (red); 'Blue Stocking' (purple); 'Croftway Pink' (pink).

Borage *Borago officinalis* Boraginaceae

Borago officinalis

A bristly-leaved annual reaching approximately 50 cm (20 in) and bearing electric blue flowers, rather reminiscent in shape of potato flowers. Borage adds delightful colour to the herb garden and the flowers may be put to good use to flavour and add interest to cold drinks.

PROPAGATE BY: seed; once established, borage will self-sow to the point of becoming invasive.

SOW/PLANT BY: hardy annual technique in flowering positions.

SPACING: 30 cm (12 in).

AFTER-CARE: none.

PEST, DISEASE OR OTHER PROBLEMS: none.

HARVESTING: flowers as they open.

STORING: freeze in ice cubes for adding to drinks.

RECOMMENDED VARIETIES: normal species only.

Pot marigold *Calendula officinalis* Compositae

The familiar traditional annual garden marigold, up to 60 cm (24 in) tall with bright orange or yellow daisy-like flowers, little used now in its traditional role as a flavouring but invaluable in the herb garden and elsewhere for its vivid colour and ease of cultivation.

PROPAGATE BY: seed; once established, marigolds will self-sow to the point of becoming invasive.

SOW/PLANT BY: hardy annual technique in flowering positions.

SPACING: 20–30 cm (8–12 in).

AFTER-CARE: none, although tall types benefit from staking.

PEST, DISEASE OR OTHER PROBLEMS: black fly (aphids) may be controlled by contact insecticides; mildew is common late in the season but seldom justifies any control measures.

RECOMMENDED VARIETIES: for purely ornamental use, the dwarf 'Fiesta Gitana' hybrids offer a range of colours on plants up to 25 cm (10 in) tall but for more traditional taller plants, 'Radio', 'Orange King' or 'Art Shades' are excellent.

Chamomile *Chamaemelum nobile* Compositae

Several quite distinct plants are called chamomile but the most important is the form of the creeping *C. nobile* with small, double white, button-like flowers. It can be used in pot pourri and for medicinal purposes but is attractive enough to include in the herb garden purely as an ornamental.

PROPAGATE BY: cuttings or division.

SPACING: 20 cm (8 in).

AFTER-CARE: clip back flowers as they fade.

PEST, DISEASE OR OTHER PROBLEMS: none.

RECOMMENDED VARIETIES: the double-flowered plant is usually called 'Flore Pleno' but the non-flowering variety 'Treneague' should be used for chamomile lawns (see p. 149).

Curry plant *Helichrysum angustifolium* Compositae

Curry plant and chives

The curry plant can be likened to a low-growing shrub, rather rosemary-like in the form of its shoots and leaves but with very soft, densely silky silver foliage. It bears a head of small, button-like golden-yellow flowers but its most characteristic feature is its strong aroma of curry.
PROPAGATE BY: cuttings.
SPACING: one specimen plant will suffice but space at 20 cm (8 in) if using the dwarf form for edging.
AFTER-CARE: clip back hard after flowering.
PEST, DISEASE OR OTHER PROBLEMS: none.
RECOMMENDED VARIETIES: apart from the normal species, the only named form usually seen is the 20 cm (8 in) tall 'Nana'.

Feverfew *Tanacetum parthenium* Compositae

A 30–60 cm (12–24 in) tall, rather woody herbaceous perennial with masses of small gold and white daisy flowers and rather deeply dissected, almost ferny foliage which betray a close relationship to the chrysanthemum. The aroma is strong and not particularly pleasant but the plant is valuable in that its leaves aid some migraine sufferers, while the golden form is an attractive ornamental.
PROPAGATE BY: seed (normal species) or cuttings.
SOW/PLANT BY: hardy annual technique in flowering positions.
SPACING: 25–30 cm (10–12 in), although only with the golden form used as edging is it likely that many will be needed.
AFTER-CARE: cut back hard after flowering.
PEST, DISEASE OR OTHER PROBLEMS: none.
HARVESTING: use leaves fresh as required.
STORING: not worthwhile.

RECOMMENDED VARIETIES: normal species or the attractive golden foliaged 'Aureum'.

Lemon balm *Melissa officinalis* Labiatae

A loose, rather woody perennial up to 1 m (39 in) tall, the normal species having little ornamental appeal although its very strong lemon scent has found a variety of uses. A 30 cm (12 in) tall golden variegated form is much more attractive.
PROPAGATE BY: seed or cuttings.
SOW/PLANT BY: hardy annual technique; germination is slow and erratic.
SPACING: one plant should suffice.
AFTER-CARE: cut back hard in autumn.
PEST, DISEASE OR OTHER PROBLEMS: none.
RECOMMENDED VARIETIES: the dwarf, variegated form 'Aurea' is the most suitable to grow.

Cotton lavender *Santolina chamaecyparissus* Compositae

A small woody, superficially lavender-like shrub but with very soft, feathery silver foliage and small, golden-yellow button flowers. Of greatest value when clipped and used as edging for knot or formal herb gardens.
PROPAGATE BY: cuttings.
SPACING: 40 cm (16 in) or 30 cm (12 in) when used as edging.
AFTER-CARE: cut back moderately after flowering and clip edging plants hard in spring. Not fully hardy so best not used as a major feature in cold gardens.
PEST, DISEASE OR OTHER PROBLEMS: none.
RECOMMENDED VARIETIES: normal species only (although there are some named forms of related species).

Rue *Ruta graveolens* Rutaceae

A 40–60 cm (16–24 in) tall, rather woody herbaceous perennial with divided, slightly leathery leaves and small, rather straggly, almost daisy-like flowers. Only really useful as a blue-leaved form that can be used as edging for formal beds.
PROPAGATE BY: cuttings.
SPACING: 35–40 cm (14–16 in) (for edging).
AFTER-CARE: clip moderately hard in spring.
PEST, DISEASE OR OTHER PROBLEMS: none.
RECOMMENDED VARIETIES: 'Jackman's Blue' has the attractive steel-blue foliage.

FRUIT have some big advantages over vegetables as edible garden crops. None is annual, most are fairly (and some very) long-lived and all require very much less routine care and attention. Against this, of course, should be set the fact that their perennial nature means that a significant area of the garden must be permanently set aside for them; and they are much more restricted in their seasonal availability.

Although most garden fruits belong to two plant families only – the rose family and the currant family – a more useful way to subdivide the different types is into the major groups of tree fruit and soft fruit, for this more meaningfully reflects the main differences in their cultivation. To these may be added two fruits that are different both in habit and cultivation, in that they are climbers.

The fruit garden

SOFT FRUIT

My comments in this section relate to all soft fruit except strawberries and blueberries, which have at least some special features that are described under their individual accounts. In general, soft fruit are slightly more shade tolerant than are most tree fruit but it is nonetheless still important to choose the sunniest available area of the garden. And because most require similar cultural treatment (and in particular, similar protection), it is sensible to group them all together in the form of a soft fruit garden. Only in very exposed coastal or high mountain gardens, or those with extremely shallow soil, are soft fruit likely to be a complete disappointment. Nonetheless, in almost every garden, some form of shelter from the wind (a hedge or fence for instance) will be beneficial in encouraging the activity of pollinating insects and in permitting vigorous shoot growth.

The ideal soil is a moisture-retentive loam with a pH of about 6.5 and, as with any perennial plant, it is important generously to incorporate organic matter into the soil before planting – it is impossible to place compost or manure in the vicinity of the plants' roots once they are established. If at all feasible, do not attempt to establish soft fruit on a site from which old fruit bushes or canes have been removed recently because there may be some carry over of viruses in the soil. Where shortage of space does make such an arrangement necessary, it is sensible to remove the soil from each planting position and swap it for fresh, obtained from elsewhere in the garden. All soft fruit are self-fertile so one plant can crop on its own and there is no need to worry about the need to grow compatible varieties.

It is unwise to be dogmatic over the ideal size for a soft fruit garden for, even if space itself is unlimited, the number of plants required and the area needed for them will be governed by the owner's preferences. Nevertheless, my own experience is that a family of four with an average fondness for soft fruit will obtain sufficient of all of the major types (to use both fresh and frozen) from an area of about 36 square metres (43 sq yds). Where space and/ or the amount of fruit needed is limited, it makes sound sense to grow red and white currants and gooseberries as cordons rather than bushes. And in similar vein, a few raspberry canes may be grouped around a single post instead of being trained more conventionally in a row against wires or a fence.

Opposite: A fan-trained 'Morello' cherry.

137

Horizontal support wires for training soft fruit – the diagonal braces are essential if the wires are to be correctly tensioned.

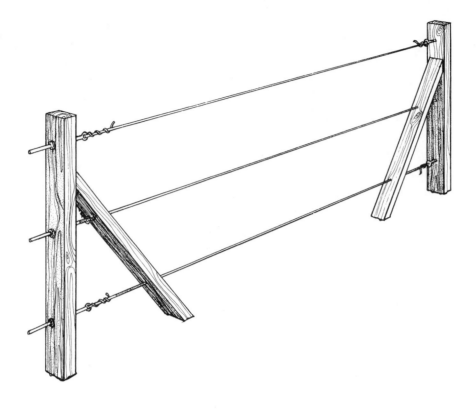

Because of the almost constant threat from birds in most parts of the country, it is wise to erect some form of permanent cage over the soft fruit garden. Such cages can be purchased in easy-to-assemble kit form, manufactured from lightweight aluminium frames and plastic netting. The internal sides of the cage itself may be used as growing space; if posts and wires are erected in front of the south and west facing sides, then blackberries and other fruits with pliable canes may be grown along them. In general, and whenever possible, rows of canes or cordons should be orientated north–south rather than east–west for maximum exposure to sunlight.

A simple fruit cage. Use wooden or aluminium posts and framework with chicken wire around the sides and lightweight plastic netting for the top.

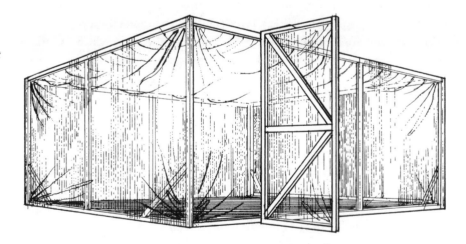

Although their demands are not constant, soft fruit benefit greatly from being given fertiliser at least at the start of each season. This need is most simply satisfied by applying a top dressing of blood, fish and bone at the rate of 80 g per square metre (2½ oz per sq yd) over the rooting area very early in the spring. Every third year, or if fruiting has been poor, a further dressing of 17 g per square metre (½ oz per sq yd) of sulphate of potash should be applied also. This should be followed by the application of a mulch of well rotted compost or manure over the moist soil. Additional water should also be applied at the time that the young fruits are beginning to swell but, if possible, this should be applied at ground level to minimise the likelihood of inducing rotting of canes and fruit.

Weed control is important among soft fruit, but not difficult. Close to the plants, annual weed growth at least will be kept in check by the moisture-retaining mulch. Between the rows, an organic matter mulch may also be laid to suppress annual weeds if sufficient mulching material is available. Failing this, a contact weedkiller or hand weeding must be used – hoeing may damage the shallow roots. Perennial weeds should be cleared as thoroughly as possible before planting but any that do persist can most readily be treated with the systemic weedkiller glyphosate.

Pest and disease problems are rarely serious among soft fruit. The two most generally encountered are grey mould on ripening fruit in damp weather, and the virus contamination that almost inevitably builds up in established plants after several years. The signs of virus are a mottling of the leaves, general stunting of the plants and gradual decline in vigour and crop production. Individual types of plant may experience other more specific problems from time to time.

Although it is possible to propagate soft fruit yourself by cuttings, layers or runners, I do not advise this. By the time that soft fruit plants are in need of replacement, they will almost certainly be contaminated with virus and new, certified virus-free stock should be obtained from a reputable supplier. Prepare the planting holes in the usual manner (p. 161) with compost and bone meal.

Careful initial training, followed by annual or, in some instances, biannual pruning is important to maintain the health and vigour of the plants. The methods to be adopted vary between the different types of soft fruit (see individual entries) but for all except free-standing bushes, it is important to have a rigid framework of horizontal wires, strained between vertical, braced upright posts (diagram).

Blackberry and hybrid berries *Rubus* spp. and hybrids
Rosaceae

Blackberries are characterised by more or less spherical black fruit and a distinctive flavour, present in wild plants but never as marked or appealing in cultivated varieties. Numerous hybrids, most with elongated red fruit, have been found or bred between blackberries, raspberries and other *Rubus* species. Many are mere curios but a small number are really well worth growing.
PLANT: in late autumn.
SPACING: in most gardens, one plant will suffice but in a row, 2.5 m (8 ft) between each must be allowed, even with the least vigorous varieties.
AFTER-CARE: cut out old canes immediately after fruiting and tie in new canes in a fan pattern. Feed and mulch in late winter.
PEST, DISEASE OR OTHER PROBLEMS: see raspberry.
HARVESTING: as the fruit attain full colour. They do not separate from the stalk or plug and should be picked with it – it is soft and does not detract from the flavour, and in any event disintegrates when the fruit are cooked.
STORING: freeze.
RECOMMENDED VARIETIES: I am convinced that 'Ashton

Tayberry

Cross', a recent selection of the wild blackberry, is easily the best garden variety; there is no other presently available that I would consider growing, although another new variety, 'Loch Ness', looks promising. Among the hybrids, I warmly recommend the tayberry (sold as the 'Medana Tayberry') and the rather similar loganberry (especially the thornless form called 'LY 654'). And although not a hybrid but a true species, the so-called Japanese Wineberry (*Rubus phoenicolasius*) with small, rich orange-coloured, rather raspberry-like fruit, and a beautiful softly prickled stem is well worth growing for ornamental as well as culinary appeal.

Blackcurrants *Ribes nigrum* and hybrids Grossulariaceae

Blackcurrant – 'Ben More'

Quite different in origin and form from red and white currants, and in need of different planting, training and pruning. The older varieties form very large bushes and should be positioned with care in small gardens. Few varieties predictably produce fruit sweet enough to eat fresh, and blackcurrants are usually considered a crop for preserving.

PLANT: in late autumn deep enough so that the soil just covers the point where the branches divide in order to encourage new, basal shoot development.

SPACING: 1.5 m (5 ft) except for the variety 'Ben Sarek' (1–1.2 m (3–4 ft)).

AFTER-CARE: prune immediately after picking or in winter by cutting back the oldest one third of the shoots to the base.

PEST, DISEASE OR OTHER PROBLEMS: aphids, mildew, virus, capsid bugs, big bud disease, grey mould, coral spot.

HARVESTING: as fruit attain full colour; it is often easier to remove entire strigs (stalks) and strip fruit from them later.

STORING: freeze.

RECOMMENDED VARIETIES: 'Ben Sarek' – mid-season, the most compact variety and ideal for garden use; 'Malling Jet' – late, but late flowering too and therefore frost resistant; 'Laxton Giant' – early, not high yielding but with very large, generally sweet fruit, an old exhibition variety to which I am very attached; 'Ben More' – a mid/late season variety with large fruit, especially suitable for cooking.

Blueberry *Vaccinium* spp. and hybrids Ericaceae

Still unfamiliar to British gardeners but widely grown in the United States and elsewhere and perfectly suitable for British gardens on naturally strongly acid, peaty soils. The fairly large size of the plants means that they are not really suitable for a peat garden or other artificially amended soil of low pH. Sometimes called the highbush blueberry, the fruit are used primarily for cooking as they tend to be rather bland when fresh. Like other soft fruit, but rather more emphatically, blueberries require sun and shelter.

PLANT: in late autumn.

SPACING: 1.5 m (5 ft).

AFTER-CARE: feed and mulch (with peat or sawdust) in early spring; never allow the plants to dry out in summer. Prune as blackcurrants.

PEST, DISEASE OR OTHER PROBLEMS: canker.

HARVESTING: as the fruit turn dark blue with a waxy bloom and part readily from the stalk – this is about seven to ten days after the blue colour first develops; regular picking is needed as the fruits ripen sequentially over a long period.

STORING: freeze.

RECOMMENDED VARIETIES: the only one that I can recommend from personal experience is 'Bluecrop', although several other American varieties are offered and may be worth trying on appropriate soils.

Gooseberry *Ribes grossularia* and hybrids Grossulariaceae

The gooseberry is best known as the most prickly of garden fruit, although one of the modern trends in gooseberry breeding is towards forms with few or no thorns. The problems in picking from so prickly a plant can be overcome partly by training the bushes as standards on a single 'leg' or, even more effectively, by training the plants as cordons or as fans. There are varieties suitable for both culinary and dessert use.

PLANT: in late autumn.

SPACING: 1.5 m (5 ft) apart (bushes); 30 cm (12 in) (single cordons); 60 cm (24 in) (double cordons); 90 cm (3 ft) (triple cordons or fans).

AFTER-CARE: prune all new side-shoots back to five leaves soon after midsummer and then back to two buds in winter, cutting back all leading shoots by half at the same time; feed and mulch in late winter.

PEST, DISEASE OR OTHER PROBLEMS: virus, mildew, gooseberry sawfly, aphids, grey mould.

HARVESTING: as the fruit reach full size and soften; some varieties turn red or yellow when ripe but others remain green, the very pale types being referred to as white.

STORING: freeze.

RECOMMENDED VARIETIES: 'Jubilee' – white, mid-season, heavy crop but really only for culinary use, a virus-free selection of the old variety 'Careless'; 'Invicta' – similar to 'Jubilee' but resistant to mildew and should be chosen where this is a problem; 'Leveller' – yellow, mid-season, good for dessert use but requires very good growing conditions and careful pruning; spreading habit and unsuitable as cordons; 'Whinham's Industry' – red, mid-season, heavy crop, very good for dessert use but prone to mildew.

Raspberry   *Rubus* spp. and hybrids   Rosaceae

Red or (in a few varieties) yellow fruit borne on more or less stiff, upright canes, although in some varieties the canes arch widely and are not suitable for small gardens. Summer fruiting types bear fruit on the previous year's canes; autumn fruiting types at the tips of those of the current year.

PLANT: in late autumn; it is easiest to prepare a trench when planting a row rather than make individual planting holes. Plant shallowly, with only about 6 cm (2½ in) of soil above the roots.

SPACING: differs slightly with variety but for all except the most vigorous types, use 15 cm (6 in) spacing within rows and 1.75 m (6 ft) between rows.

AFTER-CARE: cut out old canes on summer fruiting varieties immediately after they have fruited and tie in not more than seven new canes per plant to the support wires. On autumn fruiting varieties, cut down *all* canes to ground level in late winter. Pull out any surplus canes and also use a spade to sever any that emerge at some distance from the row. Feed and mulch in late winter; and apply sequestrene in early spring to counteract the iron deficiency and leaf yellowing to which raspberries are very prone.

PEST, DISEASE OR OTHER PROBLEMS: virus; grey mould; mildew; rust; cane blight and similar diseases; aphids; raspberry beetle.

HARVESTING: as the fruit attain full colour; they should separate readily from the stalk.

STORING: freeze.

RECOMMENDED VARIETIES: 'Glen Clova' – early season, vigorous, heavy crop, especially good for preserving; 'Malling Admiral' – mid-late season, tall canes make it less suitable for exposed areas, moderate crop, excellent flavour; 'Autumn Bliss' – the finest autumn fruiting variety and the only one really worth growing as it ripens rather earlier than most others and a reasonable crop is therefore almost guaranteed.

Red and white currants   *Ribes* hybrids   Grossulariaceae

Probably the least widely grown of the common soft fruit but with distinctive and similar flavours. Much sweeter than blackcurrants and therefore more acceptable fresh, when they add interesting colour to fruit salads, but excellent preserved also. Like gooseberries, they may be trained as bushes, cordons or fans.

PLANT: as gooseberries.

SPACING: as gooseberries.

AFTER-CARE: as gooseberries.

PEST, DISEASE OR OTHER PROBLEMS: aphids, mildew, virus.

HARVESTING: as fruit attain full colour; remove entire strigs (stalks) and strip fruit from them later.

STORING: freeze.

RECOMMENDED VARIETIES: 'Redstart' (red), 'Stanza' (red), 'White Versailles' (white).

Strawberry   *Fragaria* spp. and hybrids   Rosaceae

In many ways, strawberries are better thought of and treated as vegetables, for their cultivation and habit are quite different from that of other soft fruit. They are not long-term plants; three or four years is the effective productive life of many varieties and some are actually better grown as biennials or even annuals. They also take up a considerable area – you will require between 25 and 30 square metres (30 and 36 sq yds); and remember that, as with vegetables, you must rotate the plot when you plant fresh stock, so in effect you will need to be able to devote two or three times this area of your garden to strawberries at some time. And if you don't have sufficient room for a strawberry bed, don't bother with the crop at all – strawberries in tubs and barrels are more trouble than they are worth. The soil should be prepared as for a vegetable crop but protection from birds will be essential and is best provided by wire netting covers or by using conventional cloches which have the added advantage, of course, of encouraging earlier ripening.

PLANT: in late summer or early autumn, if possible buying individually raised, container-grown plants. Cold-stored runners may be difficult to establish, especially if they are planted in the autumn. A few varieties such as 'Sweetheart' are raised from seed but this method of raising is rarely very successful other than with the Alpine types.

SPACING: 45 cm (18 in) between plants and 85 cm (34 in) between rows.

AFTER-CARE: top dress the plants with sulphate of potash at 15 g per square metre (½ oz per sq yd) in late winter. As the fruit begin to swell, lay straw between the plants to discourage slugs and lessen the likelihood of soil and fungal spores being splashed onto the fruit. As soon as the fruit have been picked, cut off the foliage with shears to within about 10 cm (4 in) of the crown in order to stimulate new leaves to develop.

PEST, DISEASE OR OTHER PROBLEMS: virus, mildew, grey mould, slugs, aphids, red spider mite.

HARVESTING: as the fruit begin to colour; alpine varieties crop more or less continuously from spring to autumn.

STORING: freeze, although never very satisfactory and strawberries are best eaten fresh or made into preserves.

RECOMMENDED VARIETIES: a choice must be made between heavy cropping and good flavoured varieties. For flavour, I still opt for the old early-mid season 'Royal Sovereign', although plants should be discarded after two years; for high yield, my choice is 'Cambridge Favourite' or the more disease-resistant 'Silver Jubilee'. For later fruiting, try one of the new Dutch varieties such as 'Tenira' and the English 'Aromel' which is called perpetual fruiting but in fact crops twice a year and should be replaced annually. Additionally, grow a row or two of an Alpine strawberry such as 'Baron Solemacher' along the front of an ornamental bed. They are fairly shade tolerant and, because the fruit are small and well hidden by the leaves, tend to be left alone by birds.

TREE FRUIT

There is scarcely a garden that cannot grow at least some tree fruit. Apples and damsons are the toughest and are most likely to thrive in cold, exposed areas, although, of course, some shelter and the use of restricted training methods such as cordons or espaliers will also help to ensure a good crop whilst making optimum use of limited space. As with all types of tree, good and careful soil preparation will pay dividends many times over, the only exception to this rule being with figs. And despite the truth in the general maxim that a soil with a pH of about 6.5 is ideal, you will be unfortunate if you don't manage to obtain at least some fruit from trees grown on any soil likely to be found in the British Isles. Whilst it is usually safe to replant fruit trees at least close to a site from which old trees have been removed (provided no honey fungus is present), it is always unwise to plant new apple or pear trees in gardens where old trees affected with canker are present; the disease will almost inevitably spread to the new stock.

ROOTSTOCKS AND SPACINGS FOR APPLE TREES

ROOTSTOCK	CHARACTERISTICS	TREE HEIGHT AFTER TEN YEARS (m/ft)	BETWEEN TREE SPACING (m/ft)		
			Bush	*Cordon*	*Espalier*
MM 111	Vigorous	5/16½	6/20	NR	5/16½
MM 106	Semi-vigorous	3.5/11½	4.5/14½	1/3¼	4/13
M 26	Dwarfing	2.5/8	3.5/11½	1/3¼	3.5/11½
M 9	Very dwarfing	2/6½	3/10	0.75/2½	3/10
M 27	Extremely dwarfing	1.5/5	1.5/5	0.75/2½	NR

NR – not recommended

The numbers of trees to plant will depend on the amount of fruit that you require and the space that you have available. But bear in mind that with apples at least, you have a wide range of choices in the ultimate size of your trees. So, by selecting an appropriate rootstock onto which your chosen fruiting variety is grafted (see the Table), you may be able to have many more varieties than you imagined in your available space. With apples also, it is possible to buy so-called family trees, where several different varieties have been grafted onto the same roots. This neatly circumvents another complication in choosing fruit trees for your garden. For apples and pears especially are not self-fertile; in other words, another compatible variety (or, in a very few cases, two additional varieties) are needed in order for pollination and fruit set to occur. In the Table, I have indicated suitable combinations of varieties, therefore, rather than individuals.

In the early years, an annual top dressing of blood, fish and bone at about 80 g per square metre (2½ oz per sq yd) in late winter, followed by a thick organic moisture-retaining mulch is important. And of course, where fruit trees are planted in a lawn or among grass generally, an area of about 1 metre (1 yard) diameter should be kept clear (of both grass and weeds) around them. After five or six years however, it is safe to grass up to the base of the trees and to cease feeding on all except the poorest soils.

Pest and disease problems should be expected but should seldom cause alarm. Protective measures generally are only worthwhile on young plants, although a tar oil winter wash is a sound routine practice on trees of all ages. On old and established apple trees, you must accept that a proportion of the fruit will fall prey to brown rot, scab and codling moth.

Training and then, in later years, routine pruning is important with all types of fruit tree and varies rather importantly one from the other. Sadly, the self-pruning apple tree is not yet with us but whilst there are numerous pruning systems to choose from, I have described briefly the simplest of those that I have found effective for garden use. For more detail or for other pruning systems, refer to specialist literature. I recommend that apples and pears be grown as open-centred dwarf bush trees or as cordons and have shown diagrammatically how this initial training is achieved. Plums, cherries, peaches and apricots are best trained as fans and on p. 69 I have shown how to form a fan.

Forming an open-centred dwarf bush

(a) Immediately (or in the first winter) after planting a feathered maiden (a young tree with side-branches – the best type to buy), cut back the leading shoot and the side branches to their bases.

(b) In the second winter, cut back between three and five of the side-branches by one half to two thirds; cut out completely any additional side-branches.

(c) In the next winter, cut back the side branches by one half to two thirds. Thereafter, follow the pruning outlined on p. 144.

Forming a cordon

(d) Immediately (or in the first winter) after planting a feathered maiden, cut back all side-shoots more than 10 cm (4 in.) long to three buds from their bases. Do not prune the leading shoot.

(e) After the first summer's pruning (see p. 144), the tree will appear like this in its second winter.

(f) After the second summer's pruning, fruiting spurs will have begun to form and the tree will appear like this in its third winter. Thereafter, this form will be maintained by the summer pruning described on p. 144.

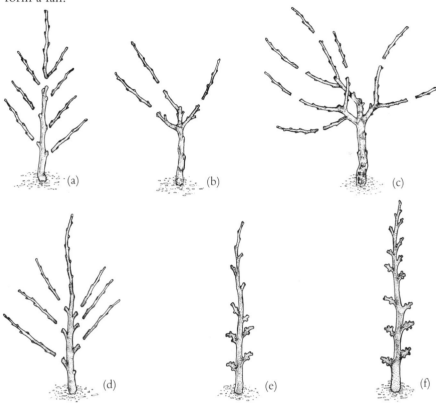

RECOMMENDED APPLE VARIETIES WITH SUGGESTED POLLINATOR VARIETIES

Dessert varieties	Recommended pollinator	
'Beauty of Bath'	'Greensleeves' or 'Idared'	Very early, yellow with red flush, poor keeper
'Blenheim Orange' (dual purpose)	'Greensleeves' plus 'Discovery' (triploid)	Mid-season, yellow with red purpose markings, heavy crop, good keeper
'Crispin'	'Greensleeves' plus 'Discovery' (triploid)	Mid-season, golden-yellow, good keeper
'Discovery'	'Greensleeves'	Early, green-yellow with red markings, the best keeper among early varieties
'Ellison's Orange'	'Greensleeves'	Early-mid-season, golden with red markings, must be eaten fresh
'Fortune'	'Discovery', 'Greensleeves' or 'James Grieve'	Early, yellow with red markings, not a good keeper
'Greensleeves'	'Discovery' or 'Grenadier'	Early-mid-season, green-gold, good keeper
'Idared'	'Discovery'	Late, yellow with red flush, good keeper
'James Grieve' (dual purpose)	'Discovery'	Mid-season, yellow with orange markings, not a good keeper

'Jupiter'	'Discovery' plus 'Spartan' or 'Sunset' (triploid)	Mid-season – late, orange over yellow, good keeper
'Kent'	'James Grieve'	Late, green with orange markings, good keeper
'Redsleeves'	'Greensleeves' or 'Fortune'	Early, red, keeps for short period
'Spartan'	'Discovery' or 'Greensleeves'	Mid-season, dark red, good keeper
'Sunset'	'James Grieve'	Mid-season, yellow with red flush, good keeper
'Tydeman's Late Orange'	'Greensleeves' or 'Spartan'	Mid-season, golden yellow with orange markings, good keeper
'Worcester Pearmain'	'Greensleeves'	Early, red over yellow, poor keeper

Cooking varieties	Recommended pollinator	
'Bramley's Seedling'	'Spartan' plus 'Discovery' (triploid)	Late, very large, green, very good keeper
'Grenadier'	'Discovery' or 'Greensleeves'	Early, yellow-green, moderate keeper
'Howgate Wonder'	'Spartan' or 'Tydeman's Late Orange'	Late, golden yellow, good keeper, very hardy
'Rev. W. Wilks'	'Idared'	Mid-season, green, moderate keeper

Apple   *Malus* spp. and hybrids   Rosaceae

Garden apple trees fall roughly into three main types, the crab, the dessert or eating apple and the more acid culinary apple or cooker (a fourth group, the very acid cider apple, is rarely grown in gardens). Some varieties are called dual purpose and are useful in limited space for they cook well but are not so acidic that they cannot be eaten fresh. Apples are amenable to a wide range of training systems, generally produce a good or even prolific crop with the minimum of attention, are available on a very wide range of rootstocks and are, all in all, the most versatile of all tree fruit.

PLANT: in late autumn.

SPACING: varies considerably depending on the rootstock and training system chosen (Table p. 142).

AFTER-CARE: Feed and mulch in late winter. Prune established cordons in late summer by cutting back all side-shoots longer than 20 cm to a point three leaves above the base and also cut back any small shoots arising from the side-shoots to one leaf above the basal leaf cluster. Once the leading shoot has reached its allotted length, treat it in the same way as the side shoots. Prune established free-standing trees by cutting back the side-shoots on each branch to two or three buds above the base in winter and shorten the leading shoots on each branch by up to one half (the less you need to cut back on established trees, the better, though vigorous trees can become out of end unless you cut back fairly hard).

PEST, DISEASE OR OTHER PROBLEMS: aphids, codling moth, red spider mite, winter moths, canker, fruit rots, honey fungus, mildew, scab.

HARVESTING: when the fruit part readily from the branch if lifted and twisted slightly; colour is no indication of maturity until you are familiar with the variety and its response to your local growing conditions.

STORING: fresh, in a uniformly cool, well ventilated place singly on slatted shelves or in slatted boxes, or in batches of about ten in clean plastic bags with small ventilation holes. Many of the later maturing varieties will remain sound on the tree through the winter.

RECOMMENDED VARIETIES: with well over 2000 existing varieties and probably around 100 readily available, choosing apples is difficult. It is compounded because many varieties will not thrive well in all areas and because the taste, even of familiar commercially grown types, may vary when grown in different parts of the country. The list that I have given therefore in the table is deliberately limited and highly personal but includes some varieties for the extremes of climate and covers most requirements in respect of use, time of maturing and keeping qualities.

Apricot   *Prunus armeniaca*   Rosaceae

In tems of cultivation, think of the apricot as like a peach, only more so. It is less hardy and it is even earlier in blossoming – the name apricot is derived from the Latin for early. In the past, apricots were much grown in greenhouses but for all practical garden purposes, they must be fan-trained against a warm south or south-west facing wall in a fairly mild area.

PLANT: in late autumn.

SPACING: 4 m (13 ft) for fan-trained plants on the rootstock 'St Julien A'.

AFTER-CARE: feed and mulch in late winter; check the pH of soils thought to be acidic and if necessary add lime in autumn to raise the alkalinity to at least pH 6.5. Provide removable protective screens of fine mesh netting or plastic sheet to place in front of the plants when the blossom opens. Hand pollinate blossom in spring. Prune established plants in spring and summer.

PEST, DISEASE OR OTHER PROBLEMS: aphids, red spider mite, bacterial canker, brown rot, peach leaf curl, silver leaf.

HARVESTING: gently feel the fruit for signs of softness close to the stalk, an indication of maturity. It helps to peg back the leaves as the fruit begin to colour in order to expose them to the maximum sunlight.

STORING: for short periods only, in refrigerator.

RECOMMENDED VARIETIES: 'Moorpark' (mid-season-late) – despite its late maturity, this is the most reliably cropping variety for gardens.

Cherry   *Prunus avium* and *P. cerasus*   Rosaceae

There are two distinct types of fruiting cherry for gardens – the sweet cherry which is a very difficult plant to grow, forming a large tree from which birds will remove all the fruit, and the acid cherry, suitable only for cooking, but much easier to grow as it produces a smaller tree. I recommend that both types be fan-trained against a wall where they can be protected with netting, although the vigour of the sweet cherry still makes it difficult to manage.

PLANT: in late autumn; acid cherries are especially suitable for north-facing walls.

SPACING: 5 m (16½ ft) for sweet cherries or 4 m (13 ft) for acid cherries, fan-trained on the semi-dwarfing rootstock 'Colt'.

AFTER-CARE: feed and mulch in late winter; check the pH of soils thought to be acidic and, if necessary, add lime in autumn to raise the alkalinity to at least pH 6.5. Provide removable protective screens of netting or plastic sheet to place in front of the plants to protect them from the birds as the fruit begin to ripen. Prune established plants in spring and summer (see Peach).

PEST, DISEASE OR OTHER PROBLEMS: aphids, birds, bacterial canker, silver leaf.

HARVESTING: when fully coloured, with the stalk intact – it is easier to cut them with scissors or snips rather than pull them.

STORING: freeze; cherries do not store well fresh.

RECOMMENDED VARIETIES: *Sweet cherry:* 'Stella' (late) – the only self-fertile sweet cherry and valuable therefore because it is often very difficult to find room for two fan-trained plants to pollinate each other. *Acid cherry:* 'Morello' – widely available and self-fertile.

Cobnuts and Filberts   *Corylus avellana* and *C. maxima*   Betulaceae

The cultivated cobnut is derived from the wild hazelnut; the filbert, with a shaggy husk, is a continental European species. Both make attractive and useful plants for the wilder, wooded areas of large gardens where they will have room to grow and also obtain the light shade and shelter needed.

PLANT: in late autumn.

SPACING: 5 m (16½ ft) – plant a small copse with a mixture of different varieties (see below).

AFTER-CARE: feed and mulch in late winter. Prune established plants biannually in winter and summer and maintain an open-centred tree with about ten main shoots.

PEST, DISEASE OR OTHER PROBLEMS: nut weevil, squirrels, mildew.

HARVESTING: when the husks begin to turn pale; this coincides with the first few nuts dropping from the trees.

STORING: dried.

RECOMMENDED VARIETIES: although nut trees are self-fertile, the male and female flowers do not always open simultaneously so it is wise to plant a mixture of varieties with slightly staggered flowering times. A useful mixture is 'Nottingham Cob' as a cobnut with 'Kentish Cob' (despite its name, actually a type of filbert) and the 'Purple-leaved Filbert', a highly ornamental plant with a more modest crop but of well flavoured nuts.

Fig   *Ficus carica*   Moraceae

Figs are hardy plants but will only produce fruit in Britain in warm, sheltered positions and are always best when fan-trained against a south or south-west facing wall. They differ from other fruit trees in two main respects – they must have poor, almost starving soil conditions and the small embryo fruit formed towards the end of one season are those that mature and ripen in the next. To satisfy the former requirement, they are best planted in a mixture of soil and rubble with their roots confined laterally by 60 cm (24 in) concrete slabs; figs may also be grown in large containers. And in order not to remove the young fruits, pruning must be performed thoughtfully.

PLANT: in spring.

SPACING: one fan-trained plant will usually suffice, for figs are self-fertile.

AFTER-CARE: apply no fertiliser but ensure that the plants are well watered as the fruit swell in early summer. Prune established plants in late spring. Cut out any branches growing directly towards or away from the wall and then, in early summer, cut back all new shoots to a point just above five leaves from the base.

PEST, DISEASE OR OTHER PROBLEMS: coral spot.

HARVESTING: when hanging down and soft, preferably at the first signs of the skin splitting.

STORING: not practicable other than for short periods in refrigerator.

RECOMMENDED VARIETIES: 'Brown Turkey' is most commonly seen and I have found it fully reliable.

Peach and Nectarine   *Prunus persica*   Rosaceae

Although peaches are often thought of as an exclusively warm-climate crop, they are in fact fairly hardy and will crop well in Britain, given shelter. It is cold springs that cause the problems and therefore, even in the south, the best conditions are provided by fan-training them against a wall; I do not recommend growing peaches as free standing trees. The nectarine is a smooth-skinned but more delicious variety of peach and is grown similarly.

PLANT: in late autumn.

SPACING: 4 m (13 ft) for fan-trained plants on the rootstock 'St Julien A'.

AFTER-CARE: feed and mulch in late winter; check the pH of soils thought to be acidic and, if necessary, add lime in autumn to raise the alkalinity to at least pH 6.5. Hand pollinate blossom in spring. Prune established fan-trained plants by cutting out in spring any shoots growing directly towards or away from the wall then, on each blossom bearing side-shoot, pinch out some of the leafy buds to leave one at the tip, one at the base (this will form the replacement side-shoot) and one in the middle. In early summer, pinch back each side-shoot to a point just above six leaves from the base. In late summer or early autumn, cut back each fruited side-shoot to its junction with the new side-shoot and then tie in this new, replacement shoot.

PEST, DISEASE OR OTHER PROBLEMS: aphids, red spider mite, bacterial canker, brown rot, peach leaf curl, silver leaf.

HARVESTING: gently feel the fruit for signs of softness close to the stalk, an indication of maturity. It helps to peg back the leaves as the fruit begin to colour in order to expose them to the maximum sunlight.

STORING: for short periods only in refrigerator.

RECOMMENDED VARIETIES: *Peaches:* 'Peregrine' (early) – a valuable variety for areas with a shorter growing season as it ripens so early; 'Rochester' (early but slightly later than 'Peregrine') – a slightly hardier American variety but I think with marginally less flavour. *Nectarines:* 'Lord Napier' (mid-season) – the most reliable and widely available variety. All peaches and nectarines are self-fertile.

Pear   *Pyrus communis*   Rosaceae

Cordon pears, grown against wall and netted

Pears are less amenable to cultivation than apples for they are slower to mature, less hardy and very difficult to grow satisfactorily in exposed gardens. There is little choice in rootstock types, none of which are very dwarfing, and the mature pear can be a very large tree. Nonetheless, when growing against a warm wall, a well trained espalier pear is a joy to behold and can yield fruit, which, when of the best varieties, is quite splendid.

PLANT: in late autumn.

SPACING: varies depending on the training system chosen (see Table p. 142 and use spacings given for apples on MM 106).

AFTER-CARE: feed and mulch in late winter. Prune cordon or espalier trees biannually in summer and winter, free-standing trees in winter only as for apples although much less pruning is needed.

PEST, DISEASE OR OTHER PROBLEMS: canker, fireblight, fruit rots, honey fungus, mildew, scab, pear midge, winter moths.

HARVESTING: pears should be picked when slightly under-ripe, when the fruit part readily from the branch if lifted and twisted slightly; most varieties turn slightly paler when ready for picking but pears mature unevenly and you should not therefore attempt to pick all of the crop at the same time.

STORING: fresh, in a uniformly cool, well ventilated place, singly on slatted shelves or in slatted boxes. Pears should preferably be stored away from apples because they must be inspected frequently and each fruit removed as it ripens and softens. Hard, cooking varieties that you may find as old trees in established gardens (but are certainly not worth planting anew) may be left on the tree over the winter and picked as needed.

RECOMMENDED VARIETIES: 'William Bon Chrétien' (early) – perhaps the most reliable early, moderately hardy dessert pear; 'Conference' (mid-season) – the best and hardiest all-round pear which is a good culinary variety and, with keeping, makes acceptable dessert fruit too. A solitary tree of 'Conference' will set some fruit on its own but is always best with another pollinator variety; 'Doyenné du Comice' (mid-late season) – the most succulent of all dessert pears but must have a warm, sunny site. In most gardens, these varieties will all pollinate each other but if you have trouble obtaining fruit set on any of them, consult a local fruit nurseryman who will suggest an additional variety appropriate to your area.

Plum (including Gage) *Prunus domestica* and Damson *P. insititia*   Rosaceae

Plums have the major advantage that, if grown as free-standing trees, once established and trained they require very little pruning. Against this must be set the fact that they always produce the best fruit in warm conditions, and in less favourable areas are much better trained against a wall as fans, although of course, the annual pruning needed is much greater. Plums suffer too in colder areas because their blossom opens fairly early in the spring and is therefore prone to late frost damage. Only two rootstocks are commonly available for garden use. Neither causes much restriction in growth, and as plums are naturally vigorous plants, they cannot really be considered suitable trees for very small gardens. Gages are small, predominantly rounded green or yellow plums with an individual flavour, and generally need more favourable growing conditions. They may be grown in the same manner as other plums. Damsons are smaller related fruit on rather hardier trees which are usually grown free-standing.

PLANT: in late autumn.

SPACING: 5 m (16½ ft) (free standing or fan-trained trees on rootstock 'St Julien A'), or 3 m (10 ft) (free standing or fan-trained trees on rootstock 'Pixy').

AFTER-CARE: feed and mulch in late winter; lightly prune established free-standing trees in spring. Prune established fan-trained plants in spring by removing any shoots growing directly towards or away from the wall, then, in summer, pinch back all side-shoots to a point just above six leaves from the base and then, immediately after the fruit have been picked, cut them back by half.

PEST, DISEASE OR OTHER PROBLEMS: aphids, brown rot, bacterial canker, honey fungus, silver leaf disease.

HARVESTING: very difficult to judge accurately because plums do not continue to ripen well once they have been picked but if they are left on the tree too long, they will succumb to birds, wasps and brown rot.

STORING: not satisfactory.

RECOMMENDED VARIETIES: 'Victoria' (mid-season) – easily the most reliable and valuable all-round variety for dessert and culinary use; 'Marjorie's Seedling' (late) – a very useful, heavy cropping all-round variety to follow on from 'Victoria'; 'Oulin's Golden Gage' (early) – the best of the widely available dessert gages; 'Merryweather' – the most prolific, easy and widely available damson with very large fruit. All of these recommended varieties are self-fertile so no pollinators are needed.

Walnut *Juglans regia* Juglandaceae

Few gardeners plant walnuts although those with larger gardens often inherit established trees. Given space, however, the walnut is worth planting provided you choose your tree carefully and have the patience to wait several years before it begins to crop.

PLANT: in late autumn.

SPACING: 5 m (16½ ft) – plant a small copse of trees to ensure pollination; with the pruning method suggested, they will stay of more or less manageable size.

AFTER-CARE: feed and mulch in late winter; continually pinch back the shoot tips to about six leaves, although leave alone the shoots bearing the male flowers. This will help induce fruiting earlier than the 10–15 years usually required. Do not attempt to prune mature trees.

PEST, DISEASE OR OTHER PROBLEMS: nut rot.

HARVESTING: as the nuts drop, for fresh use, but pick whilst still soft if they are required for pickling.

STORING: dry.

RECOMMENDED VARIETIES: there are several named varieties of walnut but these are largely of academic interest as trees hardly ever seem to be named when they are offered for sale. It is more important that you buy from an experienced fruit nursery and obtain grafted plants with the scion taken from a parent tree known to be freely fruiting. The male flowers may be recognised for they occur in typical drooping catkins, while the female flowers are in short spikes.

CLIMBING FRUIT

Grapevine *Vitis vinifera* Vitaceae

Grapevines were once very important outdoor crops in Britain and, even now, an increasing number of vineyards is to be seen. But although outdoor vines are to be found in gardens, this is not a reliable way to obtain a crop in most parts of the country and I am restricting myself therefore to describing unheated greenhouse cultivation.

PLANT: in early spring (for preference) or late autumn; much the best system is to plant just outside the greenhouse and then pass the main shoot in through a hole close to the base of the greenhouse wall. In a greenhouse with wooden or brick bases, this is simply made, but with a house that is glazed to ground level, a pane must be removed and replaced with a wooden board through which the hole can be cut. Prepare the planting position with liberal amounts of compost, broken bricks to improve drainage and 2.5–3 kg (5–6 lb) of John Innes Base fertiliser.

SPACING: one plant will suffice.

AFTER-CARE: feed and mulch in late winter; ensure that the roots are never allowed to dry out once the fruit begin to swell; Prune established plants in winter by cutting back all side-shoots to two buds from the base, where they join the main rod(s). In spring, allow one only of the new shoots to elongate from each point and tie it in to the training wires, pinching out the tip when it reaches its allotted length. Pinch out side shoots to one leaf above each flower cluster and any shoots arising from the side-shoots to one leaf from their base. Carefully snip out about half of the young fruit within each bunch with scissors.

PEST, DISEASE OR OTHER PROBLEMS: red spider mite, scale insects, grey mould, mildew.

HARVESTING: as the fruit attain full colour.

STORING: for short periods only in refrigerator.

RECOMMENDED VARIETIES: 'Black Hamburgh' (black) – probably the best and easiest all-round black dessert variety; 'Muscat of Alexandria' (white) – a superbly flavoured grape although one that will only attain full ripeness and sweetness in very warm conditions. It is improbable that you will have a sufficiently large greenhouse to produce enough grapes for wine-making, so if this is your objective, you should first ensure that you live in an area with a suitable climate and then investigate the techniques of outdoor production.

Kiwi fruit (Chinese gooseberry) *Actinidia chinensis* Actinidiaceae

---

Only since New Zealand discovered the marketable properties of this fruit has it become familiar to European consumers who now seem to want to grow it in their gardens also. It is really too vigorous for all but the larger greenhouses and must therefore be grown outside. It is generally hardier and more tolerant of cold than grapevines, although in many respects there is similarity between their cultivation.

PLANT: in early spring (for preference) or late autumn; although for large-scale production, kiwi fruit are trained against wires like vineyard grapes, the most reliable method for gardens is against a warm, tall wall.

SPACING: 6 m (20 ft), although nurseries sometimes offer a female and a male plant in the same container to ensure good pollination. These should be treated as one plant for spacing purposes.

AFTER-CARE: feed and mulch in late winter; ensure that the roots are never allowed to dry out once the fruit begin to swell; prune routinely in winter and thin and train shoots as they form during spring and summer as for grapevine.

PEST, DISEASE OR OTHER PROBLEMS: aphids, red spider mite.

HARVESTING: as the fruit attain full colour and feel slightly soft to the touch.

STORING: in refrigerator.

RECOMMENDED VARIETIES: kiwi fruits are unisexual so a male pollinator plant will be required (one male will be sufficient for up to seven females). The best fruiting female for British conditions is probably 'Hayward' and the most suitable male 'Atlas' or 'Matua', although you may find that nurseries merely offer an unnamed male clone when you purchase your fruiting variety.

The lawn

I ALWAYS find it slightly irritating when I hear gardeners complain about the chore of lawn-mowing. I realise that it can seem like nothing but a treadmill through the summer months; and of course with the milder winters that have been experienced several times recently, it can seem almost a twelve-month treadmill. But my irritation stems simply from two things, the first being that once it is mown and preferably edged too, a lawn can almost instantly bring to a garden a neatness and tidiness that nothing else can emulate; and second, because, despite the mowing, there is quite definitely no easier way of keeping an area of garden under control than by growing grass on it. For grass is the easiest of all plants to grow and it is the most efficient at suppressing weeds. And a lawn need not only be thought of as a permanent part of the garden, for in the early stages of gardening on a new site it makes a great deal of sense to grow grass over most of it, cutting beds and borders out later as time and other practicalities allow. The special feature of grass (or at least of the species used for turfing) that makes it such a useful plant is its ability to tolerate mowing. It achieves this by having the cells that are responsible for growth at the base, not the top, of the stem. If you cut off most types of plant at ground level, they will die through an inability to regenerate, but a grass will thrive on this treatment and not only grow again but also be stimulated into producing further shoots. The only other way that a plant can survive being mown is if its growing point is at the shoot tip and the shoot itself is telescoped in such a way that the whole is sunken below mowing level – this is the mechanism by which such common lawn weeds as dandelions and daisies survive.

A rustic archway provides a valuable focal point at the end of a lawn.

Grass will grow on almost any soil and on almost any type of site, although you will never have a successful lawn if the area is heavily shaded. The reason for this will be evident if you walk through a woodland; there are very few grasses growing there and those that do are in fact species that do not respond satisfactorily to mowing.

Before proceeding to describe lawn cultivation in detail, I should perhaps mention why I am confining my comments to grass, when you may have read or heard that other plants can also be used to create lawns. Such plants as thymes, some of the carpeting species of *Dianthus* and the non-flowering variety of camomile called 'Treneague' can certainly be used to create flat areas of greenery that can tolerate being walked on. But only to a very limited extent. None of them will tolerate the amount of wear and tear that grass turf can absorb. All of them look dismal in winter and will in any event only thrive in the sunniest situation and on light, free-draining soil. And all of them must be hand-weeded, for being broad-leaved plants themselves, selective weedkillers cannot of course be used on them. In short, I consider such 'lawns' to be small-scale curiosity features for large gardens rather than genuine substitutes for genuine lawns.

Having selected the area where your lawn will be laid, it is important to begin the site preparation as far in advance as is practicable. The area should be dug thoroughly, much as you would for the preparation of a vegetable garden (p. 114). If it can be double dug, so much the better, but because of the likely size of the area concerned, this is not an operation to be undertaken lightly. It is nonetheless important to remove all perennial weed growth, especially of couch grass. For whilst broad-leaved weeds can be controlled fairly satisfactorily by selective weedkillers after the lawn is established, weed grasses will be extremely difficult to eradicate. If the area is infested with couch therefore (especially on a heavy soil from which it is impossible to remove it by digging) my advice would be to begin your preparation in late spring and to use one of the systemic weedkillers, glyphosate or alloxydim

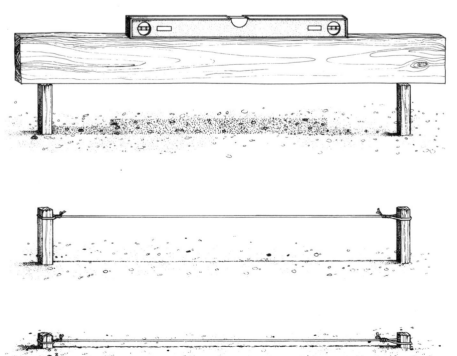

To level the site for a lawn, hammer in wooden pegs in a grid pattern over the area. Lay a plank across adjacent pairs of pegs and, on this, place a spirit level. Hammer in the pegs until the plank is horizontal and repeat this process over the whole area. Tie strings just below the top of each peg and then add soil up to the level of the strings.

sodium, throughout the summer. Then dig the area in the autumn with a view to laying the new lawn in the following spring. This may seem a long time over which to be patient but the effort will be more than repaid in the years to come.

If the site is markedly irregular, you will need to level it. This is done simply with wooden pegs and string. Hammer in the pegs 2 m (6½ ft) apart and a few centimetres deep, in a grid pattern. Lay a plank across adjacent pairs of pegs in turn, place a spirit level on top and then hammer in the pegs until all are level. Then tie string between the pegs at the lawn level required – if you tie the string at the same distance below the top of each peg, you will have a level grid pattern. Fill up to the strings with top soil; you will probably have to buy some specially for the purpose if you don't want to excavate a large hole elsewhere in the garden. Firm the soil as you fill – I find there is nothing better for this than the back of a garden rake – but always finish with a surface about 1 cm (½ in) higher than you really require, to allow for the soil settling. On a very irregularly sloping site you may need to grade the area (see diagram) but don't imagine that the surface of a good lawn must always be flat. A gentle, fairly uniform slope can be most attractive.

To grade an irregular site, use a levelled grid pattern of wooden pegs as shown on p. 149 but instead of tying string onto the wooden pegs (which would hinder the soil moving operation), simply mark the pegs at the level you wish the lawn surface to lie. Then use a rake to move the soil until it is flush with the mark on each peg – you may need to repeat the operation and raise the whole surface by a few centimetres more than you planned if you have a great deal of excess soil left over.

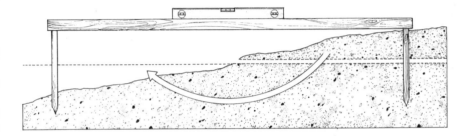

In general, the best months for laying a new lawn are April and September, although in favourable seasons turf can be laid at any time when there are no hard frosts and when rain can be expected with some confidence – artificial watering is never as effective at helping a lawn to establish. About one month before you intend to lay the lawn, give the surface a raking with a spring-tined lawn rake, carefully removing any large clods and stones. Rake alternately in directions at right angles to each other in order not to produce or accentuate any humps and hollows. Having prepared the site for your new lawn, you will need to apply a pre-sowing or turfing fertiliser and this should be done about three weeks later – or about one week before the actual start. It is simplest to use an autumn lawn feed with a relatively low nitrogen content and you should use this even if you are actually starting your lawn in the spring. Apply it at the manufacturer's recommended rate and rake it carefully into the top few centimetres of the soil.

The surface should then be firmed but this must not be done with a roller. Unless you have a very wide, lightweight roller and are skilled in using it, you will undo all your hard work and finish up with a surface like a roller-coaster track. There is no better tool for firming the surface than a pair of feet (or preferably many pairs of feet), shod in boots. Tread steadily and evenly (not with a 'heeling in' action), working your way over the surface. Tamping down the soil with the back of a garden rake may help.

Up to this stage, the operation is the same whether you intend to lay turf or sow seed, and so it is now appropriate for me to consider their relative merits. Having put down more of both in my time than I care to remember, my choice now is firmly on the side of turf. It is quicker, easier and more sure of success although it is certainly more expensive. Seedling lawns are at the mercy of the weather and the local bird population. They are also at the mercy of being swamped by weed seedlings, especially now there is no longer a suitable weedkiller available to gardeners for newly sown lawns. Nonetheless, I realise that there will be many gardeners who do still prefer seeding or who may simply have an area of potential lawn that would be prohibitively costly to turf. For them, there is now an extensive range of lawn seed mixtures, although I advise you not to become too enthusiastic about those that are offered for sowing in shade or partial shade. For the reasons that I have already indicated, the results may be marginally better than with a normal lawn seed mixture but nothing will permit you to grow a lawn satisfactorily in a woodland glade.

The principal choice to be made in seed mixtures is between those sold for fine lawns and those for lawns that will have to bear considerable wear and tear. In essence, a fine lawn seed mixture comprising various fescues and bent grasses is only worth using for a lawn that is seldom walked on. For the normal domestic lawn it is essential to choose a blend containing hard-wearing rye grasses – among which the modern hybrid varieties can give a very attractive appearance, possessing little of the coarseness of the older types. Spread the seed as uniformly as you can at the rate of about 175 g per 4 square metres (4 oz per 4 sq yds). This is actually easier than it might sound if you mark off the area into squares with string or canes, for you will find that most seed companies supply a small measure or shaker with the seed, or sometimes rather imaginatively provide a picture showing the density of seed to aim for. Although it is sometimes suggested that the seed should be left uncovered, I much prefer to spread finely sieved soil or peat over the surface so that the seed is just rendered invisible. It is then essential to provide protection from birds, and the simplest way to do this is to spread lightweight fruit cage netting over the area, supporting it on upturned plastic plant pots on the tops of canes. Use a lawn sprinkler with a very fine spray to ensure that the surface neither dries out nor is washed into ridges. The seed should germinate from 14 to 21 days later.

Lawn turf too has improved beyond recognition and I hope that the days of 'meadow turf', bought through the small advertisement columns of the local newspaper, are gone forever. Meadow turf is for grazing cattle, not for making lawns. For relatively little extra cost you can now buy specially grown turf, available in three or four different grades of fine or hard-wearing components, comparable with the seed mixtures. It is worth remembering several important things when planning to turf a lawn. The turf will be delivered in rolls which are extremely heavy, so have them dropped as close as possible to the area where they are to be laid. If you cannot lay them within about seven days, the grass will turn yellow and so they must be unrolled and stored flat – but of course you will need an area at least as large as your new lawn on which to do this. Lay the turves overlapping, rather like the bricks in a wall, and use a lawn edging iron to cut them to shape. Always stand on a plank when cutting and laying the turf to avoid damaging it. And never lay a small piece of turf at the end of a row – it will dry and shrink. Pull a full-sized piece to the edge and use a small cut-off piece to fill in the gap that this leaves. Firmly tamp down the turves with the back of a strong garden rake and brush fine soil in between them. Don't worry if you spill soil on the

Lay turves in an overlapping brick-style pattern but never use a short length at the end of a row where it will fray; move larger turves and insert the short piece in the resulting gap.

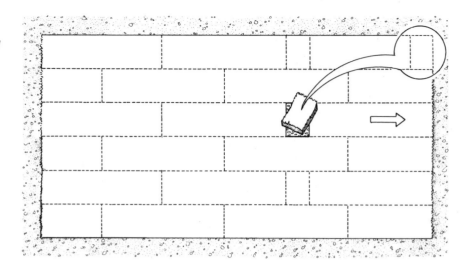

surface; the rain will soon wash it in. Use a sprinkler on the new lawn if rain doesn't fall within a few hours, and do not allow it to dry out fully for about ten days; after this time it should have taken root and can be walked on. It can be cut after about a further fortnight (preferably with a rotary mower) if the mower blades are set high.

Once established, your lawn must be given some care and attention if it is to be elevated from being merely a patch of green to a garden feature of which you can be proud. Of course, the most important routine lawn task is mowing and on p. 56 I have already given some guidance on the type of mower to choose. Try to mow at least once, and preferably twice, a week during the main growing season – from April to September in what used to be called an average year. Outside these months, the amount of mowing needed will depend on the prevailing temperature and the degree to which the grass has grown. Certainly in some recent years lawns have barely stopped growing right through the winter, and there is no reason why they should not be cut from time to time in mild periods during the winter months. But always set the cutter blades to their highest at these times – cutting the grass short when frosts are still likely is asking for trouble, in the form of the death of the leaves and consequent attack by disease-causing fungi. During the summer, however, the blades can be lowered appreciably, although I think it always unwise, other perhaps than on bowling greens, to cut grass at the lowest blade setting of all, for this merely encourages the growth of moss (see below). If your mower has a grass collector, my advice is that you should always use it; unless you are cutting almost daily, and the output of the mower therefore is of minute fragments, the mowings will be very likely to block the surface of the grass and prevent the free penetration of air and water.

It is almost impossible, in most gardens, to avoid the lawn becoming a pathway to somewhere or withstanding at least some sporting or domestic wear and tear. Where the lawn does become a regular pathway, it makes sense to accept this fact and lay either a conventional path across it or at least a series of stepping stones. But where the edges of the lawn become eroded through being stepped on or having wheeled mowers or barrows bumped over them there is another option. This is to peg heavy-duty plastic netting over the area. Special netting is sold for this purpose, and if it is laid when the lawn is wet, in autumn, it soon disappears into the surface of the turf whilst preventing it from disintegrating.

In my comments on other lawn tools, I have suggested the other important lawn care tasks – edging, raking and scarifying. But lawns must also be fed and I suggested on p. 65 that two lawn fertilisers were needed, one for spring use and one for the autumn. I am not convinced that it is worth spending money and effort on high nitrogen 'green-up' feeds for use in the summer, simply to achieve the cosmetic effect of darkening the colour of the grass. But I do delay applying the spring feed until late April or even early May when the soil is really warm and moist; and I do this not so much for the benefit of the fertiliser itself, but to ensure that the weedkiller that is combined with it is applied in conditions in which it is likely to be effective. And having done this, I usually find that no further overall weedkiller application is needed. Any weeds that do escape this treatment are dealt with later by localised application of a selective weedkiller in liquid form, either with a watering can (kept specially for the purpose) or with a weedkiller sprayer (although not with a hose-end diluter). And I mustn't forget that many gardeners today do not, in any event, seek to have weed-free lawns and find the presence of daisies or other native plants enhances their appearance.

One lawn weed, if it can be called such, causes gardeners more anguish and concern than any other. I would cherish a pound for every time that I have been asked how to rid a lawn of moss and certainly nothing brings a smile to my fellow-gardeners' faces more than when I tell them that I have moss, and plenty of it, on my own lawns. Actually, to kill moss is not difficult. Any of the modern selective moss-killers will do it, although none I think more effectively than lawn sand. But assuredly the moss will return unless it is possible to correct its underlying causes. Moss will thrive when the grass is closely mown, when the lawn is shaded and poorly drained and the grass not fed. On many lawns, the site characteristics are all but impossible to alter or correct and all I can do is to ask that you keep the problem in perspective. Don't mow too closely, aerate and scarify the lawn as frequently as you can manage, feed the grass twice a year, use lawn sand once a year to keep the moss in check; and don't lose too much sleep over the whole affair.

Apart from weeds, lawns suffer relatively little from other problems; there are few diseases and few pests likely to cause concern. Perhaps the commonest of the symptoms that you are likely to see are brown patches, although their causes are numerous. Fungal diseases are one possibility, leather-jackets or wireworms are others; but urine from bitches and spilled lawn mower petrol are at least as frequent. The more or less circular rings of toadstools called fairy rings also cause concern although I happen to find them attractive. Certainly, without wholesale excavation, you will be unlikely to be able to do anything to control them so you may as well join me and persuade yourself that they are fascinating.

Use a hosepipe and canes to mark the shape of a curved lawn edge.

The garden hedge

I DISCUSSED the value and importance of garden boundaries in general on p. 19. But I believe the hedge has a very special part to play and should be the preferred choice of boundary wherever possible; even if in some instances it must be used alongside a fence or a wall. Hedges extend the life of the garden up to its very limits and have a softness that no physical barrier ever will. They also harbour wild life, providing nesting and roosting places for birds, and shelter and homes for small mammals and countless types of insect. This is, of course, a two-edged attribute, for not all the wild life resident in the hedge is beneficial to the rest of the garden, and pest species are given shelter and overwinter quarters there too. Nonetheless, this is a small price to pay for helping ensure the survival of at least a few metres of one of the most fascinating of semi-natural habitats, one that has disappeared over vast areas of commercial farmland.

All hedges satisfy some of the most important criteria for an efficient wind protection – they are pliable and they are at least partly permeable. And because of the regular trimming that you give them, their height is very low in relation to the extent and depth of their root systems. So even in the strongest of gales, hedges are almost never damaged.

Because hedges, by their very purpose, are likely to be exposed to the full force of the wind, it is essential that species hardy enough to survive this in your area must be chosen. But I stress, hardy enough in your area, for in mild districts even such relatively tender species as fuchsias will be satisfactory. And the choice of fuchsia as a hedge raises another important issue, for whilst it does offer considerable protection against the wind, it is also a most attractive flowering plant in its own right. In mild areas, this dual role is relatively easily satisfied; there are few hedging plants that will fulfil their protective role in very exposed gardens yet still double-up as flowering

This copper beech hedge has an ornamental as well as a functional role.

shrubs. It is also worth stressing the usefulness of hedges *within* a garden too, where their role is to subdivide or even provide a low edging to some other feature. Here, toughness in the face of the wind is of much less importance and it is possible to choose plants much more positively for their attractiveness.

Perhaps the two most important criteria in choosing hedging species are first, the speed of growth, and second whether the plants should be deciduous or evergreen. Every gardener wanting to install a boundary screen desires results quickly. But unfortunately, a hedge that grows quickly enough to satisfy this requirement then continues growing quickly in its endeavour to become a tree. You must appreciate, therefore, that if your screen is to develop quickly, you will of necessity have an appreciable amount more trimming to do in future years. An evergreen hedge will of course supply you with all-year-round privacy but although a leafless deciduous hedge can, to some degree, be seen through, its windbreak effect is still perfectly adequate. The problem in selecting an evergreen hedge is that the fastest growing types are conifers which some people find dull (although I would argue against this), and which suffer from the drawback of continuing to grow quickly. The more attractive evergreens are slower growing and/or much more tender. A very valuable compromise is achieved with beech, which is fairly slow growing and, although deciduous, retains its dead leaves attractively and usefully through the winter. Hedges composed of a mixture of species are most attractive and in the Table I have suggested some possibilities.

SHRUB SPECIES COMBINATIONS SUITABLE FOR MIXED HEDGES

NATIVE SPECIES HEDGE

Alder buckthorn *Rhamnus frangula*
Beech *Fagus sylvatica*
Bird cherry *Prunus avium*
Blackthorn *Prunus spinosa*
Crab apple *Malus sylvestris*
Dog rose *Rosa canina*
Field maple *Acer campestre*
Guelder rose *Viburnum opulus*
Hawthorn *Crataegus monogyna*
Holly *Ilex aquifolium*
Hornbeam *Carpinus betulus*
Myrobalan plum *Prunus cerasifera*
Privet *Ligustrum vulgare*
Spindle *Euonymus europaeus*
Yew *Taxus baccata*

FLOWERING HEDGE

Flowering currant *Ribes sanguineum*
Forsythia *Forsythia × intermedia*
Rugosa rose *Rosa rugosa*

DWARF HEDGE

Box *Buxus sempervirens*
Lavender *Lavandula angustifolia*
Rosemary *Rosmarinus officinalis*

EVERGREEN HEDGE

Beech *Fagus sylvatica* (not strictly evergreen but retains dead foliage)
Holly *Ilex aquifolium*
Yew *Taxus baccata*

When planting a hedge, prepare the soil as thoroughly as possible – you will never have the opportunity again. This means double digging a trench and incorporating compost or well-rotted manure with a liberal dressing of bone meal. Spring is the best time to plant, and when the plants are in position, ensure that they are well watered during the first summer. Although hedges are thereafter usually neglected, it will repay you to feed with a general purpose fertiliser such as blood, fish and bone and mulch them, at least for the first few years, in order to obtain thick growth.

Buy the best quality hedging plants you can afford. If you are only planting a short run, then it is well worth choosing large, container-grown specimens. But of course if you have a hundred or more to buy, this is not realistic, and then you should buy directly from a forest nursery where the plants will be very much cheaper than from a garden centre.

The planting distance will vary with species, as I have indicated in the individual descriptions, but tall plants will always benefit from staking in the early stages. Where a particularly thick hedge for screening or perhaps protection from livestock is needed, it is worth planting a staggered double row of plants, with the distance between the two rows equal to three quarters of the distance that I recommend between the individual plants.

And so to the all important subject of trimming. You must have good equipment; good stainless steel hand shears, kept oiled and sharp, or the best powered trimmers that you can afford. For most garden hedges, powered trimmers with 35–40 cm (14–16 in) blades will be adequate. For very long hedges or those above about 1.5 m (5 ft) tall, however, 45 cm (18 in) will be very much more useful. High quality modern trimmers have built-in safety features to prevent accidental injury, but all electric models should of course be used with a mains circuit breaker. Petrol engined models tend to be more powerful but are usually very heavy to use for long periods. Always wear protective goggles and strong but flexible gloves when working. All hedge trimmings can be put through a compost shredder to make excellent compost and are most easily collected by laying old sheets or blankets alongside the hedge before you start – picking up small hedge trimmings from a gravel path is no task for a busy gardener. The frequency and timing of trimming varies from one type of hedge to the other and is mentioned in the individual descriptions. But unless you have a very good eye, it is always worth using lightweight stakes and a garden string, set with a spirit level, to ensure straight lines on formal, angularly trimmed hedges. After planting a new hedge, do not wait until the plants have attained the desired ultimate height before you start to cut. Trim them a little each year (cutting away approximately one third of the previous season's growth) to encourage bushiness.

Beech *Fagus sylvatica* Fagaceae

In many ways the ideal deciduous hedging plant, offering all-round screening by retaining its dead leaves during the winter. In spring, its fresh green colour is delightful. Its one drawback is a relatively slow growth rate.

SPACING: 30 cm (12 in).

AFTER-CARE: cut in late August and preferably late May also.

PEST, DISEASE OR OTHER PROBLEMS: beech aphid.

RECOMMENDED VARIETIES: the normal species is green leaved; *F. sylvatica purpurea* is the purple-leaved form which is very slightly slower growing.

Berberis spp.   Berberidaceae

I have eulogised over the merits of at least some berberis as shrubs on p. 170 and a few types make useful, prickly flowering hedges. They are fairly fast growing but not very dense, and apart from the more vigorous *B. stenophylla* should not be used where more than about 1.5 m (5 foot) in height is needed. Nonetheless, their prickles make them useful boundary markers and, with care and feeding, they can be very attractive with their yellow or golden spring flowers.

SPACING: 45–60 cm (18–24 in).

AFTER-CARE: trim lightly after flowering.

RECOMMENDED VARIETIES: the most vigorous hedging form is the evergreen *B. stenophylla* but the lower growing deciduous *B. thunbergii*, or its purple-leaved form *atropurpurea*, is better for small gardens. Forms of the glossy-leaved evergreen *B.* × *frikartii* and the exquisite *B. darwinii* are also sometimes sold for hedging but I find them less successful in this role.

Blackthorn, plums, sloe   *Prunus* spp.   Rosaceae

Wild plums and related species tend to be too coarse and open growing to make satisfactory hedges in small gardens although they are valuable as components of mixed farm-style hedges in more rural areas where their spring blossom makes a most attractive feature.

SPACING: 60 cm (24 in).

AFTER-CARE: trim after flowering.

RECOMMENDED VARIETIES: *P. cerasifera* (cherry plum, thorny twigs, white blossom in early spring before the leaves), the form called 'Pissardii' has dark purple leaves and pink-tinged blossom; *P. spinosa* (blackthorn, very, almost viciously, prickly, masses of white blossom in early spring, before the leaves).

Box   *Buxus sempervirens*   Buxaceae

The small evergreen leaves of box make it a good hedging plant (and useful too for topiary). It is fairly slow growing but rejuvenates moderately well when cut back hard into old wood. Box is not ideally suited for taller hedges, however, for apart from the patience needed to achieve results, it tends to open out at the base when allowed to grow much above 1.5 m (5 ft).

SPACING: 25 cm (10 in) (or 10 cm (4 in) for dwarf hedging – see below).

AFTER-CARE: trim in late May and late August.

RECOMMENDED VARIETIES: The normal species is widely sold for hedging but the best form for this purpose is 'Handsworthensis' with larger and more rounded leaves; among the several variegated forms, 'Elegantissima' and 'Gold Tip' are suitable for interplanting with the plain-leaved types in hedges – the other variegated types are less suitable in my experience; 'Suffruticosa', extremely slow growing and small leaved, ideal for dwarf hedging to edge around formal herb or other beds.

Cotoneaster spp. and hybrids   Rosaceae

Two species of cotoneaster are generally sold for hedging purposes – *C. lacteus*, evergreen with large, elliptical evergreen leaves, and *C. simonsii*, more or less evergreen in most areas but smaller, and with smaller leaves. Both have white flowers and dark red berries. Hedges of sorts can be planted with other species too, although for a distinctive ornamental rather than robustly functional appeal.

SPACING: 60 cm (24 in) (*C. lacteus* and other vigorous species); 30–45 cm (12–18 in) (*C. simonsii* and other less vigorous types).

AFTER-CARE: prune to shape in early spring and trim lightly after flowering.

RECOMMENDED VARIETIES: normal species only of *C. lacteus* and *C. simonsii* but others worth trying include *C. horizontalis* (p. 172) for a more or less two dimensional screen; *C.* × *watereri* is a fairly vigorous, semi-evergreen plant, akin to *C. lacteus* and useful for taller screening.

Escallonia hedge – Threave, Scotland

Escallonia spp. and hybrids   Escalloniaceae

Escallonias make splendid evergreen and flowering hedges in mild, especially seaside, areas; elsewhere they are almost useless for they will be killed back in hard winters. And the knowledge that they will usually regenerate is no compensation for the periodic loss of their screening effect.

SPACING: 45 cm (18 in).

AFTER-CARE: trim lightly after flowering and again in midsummer; the timing is complicated by the need to trim the foliage sufficiently near the end of the growing season for the hedge not to look unkempt during the winter, while not removing the following season's flower buds.

RECOMMENDED VARIETIES: *E. macrantha* (deep rose pink flowers) is the best hedging form although varieties such as 'Donard Seedling' (white, pink tinged) and 'C. F. Ball' (red), among others, are also sold for the purpose.

Flowering currant   *Ribes sanguineum*   Grossulariaceae

The flowering currant might not seem a very obvious hedging plant but for a tall, informal screen it can look most attractive, especially when interplanted with other ornamental species of similar size.

SPACING: 60 cm (24 in).

AFTER-CARE: trim lightly after flowering and again in late August; old plants will rejuvenate well after being cut back hard in spring.

RECOMMENDED VARIETIES: 'Pulborough Scarlet' with long, deep-red inflorescences is the best form for all purposes.

Forsythia spp. and hybrids   Oleaceae

Forsythias come in the same league as flowering currants as hedging plants. They offer relatively little screening, cannot be very closely clipped but their golden-yellow flowers are undoubtedly attractive *en masse* in the spring.

SPACING: 60 cm (24 in).

AFTER-CARE: trim lightly after flowering and again towards the end of August.

RECOMMENDED VARIETIES: the more upright-growing forms are best, *F. intermedia* 'Spectabilis' being the finest coloured of all.

Hawthorn, quickthorn *Crataegus monogyna* Rosaceae

The hawthorn or quickthorn has proved its worth over many centuries as a farm boundary fence. It is robust, dense, prickly, stock-proof and very amenable to being laid. It is also incidentally quite beautiful with its white blossom in spring. It is fairly slow to establish in the first few years but thereafter grows acceptably quickly. There is certainly nothing dainty or delicate about hawthorn and it is hardly appropriate for a small or urban garden. But for a large, rural boundary it is admirable.

SPACING: 30 cm (12 in).

AFTER-CARE: trim in early spring and again in late summer.

RECOMMENDED VARIETIES: choose the normal species only; selected forms and varieties are valuable as small trees (see p. 164) but not for hedging.

Hazel *Corylus avellana* Corylaceae

Hazel is an unusual and apparently rather odd choice for hedging but it is useful in a tall, mixed rural hedge with other native species. It is scarcely practical, however, to expect a reasonably neat hedge to be combined with a good crop of nuts, for although it is sensible and attractive to leave a small number of catkins when trimming, leaving them all will mean that so many branches are unshortened that the plant will very soon become a tree rather than a hedging shrub.

SPACING: 1 m (39 in).

AFTER-CARE: trim in early spring.

RECOMMENDED VARIETIES: choose the normal species only for hedging.

Holly *Ilex aquifolium* Aquifoliaceae

Holly hedges are probably the most impenetrable of all; and if that is your requirement, then holly should be your choice. It is fairly slow growing, especially in the early stages, but makes a valuable addition to a mixed hedge with other native species.

SPACING: 60 cm (24 in).

AFTER-CARE: trim in late summer.

RECOMMENDED VARIETIES: it is not really practical to have a trimmed holly hedge that also produces berries, for the flowers are inevitably removed in the cutting. For this reason, there is no need to choose a female form but it is worthwhile including a few plants of one of the variegated types with the normal green species to add interest.

Hornbeam *Carpinus betulus* Carpinaceae

Superficially very similar to beech although not related to it, hornbeam does not make as suitable a hedging plant for it does not retain its dead leaves through the winter as effectively. It is also much less widely available and, in consequence, is more expensive. It is worth adding nonetheless to mixed hedges of native species.

SPACING: 35 cm (14 in).

AFTER-CARE: trim in late August and preferably late May also.

RECOMMENDED VARIETIES: the normal species only is suitable for hedging.

Laurel *Prunus laurocerasus* Roseaceae

Laurel is one of the great evergreen hedging plants of the past but it has always had the drawback of the difficulty of pruning its enormous leaves. If shears are used, the leaves are cut through and become browned and untidy; while using secateurs is an almost impossible task. The only real justification for planting laurel hedges today is in gardens where they are already important features or when the intention is deliberately to recreate a Victorian period effect.

SPACING: 60 cm (24 in).

AFTER-CARE: prune in spring and preferably again in late summer.

RECOMMENDED VARIETIES: choose normal species only.

Lavender *Lavandula* Labiatae See p. 176

Lawson cypress *Chamaecyparis lawsoniana* Cupressaceae

Lawson cypress is arguably the most widely used hedging plant of all time. Its fast growth and dense screening effect have made it irresistible. But, like all fast growing plants, it requires constant attention to prevent it from becoming too tall. The argument that it is dull is hard to counter, in that it offers a wall of unrelieved and relatively uniformly textured green (although in a range of shades, depending on variety) but that could also be said of yew which is very seldom condemned in the same manner. And there are many golden foliaged forms of Lawson cypress that may either be grown alone or interplanted with green types for a more attactive effect.

SPACING: 45 cm (18 in).

AFTER-CARE: trim in late spring and again in late summer.

RECOMMENDED VARIETIES: with over 200 varieties of Lawson cypress available, it is important to choose the best form. Most good nurseries will offer their own recommendations as hedging plants but among those seen most frequently are 'Green Hedger', 'Green Pillar' and 'Golden Wonder'.

Leyland cypress × *Cupressocyparis leylandii* Cupressaceae

At once the most abused, vilified, overplanted yet under-appreciated garden plant of our time, Leyland cypress almost deserves a chapter to itself. Its outstanding feature, around which all of the emotion centres, is its speed of growth – up to 1 m (39 in) per year. There is, quite simply, no comparable plant for producing a rapid screen, and I know of gardens in exposed, upland areas that simply could not exist had not a tall hedge of Leyland cypress been planted for protection. But it must be appreciated that this growth rate will continue for many years and if this vigour is to be contained and the plant used effectively as a hedge, it must be trimmed very frequently. It is not really practicable to use for hedges less than about 2 m (6½ ft) in height; if you require a conifer screen lower than this, Lawson cypress is a much better bet. And it is not a plant for suburban gardens; you may take care of it, but those who follow you in your house may not, and it has been remarked

that suburban Britain is in serious danger of disappearing under a 30 m high forest in years to come.
SPACING: 1 m (39 in).
AFTER-CARE: do not give any fertiliser – the thing is already born with the right idea. Trim in spring, in late summer and, if possible, in midsummer too. With this degree of attention a Leyland cypress hedge can look magnificent; I have seen examples barely distinguishable from yew.
RECOMMENDED VARIETIES: the most frequently seen green foliaged form is generally sold simply under the hybrid name, although most of the plants are actually of the form called 'Haggerston Grey'. The most common golden variety, which is only marginally slower growing, is 'Castlewellan Gold'.

Lonicera nitida   Caprifoliaceae

This is a tough, shrubby honeysuckle, although few people recognise it as such. It is useful if rather unexciting for a dense, low hedge; it is unsuitable for a screen more than about 1 m (39 in) tall as it tends to open out in an unattractive manner. The leaves are tiny and bright green or, in the more commonly planted form, yellow, with silvery undersides.
SPACING: 30 cm (12 in).
AFTER-CARE: trim in late spring and, if possible, late summer.
RECOMMENDED VARIETIES: the yellow-leaved 'Baggesen's Gold' is the most widely available form, although the normal green species and its variant 'Elegant' are obtainable too.

Privet   *Ligustrum ovalifolium*   Oleaceae

The green-leaved Japanese privet has, thank goodness, now passed from favour as a hedging plant. Unlike conifers, it was truly dismal. It has a coloured form, however, that is among the most striking of golden foliaged plants and that makes an admirable boundary, if it is kept fairly low and is not so long that it dominates its vicinity. Like the green species, it will grow almost anywhere, but the yellow foliage can suffer in very hot conditions.
SPACING: 35 cm (14 in).
AFTER-CARE: trim in late spring and again in late summer.
RECOMMENDED VARIETIES: 'Aureum'.

Pyracantha spp. and hybrids   Rosaceae   See p. 177

Roses   *Rosa* spp. and hybrids   Rosaceae   See p. 193

Rosemary   *Rosmarinus* spp.   Labiatae   See p. 133

Sea buckthorn   *Hippophae rhamnoides*   Elaeagnaceae

For seaside gardeners, the sea buckthorn needs no introduction but it is scarcely known away from the coast. It is a rather elegant, fast growing, thorny deciduous shrub with narrow, willow-like silvery leaves and, when grown as a free-standing plant with male plants nearby to pollinate, the females produce masses of orange berries late in the year. Its value as a windbreak hedge in coastal gardens is considerable but, with the necessary clipping, it cannot then be expected to produce many berries.
SPACING: 60 cm (24 in).
AFTER-CARE: trim in late summer.
RECOMMENDED VARIETIES: normal species only available.

Snowberry   *Symphoricarpos* × *doorenbosii*   Caprifoliaceae

The deciduous snowberries, with their large pearly-white or pink berries, are among those plants that you either love or hate. The more upright growing forms make useful, fairly informal hedging and are often found overgrown in old cottage gardens. To help produce the so-called cottage garden style, they nonetheless make useful subjects.
SPACING: 60 cm (24 in).
AFTER-CARE: trim in late summer.
RECOMMENDED VARIETIES: although there are several named forms, the best for hedging is the upright growing, white berried 'White Hedge'.

Spiraea spp. and hybrids   Rosaceae   See p. 179

Thuja plicata   Cupressaceae

The thujas (or as they are sometimes called, the white or red cedars) are the least well known and least widely planted of the good hedging conifers. *T. plicata*, the Western red cedar, is the best for hedging, the foliage standing clipping very well and giving off a most attractive aroma. They have similar vigour to the hedging forms of Lawson cypress and must similarly be kept in check; given a choice, however, I find thujas more attractive plants.
SPACING: 45 cm (18 in).
AFTER-CARE: trim in late spring and again in late summer.
RECOMMENDED VARIETIES: choice will probably be dictated by availability. The normal species is often offered but 'Atrovirens' is a particularly good form.

Yew   *Taxus baccata*   Taxaceae

I still believe the yew to be the queen of hedging plants. Their reputation for slow growth is only founded on a slowness in the first two or three years; and that can be said of many other plants too. They have the great asset of regenerating well from the old wood, so old overgrown hedges can be rejuvenated. The only word of caution must be given when livestock are likely to gain access to the plants. All parts of the yew are poisonous but for some reason this doesn't deter cattle and horses from eating them. Yew will grow on most soils and is highly tolerant of chalk.
SPACING: 45 cm (18 in).
AFTER-CARE: trim in late spring and again in late summer.
RECOMMENDED VARIETIES: the normal species should be chosen although it is sensible to buy from a nursery that has propagated plants from cuttings of a selected strain, as plants raised from seedlings can be very variable.

Trees in the garden

I AM sure that more problems are caused through gardeners using trees incorrectly or inappropriately than arise in any other aspect of gardening. Quite simply, the reason is that trees are big and any mistakes made in choice of species or variety and in planting position are therefore magnified. Leaving aside the very small minority of gardeners who actually have space to plant woods or even copses, for the remainder, a tree is a specimen feature. And in most modern gardens, the overall space available dictates that it is a solitary feature. This being so, the tree for the modern gardener has an exacting list of attributes to satisfy.

Its size must be in proportion to the scale of the garden, so that visually it is correct. It must not be so large that it dominates the space around it to the extent that it adversely affects the growth of other plants, or poses a physical threat to the structure of the house or other buildings. It is impossible to give general advice on the planting of trees which guarantees that they will present no hazard at all to any building, but a rule of thumb that I employ is never to plant weeping willows or poplars in a garden; and never to plant any tree closer to a house than one and a half times its ultimate height.

But having a tree of the correct size is only part of the story. It must not possess other antisocial features such as large quantities of gigantic leaves that block drains and gutters and cover paths and lawns when they fall, nor give rise to sticky honeydew that cascades over people, cars and other vegetation. So much for the negative; what then are the positive attributes to consider? Perhaps the most important is that the plants should have all-year-round appeal – for after all, when it is alone or, at best, one of a very small number, a tree really must earn its keep.

The most obviously attractive parts of a tree are its leaves but other attributes to bear in mind include the length of time that these are actually present to be admired. Deciduous trees generally have more attractive leaves than evergreens but a deciduous species that comes into leaf late and sheds its foliage early is scarcely offering you very much value. Moreover, the foliage of many deciduous trees changes colour (and in a few instances, shape) as the season progresses. One that offers changing leaf interest, therefore, is especially to be cherished. Once the leaves have fallen from a deciduous tree in autumn, much interest and attractiveness may still remain in the shape of the twigs, bark and buds, although there are few trees worth growing for these attributes alone.

But almost all trees also bear flowers – collectively generally called blossom when they are present in large numbers – and many trees are chosen for their blossom alone. The other side of the coin is that many trees which are selected for a stunning floral display offer a fairly depressing spectacle for all of the months after the blossom has fallen. Flowers are followed by fruit which may also be attractive in colour and/or shape. But the period over which fruit can contribute to the appeal of a garden tree is generally limited by the local bird population who will view it, quite understandably, as a free and convenient food supply.

The traditional time for planting trees is during the dormant season, from late autumn until early spring, but this is only really relevant for bare-rooted plants. Most trees are now supplied by garden centres in containers and these can be planted at all times of the year, although establishment will still generally be more sure during the dormant period.

I cannot over-emphasise the importance of giving thorough and careful preparation to the planting position. Dig a hole approximately twice as large

Opposite: Cornus kousa 'Chinensis' – RHS Gardens, Wisley (July).

161

PLANTING TREES.

(a) Dig a hole approximately twice the size of the tree's rootball. Mix the soil removed with an equal volume of rotted manure or compost.

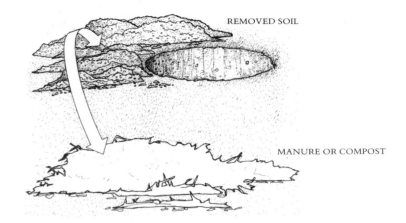

REMOVED SOIL

MANURE OR COMPOST

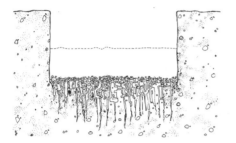

(b) Break up the soil in the bottom of the hole and gradually refill until the roots can be spread out, whilst the original soil mark on the trunk is level with the soil surface.

as the root ball of the tree and pile the soil at the side. Then mix this with a similar volume of well rotted manure or garden compost and several handfuls of bonemeal. Break up the soil in the base of the hole with a fork, then gradually refill, pressing it down gently with your boot until the remaining hole is deep enough for the tree's roots to be spread out in it while leaving the original soil mark on the trunk level with the soil surface. With a container-grown plant, simply tease away some of the roots around the sides and bottom of the compost ball as you place it in the hole. Then insert a stout stake on the windward side of the tree (to ensure that the tree is blown away from, and not onto, it). Although very short stakes have become rather popular, I prefer a purpose cut one of approximately 1.5 m (5 ft), made of treated timber, and driven at least 60 cm (2 ft) into the ground. The tree's trunk should be secured to the stake with two belt-style tree ties, one close to the top and one close to ground level. Then gradually fill in around the roots with the soil and organic matter mixture, pressing down gently with your boot. Water the area around the plant very thoroughly, then finally make a small mound of manure or compost around the base of the trunk.

The fact that trees will ultimately grow tall and appear well able to take care of themselves seems to disguise the fact that whilst they are small they need some care and attention. Trees planted in lawns or other grassed areas should have an area of approximately 1 m (3 ft) in diameter around their base kept free from grass for at least six years after planting. And this or any other area of soil around a young tree must also be kept free from weed growth. Apply a general purpose fertiliser such as blood, fish and bone around the base in late spring and then re-apply a thick organic matter mulch.

Trees should not need any routine pruning other than the removal of dead branches; nor should they suffer unduly from pests and diseases. The problem of honeydew to which I referred above arises as a result of aphid infestation and I have not recommended any of the trees that suffer seriously from this. Among common diseases, mildew and coral spot may be expected – the former must be tolerated but the impact of the latter will be diminished if dead branches are removed promptly (see p. 72). The spectre of honey fungus haunts many tree owners but this is an overestimated threat. Undoubtedly, where an old diseased tree stump is present, honey fungus may spread from it to affect living plants but some attention can prevent its affecting an entire garden – and with care and commonsense, honey fungus can be kept out of existing uncontaminated sites (see p. 84).

In my references to height in the individual descriptions, I have indicated those to be expected in average garden conditions; on very good soils and in favourable climates, growth may be faster and taller.

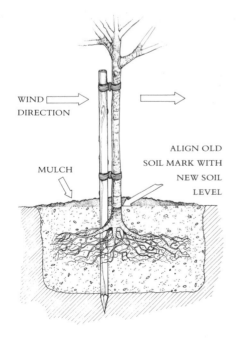

WIND DIRECTION

ALIGN OLD SOIL MARK WITH NEW SOIL LEVEL

MULCH

162   *Staking trees.*

Acacia dealbata   Silver wattle or mimosa   Leguminosae

This is the commonest and most reliable of the hardy acacias (and the one that provides the florists' 'mimosa') but it must be said that with all of these trees, hardy is a relative term. *A. dealbata* will thrive in mild (and preferably seaside) areas with some shelter provided by a building or tall wall. It then makes a lovely plant with its characteristic silvery and delicately fern-like evergreen foliage and stunning display of small, rounded, feathery, yellow, fragrant flowers in spring. Try it if you live in a favourable area but be prepared to travel to the Mediterranean to see its full glory.

HEIGHT: 6 m (20 ft) after ten years; 10 m (33 ft) ultimately (in Britain).

RECOMMENDED VARIETIES: normal species only available; other species of *Acacia* are sometimes offered but are less reliable.

Acer spp.   Maples   Aceraceae

Acer palmatum

The maples include some of the most appealing deciduous garden trees, although it is for their bark and foliage, rather than their floral features, that they should be chosen. For whilst the overall impact of a tree with unfurling leaves and opening blossom in spring is most delightful, in most species the flowers themselves are predominantly greenish and individually rather uninteresting. The most attractive feature of most maples is the colour of their leaves in autumn, although this effect is weather-dependent and the colour is invariably best in seasons (or localities, such as parts of North America) where warm days contrast with cold nights in early autumn. But *Acer* is a large genus with over one hundred species among which are many large or otherwise unsuitable types. You will, for instance, often see the sycamore (*A. pseudoplatanus*) or the field maple (*A. campestre*) offered for sale in garden centres for reasons that I find quite unaccountable. These are forest trees with no place in the modern garden. Maples in general are tolerant of most soil types but usually thrive best in slightly acid soils. Most are unsuccessful in windy or very wet sites, this being especially true of the Japanese types; the smaller forms of these can nonetheless be grown very successfully in containers.

RECOMMENDED VARIETIES: *A. griseum* (paper-bark maple) – chestnut brown, peeling bark, deep-red autumn leaves, height 4 m (13 ft) after ten years, 8 m (26½ ft) ultimately); *A. japonicum* and *A. palmatum* – Japanese maples, these two species have given rise to a huge range of tree and shrubby forms with many different leaf shapes and varying intensity of autumn colour. The named forms are invariably sold as grafted plants and are invariably expensive. **Forms of *A. japonicum*** – *aureum* – pale green in spring, yellow in summer, red-orange in autumn, height 2 m (6½ ft) after ten years, 3 m (10 ft) ultimately. **Forms of *A. palmatum*:** normal species – palm shaped green leaves, red in autumn; 'Atropurpureum' and 'Bloodgood' – palm-shaped deep-purple leaves, red and scarlet in autumn; 'Ozakazuki' – seven-lobed olive-green leaves, vivid red autumn colour, height 3 m (10 ft) after ten years, 5 m (16½ ft) ultimately; *dissectum* – finely divided, ferny green leaves, red-orange in autumn; 'Dissectum Atropurpureum' and 'Garnet' – similar but with deep-purple leaves changing to red-orange in autumn, height 1.2 m (4 ft) after ten years, 1.5 m (5 ft) ultimately; *A. maximowiczianum* (also called *A. nikoense*) – yellow flowers, leaves pale beneath, red autumn leaves, height 3 m (10 ft) after ten years, 15 m (50 ft) ultimately; *A. negundo* (box elder) – distinct foliage, not three-lobed but rather like ash, the best forms are 'Flamingo' with pale pink leaf variegation, 'Elegans' with yellow-edged, variegated leaves, although both are prone to produce shoots bearing green leaves which must be cut out, and 'Aureum' with beautiful golden foliage, no autumn colour, height 5 m (16½ ft) after ten years, 8 m (26½ ft) ultimately); *A. platanoides* 'Crimson King' – Norway maple, deep red-purple leaves, little change in autumn, the most attractive large maple for gardens, height 8 m (26½ ft) after ten years, 25 m (83 ft) ultimately, 'Drummondii' is little over two-thirds the size with pale green, yellow-edged leaves; *A. rubrum* – red maple, red flowers, vivid red, orange and yellow autumn leaves in good conditions, but not a tree for small gardens, height 8 m (26½ ft) after ten years, 23 m (76 ft) ultimately. **Snake bark maples:** *A. davidii* – greenish-purple bark with paler stripes, no autumn colour, height 8 m (26½ ft) after ten years, 15 m (50 ft) ultimately; *A. hersii* – greyish olive-green mottled bark, orange and red autumn leaves, height 8 m (26½ ft) after ten years, 14 m (46½ ft) ultimately; *A. capillipes* – reddish-purple bark with pale lines, orange and scarlet autumn leaves, height 7 m (23 ft) after ten years, 15 m (50 ft) ultimately.

Amelanchier lamarckii   Snowy mespil   Rosaceae

This is the perfect small garden tree. It is tolerant of a wide range of soils, including clay, and of a wide range of climatic conditions, including strong wind. It offers something at all seasons: delicate white blossom appears in spring, just as the dainty, elliptical leaves unfurl; these leaves turn vivid red in autumn and are accompanied by dark-red berries – provided the weather is warm and the birds sparse; in winter, the tracery of fine twigs continues the interest.

HEIGHT: 6 m (20 ft) after ten years, 8 m (26½ ft) ultimately.

RECOMMENDED VARIETIES: the related species or forms called *A. canadensis* and 'Ballerina' are inferior.

Betula spp.   Birches   Betulaceae

For too many gardeners, birches conjure up solely the native silver birch, a lovely tree in the wild, with stunning yellow autumn colour, but a liability in small gardens where it produces copious honeydew and succumbs at an early age to decay. Some of the selected forms may be suitable for larger gardens but there are much better Himalayan and American species. Unfortunately, the Himalayan species are notoriously difficult to identify accurately and may be incorrectly named in garden centres. There are also intermediate forms, which complicate the matter. They are all tolerant of a wide range of soils, although all are best on fairly well drained sites.

HEIGHT: 9 m (30 ft) after ten years, 12 m (40 ft) ultimately.

RECOMMENDED VARIETIES: under the general name of Himalayan birches, you will see *B. jacquemontii, B. utilis* and *B. ermanii*, usually grafted. *B. jacquemontii* is generally considered to have the purest white bark although the bark features do not develop fully on young trees. My favourite is *B. ermanii* which develops a pink tinge to the bark as it ages.

Caragana arborescens   Pea tree   Leguminosae

This is one of the least known yet most valuable small deciduous garden trees. It is absolutely hardy in the coldest areas and in its best forms has the most attractive soft green foliage and characteristic yellow, rather broom-like flowers.

HEIGHT: 4 m (13 ft) after ten years, 8 m (26½ ft) ultimately.

RECOMMENDED VARIETIES: 'Lorbergii', narrow, needle-like foliage; 'Walker', weeping.

Catalpa bignonioides   Indian bean tree   Bignoniaceae

Catalpa bignonioides

A striking deciduous tree with giant rounded bright-green leaves, and with flowers and fruit reminiscent of runner beans. It is fairly hardy (and also seems surprisingly drought tolerant) and makes a lovely feature on a large lawn. Its only disadvantage is that it is late into leaf and fairly early shedding them.

HEIGHT: 7 m (23 ft) after ten years, 18 m (60 ft) ultimately.

RECOMMENDED VARIETIES: normal species only is available.

Cercis siliquastrum   Judas Tree   Leguminosae

A beautiful and striking plant once mature but takes a long time to establish and also a long time before it really looks appealing. The leaves are characteristically rounded or kidney-shaped and the flowers purplish-pink and bean-like. Acid soil is needed for the plant really to give of its best.

HEIGHT: 3 m (10 ft) after ten years, 6 m (20 ft) ultimately.

RECOMMENDED VARIETIES: a white-flowered form 'Alba' is occasionally seen but for me it is the normal flower colour that is the real attraction.

Cornus spp.   Dogwoods   Cornaceae

Many of the best known dogwoods grown in gardens are truncated by hard spring pruning to form shrubs for the aesthetic appeal of the bark on their young shoots. Nonetheless, there are also several species with stunningly lovely blossom (the effect brought about by the large white bracts rather than petals) that form splendid specimens as full-sized trees. They are a diverse and valuable group of hardy deciduous plants, tolerant of a wide range of soil conditions (although generally best on slightly acid sites), among which there are types suitable for every garden.

RECOMMENDED VARIETIES: *C. alba* – hard prune in spring to encourage the production of attractively coloured (usually red) stems, height (with pruning) 1.5 m (5 ft); 'Aurea' – yellowish leaves, requires partial shade; 'Elegantissima' – silver leaf margins; 'Kesselringii' – very dark, almost black stems and dark-green leaves; 'Sibirica' (also called 'Westonbirt') – very pale young leaves, requires partial shade; 'Spaethii' – leaves with yellow margins, more compact habit than the normal species; *C. alternifolia* 'Argentea' – silver-edged leaves, red autumn colour, height 3 m (10 ft) after ten years, 5.5 m (18 ft) ultimately; *C. canadensis* – creeping ground cover habit (ultimate height 20 cm/8 in), four prominent white bracts with dark central flowers, very pretty in light woodland soil; *C. controversa* – branches in tiers giving a 'wedding cake' effect, white flowers in spring, the form called 'Variegata' with white leaf edges is exquisite, height 3 m (10 ft) after ten years, 8 m (26½ ft) ultimately; *C. florida* – four large white or pink bracts and very attractive foliage, height 4 m (13 ft) after ten years, 5 m (16½ ft) ultimately, 'Rainbow' – dark-green leaves with pale yellow-green margins; *rubra* pink bracts; *C. kousa* – four large white bracts and a partially tiered appearance, stunning when full grown and in flower, the best form is 'Chinensis' as it has larger flowers, but there are even some named selections within this also, height 3 m (10 ft) after ten years, 9 m (30 ft) ultimately; *C. mas* (cornelian cherry) – small yellow flowers on bare twigs in early spring, a good alternative to witch hazel, 'Variegata' has variegated foliage, height 4 m (13 ft) after ten years, 8 m (26½ ft) ultimately; *C. nuttallii* – four large white or pinkish bracts, rich yellow-orange autumn colour, 'Eddie's White Wonder' (probably a hybrid) has very large flowers, 'Gold Spot' has gold leaf blotches, height 4 m (13 ft) after ten years, 8 m (26½ ft) ultimately; *C. stolonifera* 'Flaviramea' – a yellow-stemmed equivalent of *C. alba*.

Crataegus spp. and hybrids   Thorns   Rosaceae

The hawthorn is too well known to need description and is a valuable hedging plant (p. 158) but it has several related forms that make glorious flowering trees. They have the advantage over flowering crab apples and cherries in suffering from far fewer pest and disease problems, they will thrive in most soils and tolerate strong winds.

HEIGHT: 6 m (20 ft) after ten years, 8 m (26½ ft) ultimately.

RECOMMENDED VARIETIES: *C. crus-galli* (white flowers, good red berries, good autumn colour, huge thorns); *C. laevigata* (also called *C. oxyacantha*) 'Paul's Scarlet' (deep-pink double flowers), 'Plena' (double white flowers), 'Rosea Flore Pleno' (pink double flowers); *C. monogyna* 'Pendula Rosea' (very hard to find but lovely weeping habit, pink flowers); *C. prunifolia* (plum-like leaves, white flowers, good red berries).

Eucalyptus spp.   Gum tree   Myrtaceae

The bluish-leaved evergreen trees of the huge genus *Eucalyptus* are synonymous with Australia and with flower arranging but they are seldom successful in British gardens. The reason is quite simply that they are not sufficiently hardy. This is unfortunate in many ways for they are quick growing and more attractive than many of the conifers that perform a similar role. Nonetheless, those flower arrangers who are besotted with the juvenile foliage will find a few species hardy enough to survive and should prune them hard in the spring, rather after the fashion of dogwoods.

RECOMMENDED VARIETIES: *E. gunnii*, rounded bluish-white juvenile foliage, green elongated mature leaves; *E. parvifolia*, narrow, elongated blue-green leaves, height (without pruning) 10 m (33 ft) after ten years, 20 m (66½ ft) ultimately (in Britain); *E. pauciflora niphophila*, greyish-green leaves, markedly pale greyish and green bark.

Gleditsia triacanthos   Honey locust   Leguminosae

This is a naturally very prickly tree that has become very popular in recent years, its attraction being the elongated, rather ash-like foliage (golden-yellow and with thornless twigs in the most popular form). It tolerates a wide range of soils, moderate exposure and full sun but suffers from the generally unappreciated drawback that it will grow much too tall for small gardens: it is too recent an arrival in our gardens for its ultimate size to be judged, but many trees are shooting upwards at an alarming rate.

HEIGHT: 9 m (30 ft) after ten years, at least 30 m (100 ft) ultimately.

RECOMMENDED VARIETIES: 'Sunburst'.

Ilex spp. and hybrids   Hollies   Aquifoliaceae

Hollies immediately conjure up images of prickly evergreen leaves, red berries and Christmas. But what a pity this is, for there are many handsome garden varieties that have no leaf prickles and, indeed, no berries by virtue of being male; and there are some, moreover, whose berries, whilst present, are not red. They will grow in almost any soil and in most situations and although hollies have one serious drawback in that most forms are fairly slow growing, this shouldn't deter anyone from having at least one representative in their garden. But remember that female forms will require a male plant nearby if they are to produce fruit.

HEIGHT: (except 'Ferox Argentea') 4 m (13 ft) after ten years, 6 m (20 ft) ultimately.

RECOMMENDED VARIETIES: *I. altaclarensis* (Highclere holly): 'Camelliifolia' – few spines, large, shining camellia-like leaves, purple shoots, red berries; 'Golden King' – few spines, shiny bright-green leaves with golden margins, red-orange berries; 'Lawsoniana' – dark-green leaves with yellow centres, orange-red berries; *I. aquifolium* (common holly): 'Argentea Marginata' – greyish-green leaves with white margins, some forms are female with orange berries; 'Argentea Marginata Pendula' – leaves dark green with white margins, red berries, weeping habit; 'Bacciflava' – bright-green leaves, yellow berries; 'Ferox Argentea' – squat shrub (ultimate height 2 m/6½ ft) with small, very prickly leaves with white margins, no berries; 'Golden Queen' – very dark green leaves, golden margins, no

berries; 'Handsworth New Silver' – narrow leaves with cream-white margins, orange berries; 'J. C. van Tol' – few spines, narrow dark-green leaves, red berries; 'Pyramidalis' – conical to pyramidal form, red berries.

Koelreuteria paniculata   Chinese rain tree or Pride of India   Sapindaceae

This is a striking if rather unkempt deciduous tree, too loose in form for small gardens but very effective in larger ones. The leaves are large and ash-like, the flowers yellow in large open heads – once seen, the name golden rain tree is readily understood. Koelreuterias will grow on most sites but are best on slightly acid, moist soils.

HEIGHT: 8 m (26½ ft) after ten years, 15 m (50 ft) ultimately.

RECOMMENDED VARIETIES: usually the normal species only is available although a fastigiate (upright) form exists and is worth looking out for.

Laburnum × watereri   'Vossii'   Leguminosae

The long, pendulous yellow flowers of the laburnum are among the most familiar sights of spring. Duty dictates that I point out how poisonous a plant this is, especially in its seeds, which are said to be curiously attractive to young children. But I grew up in a garden containing a laburnum and came to no harm because, contrary to general belief, I held no desire to eat the seeds and their pods. The decision nonetheless on whether to plant a laburnum must rest with each gardener and parent. If you do decide to grow one, give thought to the possibility of training it against a wall where it can look magnificent.

HEIGHT: 7 m (23 ft) after ten years, 10 m (33 ft) ultimately.

RECOMMENDED VARIETIES: Of the forms available, only 'Vossii' with its very long inflorescences is worth growing.

Liquidamber styraciflua   Sweet gum   Altingiaceae

Liquidambers are named from the fragrant resin produced by some species but the name is equally applicable to the glorious golden-red autumn leaf colour. I am constantly surprised that this plant is not grown in more of our larger gardens for it is tolerant of a wide range of conditions and is hardy in most areas; although admittedly it is rather vigorous.

HEIGHT: 10 m (33 ft) after ten years.

RECOMMENDED VARIETIES: normal species only is usually available although among the few named forms 'Worplesdon' has the best autumn colour.

Magnolia spp. and hybrids   Magnoliaceae

Magnolias are magnificent deciduous (or, in one notable exception, evergreen) garden trees. They have a reputation for being fussy, in requiring acid conditions, and also tender but in reality will tolerate neutral or even slightly alkaline soils. And the forms that I recommend are all reliably hardy, although of course late frost can damage the blossom. Many magnolias will become rather large plants in time and should be selected carefully, although fortunately most of the common and hardiest species remain fairly small. Many are also naturally multi-stemmed and it is a mistake to try to persuade them to form a single trunk. I must say a special word regarding *M. grandiflora*, the only evergreen species likely to be seen. This is a superb summer-flowering plant (most magnolias are spring flowering), although ultimately fairly large. Traditionally, it is grown against a tall sheltered wall (where it may be planted with no fear of damage to foundations) but it also makes an excellent free-standing tree provided the site is not too exposed. It is sensible not to buy very large plants of any magnolias for they resent root disturbance and may be difficult to establish except when small.

RECOMMENDED VARIETIES: *M. grandiflora* – evergreen, with large shiny leaves and huge creamy flowers over a long period in summer and autumn, the forms 'Exmouth' and 'Goliath' should always be chosen, for these flower at a much younger age than the species, height 4 m (13 ft) after ten years, 8 m (26½ ft) ultimately; *M. kobus loebneri* – masses of star-like flowers at an early age in spring, among the best forms are 'Leonard Messel' (pink-mauve flowers) and 'Merrill' (white flowers), height 6 m (20 ft) after ten years, 8 m (26½ ft) ultimately; *M. quinquepeta* (also called *M. liliiflora*) – slender tulip-shaped flowers in late spring, the commonest form is 'Nigra' with deep-purple outsides and pale-mauve insides to the petals, height 2 m (6½ ft) after ten years, 4 m (13 ft) ultimately; *M. soulangeana* – tulip-shaped flowers in spring, 'Alba Superba' (white with purple bases) and 'Lennei' (rose-purple outside, cream within) are perhaps my favourites but there are several other good named forms, height 4 m (13 ft) after ten years, 8 m (26½ ft) ultimately; *M. stellata* – star-like flowers at an early age in spring, 'Royal Star' (white flowers) and 'King Rose' (pink flowers) are among the best forms.

Malus hybrids   Crab apples   Rosaceae

The flowering crabs can be stunning when in blossom and they have the added advantage of producing fruit later in the year, fruit that can be very attractive as well as edible. But it must be said that they have a serious drawback; they suffer from the same mildew and scab problems as apples and in some seasons these can be seriously disfiguring. Nonetheless, most varieties are now available on the dwarfing apple rootstock M.27 (see p. 142) and this means they are among the smallest of all blossom trees and good therefore in very tiny gardens.

PEST, DISEASE OR OTHER PROBLEMS: canker, mildew, scab.

HEIGHT: depends on choice of rootstock (see p. 142).

RECOMMENDED VARIETIES: 'Golden Hornet' – white blossom, small golden-yellow fruits which hang until the winter; 'John Downie' – white blossom, orange-red fruits (the best for cooking); 'Profusion' – purple foliage, purple blossom, small red-purple fruits; *M. tschonoskii* – pink-white flowers, small yellow-brown fruit, rich orange-red autumn colour.

Parrotia persica   Hamamelidaceae

This relative of the witch hazels is a strange deciduous tree with rather coarse, toothed leaves and appealing winter flowers (although rarely produced on young plants). But it is a tree that would never be grown were it not for its ravishing yellow, orange and red autumn colour. It is very hardy but always

Parrotia persica

thrives best on acid soils.

HEIGHT: 4 m (13 ft) after ten years, 10 m (33 ft) ultimately.

RECOMMENDED VARIETIES: usually the normal species only is available although there is an attractive weeping form.

Paulownia tomentosa   Foxglove tree   Scrophulariaceae

This is an arrestingly beautiful deciduous tree, aptly named from its deep-purple foxglove-like blossom in late spring. It should be grown more widely, although ultimately it is fairly large and is really suited to milder areas, or, more pertinently, to areas with little danger of late frost. It thrives best in moist, rich soils and is fairly lime tolerant.

HEIGHT: 15 m (50 ft) after ten years, 25 m (83 ft) ultimately.

RECOMMENDED VARIETIES: normal species only available.

Photinia spp. and hybrids   Rosaceae

The evergreen photinias span the boundary between small trees and large shrubs but all share the attribute of having splendid winter foliage and young shoot colour in spring. They are tolerant of most soils although, in my experience, best with some acidity. The flowers are white and attractive but not formed consistently in all years.

HEIGHT: 2 m (6½ ft) after ten years, 4 m (13 ft) ultimately.

RECOMMENDED VARIETIES: *P. davidiana* 'Palette', *P. fraseri* 'Red Robin', vivid red shoot and leaf growth from late autumn to spring.

Prunus spp. and hybrids   Plums and cherries

This section will be one of the unexpectedly most short in the book, for I believe that the majority of flowering 'cherries' grown in gardens are unsuitable for the purpose. There are several reasons for this – they suffer from disfiguring and debilitating pests and diseases (see below), they are often utterly dismal when not in flower, the colour of their blossom blends with nothing else, and many grow extremely tall and produce extensive suckers or surface roots. The very few that I recommend are not all free from all of these problems but have at least some saving graces.

PEST, DISEASE OR OTHER PROBLEMS: aphids, bacterial canker, peach leaf curl, and, especially on the variety 'Kanzan', an ultimately fatal die-back of unknown cause.

RECOMMENDED VARIETIES: *P. hillieri* 'Spire' – pale-pink flowers, good autumn colour, upright habit, height 7 m (23 ft) after ten years, 10 m (33 ft) ultimately; *P. sargentii* – single pale-pink flowers in early spring, height 6 m (20 ft) after ten years, 10 m (33 ft) ultimately; *P. serrula* – rich, shiny, mahogany-coloured bark, contrasts wonderfully with white-barked birches, height 5 m (16½ ft) after ten years, 7 m (23 ft) ultimately; *P. subhirtella* 'Autumnalis' – small white flowers intermittently through the winter, height 5 m (16½ ft) after ten years, 8 m (26½ ft) ultimately; *P.* 'Tai-haku' – huge single white flowers, height 7 m (23 ft) after ten years, 9 m (30 ft) ultimately; *P. yedoensis* – perfumed white blossom, slightly weeping, height 7 m (23 ft) after ten years, 10 m (33 ft) ultimately.

Pyrus salicifolia 'Pendula'   Willow-leaved pear Rosaceae

For similar reasons to those I put forward against crab apples, I am not enthusiastic about ornamental pears as garden trees. This is the one exception, however, for it is one of the prettiest of weeping trees, easily mistaken for a willow because of its long, narrow, silvery leaves.

PEST, DISEASE OR OTHER PROBLEMS: canker, mildew, scab.

HEIGHT: 5 m (16½ ft) after ten years, 8 m (26½ ft) ultimately.

RECOMMENDED VARIETIES: there are no selected forms available.

Robinia pseudoacacia 'Frisia'   Leguminosae

In recent years, this yellow-green leaved deciduous tree has become one of the most fashionable species to plant in small gardens. It is undeniably pretty but will ultimately grow tall and has the serious drawback of very brittle twigs and is consequently damaged by strong winds. It also has the reputation of being difficult to establish although I have not found this to be so.

HEIGHT: 6 m (20 ft) after ten years, 12 m (40 ft) ultimately.

RECOMMENDED VARIETIES: although other forms are sometimes offered, 'Frisia' is the most reliable.

Salix spp.   Willows   Salicaceae

Whilst I have roundly condemned the planting of weeping willows (*S. chrysocoma*) in gardens, there remain several other species of this lovely genus that make excellent garden plants. They too, however, span the shrub and tree boundary and some of those listed here are small plants. They are for the most part tolerant of exposure and whilst most thrive best in fairly moist soils, this is not essential. Unfortunately, far too many small forms are offered grafted onto standard stems in 'lollipop on a stick' fashion; I recommend none of these. If you want a standard tree, then choose one naturally with a single stem or select a multi-stemmed shrub and cut out all except one. Dwarf shrubs should remain dwarf.

RECOMMENDED VARIETIES: *S. alba* 'Britzensis' – red stems, prune hard in spring; 'Vitellina' – golden stems, prune hard in spring, height (with pruning) 2 m (6½ ft); *S.* 'Boydii' – very slow growing dwarf shrub, generally producing some greyish woolly catkins, height 75 cm (30 in) after ten years, 1 m (39 in) ultimately; *S. daphnoides* – silvery catkins, deep purple stems for winter appeal, height 7 m (23 ft) after ten years, 9 m (30 ft) ultimately; *S. exigua* (coyote willow) – yellow catkins, very narrow silvery leaves, prune hard every four years, height (with pruning), 2 m (6½ ft); *S. fargesii* – deep-purple, shiny stems, purple-green leaves, lovely, height 3 m (10 ft) after ten years, 4 m (13 ft) ultimately; *S. hastata* 'Wehrhahnii' – silver catkins on almost black stems, height 1 m (39 in) after ten years, 2 m (6½ ft) ultimately; *S. helvetica* – grey woolly catkins, lovely brown winter buds, a dwarf shrub too usually seen grafted as a standard, height 1 m (39 in) after ten years, 1.5 m (5 ft) ultimately; *S. matsudana* 'Tortuosa' (cork-screw willow) – curiously twisted stems, height 6 m (20 ft) after ten years, 10 m (33 ft) ultimately.

Sorbus spp. and hybrids   Rosaceae

A most valuable and lovely genus of medium-sized deciduous trees. Some have attractive foliage, often with good autumn colours, and most have beautifully coloured fruit too. Most tolerate exposure and will thrive on most types of soil. I consider them indispensible, and the following is only a very limited selection of the many excellent named forms that you may encounter.

HEIGHT: 5 m (16½ ft) after ten years, 10 m (33 ft) ultimately (except where stated).

RECOMMENDED VARIETIES: *S. aria* 'Lutescens' (whitebeam) – silvery foliage, orange fruit; *S. aucuparia* (mountain ash), 'Asplenifolia' – fern-like leaves, red-orange fruit, 'Sheerwater Seedling' – the best form of typical mountain ash, red fruit, upright habit, 'Xanthocarpa' – yellow fruit; *S. cashmiriana* – white fruit, height 3 m (10 ft) after ten years, 4 m (13 ft) ultimately; *S. hupehensis* – white fruit; *S.* 'Joseph Rock' – yellow fruit; *S. vilmorinii* – pale-purple fruit.

Syringa spp. and hybrids   Lilacs   Oleaceae

I am still undecided about the value of lilacs as garden plants. Their foliage is dull and although their flowers are spectacular for a short period they then die depressingly. On balance I think that I would prefer to be without them except in a large garden where their out-of-season appearance can be lost amongst better things. Nonetheless, those who do enjoy them will find that they will thrive in most soils and most situations.

HEIGHT: 3 m (10 ft) after ten years, 5 m (16½ ft) ultimately (except where stated).

RECOMMENDED VARIETIES: *S. josiflexa* 'Bellicent' – arching rose-pink inflorescences; *S. meyeri* 'Palibin' – mauve-pink, dwarf habit (height 75 cm (30 in) after ten years, 1.5 m (5 ft) ultimately); *S. microphylla* 'Superba' – rose-pink, small inflorescences, dwarf habit (height 75 cm (30 in) after ten years, 1.5 m (5 ft) ultimately); *S. vulgaris* (common lilac): 'Charles Joly' (double dark purple-red), 'Katherine Havemeyer' (double pale purple), 'Madame Lemoine' (double white), 'Michel Buchner' (double pale lavender), 'Mrs Edward Harding' (semi-double, red-purple), 'Primrose' (single, pale yellow), 'Souvenir de Louis Spaeth' (single deep red).

Shrubs

THE shrub is perhaps the most important type of plant in the modern garden. In this respect, the modern garden is very different from that of a century or more ago. Then, the shrubbery was often a monotonous and rather sombre place, dominated by tough evergreens that assumed their value in the nineteenth-century urban environment because of their tolerance of the atmospheric pollution that accompanied the years following the industrial revolution. Colour in those gardens was provided by herbaceous plants or by that rather specialised group of shrubs, the roses. Today, the shortcomings in such reliance have been widely recognised and the dedicated shrubbery is a rarity to be found only in larger gardens. The modern shrub has other roles. It is at its most valuable when used to provide the permanent framework for the mixed border, where it supplies interest and attractiveness all year round, including, most importantly, in the winter when the herbaceous perennials and annuals have died down. But shrubs can also be used most valuably as individual specimens or small groups amongst other types of plant or in grass. And the interest and appeal they supply can take many forms – massed blossom or striking individual flowers, perfume, attractive bark colour or texture, leaf colour and shape, or simply the overall shape of the plant.

Much of the enhanced role that the shrub now takes has arisen because of the greatly increased role of both species and varieties now available. Much of this choice stems from the vast numbers of new introductions brought back by plant collectors from the Far East, China especially, and the careful work of selection and hybridisation that ensued in the West.

An additional but most important attribute of the shrub as a modern garden plant is its need for minimal attention. At best, shrubs benefit from annual early season mulching, a top dressing with a balanced fertiliser mixture (I strongly recommend a rose fertiliser for general application to all shrubs in the spring) and some attention to pruning. It is, however, a telling commentary on their real value that most shrubs, in most gardens, are denied all three of these in most years, and yet still give fine and rewarding displays. There are, moreover, shrubs suitable for all types of soil and for positions ranging from the most sheltered and shaded to the most exposed. Very few require staking, unless deliberately trained as standards, and in fact its requirement for a stake is a rough-and-ready way of distinguishing a tree from a shrub. (There is in fact no really hard and fast division between the two but a slightly more precise definition of a tree is that it attains a height of at least 6 m (20 ft) on a single stem.)

Most shrubs are relatively free from serious pest and disease problems, although, in common with other woody plants, almost all are unfortunately prone to honey fungus. I have not specified this within the individual descriptions, however, for I have no wish to spread alarm and despondency and dissuade gardeners from growing shrubs because of the rather slim chance that honey fungus may one day strike. Among other diseases, coral spot is perhaps the commonest, although this can generally be contained by careful garden hygiene and vigilance at cutting out the first signs of attack.

In the following lists, I have omitted roses, which I have dealt with elsewhere, and also those shrubs that are more appropriately considered in other sections. Thus, low-growing forms of *Acer*, *Cornus*, *Ilex* and *Salix*, for example, will be found in the tree section (p. 163–167), *Buxus* and *Ligustrum* among hedging plants (pp. 151–159), and several others such as *Helianthemum*, *Lavatera*, *Paeonia* and *Phlomis* among herbaceous perennials (pp. 202–213).

Opposite: Cotoneaster horizontalis

Aucuba japonica   Spotted laurel   Cornaceae

A very tough evergreen with large, oval, shiny leaves, reaching 3–4 m (10–13 ft) and one of the most valuable, if under-rated, shrubs for shady, dry and generally inhospitable places. It is almost the only shrub that I know that will grow beneath beech. A bonus is provided by the attractive red berries that hang through the winter, but male and female flowers are on separate plants so two individuals will be needed for berries to form.
PROPAGATE BY: hardwood cuttings in winter.
AFTER-CARE: none but tolerates hard cutting back if needed.
PEST, DISEASE OR OTHER PROBLEMS: none, although an inexplicable but apparently not serious blackening of the young leaf tips is very common.
RECOMMENDED VARIETIES: several variegated forms are available, in addition to the normal species. 'Crotonifolia' (male) with yellow freckled leaves is perhaps the prettiest, although 'Variegata' and 'Gold Dust', with larger blotches, have the merit of being female and therefore potentially berry-ing.

Berberis spp.   Berberidaceae

A large genus of spiny small-leaved deciduous and evergreen shrubs that includes some of the most valuable and beautiful of all garden plants. All of those that I recommend here are tolerant of a wide range of soil and site conditions, although flower production is almost always best in full sun, and the evergreens tend to brown in cold winds. Some stand hard clipping and are useful for hedging (see also p. 156) when their spiny branches help to deter intruders. Most species ultimately reach about 3 or 4 m (10 or 13 ft) but can be kept smaller by careful clipping.
PROPAGATE BY: hardwood cuttings in winter.
AFTER-CARE: none but old wood should be cut out every three or four years.
PEST, DISEASE OR OTHER PROBLEMS: none.
RECOMMENDED VARIETIES: the most important deciduous species is B. thunbergii with many forms and varieties, most notably atropurpurea with rich purple-red leaves turning flame red in autumn; 'Golden Ring' with similar, rounded leaves that develop a golden margin in warm seasons; 'Red Chief' with elongated, very vividly purple leaves and similarly coloured shoots; and 'Rose Glow' with pink and white variegated leaves. Among the evergreens, my choice is emphatically with B. darwinii, justifiably called 'the most valuable evergreen ever to grace an English garden', with more or less oval leaves, bright green above and silvery below, and masses of exquisite bright orange flowers in spring; and B. stenophylla, superficially similar to B. darwinii (which is one of its parents) but with yellow flowers. My preference is for the normal species but 'Corallina Compacta' is an appealing and curious dwarf form with buds that are bright pink before they open.

Buddleia spp.   Loganiaceae

Large, deciduous shrubs reaching 3–4 m (10–13 ft), best known for the late summer flowering forms of B. davidii, the butterfly bush, although there are other species at least as beautiful. Most are tolerant of a wide range of soil conditions and are very hardy, but flower best in full sun.
PROPAGATE BY: semi-hardwood cuttings in summer or hard-wood cuttings in winter.
AFTER-CARE: prune all growth of B. davidii to within 30 cm (12 in) of ground level in late winter; rejuvenate B. globosa on a three-year cycle, taking out the oldest third of the wood in any one year; thin out the 'crown' of B. alternifolia after flowering (when trained as a standard).
PEST, DISEASE OR OTHER PROBLEMS: none.
RECOMMENDED VARIETIES: B. alternifolia – early summer flowering with cascades of lilac, honey-scented flowers, always best when trained as a standard. B. davidii – late summer flowering, butterfly attractant, in many varieties, of which the best are 'Black Knight' (dark purple); 'Royal Red' (deep red-purple); 'White Bouquet' (the best white form with yellow centres to the flowers); 'Harlequin' is an unaccountably popular and scruffy variety with variegated leaves. B. globosa, the orange ball tree, with spherical orange-yellow flower heads in early summer, is a large, lax plant but undeniably appealing in a large garden.

Calluna vulgaris   Heather   Ericaceae

Low-growing, very hardy evergreens, barely reaching 80 cm (32 in). This is the familiar summer-flowering Scottish heather that provides such valuable ground cover on poor, acid soils; it is quite intolerant of lime. In many upland, exposed gardens, it is almost the only vegetation that will grow at all without very careful attention. Varieties exist with flower and/or foliage appeal.
PROPAGATE BY: very short semi-hardwood cuttings in summer.
AFTER-CARE: trim back with shears in spring.
PEST, DISEASE OR OTHER PROBLEMS: none.
RECOMMENDED VARIETIES: many dozens are available and new ones constantly being introduced. The following are those that have served me well – 'Alba Plena' (double white); 'Beoley Gold' (white with golden foliage); 'County Wicklow' (double pink); 'Golden Feather' (pink with golden foliage); 'Kinloch-ruel' (white with very dark green foliage); 'Peter Sparkes' (double pink); 'Robert Chapman' (double pink with yellow foliage, probably my favourite); 'Wickwar Flame' (insignificant flowers but yellow foliage that turns vivid red in winter).

Camellia spp. and hybrids   Theaceae

Camellia 'Donation'

Glorious, fairly hardy evergreens, ultimately reaching about 4 m (13 ft). Camellias are almost universally admired for their dark-green foliage and perfectly formed single or double blooms. They are bought with the best of intentions but often fail in gardens because they are not planted in acid soil and partial shade. Where the natural soil is neutral or alkaline, camellias may be grown very successfully in containers, a technique that enables them to be moved into shelter when cold winds threaten.

PROPAGATE BY: semi-hardwood cuttings in summer or leaf bud cuttings in spring.

AFTER-CARE: none but benefit from sequestered iron in early spring.

PEST, DISEASE OR OTHER PROBLEMS: late frost will damage mature buds, and bud drop is a constant problem with no certain prevention. Maintaining the soil in a thoroughly moist condition by mulching with peat will help nonetheless.

RECOMMENDED VARIETIES: C. japonica 'Adolphe Audusson' (deep red, semi-double); 'Cornish Snow' (white, single, small); 'Elegans' (peach pink, anemone-flowered – one or more rows of large outer petals with a mass of small petals and stamens within); 'Leonard Messel' (peach pink, loose paeony-flowered – a more or less loose mass of large and small petals inter-mingled with stamens); C. williamsii 'Donation' (pink, semi-double).

Ceanothus spp. and hybrids   Rhamnaceae

Deciduous and autumn-flowering or evergreen and spring-summer-flowering, the latter much less hardy and benefitting from shelter, even in mild areas; reaching 3–4 m (10–13 ft). Typically with powder-blue masses of flowers rather like lilacs, although smaller, Ceanothus are, for many people, among the glories of the garden, although personally they excite me very little.

PROPAGATE BY: semi-hardwood cuttings in summer or (deciduous forms only) hardwood cuttings in winter.

AFTER-CARE: prune deciduous forms hard in spring to within 15 cm (6 in) of base; none needed for evergreen types.

PEST, DISEASE OR OTHER PROBLEMS: none.

RECOMMENDED VARIETIES: **Deciduous:** 'Gloire de Versailles' (pale blue); 'Henri Desfosse' (deep blue). **Evergreen:** C. arboreus 'Trewithen Blue' (dark blue, probably the hardiest of the evergreens); C. impressus (deep blue, hardy, with small crinkled leaves); C. thyrsiflorus repens (deep blue, relatively wide spreading).

Ceratostigma spp.   Plumbaginaceae

Deciduous, autumn-flowering, low-growing plants, reaching at most 1 m (39 in) and with stunning, electric-blue single flowers and rich autumn leaf colours. The best results are achieved in full sun and with a slightly acid soil, but this is one plant that I would not willingly be without in any garden.

PROPAGATE BY: softwood cuttings in spring or semi-hardwood cuttings in summer.

AFTER-CARE: cut back all shoots to ground level in spring. They establish rather slowly and are best not disturbed once planted.

PEST, DISEASE OR OTHER PROBLEMS: none.

RECOMMENDED VARIETIES: differences are mainly in plant height for the flowers are all similar – C. willmottianum, the tallest and most widely available; C. plumbaginoides, lower growing.

Chaenomeles spp. and hybrids   Ornamental Quince   Rosaceae

Deciduous, spring flowering shrubs reaching about 3 m (10 ft) but of rather loose open habit and often most successful when trained two-dimensionally against a wall. The flowers are very evidently related to crab apples and range from white through pinks and creams to rich red. The fruits can be used in the same way as edible quinces but are much less palatable.

PROPAGATE BY: semi-hardwood cuttings in summer or by layering.

AFTER-CARE: on free-standing plants, cut out the oldest wood after flowering and thin out the numbers of lateral shoots. On wall-trained plants, once they have filled their allotted space, spur prune as for apples by cutting the previous season's growth back to three buds from the base after flowering.

PEST, DISEASE OR OTHER PROBLEMS: none.

RECOMMENDED VARIETIES: there are three main types – C. japonica, C. speciosa and C. superba, although nurseries often do not discriminate between them and sell plants under variety name only. For wall training especially, I recommend C. japonica (orange red); C. speciosa 'Nivalis' (white); C. superba 'Coral Sea' (pink); 'Crimson and Gold' (red flowers with gold anthers); 'Rowallane' (crimson).

Choisya ternata   Mexican Orange Blossom   Rutaceae

A low-growing (ultimately 2 m/6½ ft) evergreen, summer-flowering shrub with very fragrant, orange-perfumed flowers held in flat inflorescences above glossy, oval leaves. It is attractive enough in bloom and tolerates both sun and partial shade, but is rather boring and laurel-like for the remainder of the year.

PROPAGATE BY: semi-hardwood cuttings in summer or hard-wood cuttings in winter.

AFTER-CARE: remove the oldest one third of the wood after flowering each year.

PEST, DISEASE OR OTHER PROBLEMS: none.

RECOMMENDED VARIETIES: apart from the normal species there is a smaller, golden-foliaged form called 'Sundance'. This is evidently much admired because it has become very popular but it is less hardy and to me looks merely bilious.

Conifers (dwarf)

I have included this rather varied group of plants here for a number of reasons. These are the dwarf forms of the many coniferous trees that, full size, generally have little place in the garden but in their abbreviated dimensions make useful shrubs. They do not, of course, have flowers and their appeal derives almost entirely from the colour and shape of their needles and their overall form. They are not, let it be said, to everyone's taste and I would certainly baulk at using them with heathers and similar plants to create a garden, as some people have done, that excludes almost everything else. Nonetheless, dotted among other vegetation, their rather special forms can be most useful. They are tolerant of most types of soils, although they are generally more successful on acidic types and tend to turn yellow on alkaline ones.

PROPAGATE BY: semi-hardwood cuttings in late summer but this is not easy and a mist propagation system is needed for consistent success.

AFTER-CARE: none.

PEST, DISEASE OR OTHER PROBLEMS: red spider mite can be troublesome in hot dry seasons.

RECOMMENDED VARIETIES: there are hundreds, if not thousands, of varieties, generally with names in inverse proportion to their size. If you require something out of the ordinary, then I advise you to visit a specialist nursery. Rather than mention individual varieties that you may well be unable to obtain, therefore, I shall indicate the main types. **Abies** spp. (firs): typically Christmas tree like in general form, often with rather sharp, short, stiff needles. There are good golden, silvery and green needled types and some good prostrate forms. The group includes, in *A. koreana*, the conifer that produces cones at a younger age than almost any other. **Cedrus** spp. (cedars): there are a few soft-needled, golden and sometimes weeping forms. **Chamaecyparis** spp. (cypresses): a huge group of mainly upright, conical or domed-shaped plants with frond-like green or yellow shoots and no obvious needles. **Cupressus** spp. (cypresses): similar to *Chamaecyparis* but including some very good prostrate types. **Juniperus** spp. (junipers): another huge group with some very good prostrate and semi-prostrate forms as well as some excellent conical varieties with green, bluish or gold foliage and very short, often rather prickly needles. **Larix** spp. (larches): my favourite conifers, deciduous and with beautiful soft needles but with only one or two dwarf types. **Picea** spp. (spruces): Christmas tree or pyramidal shapes in general, with short, often prickly needles and a range of green, bluish and yellow colours. **Pinus** sp. (pines): generally long (and sometimes very long), fairly soft needles and upright or domed habit with a range of green and golden colours; a superb group. **Taxus baccata** (yew): not really dwarf but some very slow growing pillar-like plants in green or gold. **Thuja** spp. (red cedars): soft, scented foliage and some beautiful dome-shaped plants with green or golden colours.

Cotinus coggygria and related spp.　Smoke Bush Anacardiaceae

A deciduous shrub reaching 6 m (20 ft), with very attractive autumn colours, broadly oval leaves and unusual, feathery inflorescences that are produced best in full sun. It is said that the dark-leaved forms turn green in the shade but I have never found this so and, in fact, if you are prepared to sacrifice some flower production, this makes a useful shrub for light shade.

PROPAGATE BY: layering.

AFTER-CARE: either leave unpruned if space permits or remove the oldest one third of the wood after flowering each year.

PEST, DISEASE OR OTHER PROBLEMS: none.

RECOMMENDED VARIETIES: the normal species provides good inflorescences and green foliage; 'Royal Purple' is my choice for deep-purple leaves and flame-red autumn colour.

Cotoneaster spp.　Rosaceae

A large and very useful group of deciduous and evergreen shrubs, covering a range of forms from low growing, ground hugging species to 4 m (13 ft) tall shrubs, and including several that are very useful trained against walls and a few that make striking hedges. The flowers are almost always insignificant (although often very effective as bee-attractants), but the real glory of many types lies in their red, orange or yellow berries

and also in the autumn foliage colours of the deciduous species.

PROPAGATE BY: semi-hardwood cuttings in summer or hardwood cuttings in winter.

AFTER-CARE: no pruning is required routinely but most forms will tolerate being cut back for rejuvenation or to keep them within bounds; those trained against walls and as hedges may be clipped.

PEST, DISEASE OR OTHER PROBLEMS: none, although birds are greatly attracted to the berries.

RECOMMENDED VARIETIES: **Deciduous types:** *C.* 'Coral Beauty', spreading, low growing, pink-red berries, small, greyish oval leaves; *C. horizontalis*, small leaves, herringbone branching pattern, rich red berries and red autumn colours; *C. simonsii*, upright growth and good as informal hedge, white flowers in spring followed by red berries. **Evergreen types:** *C. dammeri*, wide spreading, low growing, self-layers readily and good ground cover, red autumn berries; *C. microphyllus*, tiny dense, glossy dark-green leaves, rather large, red berries, mound forming and makes good ground cover; *C. wateri*, 'Pendulus' (often called 'Hybridus Pendulus'), spreading shrub with attractive reddish leaf stalks and bright-red autumn berries, most often seen grafted as a small standard tree but I am not sure if I like this; *C.* 'Rothschildianus', superb tall shrub with narrow, elongated leaves and yellow autumn berries; *C. salicifolius* 'Floccosus', narrow, elongated leaves, shiny above and white below with red autumn berries, one of the most undervalued plants for covering a shady wall.

Cytisus spp. and hybrids　Brooms　Leguminosae

Deciduous spring- or summer-flowering shrubs with pea-like flowers, ranging from low-growing forms, more or less suitable as ground cover, to one magnificent species 6 m (20 ft) tall. They are all fairly hardy and tolerant of a wide range of soils, although most thrive best in full sun in slightly acid conditions; most too are unlikely to succeed on heavy, wet soils.

PROPAGATE BY: semi-hardwood cuttings in summer or hardwood cuttings in winter.

AFTER-CARE: do not respond well to pruning; old, leggy specimens should be replaced.

PEST, DISEASE OR OTHER PROBLEMS: none.

RECOMMENDED VARIETIES: **Low growing, ground cover types:** *C. beanii*, yellow, mound-forming; *C. kewensis*, cream-yellow, creeping; **Medium sized types:** *C.* 'Andreanus' (red and yellow); *C.* 'Killiney Red' (red); *C. praecox* 'Albus' (white); 'Allgold' (yellow-gold); *C. scoparius* (yellow and white); *C.* 'Windlesham Ruby' (brown-red). **Tall type:** *C. battandieri*, Pineapple or Moroccan Broom (large yellow, pineapple perfume).

Daphne spp. and hybrids　Thymeliaceae

Deciduous or evergreen, low growing (1–2 m/3¼–6½ ft) early spring flowering shrubs with small, sometimes rather attractive greenish, white or pinkish flowers and, usually, very strong sweet perfume. Most daphnes are hardy and require partial shade and a humus-rich soil; they are especially valuable when placed close to a path, doorway or garden seat where their perfume can best be appreciated.

PROPAGATE BY: semi-hardwood cuttings in summer.

AFTER-CARE: no pruning required but respond well to early season mulching.

PEST, DISEASE OR OTHER PROBLEMS: none.
RECOMMENDED VARIETIES: **Deciduous types:** *D. blagayana* (cream-white); *D. burkwoodii* (pale pink, large clusters); *D. mezereum* 'Alba' (white). **Evergreen types:** *D. cneorum* (rich pink); *D. laureola* (greenish, a lovely native woodland plant); *D. tangutica* (dwarf, white/pink-purple).

Elaeagnus spp. and hybrids Elaeagnaceae

Although there are deciduous species, it is the evergreen forms that are of greatest value in the garden, offering an attractive range of foliage colours. Unfortunately, the summer flowers are insignificant (although fragrant in some types) but for hardy, medium-sized (reaching 3 m/10 ft) plants for winter leaf appeal in most sites in most gardens, elaeagnus take some beating.
PROPAGATE BY: semi-hardwood cuttings in summer, hardwood cuttings in winter or by layering.
AFTER-CARE: cut out green-leaved shoots on variegated forms.
PEST, DISEASE OR OTHER PROBLEMS: none.
RECOMMENDED VARIETIES: *E. ebbingei* (yellow flowers, scented); 'Gilt Edge' (golden leaf edges); 'Limelight' (golden blotches on leaves); *E. pungens* 'Maculata' (golden leaf blotches that intensify in winter; invaluable for winter colour).

Erica spp. and hybrids Heaths Ericaceae

Erica carnea 'Vivellii'

Invaluable low-growing evergreen plants for flower and leaf appeal on poor acid soils, although the autumn-, winter- or spring-flowering forms of *E. carnea* and, to a lesser extent, *E. darleyensis* are tolerant of quite high levels of alkalinity. Even in very alkaline gardens, however, the rewards offered by summer-flowering heaths alone justify the construction of a small peat bed.
PROPAGATE BY: short semi-hardwood cuttings in summer or, very easily, by layering – peg down shoots and mound soil in the centre of old clumps.
AFTER-CARE: trim with shears after flowering.
PEST, DISEASE OR OTHER PROBLEMS: none.
RECOMMENDED VARIETIES: there are several hundred varieties and the following small selection represents merely my prime choices: *E. cinerea* 'Alba Minor' (white, compact); 'C. D. Eason' (dark red-pink); 'Eden Valley' (lavender and white); 'Foxhollow Mahogany' (mahogany-purple-red); 'Pink Ice' (rich pink); 'Velvet Knight' (dark purple); *E. carnea* (sometimes called *E. herbacea*) 'Ann Sparkes' (purple-red, yellow-bronze foliage);

'Myretoun Ruby' (deep red); 'Pink Spangles' (pink); 'Springwood White' (white; very good close ground cover); 'Vivellii' (red flowers, bronze foliage, slower growing); *E. darleyensis* 'Arthur Johnson' (rose pink, vigorous); *E. vagans* 'Mrs D. F. Maxwell' (pink; an outstandingly good variety).

Escallonia spp. and hybrids Escalloniaceae

Evergreen, glossy-leaved summer-flowering shrubs, reaching 3 m (10 ft) and especially valuable as hedging plants in seaside gardens, although they can be grown successfully as specimens too. They are prone to damage from cold winter winds but usually regenerate.
PROPAGATE BY: semi-hardwood cuttings in summer or hardwood cuttings in winter.
AFTER-CARE: cut out the oldest third of the shoots on specimen plants after flowering each year; clip hedges immediately after flowering.
PEST, DISEASE OR OTHER PROBLEMS: none.
RECOMMENDED VARIETIES: *E.* 'Apple Blossom' (soft pink); *E.* 'Donard Seedling' (white, pink-tinged); *E.* 'Iveyi' (white); *E. langleyensis* (rich pink, floriferous); *E. macrantha* (deep pink; best for seaside hedging).

Euonymus spp. Spindles and others Celastraceae

Deciduous or evergreen, some reaching 3 m (10 ft) and valuable for hedging, although with several low-growing, ground-cover types too. This is a versatile genus which should have at least some representatives in every garden. They are undemanding of site and aspect.
PROPAGATE BY: semi-hardwood cuttings in summer, hardwood cuttings in winter or by layering.
AFTER-CARE: clip hedging forms twice a year; remove old wood periodically on large, established specimens and cut back upright shoots on ground cover forms in spring.
PEST, DISEASE OR OTHER PROBLEMS: mildew on *E. japonicus*.
RECOMMENDED VARIETIES: **Deciduous type:** *E. europaeus* 'Red Cascade' (selected form of native spindle bush with red fruits and good autumn colour). **Evergreen types:** *E. fortunei* (ground cover) 'Emerald Gaiety' (ground hugging, white and green leaf patterning); 'Emerald 'n' Gold' (an appalling name for a pretty plant with pale green and yellow leaves); 'Silver Queen' (pale-green leaves with white margin, most pronounced in summer); 'Sunspot' (the best golden blotched form with contrasting dark-green leaf areas); *E. japonicus* (dark-green glossy leaves, not an especially attractive plant but a remarkably effective dense hedge, especially for seaside areas; often planted as a screen around public lavatories).

Forsythia spp. and hybrids Oleaceae

Invaluable deciduous plants for bright yellow or gold spring flowers. Hardy and tolerant of most soil types but will not flower effectively unless in full sun. Reach 4 m (13 ft) although some low-growing forms exist too.
PROPAGATE BY: semi-hardwood cuttings in summer or hardwood cuttings in winter.
AFTER-CARE: cut out the oldest third of shoots each year.

Wall-trained plants should be pruned or clipped after flowering.
PEST, DISEASE OR OTHER PROBLEMS: none.
RECOMMENDED VARIETIES: *F. intermedia* 'Spectabilis' (golden yellow; quite the best forsythia in my experience); 'Lynwood' (free flowering but colour inferior to 'Spectabilis').

Fuchsia spp. and hybrids   Onagraceae

The fuchsia is best known as a half-hardy plant for indoor or conservatory use or for planting in bedding schemes or containers. I describe varieties suitable for the latter purposes on p. 219 but here I am concerned with the fewer but nonetheless very valuable hardy species. In mild and maritime areas, they are well known and extremely useful for hedging but in many other districts, too, they can make important contributions to small shrubberies and mixed borders.
PROPAGATE BY: shoot tip cuttings in spring or semi-hardwood cuttings in summer.
AFTER-CARE: in mild areas, leave unpruned (or clip hedges) but elsewhere, they will die down in winter, although the dead shoots should not be removed until spring.
PEST, DISEASE OR OTHER PROBLEMS: whitefly.
RECOMMENDED VARIETIES: *F.* 'Genii' (red and purple with yellowish foliage); *F. magellanica* 'Alba' (white with pink tinge); 'Riccartonii' (red and purple, the commonest hedging form); 'Versicolor' (red and purple with silvery foliage); *F.* 'Mrs Popple' (red and violet; perhaps the hardiest of all); *F.* 'Tom Thumb' (red and purple, dwarf, compact).

Genista spp.   Brooms, gorses   Leguminosae

Deciduous, summer-flowering shrubs with yellow, pea-like flowers and small, elongated leaves which tend to be hidden by the masses of blossom. Normally reach about 1–1.5 m (3–5 ft), although *G. aetnensis* is almost tree-sized. They are widely tolerant of soil and aspect but, like the *Cytisus* brooms, thrive best in full sun and resent heavy, wet conditions.
PROPAGATE BY: semi-hardwood cuttings in summer or hardwood cuttings in winter.
AFTER-CARE: none, resent pruning.
PEST, DISEASE OR OTHER PROBLEMS: none.
RECOMMENDED VARIETIES: *G. aetnensis* (ultimately reaches 5 m (16½ ft) with widely arching branches; spectacular when in flower); *G. hispanica* (useful for a low, ornamental hedge but prickly); *G. lydia* (mound-forming); *G. pilosa* 'Lemon Spreader' (mound-forming); *G. tinctoria* 'Royal Gold' (larger flowers than most).

Hamamelis mollis   Witch Hazel   Hamamelidaceae

Large, deciduous shrubs, at maturity almost tree-like, and treasured for their highly individual winter flowers borne on bare branches. Some also have an attractive perfume but they are not easy plants to grow and are always most successful in fairly mild areas with acid soils. Being grafted, they are expensive to buy and are scarcely worth the experiment unless you know of successfully established plants in your area.
PROPAGATE BY: layering; but very difficult which is why nurseries graft them.
AFTER-CARE: none.

PEST, DISEASE OR OTHER PROBLEMS: none.
RECOMMENDED VARIETIES: 'Pallida' – pale-yellow flowers and very good autumn leaf colour.

Hebe spp. and hybrids   Scrophulariaceae

Hebe pinguifolia 'Pagei'

Summer-flowering evergreens, reaching at most 1.5 m (5 ft) but with some dwarf forms also. Most are characterised by elongated leaves and by elongated inflorescences of purple or whitish flowers, but also by their relative non-hardiness. They are well worth growing but remain risky in colder areas where they should not be used in such a way that their loss in a cold winter would have a major impact on the garden.
PROPAGATED BY: semi-hardwood cuttings in summer.
AFTER-CARE: trim lightly in spring; old plants can be rejuvenated by cutting back to about 30 cm (12 in) above ground level.
PEST, DISEASE OR OTHER PROBLEMS: none.
RECOMMENDED VARIETIES: *H. albicans* 'Red Edge' (dwarf, white flowers, red-edged leaves); *H. armstrongii* (olive-green, whipcord-like foliage, quite distinct); *H. cupressoides* 'Boughton Dome' (cypress-like silvery-green foliage); *H.* 'Karl Teschner' (violet blue, almost prostrate); *H.* 'Marjorie' (pale violet, especially hardy); *H.* 'Midsummer Beauty' (blue-pale purple); *H.* 'Mrs Winder' (blue-mauve, purplish leaves); *H. pinguifolia* 'Pagei' (low-growing or mound-forming; rounded masses of white flowers, good for the rock garden); *H. rakaiensis* (bright-green foliage, dome-forming); *H. salicifolia* (white, one of the hardiest).

Hibiscus syriacus   Malvaceae

Late-summer or autumn-flowering deciduous shrubs, reaching 2–3 m (6½–10 ft) and closely related to the tender greenhouse or indoor species. The outdoor hibiscus is greatly underrated and is much hardier than may be imagined, although it is prone to late frost damage in cold areas. The freely produced open cup-shaped flowers readily betray their relationship to mallows and lavateras.

PROPAGATED BY: semi-hardwood cuttings in summers.

AFTER-CARE: none.

PEST, DISEASE OR OTHER PROBLEMS: none.

RECOMMENDED VARIETIES: the wild species has a very wide range in flower colour from white through various reds and purples and includes some striped types. This range is reflected in the many named forms of which the best and most widely available are: 'Blue Bird' or 'Oiseau Bleu' (blue violet); 'Hamabo' (pale rose-pink with darker centres); 'Red Heart' (white with central red spot); 'William E. Smith' (white, uncommon but the best single white); 'Woodbridge' (vivid reddish-pink).

Hydrangea spp. and hybrids   Hydrangeaceae

Summer or autumn flowering deciduous shrubs, reaching 3–4 m (10–13 ft). Traditionally associated with mild seaside areas, the genus Hydrangea is grossly misrepresented in most gardeners' minds by the red (on alkaline soils) or blue (on acid soil) flowered mop-head forms of H. macrophylla. These are endearing enough (although the blues are so fierce as to appear artificial) but there are several other, much better, related species, suitable for almost all soils and situations, provided moderate shelter can be given from cold winds.

PROPAGATE BY: semi-hardwood cuttings in summer.

AFTER-CARE: provide protection for the crowns in winter by mounding compost around them. Prune the mop-head and lace-cap forms of H. macrophylla in spring by cutting back the oldest one third of the shoots to a bud close to the base and cutting off the dead flower heads on the remainder (do not remove these in the autumn) to a strong pair of leaves about one third down the shoot. Other types require no pruning. On alkaline soils, the unaccountably appealing blue colour of H. macrophylla varieties can be obtained by applying proprietary blueing powder (aluminium sulphate) to the soil in accordance with the manufacturer's directions.

PEST, DISEASE OR OTHER PROBLEMS: none.

RECOMMENDED VARIETIES: (colours on alkaline/acid soils where appropriate): H. macrophylla (mop-head types): 'Ami Pasquier' (red/purple); 'Ayesha' (pink/lilac); 'Blue Prince' (deep pink/clear blue); 'Generale Vicomtesse de Vibraye' (pink/clear blue); 'Madame Emile Mouillière' (white or pale pink/white). **Lace-cap types:** 'Blue Wave' (also called 'Mariesii Perfecta') (pink/electric blue); 'Lanarth White' (pink/blue with outer florets almost always white); H. arborescens (15 cm (6 in) diameter cream-white flower heads; not common but worth looking for); H. aspera (the most glorious of the lace-caps with pink-lilac ray florets – the form called 'Villosa' or H. villosa is widely available); H. involucrata 'Hortensis' (small double pink-white flowers); H. paniculata (elongated, fluffy white flower heads, glorious but only choose the variety 'Grandiflora'); H. quercifolia (white flowers and huge, oak-like leaves with lovely autumn colour; slightly tricky to establish but my favourite of all hydrangeas, the normal species is superior to named forms); H. sargentiana (lace-cap white-pink flowers); H. serrata (flowers in large flattish or slightly rounded clusters) 'Blue Bird' (pink/blue), 'Grayswood' (pale pink/pink), 'Preziosa' (pink/pink).

Hypericum spp. and hybrids   Guttiferae

Evergreen or deciduous summer-flowering shrubs, more of use than ornament. The taller forms reach 2 m (6½ ft) but the most familiar type, H. calycinum, is a lower growing ground-cover species of legendary invasiveness.

PROPAGATE BY: semi-hardwood cuttings in summer, hard-wood cuttings in winter or by layering.

AFTER-CARE: cut out the oldest one third of the shoots in spring, although if old plants are cut back entirely to ground level, they will usually regenerate satisfactorily.

PEST, DISEASE OR OTHER PROBLEMS: rust disease is becoming increasingly serious and is yet another reason for choosing other shrubs for your garden.

RECOMMENDED VARIETIES: if you must have a vigorous yellow-flowered ground-cover plant for the less important areas of your garden, then H. calycinum will be your choice; otherwise restrict yourself to H. 'Hidcote', the best of the flowering varieties but apt to become large and leggy if left unpruned.

Jasminum spp. and hybrids   Oleaceae

Invaluable evergreen or deciduous flowering shrubs reaching 3–4 m (10–13 ft) with species suitable for winter or summer. Most are grown against the protection of a wall, for they are rather weak-stemmed and in need of support. Almost any soil and situation suits them, although the common white-flowered and perfumed summer jasmine is rather tender, and all flower best in full sun.

PROPAGATE BY: semi-hardwood cuttings in summer or hard-wood cuttings in winter.

AFTER-CARE: J. officinale requires no pruning other than the removal of frost-damaged shoots; J. nudiflorum and similar species can be pruned in three main ways: when trained against a wall, they can be clipped fairly hard after flowering, provided some of the oldest shoots are cut back to ground level every year; or the dead flowering shoots may simply be pruned back, a laborious task. When grown as a free-standing shrub, leave the dead flower shoots to wither and merely carry out the removal of the oldest one third of the main shoots each year.

PEST, DISEASE OR OTHER PROBLEMS: none.

RECOMMENDED VARIETIES: J. officinale (white summer jasmine), the normal species is much prettier than the variegated forms but 'Grandiflorum' (also called J. officinale affine) is a splendid, large-flowered type, although even less hardy; J. nudiflorum (yellow-flowered winter jasmine); J. humile, usually seen in the form called 'Revolutum' (sometimes called J. reevesianum), is an attractive late-spring or early-summer-flowering species with large yellow flowers; J. × stephanense is a scrambling or almost climbing hybrid with pinkish flowers in summer.

Kerria japonica   Jew's Mallow   Rosaceae

A deciduous, spring-flowering shrub with yellow blooms, suitable for almost any soil and any situation and particularly useful for its upright, almost raspberry-cane-like habit which

enables it to be fitted into a small space amongst other plants.
PROPAGATE BY: semi-hardwood cuttings in summer, hardwood cuttings in winter or by layering.
AFTER-CARE: cut out the oldest one third of the shoots each spring after flowering.
PEST, DISEASE OR OTHER PROBLEMS: none.
RECOMMENDED VARIETIES: the form most commonly seen is the double-flowered 'Pleniflora' (also called 'Flore Pleno') but the single-flowered, normal species is pretty too. The variegated foliaged type, 'Variegata', is a feeble looking, pathetic thing.

Lavandula spp. and hybrids   Lavender   Labiatae

Very familiar deciduous or evergreen low-growing summer-flowering shrubs, some reaching about 1 m (39 in) if unpruned, but all benefit from annual pruning. Some species make valuable low hedges (p. 158). There is a much wider range in flower colour and plant size than is generally appreciated.
PROPAGATE BY: semi-hardwood shoot cuttings in early summer or hardwood cuttings in winter.
AFTER-CARE: prune lightly in spring (although old plants can be rejuvenated by hard pruning at this time) and then trim again after the flower heads have faded, cutting slightly beyond the flowers themselves and into the shoot wood.
PEST, DISEASE OR OTHER PROBLEMS: none.
RECOMMENDED VARIETIES: *L. angustifolia* (also called *L. officinalis* or *L. spica*, Old English lavender) 'Alba' (white); 'Grappenhall' (lilac); 'Hidcote' (deep violet-blue, compact and a good hedging plant); 'Munstead' (lavender blue, compact, a good hedging plant); *L. latifolia* 'Loddon Pink' (pink blue, with long flower stalks); *L. pinnata* 'Rosea' (pink-blue, compact); *L. stoechas* (French lavender, evergreen, dark purple, curious flask-like flower heads).

Leucothoe fontanesiana   Ericaceae

An evergreen shrub ultimately reaching 1.5 m (5 ft) but spreading rather widely, with long, drooping branches and attractive narrowly elliptical leaves with drooping white inflorescences in spring. It requires moist acid, or at least neutral, soil and partial shade.
PROPAGATE BY: softwood shoot cuttings in early summer or by layering.
AFTER-CARE: cut out the oldest one third of the shoots in spring once plants are well established.
PEST, DISEASE OR OTHER PROBLEMS: none.
RECOMMENDED VARIETIES: the normal species and a form called 'Rainbow' with rather pretty yellowish and pink leaf flecking are widely available.

Leycesteria formosa   Himalayan honeysuckle   Caprifoliaceae

An invaluable and very easy deciduous shrub, reaching 2–3 m (6½–10 ft) and bearing unusual hanging inflorescences of white flowers with dark red-purple bracts in late summer followed by dark-purple fruit. It is tolerant of moderate shade and as it should be pruned hard every year will never become out of hand.

PROPAGATE BY: softwood shoot cuttings in early summer or by seed.
SOW/PLANT BY: tree and shrub technique with stratification.
AFTER-CARE: prune all growth to the base in early spring.
PEST, DISEASE OR OTHER PROBLEMS: none.
RECOMMENDED VARIETIES: no named forms available.

Lonicera spp.   Shrubby honeysuckles   Caprifoliaceae

Evergreen or deciduous shrubs ranging in size from ground-cover species through medium-sized species suitable for hedging to plants reaching 3–4 m (10–13 ft). Those suitable for hedging are described on p. 159 as I do not find them inspiring enough to consider as specimen shrubs. Here, therefore, I shall restrict myself to the ground-cover foliage species and a few striking and greatly neglected flowering shrubs. Although of the same genus as the climbing honeysuckles, most of the shrubby species do not have such spectacular flowers, although there is usually perfume, the colour range is similar and on close inspection the relationship will be evident.
PROPAGATE BY: semi-hardwood cuttings in summer or hardwood cutting in winter.
AFTER-CARE: no pruning is required although old woody shoots should be cut out from time to time.
PEST, DISEASE OR OTHER PROBLEMS: mildew in sheltered situations.
RECOMMENDED VARIETIES: *L. fragrantissima* (semi-evergreen, tiny, scented cream flowers through the winter); *L. purpusii* (similar to *L fragrantissima* but generally larger although more sparsely flowering); *L. involucrata* (deciduous, yellow flowers with red bracts in early summer); *L. maackii* (stunningly lovely but seldom seen, scented white-yellow flowers in serried ranks in summer); *L. pileata* (semi-evergreen, flowers small and yellowish in summer but of greatest value as a fairly low-growing ground-cover plant for large areas).

Mahonia spp. and hybrids   Berberidaceae

Evergreen shrubs, some reaching 4 m (13 ft) and valuable for their shade tolerance and, in most of the best species, for their scented yellow winter flowers. The leaves are often characteristically dark green and glossy with more or less spiny margins.
PROPAGATE BY: semi-hardwood cuttings in late summer.
AFTER-CARE: no pruning is required, although old woody shoots should be cut out from time to time.
PEST, DISEASE OR OTHER PROBLEMS: rust can occasionally be troublesome on some forms.
RECOMMENDED VARIETIES: *M. aquifolium*, oregon grape, very tough and tolerant of extreme shade and dryness; invaluable for mass planting as ground cover in such conditions; the form called 'Apollo' is less invasive and better as a specimen plant; *M. wagneri* 'Undulata' is similar to the preceding but has slightly wavy leaves and requires rich, moist soil; *M. japonica*, taller with large slightly glaucous leaves and long arching, richly scented inflorescences; *M.* 'Charity' is similar to *M. japonica*, one of its parents, but with more upright inflorescences, a characteristic derived from its other parent, the almost equally lovely but less hardy *M. lomariifolia*.

Philadelphus spp. and hybrids   Mock oranges
Philadelphaceae

Philadelphus 'Belle Etoile'

Extremely beautifully flowered deciduous shrubs, ranging from 1 to 5 m (3 to 16½ ft) and all characterised by very fragrant white summer blossom. The foliage is usually elongated oval in form and relatively uninspiring, with the notable exception of one fine golden variety. If the mock oranges have a disadvantage, it is that most have a rather stiff, stark twiggy appearance in the winter; but that could be said of many other shrubs too and the heavenly summer perfume is admirable compensation. They are tolerant of a wide range of soils, although they thrive best in well drained conditions in full sun or light shade.

PROPAGATE BY: semi-hardwood cuttings in summer or hardwood cuttings in winter.

AFTER-CARE: cut out the oldest one third of the shoots on established plants every year after flowering.

PEST, DISEASE OR OTHER PROBLEMS: aphids are almost ubiquitous.

RECOMMENDED VARIETIES: 'Manteau d'Hermine' (1–1.5 m (3–5 ft), double white); 'Belle Etoile' (1.5 m (5 ft), single white with dark-purple central spot); 'Beauclerk' (2–3 m (6½–10 ft), single white with pinkish centre); 'Virginal' (4 m (13 ft), double white); *P. coronarius* 'Aureus' (3 m (10 ft), single white but really grown for its golden/pale-green foliage).

Pieris spp. and hybrids   Ericaceae

Invaluable evergreens reaching 2–3 m (6½–10 ft) and grown for both foliage and flowers on shaded, moist acid soils. The white spring flowers hang down in delightful cascades while the foliage and shoots in the best forms change colour from a vivid red to dark green as they mature.

PROPAGATE BY: semi-hardwood cuttings in summer or by layering.

AFTER-CARE: none.

PEST, DISEASE OR OTHER PROBLEMS: none.

RECOMMENDED VARIETIES: *P. floribunda* (hardier than most forms); *P.* 'Forest Flame' (hardy and with very vivid red young shoots); *P.* 'Firecrest'; *P. japonica* 'Purity' (notably long inflorescences).

Potentilla spp. and hybrids   Shrubby cinquefoils
Rosaceae

Low-growing, more or less compact deciduous shrubs for flowering through long periods of the summer. The conspicuous single flowers occur in a wide range of colours, although that of some of the most recent introductions fades in the full sun that most potentillas require. They comprise, nonetheless, a most useful group of small shrubs for fairly light soils, the drawbacks being simply that they lack perfume and have a decidely dead appearance in winter.

PROPAGATE BY: semi-hardwood cuttings in summer, hardwood cuttings in winter, by layering or by division.

AFTER-CARE: the smaller forms require little or no pruning, although larger plants should have the oldest one third of the shoots cut back to the base in the spring. Very old plants can sometimes be rejuvenated by cutting them back fully to the base.

PEST, DISEASE OR OTHER PROBLEMS: none.

RECOMMENDED VARIETIES: *P.* 'Daydawn' (pink-peach); *P.* 'Goldfinger' (large, golden yellow); *P.* 'Manchu' (prostrate, pure white); *P.* 'Primrose Beauty' (clear primrose yellow); *P.* 'Tilford Cream' (cream-white).

Pyracantha spp. and hybrids   Firethorns   Rosaceae

Evergreen shrubs grown essentially for their very attractive winter fruits. They can reach 4 m (13 ft) or more and are usually most successful when trained against a wall or as a free-standing feature around a pillar or similar support. They are at their best in full sun and suffer mainly from an uninteresting appearance when not in flower or fruit, from the attentions of birds which can rapidly strip the berries and also from a rather vicious thorniness.

PROPAGATE BY: semi-hardwood cuttings in summer.

AFTER-CARE: prune wall-trained plants in early spring to lessen the loss of too many of the season's flowers and berries. Free-standing plants required no pruning but can be shaped if necessary in spring.

PEST, DISEASE OR OTHER PROBLEMS: none.

RECOMMENDED VARIETIES: *P. coccinea* 'Lalandei' (reddish-orange fruits, upright habit); *P.* 'Orange Glow' (reddish-orange fruits); *P.* 'Red Column' (red fruits, upright habit); *P. rogersiana* (reddish-orange fruits, good for more shaded positions); *P.* 'Soleil d'Or' (vivid golden-yellow fruits).

Rhododendron spp. and hybrids   Ericaceae

Evergreen shrubs occurring in a vast range of sizes from dwarf rock-garden species to small trees, all with an absolute requirement for strongly acid soils. The genus rhododendron also includes the evergreen and deciduous forms popularly called azaleas. Generally, the flowers are recognisably similar and occur in large, more or less rounded inflorescences, although some of those with more elongated bell-shaped flowers can be confusing. The colour range is very wide, including white, yellows, oranges and mauve verging on blue. Many rhododendrons are hardy (most notably the group called 'the hardy hybrids'), although many others (including most of the very large and also, unfortunately, most of the perfumed species) can only be grown satisfactorily in mild areas or indoors. The true rhododendrons are woodland plants and must have moist conditions and some shade. This is less true of the azaleas, however, which will often thrive in full sun. Although it is often said that rhododendrons are magnificent for only a few weeks of the year and display nothing but dismal foliage thereafter, there are many types which have leaves interestingly adorned with felt-like or other coverings. They also have the merit of being virtually self-sufficient and are quite indispensible for any garden on an acid soil.

PROPAGATE BY: semi-hardwood cuttings in summer or hardwood cuttings in winter but extremely difficult for many types.
AFTER-CARE: no pruning is needed but remove dead flower heads if practicable, although take care not to damage the shoot apex.
PEST, DISEASE OR OTHER PROBLEMS: leaf spotting of many forms is very common but unimportant.
RECOMMENDED VARIETIES: the choice is vast; there are around 3000 species and hybrids of rhododendron and azalea in cultivation (and yet more species in the wild), although many are obtainable only from specialist nurseries. The very limited selection that follows is essentially taken from the most widely available types and is based on those of which I have some experience. I have excluded those suitable only for very mild and very large gardens and have concentrated instead on the hardiest and smaller types and have included some dwarf enough to make an attractive display in a small peat bed such as could be built in almost any garden, irrespective of the natural soil.
True rhododendrons: R. impeditum (dwarf, mauve blue); R. pemakoense (1 m (39 in), bell-shaped, lilac-purple); R. williamsianum (1 m (39 in), bell-shaped, pink); R. yakushimanum (1 m (39 in), bell-shaped, rose-pink buds, opening pink-white; a magnificent small shrub, expensive but far superior to the hybrids derived from it); R. 'Blue Tit' (1 m (39 in), lavender-blue); R. 'Bow Bells' (1 m (39 in), loose, markedly bell-shaped, pink); R. 'Britannia' (3 m (10 ft), crimson); R. 'Chikor' (dwarf, yellow); R. 'Elizabeth' (1.5 m (5 ft), dark red); R. 'Gomer Waterer' (3 m (10 ft), white with pink and yellow flushes); R. 'Hummingbird' (1 m (39 in), bell-shaped, scarlet); R. 'Lord Roberts' (3 m (10 ft), crimson with black blotches); R. 'Sappho' (3 m (10 ft), mauve buds, opening white with purple flush and a black blotch).
Azalea hybrids: (Evergreen – 1 m/39 in) 'Addy Wery' (dark red); 'Blaauw's pink' (pink); 'Blue Danube' (mauve-blue); 'Hinode-giri' (crimson); 'Hino-mayo' (pink); 'Kure-no-yuki' (white); 'Mother's Day' (red); 'Orange Beauty' (orange); 'Vuyk's Scarlet' (red). (Deciduous – 2–2.5 m/6½–8 ft) 'Berryrose' (pink flushed yellow); 'Cecile' (salmon pink); 'Gibraltar' (orange flushed yellow); 'Homebush' (pink); 'Persil' (white flushed orange); 'Strawberry Ice' (pink with yellow flush).

Ribes spp. and hybrids   Flowering currants
Grossulariaceae

Deciduous or evergreen shrubs, reaching 2.5–3 m (8–10 ft) and sometimes maligned for their rather unappealing scent but nonetheless very easy to grow and with attractive pendant spring inflorescences. They will thrive in most soils and most conditions, although R. speciosum, the real glory of the genus, must have shelter and prefers an acid soil.
PROPAGATE BY: semi-hardwood cuttings in summer or hardwood cuttings in winter.
AFTER-CARE: cut out the oldest one third of the shoots after flowering in spring; old plants can be rejuvenated at the same

time by cutting back even more of the shoot growth.
PEST, DISEASE OR OTHER PROBLEMS: none.
RECOMMENDED VARIETIES: R. odoratum, buffalo currant, spicy scented yellow flowers; R. sanguineum, flowering currant, long inflorescences, 'Album' (white); 'King Edward VII' (red, lower growing than most); 'Pulborough Scarlet' (red, very long inflorescences); R. speciosum, fuchsia-flowered gooseberry (exquisite, aptly described by its name – red fuchsia-like flowers, gooseberry-like leaves).

Rubus spp. and hybrids   Flowering brambles
Rosaceae

Deciduous scrambling shrubs, some useful as ground cover, others upright and rather stiff-caned. Some are valuable for their flowers, others for their attractive white stems. These are not plants for the small neat garden for their growth habit is too unruly, but they are very hardy and tolerant of most soils and situations.
PROPAGATE BY: semi-hardwood cuttings in summer, hardwood cuttings in winter or by layering.
AFTER-CARE: cut out the oldest one third of the shoots after flowering.
PEST, DISEASE OR OTHER PROBLEMS: none although rust may occasionally be troublesome.
RECOMMENDED VARIETIES: R. cockburnianus (vivid white stems); R. thibetanus (stiff brownish canes with a white bloom); R. tricolor (ground cover, even in shade, although not successful in very dry situations; with attractive reddish stems and bristly, dark-green leaves); R. tridel 'Benenden' (large white flowers with vivid yellow stamens); R. ulmifolius 'Bellidiflorus' (very pretty but vigorous scrambler with double pink flowers and acceptable bramble fruit).

Sambucus spp.   Elders   Caprifoliaceae

Deciduous shrubs, related to the weedy elderberry and grown principally for their foliage. They are certainly at home in almost any situation but must be pruned carefully to maintain the attractive appearance, and the golden forms are rather prone to wind scorch. I can never grow any of them without thinking of the number of wild elders that I have dug out in my time.
PROPAGATE BY: semi-hardwood cuttings in summer or hardwood cuttings in winter.
AFTER-CARE: cut out the oldest one third (or all in the case of the golden-leaved forms) of the shoots in spring.
PEST, DISEASE OR OTHER PROBLEMS: aphids.
RECOMMENDED VARIETIES: S. nigra 'Purpurea' (dark-purple leaves); 'Aurea' (golden leaves); S. racemosa 'Plumosa Aurea' (deeply divided, fern-like golden foliage).

Skimmia spp. and hybrids   Rutaceae

Evergreen, low growing shrubs reaching 1 m (39 in) but only really at their best on acid soil and in partial shade. The main attraction lies in the bright-red fruit but not all types are hermaphrodite so it is important in such cases to plant both male and female plants. The foliage is also very prone to bleach, especially in bright sun.
PROPAGATE BY: semi-hardwood cuttings in summer or hard-

wood cuttings in winter.

AFTER-CARE: none.

PEST, DISEASE OR OTHER PROBLEMS: none.

RECOMMENDED VARIETIES: *S. japonica*, 'Fragrans' (male); 'Nymans' (female); *S. rogersii* (female); *S. reevesiana* (hermaphrodite).

Spiraea spp. and hybrids   Rosaceae

Deciduous shrubs ranging from low growing species around 0.5–1 m (20–39 in) to over 2 m (6½ ft) tall. They require sun and prefer light soils; they flower in spring or early summer and are easy to grow. The white-flowered forms are most attractive and worthy of a place in any garden but I cannot love the lurid pinks and reds which I find extremely hard to blend with anything else; some have inflorescences very like the similarly coloured astilbes, which I dislike above most things. There are even forms with sickening mixtures of red, pink and white flowers on the same plant.

PROPAGATE BY: semi-hardwood cuttings in summer, hardwood cuttings in winter or by division, which is remarkably successful for a shrub.

AFTER-CARE: varies with type: cut out the oldest one third of the shoots after flowering (Method 1), cut down almost completely to ground level (Method 2) or do not prune at all.

PEST, DISEASE OR OTHER PROBLEMS: none.

RECOMMENDED VARIETIES: *S. bumalda* (if you must have the lurid dwarfs) (0.5 m (20 in), pruning method 2) 'Anthony Waterer' (pink-red); 'Gold Flame' (pink-red with golden foliage); *S. arguta* (bridal wreath, 2 m (6½ ft), white, lovely in full blossom, pruning method 1); *S. nipponica* 'Snowmound' (2 m (6½ ft), arching branches, white, pruning method 1).

Stephanandra spp.   Rosaceae

Stephanandra tanakae

Underappreciated deciduous shrubs of great value and attractiveness, one a mound-forming variety with year-round interest, and the other a 3 m (10 ft) tall plant with special appeal for its rich brown bare stems. They are very hardy and easy to establish in almost any soil.

PROPAGATE BY: semi-hardwood cuttings in summer or by layering.

AFTER-CARE: cut out a proportion of the oldest wood each spring; *S. incisa* 'Crispa' can become very congested in time.

PEST, DISEASE OR OTHER PROBLEMS: none.

RECOMMENDED VARIETIES: *S. incisa* 'Crispa' (moundforming, very good ground cover with small, hawthorn-like leaves); *S. tanakae* (green-white spring flowers, mahoganybrown winter stems).

Stranvaesia (sometimes called *Photinia*) *davidiana*   Rosaceae

Semi-evergreen, useful if unexciting plant reaching 5–6 m (16½–20 ft) and grown most for its red autumn fruits. Stranvaesias are best grown in massed plantings in semi-wild gardens for they do not really have enough intrinsic merit to be used as specimens.

PROPAGATE BY: soft wood cuttings in early summer or, better, by layering.

AFTER-CARE: none.

PEST, DISEASE OR OTHER PROBLEMS: fireblight; should not therefore be grown close to fruit trees, especially pears.

RECOMMENDED VARIETIES: normal species is the best form available.

Viburnum spp. and hybrids   Caprifoliaceae

A large genus containing many deciduous and evergreen species with a considerable range of uses in the garden. They are tolerant of a wide range of soils and conditions and all of those recommended here are perfectly hardy. The group is most usefully divided into the winter/early-spring-flowering types, the later-flowering types, the large-leaved evergreen foliage types (which are the least appealing visually but useful for screening purposes), and the deciduous ornamental fruiting types. There can be scarcely any garden that would not be enhanced by at least one type of viburnum.

PROPAGATE BY: try soft wood cuttings in early summer, semi-hardwood cuttings later in summer, hardwood cuttings in winter or layering. Some methods are better with some types than with others but some are notoriously difficult to root and commercially are grafted.

AFTER-CARE: leave unpruned until established then cut out up to one third of the oldest shoots each year after flowering.

PEST, DISEASE OR OTHER PROBLEMS: none.

RECOMMENDED VARIETIES: **Winter/early-spring-flowering**: *V. bodnantense* 'Dawn' (4m (13 ft), masses of pinkish spherical inflorescences on bare twigs, indispensible for the winter garden); *V. burkwoodii* (2 m (6½ ft), masses of fragrant white flowers, semi-evergreen); *V. carlcephalum* (2 m (6½ ft), similar to preceding but deciduous); *V. carlesii* (2 m (6½ ft), white, strongly and sweetly scented flowers, rounded greygreen leaves with felted undersides, deciduous, with good autumn colour; there are many inferior forms, the best is 'Aurora'); *V. tinus* (still sometimes called *laurustinus*) 'Eve Price' (2–3 m (6½–10 ft), white-pinkish scented flowers through the winter, small glossy evergreen leaves).

Later-flowering types: *V. plicatum* snowball tree (4–5 m (13–16½ ft), deciduous, hydrangea-like white or pink lace-cap or mop-head inflorescences), 'Lanarth' (white, lace-cap in pronounced tiers); 'Mariesii' (white, lace-cap, in pronounced tiers); 'Grandiflorum' (white-pink, mop-head, good autumn leaf colour); *V. tomentosum* (white, lace-cap, good autumn leaf colour).

Evergreen foliage types: *V. rhytidophyllum* (5 m (16½ ft), large creamy inflorescences in spring, leaves glossy with felted under-

179

sides, red winter berries); *V. davidii* (1.5–2 m (5–6½ ft), elongated, rather matt leaves and clusters of tiny, elongated dark-blue fruits in autumn; unisexual so both male and female clones will be needed).

Ornamental fruiting types (reaching 4 m/13 ft): *V. lantana* (wayfaring tree, white summer flowers followed by bright-red fruit that gradually darken to black); *V. opulus*, guelder rose, 'Aureum' (large white summer flowers followed by red fruit and with yellow young shoots in spring); 'Notcutt's Variety' (large white summer flowers of lace-cap type, followed by bright-red fruit, the best red fruiting form); 'Xanthocarpum' (as preceding but with golden fruit).

Vinca spp.   Periwinkles   Apocynaceae

Evergreen ground-cover plants with rather sparse but attractive blue flowers. These are most useful for covering dry, difficult areas beneath trees. The larger species can become rather straggly and invasive although not aggressively so; its main drawback is its susceptibility to a rust disease for which there is no effective treatment.

PROPAGATE BY: soft-wood cuttings in early summer or by layering (layers form naturally very readily).

AFTER-CARE: trim (or strim) back to ground level in spring (large species) or trim lightly (small species).

PEST, DISEASE OR OTHER PROBLEMS: rust on *V. major*.

RECOMMENDED VARIETIES: *V. major* (large leaves, vigorous); *V. minor* 'Aureovariegata' (yellow leaf blotches); 'Bowles Variety' (larger flowers); 'Variegata' (white leaf variegation).

Weigela spp. and hybrids   Caprifoliaceae

Dual-purpose deciduous shrubs grown for flower and foliage effect and ranging up to about 2.5 m (8 ft). Useful if mostly undistinguished would summarise them. They are suitable for all except very wet soils and are always most successful in full sun. The loveliest colours are the really deep reds and the pinks; there is at least one recent introduction with a sickening mixture of cream and pink flowers that, once seen, is best forgotten.

PROPAGATE BY: semi-hardwood cuttings in early summer or hardwood cuttings in winter.

AFTER-CARE: remove about one third of the oldest shoots on established plants after flowering.

PEST, DISEASE OR OTHER PROBLEMS: none.

RECOMMENDED VARIETIES: 'Abel Carriere' (2 m (6 ft), red with yellow throat); 'Bristol Ruby' (1.5 m (5 ft), rich red); 'Florida Variegata' (2 m (6½ ft), pink flowers, white leaf margins, my favourite); 'Newport Red' (1.5 m (5 ft), dark red); *W. florida* (2–2.5 m (6½–8 ft) 'Aureovariegata' (pink, yellow leaf variegation), 'Foliis Purpurea' (pink-purple, purplish leaves); *W. middendorffiana* (yellow/orange, widely arching branches).

Climbing plants

Wisteria sinensis

CLIMBING plants add the vertical dimension to the garden. Naturally, they grow with the support of other vegetation – over trees and shrubs, for instance, over rock faces or, sometimes, scrambling along the ground and even forming a knotted mound as they entwine amongst themselves. But they all share the feature of having stems that are too weak to support them. There are a few climbing fruits and vegetables that I have dealt with in their respective chapters but the most important role for climbers in the garden is as ornamentals.

In gardens, there are essentially two ways in which climbers can be supported – either by growing them over other plants, much as they grow naturally, or more precisely trained up such artificial supports as trellises, fences, archways or pergolas. I have described such supports in detail elsewhere (p. 189) but in general, the unashamedly artificial types are most appropriate for the small or formal garden, leaving the more natural 'free rein' approach to larger and preferably fairly well wooded gardens. Bear in mind too that some types of climber are intrinsically more appropriate to the formal, trained situation – the less vigorous species of clematis, for instance, are very effective when grown on a trellis, whereas the unkempt, scrambling honeysuckle rarely is.

Many types of climber are naturally plants of the woodland and many, therefore, are fairly shade tolerant, although you should be aware that some require shade at the roots but will only flower satisfactorily if their upper parts are in full sun. As with other types of garden ornamentals, there are climbers adapted to most types of soil but almost all will benefit from careful attention being given to soil preparation before planting. The base of a wall, hedge, fence, tree or other support is almost inevitably dry and often impoverished too. Thorough incorporation of organic matter, regular feeding (using liquid fertilisers during the growing season) and watering are most important, therefore.

The more formally trained climbers require regular attention to pruning and training and also tying to their supports. Care must be taken, too, to ensure that the support ties are checked annually – a rapidly growing climber such as a wisteria also grows considerably in girth too and a wire that was loose in one autumn can be almost a garotte by the next.

Largely because of the shelter afforded by the supports, climbing plants as a group tend to be rather prone to pests and diseases – the shelter and warmth accorded the plants is accorded to their problems too. Among pests, red spider mite and aphids, whilst among diseases, mildew, will require watching carefully and probably need regular control.

Although most familiar climbing ornamentals are perennial, there is a surprising number of climbing hardy or half-hardy annuals too that can be used to provide rapid summer cover for fences or to add appeal to otherwise boring evergreen trees or hedges. A few, even of the half-hardy types, will self seed in the garden. As a group, perennial climbers of all types, especially the natural species, tend to be fairly easy to propagate, their pliable shoots being amenable to forming roots both as cuttings and as layers. Among the common garden climbers clematis cuttings require special attention, the majority rooting most readily when taken inter-nodally (that is, when they are cut between, rather than just below, the leaf clusters).

Climbing plants climb in several rather different ways. Some merely twine themselves around their supports; sometimes it is the stem and sometimes the leaf stalk that fulfills this role and there is unaccountable variation between different plants in their propensity for twining clockwise or anticlockwise. Yet other species have stem ends or leaf stalks modified to form specialised grasping tendrils while a few, ivies most notably, have modified aerial roots with minute suckers.

The one important group of climbing plants that I have excluded from the following list is roses which I have dealt with in detail on pp. 193–199.

Actinidia kolomikta   Actinidiaceae

Actinidia kolomikta

A deciduous twining perennial, closely related to the kiwi fruit but grown for its attractively patterned heart-shaped leaves on which the terminal half is coloured creamy white and pink. Ultimately reaches 3–4 m (10–13 ft). The leaf colouration may take several years to develop fully and is then always best in the early part of the season and when the plant is grown against a warm wall.
PROPAGATE BY: semi-hardwood cuttings in late summer or by layering.
AFTER-CARE: cut out long straggly shoots in summer and cut back a proportion of the long side growths to two buds in late winter to maintain the plant's framework.
PEST, DISEASE OR OTHER PROBLEMS: none.
RECOMMENDED VARIETIES: no named forms are available.

Akebia quinata   Lardizabalaceae

A vigorous twining perennial, evergreen in mild winters and reaching 10 m (33 ft) if not pruned. The stems fix themselves firmly to their supports and the plant is ideal for covering large walls or stout fences where it can be given free rein. Tolerant of north- or east-facing situations. Small, deep purple, spicy fragrant flowers are borne in hanging racemes in spring. Occasionally, purple-grey, sausage-like fruits are produced.
PROPAGATE BY: semi-hardwood cuttings in late summer or by layering.
AFTER-CARE: little pruning is needed but the plants should not be disturbed once established.
PEST, DISEASE OR OTHER PROBLEMS: none.
RECOMMENDED VARIETIES: no named forms are available.

Aristolochia macrophylla   Dutchman's Pipe   Aristolochiaceae

A vigorous deciduous twining perennial, reaching 8–10 m (26½–33 ft), hardy only in sheltered south-west or west-facing positions. The early summer flowers are greenish yellow and purple and lack petals but bear inflated and curved sepals to produce a form that gives rise to the plant's common name. They are curious but scarcely lovely, although the plant is well worth growing for its attractive foliage and its aromatic bark.
PROPAGATE BY: semi-hardwood cuttings in late summer or by division.
AFTER-CARE: little pruning is needed but straggly shoots should be cut back after flowering.
PEST, DISEASE OR OTHER PROBLEMS: none.
RECOMMENDED VARIETIES: no named forms are available.

Campsis radicans   Trumpet Vine   Bignoniaceae

A vigorous deciduous self-clinging perennial with aerial roots, reaching 10–12 m (33–40 ft), hardy in many areas if grown against a fairly warm wall. The orange and scarlet flowers that give the plant its name are borne in terminal clusters in late summer or autumn and are stunningly beautiful.
PROPAGATE BY: semi-hardwood cuttings in late summer.
AFTER-CARE: although self-clinging, the weight of the plant, once established, may be so great that it pulls itself away from the wall if not pegged. Prune back lateral shoots to two buds in early spring.
PEST, DISEASE OR OTHER PROBLEMS: none.
RECOMMENDED VARIETIES: 'Flava' or 'Yellow Trumpet' has yellow flowers. The beautiful hybrid 'Madame Galen' is also sometimes available, a cross between *C. radicans* and its less hardy relative *C. grandiflora*.

Celastrus orbiculatus   Celastraceae

A vigorous deciduous twining perennial, reaching 14 m (46½ ft), hardy, tolerant of north- or north-east-facing positions and valuable for covering old walls, trees and large pergolas. The flowers are insignificant but the glory of *Celastrus* is its small, black, spherical fruits which burst to reveal golden-yellow inner sides and masses of scarlet seeds. These fruits hang on the plants during the winter and are rarely taken by birds, making it an invaluable subject for the winter garden.
PROPAGATE BY: semi-hardwood cuttings in late summer. Plants raised from seed will not usually set fruit (see below).
AFTER-CARE: prune to shape if necessary in late winter.
PEST, DISEASE OR OTHER PROBLEMS: none.

RECOMMENDED VARIETIES: almost invariably, plants raised from seed are unisexual and will not form fruit without a partner, which must, of course, be of the opposite sex. But hermaphrodite clones are available, so to avoid the lottery, buy plants specifically so labelled.

Cobaea scandens　Cup and saucer vine　Polemoniaceae

A vigorous tender tendril perennial, usually grown as an annual when it reaches about 3 m (10 ft). The bell-like flowers are borne on long stalks and gradually change colour from greenish white to purple as they age. The petals are surrounded by the green sepals, resulting in an appearance that has given rise to the plant's common name. Particularly attractive when trained over a trellis.
PROPAGATE BY: seed.
SOW BY: half-hardy annual technique at high temperature in late winter.
TRANSPLANT: after the danger of frost has passed.
AFTER-CARE: pinch out shoot tips regularly to maintain a neat appearance.
PEST, DISEASE OR OTHER PROBLEMS: none.
RECOMMENDED VARIETIES: no named forms are usually available although a flowered variant is offered occasionally.

Clematis spp. and hybrids　Ranunculaceae

Deciduous or evergreen twining perennials, some reaching 8 m (26½ ft) or more. Clematis are the most familiar and most widely grown of all climbers, and probably available in the greatest range of varieties too. I am reluctant to call them the most useful, however, for I am sure that it is merely because clematis are thrust at gardeners from all sides that many other, very worthy plants are not grown. Many clematis are also straggly and unkempt, most lack perfume, and almost all require rather careful pruning to give of their best. Nonetheless, many are undeniably lovely, and they are certainly with us to stay. Their soil requirements are similar – alkalinity is preferred although not demanded, shade at the roots is very beneficial and all benefit from (although seldom receive) liquid feeding. Some species are best in full sun but many in fact produce their most intense flower colour in partial shade and are useful for north- or even east-facing walls. All require some support which is most readily provided by trellis or plastic clematis netting. A few types are best grown as herbaceous perennials (p. 205).
PROPAGATE BY: semi-hardwood cuttings in summer or by layering.
AFTER-CARE: there are three important pruning methods, designated groups 1, 2 and 3. Group 1 – cut back immediately after flowering: the weaker growing varieties need little more than a tidying up but strong growers such as *C. montana* may be cut back very hard; Group 2 – prune lightly in early spring (cut away about one quarter of the total growth); Group 3 – prune hard in early spring, cutting back almost to the base of the previous year's growth, and to within about 80 cm of soil level.
PEST, DISEASE OR OTHER PROBLEMS: aphids, clematis wilt, mildew.
RECOMMENDED VARIETIES: *C. alpina* – relatively restrained growth, good for north walls, bell-shaped flowers in spring (Pruning Group 1) – 'Frances Rivis' (large purple flowers); 'White Moth' (double white flowers); *C. armandii* – evergreen, spring flowering, best on a warm wall in mild areas, medium-sized open flowers (Pruning Group 1) always choose the named

forms 'Snowdrift' (white) or 'Apple Blossom' (white-pink); *C. campaniflora* – tiny bell-shaped pale-blue flowers in late summer (Pruning Group 2); *C. jackmannii* – the original hybrid has velvety-purple flowers through the summer but there are other good varieties in this group (Pruning Group 2): 'Comtesse de Bouchard' (rose-pink); 'Hagley Hybrid' (pale pink); 'Perle d'Azur' (pale blue; arguably, although slightly unaccountably, the most popular of all clematis); *C. macropetala* – similar to *C. alpina* (Pruning Group 1) – the normal blue-flowered species and the pink 'Markham's Pink' are the best; *C. montana* – very vigorous, spring flowering, needs space (Pruning Group 1): 'Elizabeth' (pale pink with perfume – a rarity in clematis); var. *rubens* (rose-red with reddish-purple young growths and foliage); 'Tetrarose' (large, purple pink); *C. tangutica* – late summer flowering, yellow or orange (Pruning Group 3): choose the normal, yellow-flowered species and the orange peel clematis 'Bill Mackenzie' (still called *C. orientalis* by many nurseries) (thick orange peel-like flowers); *C. viticella* – late summer flowering with open but nodding flowers (Pruning Group 2): 'Ernest Markham' (purple-red); 'Mme Julia Correvon' (rich deep purple); 'Ville de Lyon' (bright red with yellow stamens). Large-flowered hybrid clematis – mostly early-summer flowering (Pruning Group 2): 'Dr Ruppel' (pink with darker pink stripes); 'Lasurstern' (blue-purple with yellow stamens); 'Marie Boisselot' (double white); 'Nelly Moser' (pale pink with darker pink stripes); 'The President' (rich violet purple, very long flowering period); 'Vyvyan Pennell' (deep violet-blue with reddish centres); 'W.E. Gladstone' (lilac with purple anthers).

Eccremocarpus scaber　Glory vine　Bignoniaceae

A fairly vigorous, fairly hardy evergreen tendril perennial, usually grown as an annual when it reaches 3–4 m (10–13 ft). The tubular, yellow-orange flowers are borne in nodding racemes throughout the summer. Even in mild areas, where the plant will survive as a woody rootstock over winter, it is often short-lived and is much better managed as an annual. The growth is always straggly so *Eccremocarpus* is invariably at its best in a semi-natural planting, but its flowers are striking and have the great merit of being borne for a very long period.
PROPAGATE BY: seed; quite commonly self sows in the garden.
SOW BY: half-hardy annual technique at moderate temperature in late winter.
TRANSPLANT: after the danger of frost has passed.
AFTER-CARE: none.
PEST, DISEASE OR OTHER PROBLEMS: none.
RECOMMENDED VARIETIES: the normal species is the best form commonly available, although mixed hybrids bearing such names as 'Mardi Gras' and 'Fireworks' will produce pinks and reds as well as oranges and yellows, if that is your fancy.

Fallopia baldschuanica　(= *Polygonum baldschuanicum*)
Russian Vine, Mile a Minute Vine　Polygonaceae

An exceedingly vigorous, deciduous, twining climber, capable of reaching 12 or 15 m (40 or 50 ft) very rapidly. Whilst the massed greenish-white inflorescences are undeniably attractive in summer, admiration for them should be kept in check. For in almost any situation and any soil this plant will rapidly take over. It has its uses where you may wish to cover some unsightly structure well away from other cultivated plants, but as an ornamental for normal gardens it is best forgotten.

PROPAGATE BY: semi-hardwood cuttings in late summer.
AFTER-CARE: the machete rather than the secateurs or shears is the tool needed to contain the growth.
PEST, DISEASE OR OTHER PROBLEMS: none.
RECOMMENDED VARIETIES: no named forms available.

Hedera spp.   Ivies   Araliaceae

Evergreen self-clinging perennials with aerial roots. Although ivies as flowering plants have nothing to commend them, they are the most generally valuable evergreen foliage climbers. Several species are available in an enormous range of varieties and almost all have the advantages of thriving even in poor soil, of growing in very dense shade and of being pest and disease free. Contrary to popular belief, ivies will not harm sound bricks and mortar although, in common with other climbers, they can damage old crumbly walls and cause problems if allowed to penetrate beneath tiles.
PROPAGATE BY: semi-hardwood cuttings in late summer or by layering.
AFTER-CARE: clip back straggly growths in summer to maintain shape; cut out green-leaved or normal-leaved shoots on named forms.
PEST, DISEASE OR OTHER PROBLEMS: none.
RECOMMENDED VARIETIES: *Hedera helix* (common ivy), predominantly small leaves, the most tightly clinging form – 'Buttercup' (pale-green or yellow leaves); 'Digitata' (large, deeply lobed leaves); 'Glacier' (the best of the forms with silver-splashed leaves); 'Goldheart' (dark-green leaves with central golden splash); *H. canariensis* (Canary Island ivy) – large, unlobed leaves, slightly less hardy than *H. helix*: 'Gloire de Marengo' (green leaves with cream margin and a large patch of silver grey between the veins); *H. colchica* (Persian Ivy) – large, unlobed, leathery leaves: 'Dentata Variegata' (dark-green leaves with cream margin and irregular grey-green patches); 'Sulphur Heart' (often called 'Paddy's Pride') – pale-green leaves with irregular yellow or paler green central blotches.

Humulus lupulus and *H. japonicus*   Hop   Cannabidaceae

H. lupulus is a fairly vigorous twining herbaceous perennial reaching 6 m (20 ft). This is the native hop, the same species as is used in brewing. It is a rather unkempt and straggly species but its golden form is very appealing in fruit when growing in a semi-natural habitat, where it will tolerate partial shade. The flowers are insignificant but the green fruits or 'cones' which form late in the summer are most attractive. *H. japonicus*, the Japanese hop, is an inferior plant, reaching 3 m (10 ft) but it is barely perennial in Britain and best grown as an annual.
PROPAGATE BY: seed (*H. japonicus*) or by basal or Irishman's cuttings (*H. lupulus*).
SOW BY: half-hardy annual technique at moderate temperature in early spring.
TRANSPLANT: after the danger of frost has passed.
AFTER-CARE: cut down perennial forms in autumn; mulch and
feed in early spring.
PEST, DISEASE OR OTHER PROBLEMS: none.
RECOMMENDED VARIETIES: the best perennial form is 'Aureus'. The best of the forms to raise from seed is the variegated type called 'Variegatus'.

Hydrangea petiolaris   Climbing hydrangea   Hydrangeaceae

A deciduous, self-clinging perennial with aerial roots, reaching 15 m (50 ft) in good soil. This is a very useful plant, especially for north- or east-facing walls. It is easily pruned to confine it to its allotted area and although deciduous, its reddish peeling shoots are attractive even out of leaf. The dull white flowers are borne in early summer in flat-topped inflorescences of typical hydrangea form, although they tend not to form until the plant is well established.
PROPAGATE BY: semi-hardwood cuttings in late summer.
AFTER-CARE: prune out straggly growths in summer and shorten long side shoots to two buds in the spring.
PEST, DISEASE OR OTHER PROBLEMS: none.
RECOMMENDED VARIETIES: no named forms are available.

Ipomoea spp.   Morning Glory   Convolvulaceae

Fairly vigorous, tender perennial herbaceous climbers reaching about 4–5 m (13–16½ ft) and grown in gardens as annuals. These are the ornamental, trumpet-flowered relatives of the bindweed but, not being hardy, they will never become a problem. Morning glories revel in sunshine and are best planted in relatively informal situations where they may be used to conceal wire netting or similar eyesores, but resist the temptation to grow them up plastic netting from which they cannot be removed without damaging the netting itself. The rich purple-coloured forms are also very attractive when allowed to grow with or through pink and red shrub roses.
PROPAGATE BY: seed.
SOW BY: half-hardy annual technique at moderate temperature in early spring.
TRANSPLANT: after the danger of frost has passed.
AFTER-CARE: none.
PEST, DISEASE OR OTHER PROBLEMS: none.
RECOMMENDED VARIETIES: seed is offered of several species and hybrids derived from them but the best by far is 'Heavenly Blue' – a deep sky-blue with whitish centres.

Lathyrus spp.   Sweet pea   Leguminosae

Lathyrus latifolius

The familiar garden sweet pea, derived from *L. odoratus*, is an invaluable tendril annual that responds especially well to very good soil preparation. Trenching is only worthwhile if you intend to grow flowers for exhibition, but thorough incorporation of organic matter in the autumn will certainly pay dividends, even with normal garden plants. There are many ways to support sweet peas – a wigwam of twigs or canes, against plastic clematis netting along a wall or fence, through tall shrubs or, very effectively, with a cylinder-shaped arrangement of canes or a tube of netting. But the annual sweet pea has two less widely grown perennial relatives, *L. grandiflorus* and *L. latifolius*, that are very useful for the informal, cottage-style garden where they will reward you with flowers for year after year; I know of one that has been neglected to the point of abuse and must be almost a century old yet still produces stunning displays.

PROPAGATE BY: seed or by division in spring (perennials).

SOW BY: hardy annual technique at moderate temperature in autumn or early spring. Soak the seeds for 24 hours before sowing and if by this time any have failed to swell (as may happen with dark-coloured seeds), nick them with the point of a sharp knife on the side opposite the 'eye' (p. 104).

TRANSPLANT: after hardened off. When transferring seedlings to individual pots, nip the end from the tap root to encourage a better root system and then, when the plants have two true leaves, pinch out the shoot tip.

AFTER-CARE: do not allow the roots to dry out – use mulch and regular watering. Cut down perennial species in autumn.

PEST, DISEASE OR OTHER PROBLEMS: mildew; root rot if grown repeatedly on the same site or in very wet, cold conditions.

Wigwam of canes to support sweet peas.

RECOMMENDED VARIETIES: there are several distinct types of sweet pea and a huge range of varieties but for garden ornament, perfume and/or use as cut flowers, the choice really lies with the normal garden standard or Spencer varieties, with up to five flowers per stem, the Galaxies with up to eight flowers, the Dwarfs, which reach barely 30 cm (12 in) height and are useful for containers, and the Intermediates which manage around 1 m (39 in). My personal preferences are: **Spencers**: 'Royal Wedding' (white); 'Sally Unwin' (pink); 'Sheila Maqueen' (salmon-orange); 'Lady Fairbairn' (lilac-pink); 'Blue Danube' (blue-mauve); 'The Doctor' (mauve); 'Milestone' (dark maroon). **Galaxy**: usually available in mixtures only. **Dwarfs**: 'Bijou' – a widely available mixture. **Intermediates**: 'Jet-Set' – usually only available as a mixture. The perennial species *L. grandiflorus* exists only as the pink- and purple-flowered species but *L. latifolius* has several forms of which the best are 'Albus' (white) and 'Splendens' (deep pink).

Lapageria rosea   Chilean bell flower   Smilacaceae

Evergreen, twining perennial reaching 5 m (16½ ft); rather tender and only successful in moist, rich acid soils but truly lovely and well worth trying. The flowers are elongated, waxy bells, borne in groups of two or three close to the shoot tips.

PROPAGATE BY: seed or layering.

SOW BY: half-hardy annual technique after washing the fresh seed in several changes of water for two days to remove the inhibitor.

AFTER-CARE: prune very lightly after flowering to maintain shape.

PEST, DISEASE OR OTHER PROBLEMS: none.

RECOMMENDED VARIETIES: although raising from seed is reliable, you may not obtain a particularly good form this way as only the white-flowered 'Alba' seems to come true. If buying a plant, therefore, be certain to choose any of several named forms (there are pink-flowered types among them).

Lonicera spp.   Honeysuckles   Caprifoliaceae

Lonicera × *tellmanniana* and *Clematis* 'Lasurstern'

Deciduous or evergreen twining perennials reaching 10 m (33 ft) (although with some shrubby species too – see p. 176). Honeysuckles are very familiar garden plants, although the wide range of species and varieties is not often appreciated. The deciduous forms are all hardy but always look best when grown in a semi-natural woodland situation where their roots can be shaded but their upper parts reach the sunlight to flower. They are very difficult to restrain and prune neatly against a house wall or similar formal situation. The evergreen species are all unfortunately only hardy enough for sheltered situations in milder areas or have relatively insignificant flowers, and my advice is to grow only the deciduous species and hybrids.

PROPAGATE BY: semi-hardwood cuttings in summer or by layering.

AFTER-CARE: prune lightly after flowering to remove straggly growths and maintain shape.

PEST, DISEASE OR OTHER PROBLEMS: aphids, mildew.

RECOMMENDED VARIETIES: *L. periclymenum* (common honeysuckle) – 'Belgica' (early Dutch), purple-red flowers fade to pink-yellow, early summer and 'Serotina' (late Dutch), dark-purple flowers in late summer; *L. caprifolium* – the normal species is better than the few named forms (and perhaps the best of all honeysuckles) with yellowish, pink-tinged flowers and superb perfume; *L. japonica* (Japanese honeysuckle) with white flowers that turn yellow as they age – 'Halliana' is the best form; *L. tellmanniana* – beautiful yellow flowers that are cupped by the uppermost leaves; *L. brownii* (scarlet trumpet honey-suckle) – almost evergreen in mild areas; 'Dropmore Scarlet' with rich orange flowers and a long flowering season is the most widely available and best coloured form but, unfortunately, none have perfume.

Parthenocissus spp. Vitaceae

A genus of several very lovely and closely related, more or less self-clinging, deciduous, tendril perennials with palmate leaves, including the Virginia Creeper. All have insignificant flowers but the foliage is very attractive and usually displays stunning autumn colours. All are fairly vigorous and reach from 10–20 m (33–66 ft). They are of greatest value when allowed free rein over tall walls, although they should not be allowed to become established on crumbling brickwork or mortar.

PROPAGATE BY: semi-hardwood cuttings in late summer or by layering.

AFTER-CARE: clip rather than prune established plants in summer to keep them within bounds.

PEST, DISEASE OR OTHER PROBLEMS: none.

RECOMMENDED VARIETIES: *P. quinquefolia* (Virginia Creeper) – five-lobed leaves and sticky suckers on the tendrils; *P. inserta* – five-lobed leaves but with simply twining tendrils and therefore needs more support; *P. henryana* – large three- to five-lobed leaves of beautiful greenish-bronze with contrasting reddish veins; *P. tricuspidata* (Boston ivy) – three-lobed leaves, very tightly self-clinging and with vivid red autumn colour; the form called 'Veitchii' has slightly smaller leaves and is the best *Parthenocissus* for neatly covering a large wall.

Passiflora caerulea Passion flower Passifloraceae

A more or less evergreen, moderately hardy tendril perennial reaching about 5 m (16½ ft). The foliage is uninteresting but the flowers are both intriguingly complex and staggeringly beautiful. Passion flowers always thrive best on a warm south- or south-west-facing wall, although, even here, they can be cut back by hard frosts. Confining the roots, in much the same manner as is done with figs (p. 145), will help to encourage flowering. After warm summers, fruits may form but although they are edible when ripe, they have nothing to commend them – the true edible passion fruit is from a related species.

PROPAGATE BY: semi-hardwood cuttings in late summer; plants grown from seed are generally inferior, although occa-sionally some interesting variants arise.

SOW BY: half-hardy annual technique in spring.

AFTER-CARE: prune out dead or straggly shoots in spring to maintain shape.

PEST, DISEASE OR OTHER PROBLEMS: red spider mite, virus (which may render the plants more susceptible to frost injury).

RECOMMENDED VARIETIES: the only named form likely to be found is the very beautiful white-flowered 'Constance Elliott'.

Schizophragma hydrangeoides Hydrangeaceae

Schizophragma hydrangeoides 'Roseum'

A deciduous, self-clinging perennial with aerial roots, reaching 12 m (40 ft). It is often confused with *Hydrangea petiolaris*, to which it is related, and in fact is sometimes sold as such. It is indeed similarly useful and has the advantage that it is reputed to flower at an earlier age, although I am not entirely convinced of this. The main difference between the two is that the large (sterile) flowers of *Schizophragma* have only one elongated petal-like sepal; the climbing hydrangea has three to five.

PROPAGATE BY: semi-hardwood cuttings in late summer.

AFTER-CARE: prune out straggly growths in summer and shorten long side shoots to two buds in the spring.

PEST, DISEASE OR OTHER PROBLEMS: none.

RECOMMENDED VARIETIES: no named forms usually avail-able, although an appealing pink-flowered variant called 'Roseum' does exist.

Solanum crispum Solanaceae

An evergreen, twining perennial reaching about 6 m (20 ft) and one of the loveliest of purple-flowered climbers. The flowers are very evidently potato-like and are produced in large clusters throughout the summer. Although a plant with a rather untidy, scrambling nature, it nonetheless looks very effective when trained, with ample support wires, against a warm wall. It only really succeeds in fairly mild areas and is invariably better on an alkaline soil.

PROPAGATE BY: semi-hardwood cuttings in later summer.

AFTER-CARE: prune out straggly growths in summer and shorten long side shoots to two buds in the spring; but take care handling the foliage as some people develop an allergic rash.

PEST, DISEASE OR OTHER PROBLEMS: red spider mite.

RECOMMENDED VARIETIES: always choose the variety called 'Glasnevin' which is slightly hardier than the normal species and has a longer flowering period.

Trachelospermum asiaticum and T. jasminoides
Star jasmines   Apocynaceae

Evergreen, self-clinging perennials reaching 6–9 in (20–30 ft); among the very few fairly hardy, flowering and scented evergreen climbers. The leaves are oval, shiny and leathery and the summer flowers very jasmine-like; creamy-yellow in *T. asiaticum*, white but with better perfume in the slightly less hardy *T. jasminoides*. They require some shelter and always succeed best on a warm, south-facing wall in milder areas.

PROPAGATE BY: semi-hardwood cuttings in late summer or by layering; in common with almost all plants that produce a milky sap, they do not strike very readily from cuttings and layering is probably more certain.

AFTER-CARE: prune very lightly after flowering to maintain shape.

PEST, DISEASE OR OTHER PROBLEMS: none.

RECOMMENDED VARIETIES: named forms of *T. jasminoides* are sometimes offered, including one with variegated leaves, but I find the normal species more attractive.

Tropaeolum spp.   Climbing nasturtiums and Canary creeper   Tropaeolaceae

Tropaeolum speciosum

Annual or herbaceous twining perennials reaching 2–3 m (6½–10 ft). There are three main groups of these very useful climbers with vivid orange or yellow flowers – first, *T. majus* (in fact, a mix of hybrids) is the annual nasturtium which rapidly covers almost anything and flowers profusely (with edible blooms that adorn summer salads) provided it is sown in very poor soil. In rich conditions, it will produce only leaves. The second group comprises *T. peregrinum*, the yellow-flowered canary creeper, a perennial usually grown similarly to *T. majus*

as an annual. The third group comprises the two herbaceous perennials, *T. speciosum*, the very hardy Scots or Chilean Flame Flower, and the less hardy *T. tuberosum*. The former is especially valuable for planting where it can romp over tall evergreen hedges or coniferous trees.

PROPAGATE BY: seed (*T. majus* and *T. peregrinum*); root cuttings in winter or layering with the two perennials. *T. tuberosum* can also be propagated by means of its tubers.

SOW BY: hardy annual technique in spring.

AFTER-CARE: cut down perennial forms in autumn.

PEST, DISEASE OR OTHER PROBLEMS: aphids.

RECOMMENDED VARIETIES: named forms of the perennials have no particular merit and among the climbing varieties of the annual nasturtium you will probably be restricted to something called 'Tall Mixed'.

Vitis spp.   Vines   Vitaceae

More or less self-clinging, deciduous, tendril perennials closely related to the grapevine and also related to *Parthenocissus*. *V. coignetiae* is perhaps the most imposing of all vines. It is very vigorous, reaching 15 m (50 ft) and has very large, more or less heart-shaped leaves that assume magnificent autumn colours; but it does need space to display its charms. 'Brandt' is a grape very similar to the true grapevine but bearing very small fruit; it has long been popular as an ornamental for it too has splendid autumn colours. Its origin is unknown but modern catalogues may list it as *V. betulifolia* 'Brandt'.

PROPAGATE BY: semi-hardwood cuttings in late summer, short hardwood cuttings in winter or by layering.

AFTER-CARE: clip rather than prune established plants of *V. coignetiae*; prune 'Brandt' as a grapevine (p. 147).

PEST, DISEASE OR OTHER PROBLEMS: red spider mite, mildew.

RECOMMENDED VARIETIES: there are no named forms of *V. coignetiae*, and 'Brandt' is unique.

Wisteria spp.   Leguminosae

Magnificent deciduous twining perennials, often referred to as the queens of climbers. There are two common species, differing mainly in the number of leaflets to each leaf. Wisterias always look best when trained against a tall, preferably old wall, and whilst they undeniably flower better in full sun, they will thrive, but less floriferously, on a north-facing wall too. They may also be trained as standards, the weak stems being allowed to twine around a stout central support. The main frustration with wisterias is that they rarely flower when under five years of age.

PROPAGATE BY: semi-hardwood cuttings in late summer.

AFTER-CARE: prune back long whippy shoots to six buds in summer and then to two buds in winter. Apply sulphate of potash in early spring to encourage flowering on young plants.

PEST, DISEASE OR OTHER PROBLEMS: none.

RECOMMENDED VARIETIES: *Wisteria floribunda* (about 10 m/33 ft) – much the best is 'Macrobotrys' (also called 'Multijuga'), with inflorescences up to 1 m (39 in) long; *W. sinensis* (20 m (66 ft) or more) – usually only the normal species is offered but 'Alba' with white, strongly perfumed flowers is extremely attractive too.

Supports for climbing and other plants

Clematis 'Comtesse de Bouchard'
(on tree)

I T MIGHT at first sight seem a trifle odd to devote a separate account to so specific a subject. But I consider climbing plants of all types to be extremely important and valuable in gardens. And yet, in the majority of instances, they seem to be supported inadequately, inappropriately or in ways that do not make the most of the tremendous potential that their life form offers.

Naturally, climbing plants climb over other plants, over themselves to form a huge rounded heap of growth or over rocks or other inanimate structures. And it is perhaps in allowing climbing plants to do what comes so naturally to them, and to climb over each other, that gardeners are least adventurous. In a large and relatively informal garden, living trees provide excellent supports for climbers, although it is important to match the vigour of the climber with the robustness of the tree. The twining embrace of a honeysuckle, for instance, can be lethal to a young sapling, whereas a relatively mature trunk can withstand it with impunity. Conversely, an annual climber such as a climbing nasturtium, or a herbaceous one such as the hop, which dies down at the end of the season, can be used to grow up and through other relatively fragile vegetation. In general, my advice would be not to use a climber such as a honeysuckle, with a perennial woody structure that is rarely if ever cut back, on a supporting plant, tree or shrub less than ten years old.

In the early stages of growing almost any climber up a tree or large

189

Rustic poles used to build an arch.

shrub, it will be necessary to give it a little encouragement by tying it loosely to the trunk or stem. And I stress loosely – please don't hammer nails into the wood. I have found that a small piece of plastic clematis support netting tied to the trunk often provides just the right incentive for climbers to climb, although a few self-clinging plants, most notably those with aerial roots such as ivies, will obstinately refuse to cling until they are ready to do so. They form a mound of growth at the base of their supporting host and then, after perhaps two or three years, decide that the time has come to take off.

I have mixed feelings about using dead trees, left where they have died, as plant supports. If you leave a length of trunk several metres tall, it will inevitably decay after a few years and topple over, taking your carefully nurtured climber with it. Stumps too will rot in time, and in general I much prefer to see stumps removed or ground down because of the potential they offer for honey fungus to establish itself in an otherwise healthy garden. But where there is a very large stump or very old stump that cannot be removed, it does make sense to allow ivies or other closely matted climbers to grow over it.

But dead trees, in the shape of what are euphemistically called rustic supports, are excellent for climbing plants of many different types. Ensure that any timber you use has been treated with preservative, especially at the lower end where it is in the soil. Then form a further protective covering by wrapping the base in a plastic bag or sheet but retain an open top to the plastic sheath in order not to bottle up any moisture within. I never use concrete to anchor wooden plant supports, much preferring to ram soil around them. This is secure enough if at least 60 cm (24 in), and preferably 1 m (39 in), of the post is buried. Inevitably the support will rot in time, but removing a mass of concrete is much more likely to damage the roots of the established climber. Rustic poles of this type can be utilised in various ways. Used singly, they are ideal for supporting the less vigorous climbing roses (or rather lax, tall-growing shrub roses) which are often referred to as pillar varieties. For this purpose, it is sensible to use the more robust types of timber – slim poles look slightly odd when employed in this manner. But the more orthodox poles of about 6–8 cm (2½–3½ in) in diameter are excellent for forming the basis of rustic archways or pergolas.

I find that archways are invaluable for changing the emphasis of one part of the garden – at the entrance to a herb garden or vegetable plot, for instance, or simply at the turn in a path where the view through the arch will instantly bring added interest. Pergolas are rather more ambitious structures, generally used to surround a paved or gravelled courtyard or to line a more formal and large-scale pathway. It is generally best not to try to grow different types of climber up each vertical of a pergola, for you will merely end up with a hotch-potch. But growing a small range of varieties, of a small number of types of plant, to provide you with a prolonged flowering season is an excellent notion. And remember too that pergolas, archways or other structures do allow you scope to grow one climber through another – growing clematis through old roses is an excellent example. One type of rustic plant support that is not used nearly as much as it might be is the tripod. Placed within a large border, a 2 m (6½ ft) tall tripod of rustic poles might look a little bare and bald when new but provides a wonderful feature at the height of summer when it is clothed in flowering growth. And smaller tripods of slim rustic timbers with horizontal pieces close to the top offer the ideal method of support for any shrub rose.

Of course, it is perfectly possible to construct all or any of the supports that I have mentioned from sawn and squared rather than round and rustic timber but to my mind they seldom look as attractive. Sawn timber comes into its own for trellis work, however, and there are many ways in which this can be used. The conventional trellis panel fixed to a wall is the obvious one, although here, as with all uses of trellis, do choose carefully. The most attractive, least assertive visually is the diamond patterned trellis, but much of that sold to gardeners is too fragile for the purpose and will disintegrate within a few seasons. You may even prefer to use plastic rather than wooden trellis, although I hope that I can dissuade you from doing this too frequently; as will, I hope, be apparent by now, I am no lover of plastic horticulture and as this is my book, I shall say so. Whatever form of trellis you use, do be sure that it is fixed securely to the wall by means of battens and not attached directly to the brickwork. It is essential to allow air flow around and through your climbers if mildew and other diseases are not to become serious problems. Trellis can also be used to make a free-standing support if it is attached to a secure wooden framework, although this really must be very robust to withstand winter winds. And don't forget how valuable trellis can be surmounting fence panels, where a 30 cm (12 in) tall addition will soften the overall impact even of a really severe fence. But the use of trellis on top, with the added weight both of the trellis itself and any plants climbing through it, is a further reason for ensuring that the fence posts are very firmly secured (p. 20).

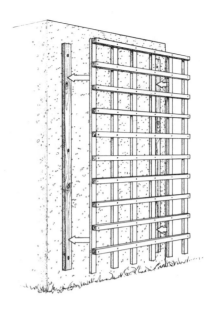

Fixing trellis to a wall with the aid of battens.

The other options for attaching plants to walls are lead-headed nails or related modern proprietary fixings, or wires. Lead-headed or similar nails are ideal for climbers such as established wisterias, where there is extensive and fairly irregular growth of a large and robust plant. A system of wires is ideal if you are in a position to begin training a fairly vigorous climber from scratch and this is the method I much prefer to use with climbing roses. Be sure to use strong, plastic-coated training wire that can withstand the strain of being pulled taut. And do use screws or other very secure fittings plugged into the brick or stonework.

You will also need wires for training plants in the kitchen garden and I have mentioned them in connection with soft fruit canes in particular. Here, where it is improbable that the supports will be secured against a wall, it is essential to use firm posts (rustic I hope), braced with diagonals so that they too will enable the wires to be pulled tight.

Trees must be supported with firm stakes and I have discussed this in relation to tree planting on p. 162, but it should be remembered that fruit trees on the very dwarfing rootstock will require support throughout their lives. With taller trees, the stakes may safely be removed when the plant reaches about 3 m (10 ft) in height. Stakes or stout canes have also been used traditionally to support the taller types of herbaceous plant such as lupins, delphiniums and lilies but I have always found them ugly and ungainly when used in this way. I am now converted to modern 'invisible' wire supports of which there are several types, the general principle being that the unobtrusive supports are put in place whilst the plants are young and gradually become obscured as the stems and leaves develop. They are neat, inexpensive, re-usable and very effective. Some supports will be needed too in the vegetable and kitchen gardens and greenhouse for use with such plants as runner beans, peas, sweet peas and tomatoes, but I have outlined the various options and those that I recommend in the appropriate detailed accounts.

I RECALL having read once that 80 per cent of British gardens contain at least one rose. This is a readily believable statistic for there are species or varieties of roses appropriate to almost every type of garden, large or small. It is perhaps easiest to begin, therefore, by mentioning the two unusual situations where they are least likely to succeed. Strongly acid soils and very cold, windy and exposed gardens will not suit them, although even here, soil improvement with organic matter and lime, or the provision of some robust shelter, should enable a few representative types to be grown.

The ideal conditions for most types of rose are met essentially by a moisture-retentive soil. Conventional gardening wisdom tells us that a clay soil is a prerequisite for successful rose cultivation. But whilst this type of soil probably gives the best results most easily, any soil, even a light sand, can be rendered suitable for rose growing if large quantities of organic matter, in the form of well rotted manure or garden compost, are dug in in advance of planting and a thick organic mulch is applied routinely to the soil surface both in spring and autumn.

Planting of roses is much the same as the planting of other types of flowering shrub (p. 169), as is their subsequent feeding – a top dressing of a proprietary rose fertiliser should be applied around the plants in spring, just before growth starts, and again shortly after midsummer. In many instances, this second feeding will follow the dead-heading that is performed after the first flush of flowers has faded.

The pruning of roses perplexes many gardeners, but whilst the dedicated rosarian or exhibitioner develops slightly different methods for different varieties, perfectly splendid garden roses can be produced by following some very simple, general rules. In most instances, the type of pruning is related to the overall group within which any particular rose variety falls. And here, too, I shall generalise and use three main groups – modern bush roses, shrub roses, climbers and ramblers.

One matter related to pruning that is applicable to most roses is that of suckers – shoots that arise from below soil level close to the base of the plant and display foliage (and flowers if they are allowed to grow large enough) different from those of the variety itself. Suckers form because most roses are not grown on their own roots but grafted onto a rootstock of a different variety. Allowed to remain, the rootstock shoots will gradually take over and not only appear unsightly but seriously weaken your plant. They must be removed by pulling them away from below ground level. If they are too tough to be pulled, they may be chopped, but a clean cut is merely likely to stimulate them to grow anew.

And so to a survey of the main groups of roses that you are likely to encounter. Modern rose bushes comprise the majority of the roses that you will see in gardens and also in massed displays in public parks. These roses are subdivided into hybrid teas (now more correctly called large-flowered roses) and floribundas (now more correctly called cluster-flowered roses, although neither of these new terms has really captured the imagination of the gardening fraternity). Hybrid teas usually have fairly large and quite often scented flowers borne singly on their stems; the floribundas have clusters of blooms that individually are usually smaller and have less, if any, perfume. Both hybrid teas and floribundas include varieties representative of the fullest range of rose colours, from white through creams, yellows and oranges to pinks and reds and including some with flowers of mixed colour. Almost all bloom throughout the summer – either on and off or more or less

Roses

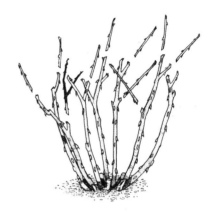

PRUNING HYBRID TEA ROSES.

(a) Remove dead and diseased shoots and those that cross over. Cut back remaining shoots by about half – more for a weak-growing variety and less for a strong-growing variety.

(b) Tip back all shoots in autumn to avoid damage by winter winds.

Opposite: Rosa 'Fragrant Cloud'.

PRUNING FLORIBUNDA ROSES.

(a) Remove one third of the old wood to the base in spring.

(b) Cut back the remaining shoots by one third.

(c) Tip back all flowering shoots and very long stems at the end of flowering.

continuously. A few types attain around 1.5 or 2 m (5 or 6 ft) in height but most are considerably smaller, although, as the diagrams show, all must be accorded a very positive annual pruning if they are to give of their best.

One rather individual type of rose that is conveniently grouped with the modern bush roses is the miniature – or, as they are sometimes called, pot or patio roses. These rarely exceed 45 cm (18 in) in height and many are much smaller than this. They tend to have a rather congested, twiggy nature and bear masses of tiny flowers, generally in floribunda style, although there are a few exquisite little varieties that are, to all intents and purposes, perfectly scaled-down hybrid teas with beautifully formed blooms.

Modern bush roses tend to polarise gardening opinion like few other plants – I hear frequently from equal numbers of those who love or loathe them. I am sure, however, that much of the evident dislike for these roses comes more from the way in which they are grown than from the individual plants themselves. For the massed rose beds so beloved of municipal park gardeners are understandably not to everyones's taste; they may be fine for large public places but can dominate a small home garden. And they can look unutterably dismal in winter. But use an individual hybrid tea or floribunda, or a group of three plants of one variety amongst other types of plant in a mixed border, and they can be most effective. I grow several varieties in this manner and I also have bush roses growing as specimens through gravel, forming a backdrop to a shrubbery, among lavender and herbs and even dotted among the lettuces and carrots of my kitchen garden. Use your imagination and choose carefully, and the modern bush rose can be a most valuable plant in almost any garden. The miniature roses are, however, rather a different proposition and here I do find that a small bed devoted to them makes sound sense – perhaps a raised bed where they can be brought closer to eye level.

Shrub roses comprise a large and highly varied group but they are generally very different in appearance and require different pruning from the modern bush types. Think of them as flowering shrubs that happen to be roses and you will then not be surprised to learn that they have fairly clearly defined and often rather short flowering seasons, and that they require only a modest amount of pruning; the fairly general shrub pruning maxim of cutting out the oldest third of the shoots every spring is not a bad one to follow, although the plants can in practice be left virtually unpruned for several years. Shrub roses as a group are often called old or old-fashioned roses, and certainly many of the loveliest varieties have been with us for hundreds of years. There are, nonetheless, modern shrub roses too, and there are also a few wild shrub rose species that are well worth growing in their natural, unaltered form. For most shrub roses, the peak of blooming comes in June when a massed border of these plants with their predominantly red, pink and white blooms and strong perfume can be overwhelmingly lovely. Many shrub roses are tall – 2 or 3 m (6½ or 10 ft) is not unusual – although there are lower growing forms too, and I have included some of these among my recommendations for they are especially valuable in small gardens. In the listings, I have indicated to which of the numerous shrub rose groups each of my suggestions belongs, in the hope that when you find a type that appeals to you especially, you will search out other less well known varieties in the same groups. Whilst shrub roses may be used in the garden in much the same manner as the modern bush roses – scattered amongst other plants or massed in beds – consider the possibility of using some in a rather different way; many of the more robust types, the forms of *R. rugosa* especially, make excellent and attractive hedges.

Climbing roses include the widest range of types of all, for almost every main group includes some climbing forms. There are, therefore, climbing forms of many hybrid teas and floribundas, climbing types within most of the many forms of shrub rose, climbing species, and even some climbing miniatures. In general, the flowering period of a climber is similar to that of the remainder of the group to which it belongs – the climbing forms of modern roses, therefore, tend to bloom for much longer than the climbing forms of shrubs. Even more than shrub or bush roses, however, climbers should be chosen carefully, for the range in their vigour is enormous and varies from those that are little more than rather tall, weak-stemmed shrubs (and are ideal, therefore, for training against pillars) to monsters that can attain 15 m (50 ft) or more and are perfectly capable of producing shoots 7 m (23 ft) long in a single season. As with other types of climbing plant (see p. 182), the more vigorous and more unkempt climbing roses are best grown as they would grow naturally, up and over trees, leaving the less vigorous and more easily constrained types for trellises and similar supports. In general, climbing varieties of hybrid tea and floribunda roses should be pruned similarly to their bush equivalents. Rambling roses, which almost invariably bloom once only in early summer, are slightly different however and are pruned immediately after flowering. Most rambler varieties should be pruned as shown in the diagram, the flowered shoots being cut back to the main shoot from which they arise; although a few varieties, such as the old favourite 'Albertine', must have the entire old shoot on which the flowers arose cut back right to the base, in exactly the same way as a raspberry cane is cut back after fruiting.

Before leaving the various rose categories, I should say something about standard and half-standard roses, for there is commonly confusion about these in gardeners' minds. They are roses grafted onto upright stems or trunks – approximately 1.2 m (4 ft) tall for standards and approximately 85 cm (34 in) for half-standards. No varieties are available only in this form,

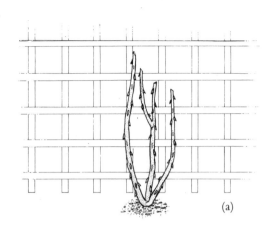

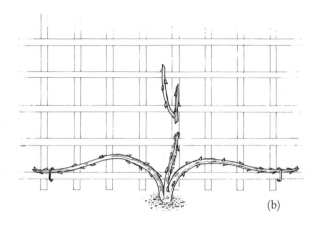

TRAINING AND PRUNING A
RAMBLER ROSE
(a) Newly planted.
(b) Initial training.
(c) After first flowering season – old
flowered shoots cut back to main framework.
(d) After second flowering season – old
flowered shoots cut back to main framework.

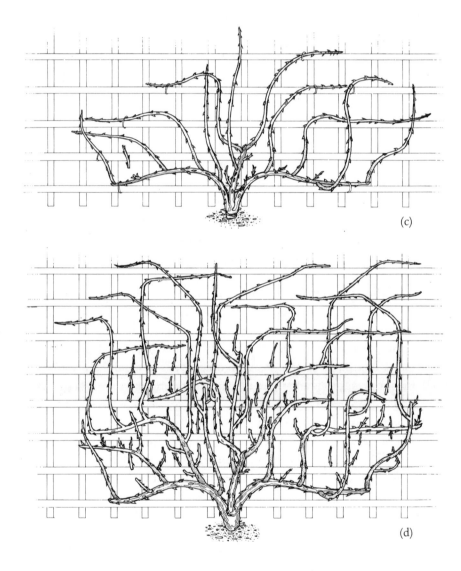

but some are more amenable than others to being grown in this way; the lovely weeping standards, in which the shoots arch downwards, are almost always formed from rambler varieties. Because of the labour involved in the grafting process and the time taken to grow the rootstocks, standard and half-standard plants tend to be fairly expensive, and demand always exceeds supply, so you will need to order well in advance. Prune standards and half-standards as you would the same plant growing in the normal manner.

Apart from the necessity for pruning and feeding, rose growing also demands rather more than the average amount of attention to pest and disease control. Mildew, black spot, aphids and, to a lesser extent, rust will sap the vigour of almost all types of rose unless routine controls are applied. Whilst some rose varieties exhibit some resistance to the three main diseases (and I have indicated this where appropriate), resistance alone is very seldom sufficient to give adequate protection; and yellow roses especially display very little resistance to black spot, which is almost always a problem on them. Moreover, miniature roses have an inverse relationship to disease – in general, the smaller they are, the more disease-prone they tend to be and certainly the greater is the impact of disease upon them. Overall, therefore, I am bound to admit that the roses are among the very few plants in my garden that must be sprayed with chemicals as a matter of routine.

To make a selection of rose varieties from the bewildering range of around 2000 currently available is extremely difficult. No one has even seen them all and few people have grown more than a small percentage. As elsewhere in the book, therefore, I have selected some with which I am very familiar (in almost all instances having grown them personally) that seem representative of the overall types and colours in existence and, wherever possible, that have few problems attached to their cultivation.

MODERN BUSH ROSES

Hybrid Teas

WHITE: 'Pascali' (long straight stems and good rain resistance); 'White Wings' (one of those rarities, a single hybrid tea, but a glory with chocolate brown anthers; a rose I would never be without).

YELLOW: 'Diorama' (good rain resistance and a long flowering season); 'Grandpa Dickson' (good rain resistance, a long flowering season and, for a yellow, tolerable resistance to black spot); 'King's Ransom' (very full blooms and an abundance of richly coloured petals); 'Peace' (beyond compare, large blooms with petals fading to pink at the edges; if only it had perfume); 'Sutter's Gold' (rather short-lived flowers, slightly straggly ragged blooms but with more scent than any other yellow hybrid tea that I know).

ORANGE: 'Doris Tysterman' (moderately sized blooms, average scent, some susceptibility to mildew but an appealing shade for an orange, which is my least favourite rose colour); 'Mrs Oakley Fisher' (another single and another beauty with coppery-orange petals and amber stamens); 'Whisky Mac' (a rather special amber-gold colour, compensation for this being a rather difficult rose to grow well, for it must have good conditions).

PINK: 'Blessings' (very floriferous, moderately sized blooms, moderate scent); 'Dainty Bess' (a single gem, silver-pink petals, golden stamens and perfume); 'Elizabeth Harkness' (a special colour – cream white with a pink flush, due for a comeback); 'Madame Butterfly' (soft pink with touches of yellow and lovely fragrance, old but still a delight); 'Mischief' (masses of moderately sized, rich coral-pink blooms but rather disease prone); 'Silver Jubilee' (rich silvery pink with peach flushes, masses of large fragrant blooms, the finest hybrid tea of recent times).

RED: 'Alec's Red' (masses of very full deep-red blooms with rich perfume; the finest of the numerous red hybrid teas); 'Ena Harkness' (a rose that many fault for its weak flower stalk, but of a rich deep crimson colour and with fine fragrance); 'Fragrant Cloud' (a rather assertive coral red and somewhat variable in colour but very floriferous and richly fragrant); 'Josephine Bruce' (very dark crimson, a beautiful shape and rich perfume); 'National Trust' (very full, rich red blooms but sadly no perfume).

OTHER COLOURS: 'Piccadilly' (scarlet and yellow, no fragrance but the best with this colour combination); 'Rose Gaujard' (unique colours – rose-red petals with striking silver undersides, little perfume).

WHITE: 'Iceberg' (unquestionably the best white floribunda and one of the best of any colour, with masses of loose blooms but little perfume); 'Margaret Merril' (not pure white, having a flush of pink in the centre, but with rich perfume although little rain resistance).

YELLOW: 'Allgold' (a very long flowering season and excellent rain resistance); 'Arthur Bell' (probably the best all-round yellow floribunda with good rain resistance, moderate perfume and reasonable disease resistance); 'Korresia' (another excellent all-round rose with slightly fuller blooms); 'Mountbatten' (a wonderful rose for a larger garden, a tall plant with very full blooms, the yellow equivalent of 'Queen Elizabeth', sometimes classed as a shrub).

ORANGE: 'Glenfiddich' (amber gold, very floriferous); 'Orange Sensation' (vivid orange, semi-double, a very assertive plant but reliable if you need this colour); 'Southampton' (apricot orange with a reddish flush, rather tall and upright of habit).

PINK: 'City of Leeds' (rich salmon pink, very floriferous and a good variety for massed planting, at its best in public parks); 'Pink Parfait' (semi-double blooms in a rather appealing mixture of different pink shades, very floriferous); 'Queen Elizabeth' (unrivalled, tall, with beautifully formed blooms of clear pink, very vigorous, disease resistant).

RED: 'Beautiful Britain' (orange red, floriferous, another variety for the massed planting); 'Lili Marlene' (deep velvet red, particularly easy and reliable); 'Matangi' (vivid vermilion with silver undersides to the petals, unique if curious).

OTHER COLOURS: 'Masquerade' (a rose that I can happily live without but I recommend it for those many gardeners who love such colour combinations – bright yellow petals that gradually change through pink to red); 'Sweet Dream' (a low growing variety in a lovely apricot shade, good rain resistance).

MINIATURES: 'Baby Masquerade' (a tiny version of its floribunda namesake); 'Cricri' (salmon pink); 'Dresden Doll' (a little gem, a miniature pink moss rose); 'Easter Morning' (the best of all, ivory white); 'Magic Carousel' (very long flowering and rather taller than most, white petals with pink tips); 'Pour Toi'

Rosa 'Iceberg'

(white with yellow centres); 'Yellow Doll' (the best miniature yellow, but a martyr to black spot).

SHRUBS

WHITE: 'Blanc Double de Coubert' (Hybrid Rugosa, nearly fully double, rich perfume but a tendency for the petals to stain brown); 'Madame Hardy' (Damask, fully double with green central 'eye', rich perfume); 'Nevada' (*R. moyesii* hybrid, very tall, single with brownish stamens); 'Pax' (Hybrid Musk, semi-double, cream-white with golden stamens, tall); 'Schneezwerg' (Hybrid Rugosa, single, medium height).

YELLOW: 'Canary Bird' (form of *R. xanthina*, single, very early, tall); 'Dunwich Rose' (form of *R. pimpinellifolia*, single, mound-forming, lovely perfume); 'Francesca' (Hybrid Musk, semi-double, medium height); 'Frühlingsgold' (Modern Shrub, almost single, fairly early, tall).

ORANGE: none.

PINK: 'Ballerina' (Modern Hybrid Musk, single, pink, very floriferous and invaluable for its rain tolerance, fairly low growing); 'Fantin Latour' (form of *R. centifolia*, exquisite, double, shell pink with flowers like tissue, intense perfume); 'Frau Dagmar Hastrup' (Hybrid Rugosa, fairly low growing, single, fine perfume and good autumn hips); 'Great Maiden's Blush' (Alba, double, pale shell pink, rich perfurme); 'Madame Isaac Pereire' (Bourbon, loose, double, rich deep pink, intense perfume); 'Nozomi' (Modern Procumbent, very pale pink, double, valuable as ground cover); 'Raubritter' (form of *R. macrantha*, silver pink, semi-double, more or less prostrate); 'The Fairy' (Polyantha, semi-double, low growing, useful for coming late into bloom).

RED: *Rosa moyesii* (Species, single, rich crimson, tall, lovely autumn hips); 'Roseraie de l'Hay' (Hybrid Rugosa, rich deep crimson, semi-double, strongly perfumed, tall); 'Tuscany Superb' (form of *R. gallica*, semi-double, very deep crimson with golden stamens, rich perfume, medium height); 'William Lobb' (Moss, semi-double, magenta and pink, strongly perfumed, medium height with the typical moss rose characteristic of soft, moss-like prickles).

OTHER COLOURS: 'Buff Beauty' (Modern Hybrid Musk, double, exquisite apricot, rich perfume); 'Perle d'Or' (form of *R. chinensis*, cream-buff, double, tiny flowers on fairly low-growing, twiggy stems).

WHITE: 'Félicité et Perpétue' (form of *R. sempervirens*, small double flowers with suggestion of pink, few thorns, vigorous (5 m/16½ ft); 'Iceberg' (Climbing Floribunda, the flowering characteristics of the bush form but vigorous, 6 m/20 ft); 'Madame Alfred Carrière' (Noisette, loose double blooms, good perfume, a delight in an old garden, fairly vigorous, 4 m/13 ft); 'The Garland' (Climbing Musk, tiny, semi-double blooms, strong perfume, very vigorous, 5 m/16½ ft).

YELLOW: 'Golden Showers' (Modern Climber, loose double, golden blooms, 3 m/10 ft); 'Maigold' (*R. pimpinellifolia* hybrid, semi-double, very floriferous, very early, 4 m/13 ft).

ORANGE: 'Schoolgirl' (Modern Climber, arguably the only reliable orange climber, loose semi-double blooms, fairly vigorous 3 m/10 ft).

PINK: 'Aloha' (Modern Climber, fully double, rich deep coppery pink, lovely perfume, very disease resistant, 3 m/10 ft (ideal for pillars), my perfect modern climbing rose for limited space); 'American Pillar' (Rambler, single, pink with white centres, fascinating but can be damaged by rain, 5 m/16½ ft); 'Constance Spry' (Modern Climber, double, shell pink, rich spicy perfume, lovely but vigorous, 6 m/20 ft), 'The New Dawn' (Rambler, semi-double, pale pink, some perfume, probably the best of all ramblers, 3 m/10 ft); 'Zéphirine Drouhin' (Climbing Bourbon, semi-double, rose pink, perfumed, very prone to mildew but valuable for being thornless and useful, therefore, by doors or pathways, 3 m/10 ft).

RED: 'Danse du Feu' (Modern Climber, lurid orange-red, floriferous, lovely if you need this colour, 4 m/13 ft); 'Josephine Bruce' (Climbing Hybrid Tea, characteristics of the bush form, 5 m/16½ ft); 'Paul's Scarlet Climber' (Unknown affinities, semi-double, very floriferous, 3 m/10 ft).

OTHER COLOURS: 'Gloire de Dijon' (Climbing Tea, wonderful, peach-yellow, perfumed, rather disease-prone and much hardier than often claimed, 4 m/13 ft); 'Handel' (Modern Climber, a rose that I cannot abide but it is probably the most popular of all climbers so this must say more about me and my general dislike of picotee flowers than it does about the rose, semi-double, silver-white petals with reddish edges, 4 m/13 ft); 'Lady Hillingdon' (Climbing Tea, has much in common with

Rosa 'Aloha'

'Gloire de Dijon' but with much neater flowers and I love it equally, hardy in a sheltered part of my fairly cold Midland garden so do give it a try, 5 m/16½ ft).

Rosa 'American Pillar'

Rosa 'Zéphirine Drouhin'

Herbaceous perennials

I THINK that the herbaceous perennial is at the same time one of the most useful yet also one of the most troublesome plants in the modern garden. The name perennial suggests that such plants may be left undisturbed for many years, as indeed they can, although I must stress that being perennial is not the same as being immortal. For after four or five years, almost all types of herbaceous perennial will require some rejuvenation, as I shall explain shortly. However, being not only perennial but also herbaceous brings with it certain special problems. For whilst a tree or a shrub maintains its perennial nature through a permanent, above-ground, woody framework, and a bulbous plant survives discreetly below ground, its leafy parts generally having shrivelled to nothing, a herbaceous perennial has an inconvenient in-between life style. It dies down to a rootstock, in effect a clump of roots with a crown at or just below the soil surface, leaving a mass of dead stems above ground. And the herbaceous rather than woody nature of the above-ground structure is, I think, the cause of the most labour-demanding aspect of herbaceous perennial gardening for, in many instances, the stems are inadequate fully to support the flower heads. Most herbaceous perennials, therefore, require some form of support, and on p. 191 I have outlined the systems that I have found to be most effective.

From what I have written so far, you may be forgiven for thinking that whilst I have not exactly damned herbaceous perennials, I have treated them as necessary evils. In practice, I consider them both beautiful and indispensable but I feel duty bound to put them some way behind shrubs (although well ahead of annuals) in their requirements for continuing attention. I have been particularly conscious, nonetheless, in my lists of recommended varieties to select those that do have the least need for staking or other chores.

Like annuals, herbaceous perennials offer you nothing in the winter (with the possible exception of those few with particularly striking dead flower or seed heads that may be left for their aesthetic appeal or as food for birds until wind and rain lay them low). Herbaceous perennials must be used with care in the garden, therefore, because, being generally large plants, the gap they leave out of season is also a large one. In times past whole vast borders were devoted solely to such plants – the herbaceous border, much loved of Gertrude Jekyll and her nineteenth- and turn-of-the-century contemporaries, was, at its best in summer, one of the greatest glories that the English garden has ever seen. But such a feature slowly fell from favour, partly through its great labour intensiveness and partly through its depressing appearance in winter. A huge, dead area of soil might be overlooked in the extensive grounds of a country house, but it would occupy an unacceptably large slice of the plot of the modern home gardener.

Today, therefore, herbaceous perennials are seldom planted in beds or borders to the exclusion of other plants. Most commonly, they are integrated with shrubs in what has become known as the mixed border, the shrubs providing a permanent above-ground framework. Even here, nonetheless, it is important to select herbaceous varieties with complementary colours and flowering times and to choose carefully the taller varieties for planting at the back and sides of the border with the lower growing ones in the centre and front. And even in a small garden, there will be a few instances where a modest group or even a single specimen herbaceous perennial may be used to good effect – growing through a gravelled area, for instance, where perennial ornamental grasses can look most attractive. But herbaceous perennials are not in general satisfactory plants for containers.

Seed catalogues have large sections devoted to herbaceous perennials and it may be thought, therefore, that the best way to raise them is from seed. In general, I find that it is not. The best (in the sense of most attractive or functionally useful) varieties cannot usually be raised in this manner. They have to be propagated vegetatively and thus must be purchased from nurseries or garden centres as plants. Where there are exceptions to this general rule, I have mentioned them in my individual descriptions, although I must add one rather important group of exceptions. For many people (me included) there is an appeal in growing plants in their wild form, and there are many species that have never been subjected to hybridisation and selection and exist, therefore, only in their natural, unaltered state. A great many, indeed the majority, amongst them do not have the mass appeal that attracts those nurserymen who cater for the mass market. Inevitably, therefore, plants of these species should be sought from specialist suppliers or, to return to my main point, you may raise them yourself from seed (which may in turn have to be obtained from a specialist rather than a mass market company). By and large, you will succeed best if you use the hardy annual technique (p. 99), but always grow on the young plants in pots for at least a season before planting them out in the garden. This will ensure that they are robust and have a strong enough root and crown system to enable them to survive.

When planting any herbaceous perennials in the garden, follow the same general technique as I have outlined for trees and shrubs (p. 161), ensuring that the prepared planting hole has a volume approximately twice that of the plant's root ball. If you are planting or replanting an entire border from scratch, it makes sense, nonetheless, to adopt the same technique as I suggest for preparing vegetable beds – double digging (p. 58). In suggesting this I understand the effort involved, indeed I wince at it. But the chances are that you will prepare a new mixed border on only a few occasions in a gardening lifetime, so it really is worthwhile doing it properly.

Apart from the routine staking and fairly regular division of the plants that I mentioned earlier (to be done in the manner that I described on p. 106), herbaceous perennials require further attention in the shape of feeding, watering and mulching. Feeding should take the form of a twice-yearly dressing with a general purpose balanced fertiliser such as blood, fish and bone. Apply it first as growth begins in the spring and then again around mid-summer, on each occasion at the rate of approximately 100–125 g/ square metre (3–4 oz/sq yd). Following the first feeding, and while the soil is still moist, apply a thick organic mulch around the plants or, if you have sufficient organic matter available, over the entire bed. Thorough mulching at this stage should make the consequences of any water shortage later in the summer less serious but if watering regulations do permit the use of hoses and sprinklers, don't neglect the perennials when you are watering other parts of the garden.

In the early autumn, the above-ground growth should be cut down and then preferably shredded and composted – it makes an excellent blend when forked into the compost bin with grass cuttings. Where dead heads remain with masses of seeds, however, or where the dead stems have a particularly attractive appearance, there is no harm and every merit in leaving them at least for a few months for your own and the local bird population's delight.

The relatively close positioning of herbaceous perennials that is desirable to achieve the dramatic effect of massed blooms means that they can be prone to rather more than their fair share of pests and diseases. Among pests, aphids are especially troublesome, while among diseases, mildew can be very damaging, especially in a dry summer. Although I can offer little in the way of resistance to aphids, whenever possible I have recommended varieties that do have some resistance to mildew.

Acanthus spp.   Bear's Breeches   Acanthaceae

Despite having been cultivated since the sixteenth century, the robust, 1.2 m (4 ft) tall spikes of *Acanthus* flowers with their large spiny leaves still turn heads and lead to queries of 'Whatever is that?' The individual mauve and white mid- to late-summer flowers are lipped and somewhat pea-like but, despite its dramatic appearance, this is a rather gaunt plant that really must be placed towards the back of a fairly large border.
OBTAIN AS: plants or seed (normal species only).
PEST, DISEASE OR OTHER PROBLEMS: none.
RECOMMENDED VARIETIES: the normal species is widely available but a group of selected forms called 'Latifolius' is also sometimes seen. *A. longifolius* (sometimes called *A. balcanicus* or *A. hungaricus*) is rather lower growing while *A. spinosus* is rather more robust and stately.

Achillea spp. and hybrids   Compositae

I am no great lover of achilleas because they remind me too much of the hours that I have spent eradicating *A. millefolium* from my lawn. The best cultivated forms are taller (90 cm (3 ft) or even more) with large closely knit heads of small, closely knit flowers from mid-summer onwards. The yellow forms are striking enough and useful for mixing with other, more classical things at the back of the border but some of the slightly shorter modern hybrids and the cultivated varieties of *A. millefolium* are nothing but bilious in appearance.
OBTAIN AS: plants.
PEST, DISEASE OR OTHER PROBLEMS: none.
RECOMMENDED VARIETIES: *A.* 'Coronation Gold'; *A. filipendulina* 'Cloth of Gold', 'Gold Plate'.

Aconitum spp.   Monkshood   Ranunculaceae

The monkshood is an ancient, slightly sinister and distinctly poisonous plant. But in spite (or perhaps because) of this I find them intriguing. The flowers are deeply hooded, typically a dark, ominous purple, and carried on spikes usually reaching around 1.5 m (4 ft) in height but taller still in some species. I find that they always thrive best in damp, rich soil and preferably in the partial shade of other taller plants. Incidentally, despite their name, they should not be confused with the plant generally called aconite which is, more accurately, *Eranthis hyemalis* (p. 231).

OBTAIN AS: plants or seeds (species only).

PEST, DISEASE OR OTHER PROBLEMS: none.

RECOMMENDED VARIETIES: *A.* 'Bressingham Spire' (90 cm (3 ft), deep violet, a lovely plant); *A.* 'Ivorine' (90 cm (3 ft), ivory flowers); *A. napellus* (blue flowers or white in variety 'Albidum'); *A. volubile* (2.5 m (8 ft) with weak stems, best allowed to fall through the branches of a tall shrub, lilac flowers).

Alchemilla mollis   Lady's Mantle   Rosaceae

There is no better deciduous ground-cover perennial than *Alchemilla* for, although it offers nothing in winter, its deliciously lime-green foliage and feathery greenish-yellow flowers are exquisite in summer. The leaves have a rather special facility for trapping beads of dew or rain and this adds further to their appeal. In the border, such ground-cover plants are naturally better at the front but I find this is an especially useful plant for the slightly more informal or unkempt areas. It is especially valuable in partial shade.

OBTAIN AS: seed or plants.

PEST, DISEASE OR OTHER PROBLEMS: none.

RECOMMENDED VARIETIES: the normal species is almost invariably the form that is seen, although its slightly less robust relative *A. alpina* is valuable for smaller gardens.

Althaea officinalis   Hollyhock   Malvaceae

Whatever is to be done about the hollyhock? It has been part of English gardens for so long but its almost inevitable affliction with rust means that it now disappoints more frequently than it satisfies. I have no real answer to this, other than to use the recommended routine fungicide spray (p. 83) and/or to grow them from seed as biennials rather than as perennials. If you *can* succeed with them, I would ask you to take account of the fact that hollyhocks are among the few herbaceous perennials that always look at their best when away from the border. Their traditional home is in a small group close to the house wall.

OBTAIN AS: seed or plants.

PEST, DISEASE OR OTHER PROBLEMS: rust.

RECOMMENDED VARIETIES: the normal species is frequently available both as seed and plants but there are also several seed mixtures worth trying. Avoid if you can the dwarf seed-raised forms such as 'Majorette' which bear little resemblance to the hollyhock that we all know and love.

Anemone hybrida   Ranunculaceae

The genus *Anemone* is a large one, including several quite distinct groups of plants. The relatively low-growing forms raised from corms are considered on p. 229 but there is one extremely useful group of taller-growing forms that reach about 60 cm (2 ft). Commonly called Japanese anemones, they offer delicately attractive blooms in late summer and well into the autumn and suffer only from the drawback of being somewhat invasive. For this reason, they need careful attention and regular division as border plants, but I find them particu-

Anemone hybrida

larly useful when grown as a discrete group in a gravelly corner or other situation where they can be allowed free rein.

OBTAIN AS: seed or plants (best forms are only available as plants).

PEST, DISEASE OR OTHER PROBLEMS: none.

RECOMMENDED VARIETIES: 'Honorine Jobert' (white, single, much the loveliest); pink coloured forms are also widely available but not remotely as pretty.

Aquilegia spp. and hybrids   Columbine   Ranunculaceae

The tall-stemmed, early summer flowering aquilegias are among the cottage garden indispensables, although there are numerous low-growing species too, suitable for the alpine garden. The old border forms have the major advantage of seldom requiring staking, although they soon flop and succumb to mildew once the flowers have faded, and the dead stems should be cut back promptly therefore.

OBTAIN AS: seed or plants.

PEST, DISEASE OR OTHER PROBLEMS: aphids, mildew (although seldom sets in early enough to affect flowering).

RECOMMENDED VARIETIES: *A. canadensis* (35 cm (14 in), slender stems, less robust overall, with red and yellow bi-coloured flowers); *A. vulgaris* (60 cm (2 ft), the wild columbine, available as mixtures including the beautiful mauve, white and pinkish flowered double forms often called granny's bonnets; the form with double green and red flowers called 'Nora Barlow' belongs here. It is a lovely cottage garden flower, although not nearly as old a variety as is sometimes claimed).

The McKana hybrids are a group of rather weak stemmed and sometimes bizarrely coloured forms that I find distinctly unattractive.

Artemisia spp. and hybrids   Wormwood   Compositae

The best-known artemisias are probably the herbs lad's love and tarragon, but there are several other species, characterised by finely divided, often silvery foliage, that are useful border plants. Their flowers are usually insignificant but they act as a visual foil to plants with brightly coloured flowers and were much used by Jekyll towards the sides of her herbaceous borders to counter the hot and fiery hues in the centre. They are, ideally, plants of light dry soils and sunny situations and may be damaged in hard winters.

OBTAIN AS: seed or plants.

PEST, DISEASE OR OTHER PROBLEMS: none.

RECOMMENDED VARIETIES: A. absinthum 'Lambrook Silver' (50 cm (20 in), very finely divided, green-silver foliage); A. arborescens 'Faith Raven' (1 m (39 in), shrubby, silvery white foliage); A. 'Powis Castle' (1.2 m (4 ft), silver-grey foliage); A. schmidtiana 'Nana' (60 cm (2 ft), mound-forming, silvery-grey foliage).

Aster spp. and hybrids   Compositae

Asters appear under two other headings – as bedding plants and as alpines. The asters in this section are those border perennials most commonly referred to as Michaelmas daisies. Their daisy-like flowers in shades of mauve and pink are among the most familiar and best loved sights of early autumn. The traditional Michaelmas daisies, however, of the species A. novi-belgii, are equally traditionally devastated by mildew and most of my recommendations are derived from other, related species of similar form.

OBTAIN AS: plants.

PEST, DISEASE OR OTHER PROBLEMS: mildew.

RECOMMENDED VARIETIES: Forms of A. amellus: 'King George' (blue-lilac), 'Nocturne' (lavender), 'Violet Queen' (low growing, deep violet). A. frikartii 'Monch' (blue-lilac with yellow centres). Forms of A. novae-angliae: 'Alma Potschke' (rich pink), 'Herbstschnee' ('Autumn Snow') (white), 'September Ruby' (deep red). Forms of A. novi-belgii: 'Ada Ballard' (mauve-blue), 'Little Pink Beauty' (pink). A. thompsonii 'Nanus' (low-growing, lilac).

Astilbe hybrids   Saxifragaceae

I have forced myself to include astilbes for I know that many gardeners love them, although personally I cannot abide their artificial-looking plumes and, in many cases, luminous colours. They are really at home in moist soil and are most frequently used around pools and bog gardens. Their advantage is their strong, stout stems that need no staking.

OBTAIN AS: plants.

PEST, DISEASE OR OTHER PROBLEMS: none.

RECOMMENDED VARIETIES: 'Bressingham Beauty' (pink), 'Deutschland' (white), 'Federsee' (red), 'Snowdrift' (white).

Astrantia spp.   Umbelliferae

Astrantias are among the unsung beauties of the herbaceous world. Their flowers are not striking but when seen at close quarters, the mass of stamens and simple pale pointed petals are undeniably lovely. They are also exquisite in simple cut-flower arrangements, with strong 60 cm (2 ft) tall stems. I find astrantias particularly useful in partial shade, an unusual attribute among herbaceous perennials of this height.

OBTAIN AS: plants.

PEST, DISEASE OR OTHER PROBLEMS: none.

RECOMMENDED VARIETIES: A. major (60 cm (2 ft), greenish-pink flowers; the forms 'Rosea' and 'Rubra' have more reddish flowers but to my mind are less attractive); 'Marjory Fish' (now regrettably called 'Shaggy') is a particularly fine variety.

Bergenia spp. and hybrids   Saxifragaceae

Bergenias, or to give them their rather descriptive popular name of elephant's ears, are extremely useful plants in providing ground-cover in shady places, especially where some moisture is present. Some varieties have the added attraction of beautifully coloured foliage and imposing flower spikes also.

OBTAIN AS: plants.

PEST, DISEASE OR OTHER PROBLEMS: none.

RECOMMENDED VARIETIES: B. 'Bressingham White' (green leaves, white flowers); B. 'Bressingham Ruby' (rich green leaves which turn deep purple in winter, rich deep-red flowers); B. cordifolia purpurea (purple leaves, pink flowers); B. 'Silberlicht' (green leaves, white flowers).

Calamintha spp.   Labiatae

Common but none the worse for that, Calamintha has many advantages. The rich blue or purple flowers last for ages and the plant provides wonderful ground-cover at the front of a border. The species of Calamintha are rather similar to the true catmints, Nepeta spp. (p. 211). Both genera are vigorous and should be divided every two years.

OBTAIN AS: seed or plants.

PEST, DISEASE OR OTHER PROBLEMS: none.

RECOMMENDED VARIETIES: C. grandiflora (purple flowers); C. nepetoides (also called C. nepeta nepeta, powder-blue flowers).

Campanula spp.   Bell flowers   Campanulaceae

There are some very attractive low-growing campanulas suitable for the alpine garden (p. 239), but the tall-growing species that reach between 50 and 100 cm (20 and 40 in) have a role in the mixed border. I am nonetheless in two minds about their value, for whilst the flowers are undeniably attractive, the stems of many are prone to flop, with the bend starting almost at soil level, and in consequence they are all but impossible to stake effectively unless you arrange tier upon tier of perforated wire supports.

OBTAIN AS: plants.

PEST, DISEASE OR OTHER PROBLEMS: slugs.

RECOMMENDED VARIETIES: C. lactiflora (1.2 m/4 ft) alba (white), 'Loddon Anna' (pink); C. latifolia (1.2 m/4 ft) alba (white), 'Brantwood' (purple); C. persicifolia (1 m/39 in) (lilac-blue), alba (white), 'Fleur de Neige' (double, white), 'Pride of Exmouth' (double, powder blue), 'Telham Beauty' (powder blue).

Centranthus ruber spp.   Valerian   Valerianaceae

This is the 1 m (39 in) tall valerian, so beautiful when seen in its natural habitat, growing on and from the cracks of old walls. These, or the wilder parts of the garden, are really its ideal habitat, for it self-seeds wickedly, but it has a place in the mixed border provided you are really ruthless in pulling out the seedlings.

OBTAIN AS: seed or plants.

PEST, DISEASE OR OTHER PROBLEMS: none.

RECOMMENDED VARIETIES: the normal species is red, but there is a common white form 'Alba'.

Chrysanthemum spp. and hybrids   Compositae

The botanical genus Chrysanthemum has been rent asunder in recent years, its species dispersed to such unfamiliar and unfriendly names as Argyranthemum, Dendranthema, Leucanthomella and, awful to tell, Nipponanthemum. I shall spare you all of this misery, however, and stick with the name you know and love, but undeniably, the group is diverse and its splitting into several parts is understandable. I shall restrict myself here to the clump-forming border perennials of shasta daisy type, the rather more compact varieties of C. rubellum and the traditional, multi-headed spray chrysanthemums of various flower form. I shall not consider the more specialised growing of so-called florists' or disbudded chrysanthemums, almost invariably raised under some protection for exhibition or other display purposes. Nonetheless, in all except very mild areas, I prefer to lift all types of border chrysanthemum in the autumn except the shasta daisies. Cut back the above-ground growth and store the stools (rootstocks) until spring in slightly damp peat or similar medium in boxes in a place protected from frost.

OBTAIN AS: plants.

PEST, DISEASE OR OTHER PROBLEMS: slugs, rust, mildew.

RECOMMENDED VARIETIES: **C. rubellum** 'Clara Curtis' (deep pink), 'Duchess of Edinburgh' (copper red), 'Mary Stoker' (cream-yellow). **C. superbum** (90 cm (3 ft) double white shasta daisy) 'Esther Read', 'Wirral Supreme'. **Spray chrysanthemums**: there are vast numbers of spray chrysanthemum varieties and to single out a few would be pointless. Moreover, as individual chrysanthemum-raising nurseries each produce their own ranges, your choice will usually be limited by the source from which your garden centre or nursey obtains its stock. Nonetheless, of those that I have grown, the Pennine and Wessex ranges have proved particularly attractive and reliable.

Cimicifuga spp.   Ranunculaceae

Cimicifugas do have an English name and although it is rarely used, it is descriptive – bugbane – for they have a curious bug-like smell. They are attractive late summer blooming plants with slender, candle-like spikes of white flowers and, depending on the species chosen, may be used in the centre or at the back of the border provided you are prepared to stake carefully, for they are inherently weak.

OBTAIN AS: plants.

PEST, DISEASE OR OTHER PROBLEMS: none.

RECOMMENDED VARIETIES: C. racemosa (1.5 m/5 ft); C. ramosa 'Atropurpurea' (2.2 m (72 ft), purple stems and foliage, very striking but very slender); C. simplex 'White Pearl' (1.2 m (4 ft), purple stems).

Clematis spp.   Ranunculacea

To the modern gardener, clematis are thought of exclusively as climbers but in the nineteenth century they were important border plants, the long stems being pegged down to form a mound of growth. Today, they still have a role in the border but it is achieved by using a few select forms that are less rampant and are usually called herbaceous clematis. It is pointless to try to keep them too neat and tidy – provide them with twigs or other support much as you do for peas.

OBTAIN AS: plants.

PEST, DISEASE OR OTHER PROBLEMS: slugs, clematis wilt.

RECOMMENDED VARIETIES: C. heracleifolia 'Wyevale' (1 m (39 in), dark-blue, tubular flowers, late summer-autumn); C. integrifolia (80 cm (32 in), deep-blue bell-shaped flowers, summer).

Dahlia hybrids   Compositae

You either love or loath them but they can't be ignored. The tuber-forming large flowering half-hardy dahlias have a fanatical following among some gardeners who grow them in vast monoculture beds where they are staked like trees. But in fact, they have their uses in the mixed border too where they will thrive with rather less dramatic stakes and add a startling array of colour to the late summer border and of course, make fine cut flowers. Not least among their attributes is their colour range which contains most shades except blue and also, incidentally, some of the most appalling bicolours I have ever seen. Although many people think automatically of dahlias as large flowered decoratives, there are several other very attractive flower shapes, including some very small ones.

OBTAIN AS: tubers or young plants; tubers may be planted about three weeks before the danger of the last frost has passed, but plants, suitably hardened off, not until after. When autumn frost kills off the foliage, cut down the tops to leave about 15 cm of stem, lift the tubers with a fork, carefully poke away excess soil, stand them upside down for about one week to drain and then store them in dry peat or newspaper bags in a frost free place until spring.

PEST, DISEASE OR OTHER PROBLEMS: slugs.

RECOMMENDED VARIETIES: Giant and Large flowered decoratives (blooms up to 35 cm diameter) – 'Hamari Girl' (pink), 'Lavengro' (lavender and bronze – prettier than it sounds), 'Night Editor' (deep purple), 'Silver City' (white); Medium and Small flowered decoratives (blooms 10–20 cm diameter) – 'Alloway Cottage' (yellow with pink flush), 'Edinburgh' (purple with white tips), 'Evelyn Foster' (white), 'House of Orange' (orange), 'Rothesay Robin' (deep pink); Miniature flowered decoratives (blooms up to 10 cm diameter) – 'Chorus Girl' (pink); Pompons (tightly held petals on almost spherical blooms up to 5 cm diameter) – 'Rhonda' (lilac and white), 'Small World' (white), 'Willo's Violet' (shades of violet); Cactus flowered (spiky head form, ranging in size from miniature (under 10 cm diameter) to giant (30 cm) – 'Polar Sight' (giant, white), 'Banker' (medium, red), 'Klankstad Kerkrade' (small, yellow); Semi-cactus flowered (intermediate between cactus and decorative) – 'Vantage' (giant, yellow), 'Reginald Keene' (large, bronze-orange), 'Snip' (miniature, bronze-orange); Miscellaneous and collerette – 'Bishop of Llandaff' (my favourite dahlia, dark reddish foliage, single red flowers), 'Chimborazo' (red and yellow, single, vulgar but with an undoubted charm).

Delphinium hybrids   Ranunculaceae

The word stately is inextricably associated with the tall flower spikes of delphiniums, although there is now a range of forms with heights from about 90 cm up to almost 3 m (3–10 ft). They all benefit from being staked, although the shorter varieties will manage without in sheltered situations and when among other plants in the centre of the border. It is advantageous, although not essential, to remove the weaker shoots early in the season to leave no more than four per plant for maximum performance.

OBTAIN AS: plants.

PEST, DISEASE OR OTHER PROBLEMS: slugs, mildew.

RECOMMENDED VARIETIES: *Shorter growing forms*: 'Blue Fountains' (mixture of blues), 'Blue Tit' (dark blue), 'Mighty Atom' (lilac). *Taller growing forms*: Pacific hybrids (generally up to 1.5–2 m/5–6½ ft) – 'Astolat' (pink), 'Black Knight' (dark blue), 'Galahad' (white); taller forms other than Pacific Hybrids (up to 3 m/10 ft) – 'Butterball' (cream), 'Vespers' (mauve). The Belladonna hybrids are plants of medium height but spindly appearance.

Digitalis spp. and hybrids   Foxgloves   Scrophulariaceae

The foxglove is among the best loved of native plants and it has a useful role to play in the garden, especially in slightly shaded, more wild areas. The native species *D. purpurea* occurs in both purple and white forms and self seeds with abandon. The white gene is recessive and to maintain a population of white plants in a garden, therefore, it is necessary to remove all purple-flowered seedlings before the flowers have opened sufficiently for bees to have removed some pollen. Generally, foxgloves are biennial or short-lived perennials but if you are fortunate, they will continue to grow from the same clump by the formation of offsets. In addition to the native species, there are several other attractive species, although none are long-lived.

OBTAIN AS: seed or plants.

PEST, DISEASE OR OTHER PROBLEMS: none.

RECOMMENDED VARIETIES: *D. grandiflora* (60 cm (2 ft), yellow); *D. lanata* (purple or white); *D. mertonensis* (75 cm (30 in), rosy pink); *D. parviflora* (flowers small, brown-purple); *D. purpurea* (1.2–1.5 m (4–5 ft), purple or white in form 'Alba'; there are also selected colour strains called 'Excelsior Hybrids' and a variety called 'Foxy', a low growing plant with revolting 'strawberries and cream' coloured flowers).

Doronicum spp.   Leopard's bane   Compositae

I am not sure how many of the gardeners who grow doronicums would recognise the name leopard's bane but I find this a useful if fairly unremarkable plant for bringing some yellow into the early summer border. The flowers are characteristically daisy-like and single.

OBTAIN AS: plants.

PEST, DISEASE OR OTHER PROBLEMS: mildew, although it usually sets in too late to affect flowering.

RECOMMENDED VARIETIES: *D. orientale magnificum* (sometimes called *D. caucasicum*); *D. plantagineum* 'Excelsum' (usually called 'Harpur Crewe').

Euphorbia spp.   Spurges   Euphorbiaceae

The spurges are unusually appealing because their flowers are individually quite undistinguished, lacking petals and having small, greenish petal-like bracts. *En masse*, however, the flower heads have a remarkably attractive appearance and the oppositely arranged pairs of leaves display considerable variety. There is variety too in the preferred habitats, many species revelling in hot sun and dry soil while a few, most notably *E. amygdaloides robbiae*, are most useful for shady places.

OBTAIN AS: seed (true species only) or as plants.

PEST, DISEASE OR OTHER PROBLEMS: aphids.

RECOMMENDED VARIETIES: *E. amygdaloides robbiae* (45 cm (18 in), dark-green foliage, shade tolerant); *E. characias* (1 m (39 in), shrubby, yellow-green flowers with reddish centres), *wulfenii*, more robust with larger, pillowy flower heads; *E. cyparissias* (30 cm (12 in), pale-green, useful as ground cover); *E. griffithii* 'Fireglow' (75 cm (30 in), vivid red-orange bracts); *E. myrsinites* (15 cm (6 in), blue-green foliage, useful ground cover); *E. polychroma* (45 cm (18 in), bright-green foliage and vivid yellow-green flower heads); *E. sikkimensis* (1.2 m (4 ft), reddish young growths in spring, vivid green-yellow flower heads later).

Ferns   Polypodiaceae

I have mentioned one or two small species of fern as suitable for the alpine or peat garden but there are other, taller growing forms that are appropriate in the mixed border and in more informal plantings too. Almost without exception (that exception being *Polypodium vulgare*), ferns will not thrive in dry situations and a well mulched, moist organic soil suits them ideally. The species suitable for gardens represent several genera but the most useful division is into evergreen and deciduous types. They may not have flowers but their foliage is beautiful and this is one group of plants that my garden would be much poorer without. There are hundreds of forms of some species and you would be wise to seek out a specialist fern nursery for the best choice.

OBTAIN AS: plants.

PEST, DISEASE OR OTHER PROBLEMS: none.

RECOMMENDED VARIETIES: *Adiantum* spp. (Maidenhair ferns): *A. pedatum* (20 cm/8 in), *A. pedatum subpumilum*, also called *A. aleuticum*, (15 cm (6 in), compact, superb), *A. venustum* (25 cm (10 in), carpeting habit). *Athyrium filix-femina* – numerous forms with distorted and crested fronds, 'Victoriae' (90 cm/3 ft) is the loveliest. *A. nipponicum pictum* (70 cm (28 in), bronzed fronds). *Blechnum penna-marina* (15 cm (6 in), creeping, deeply toothed fronds, evergreen). *Dryopteris erythrosora* (55 cm (22 in), coppery-pink young fronds), *D. wallichiana* (80 cm (32 in), upright habit, black scaly frond stems). *Matteuccia struthiopteris* (60 cm (24 in), creeping rhizomatous habit with vase-shaped plants arising at intervals). *Osmunda regalis* (1.5 m (5 ft), superb, coarsely indented fronds for very moist places). *Phyllitis scolopendrium* (hart's tongue, 60 cm (24 in)), entire, strap-like leaves with numerous variants having crests or other ornamentation on the fronds, evergreen. *Polypodium vulgare* (30 cm (12 in), typically with entire, not toothed, fronds, but twisted forms occur, evergreen). *Polystichum setiferum* (1 m (39 in) highly indented fronds, especially lovely in the twisted, compact form *divisilobum*, evergreen).

Filipendula spp.   Meadow sweet   Rosaceae

Feathery flower heads from midsummer onwards, deeply divided leaves and a general preference for moist conditions are the characteristics of the meadow sweets. They are really most appropriate for the edge of a water or wild garden and only justify their place in a border if it is a very large one when they will usefully contribute to the overall effect.

OBTAIN AS: plants.

PEST, DISEASE OR OTHER PROBLEMS: none.

RECOMMENDED VARIETIES: *F. rubra* 'Venusta' (2 m (6½ ft), pink flowers); *F. ulmaria* (1 m (39 in) or 45 cm (18 in) in the golden-foliaged form 'Aurea').

Geranium spp. and hybrids   Cranesbills   Geraniaceae

The hardy geraniums are, I am sure, one of the three or four most valuable groups of herbaceous perennials. They offer a long flowering season, ease of cultivation, fairly rapid growth, a range of delightful colours and a range of habits too, including some fine ground-cover species. Few require staking but most of the larger types must be divided every two or three years.

OBTAIN AS: plants.

PEST, DISEASE OR OTHER PROBLEMS: none.

RECOMMENDED VARIETIES: *G. cinereum subcaulescens* (15 cm (6 in), magenta with black centres), 'Apple Blossom' (pink), 'Ballerina' (white with red-purple markings); *G. dalmaticum* (25 cm (10 in), pink, or white in form 'Album'); *G. endressii* 'Wargrave Pink' (45 cm (18 in), pink); *G.* 'Johnson's Blue' (40 cm (16 in), powder blue); *G. himalayense* 'Plenum' (25 cm (10 in), double purple); *G. macrorrhizum* 'Ingwerson's Variety' (25 cm (10 in), pale lilac, excellent ground cover for shade); *G. oxonianum* 'Claridge Druce' (75 cm (30 in), lavender, vigorous, self-seeds readily); *G. phaeum* (75 cm (30 in), deep purple, superb in shade); *G. pratense* 'Mrs Kendall Clark' (70 cm (28 in), clear blue); *G. procurrens* (10 cm (4 in), magenta); *G. pylzowianum* (20 cm (8 in), pink, beautifully mottled foliage); *G. riversleaianum* 'Russell Prichard' (20 cm (8 in), magenta); *G. sanguineum* (20 cm (8 in), magenta), *lancastriense* 'Splendens' (flowers larger, pink); *G. wallichianum* 'Buxton's Variety' (also called 'Buxton's Blue') (25 cm (10 in), blue, white centres).

Geum spp.   Rosaceae

The cultivated geums have stayed closer in general form to the familiar native species than have many other types of herbaceous perennial. There are both singles and doubles but the singles, with their characteristically rosaceous flowers, are perhaps the prettier. They are useful plants for close to the front of a large border in a sunny position on light soil, where they contribute usefully to the overall effect, although they are scarcely good enough to be made features.

OBTAIN AS: plants.

PEST, DISEASE OR OTHER PROBLEMS: none.

RECOMMENDED VARIETIES: *G.* 'Georgenberg' (30 cm (12 in) deep yellow); *G. quellyon* 'Mrs Bradshaw' (60 cm (24 in), semi-double red, an old variety and the most popular); *G. rivale* 'Album' (30 cm (12 in), white), 'Lady Stratheden' (60 cm (24 in), double yellow), 'Leonard's Variety' (30 cm (12 in), red); 'Lionel Cox' (30 cm (12 in), pink).

Grasses   Gramineae

Cortaderia selloäna

The lawn is not the only place in the garden for growing grasses. There are several grass genera and species, both perennial and annual, that make attractive additions to the mixed border and also, incidentally, to other garden situations – in corners, among gravel or between paving stones, for instance. Clearly the species to be chosen for this purpose should be clump, rather than matted turf-forming, but their ornamental appeal can come from attractively coloured (often variegated) foliage or from the delicacy of their flower and seed heads. Most thrive best in full sun on well-drained soils and a few will self-seed, although none of those that I recommend are likely to become a nuisance in this respect. Among the herbaceous grasses, I am including some of the woody species, familiarly known as bamboos, although unfortunately very few of these are suitable for the British climate.

OBTAIN AS: seed (true species) or as plants.

PEST, DISEASE OR OTHER PROBLEMS: none.

RECOMMENDED VARIETIES: *Alopecurus pratensis* 'Aureomarginatus' (30 cm (12 in), flower stalks to 75 cm (30 in), yellow and green striped leaves, soft, dense flower heads, my favourite variegated grass); *Arundinaria* spp. (several of these bamboos have now been reclassified under other generic names but I can think of few garden centres that will pay any attention) – *nitida* (5 m (16½ ft), purple canes, green leaves), *variegata* (1.25 m (50 in), pale-green canes, dark-green and white striped leaves), *viridistriata* (1 m (39 in), purple canes, yellow and green striped leaves); *Avena candida* (now called *Helictotrichon sempervirens*) (1.2 m (4 ft), grey-blue leaves, arching flower stalks); *Cortaderia selloana* (pampas grass – always buy a named form, plants raised from seedlings are notorious at not flowering reliably. At the end of the season, pull out old foliage, with strong gloves, do not set fire to the clump – 'Pumila' (1.75 m (6 ft), compact, reliable flowering), 'Sunningdale Silver' (1.5 m (5 ft), flower stalks to 2 m (6½ ft), sharp-edged leaves, cream flower heads); *Elymus magellanicum* (often called *Agropyron magellanicum* (30 cm (12 in), silver-blue); *Festuca glauca* (25 cm (10 in), steel blue, arching flower stalks); *Hakonechloa macra* 'Alboaurea' (35 cm (14 in), green and white striped leaves); *Holcus mollis* 'Albovariegatus' (25 cm (10 in), silver-grey variegation); *Molinia caerulea* 'Variegata' (60 cm (24 in), green and yellow striped leaves, purple flower stalks); *Stipa gigantea* (45 cm (18 in), flower stalks to 2.5 m (8 ft), green leaves, silvery flower heads).

Helleborus orientalis (purple form)

Gypsophila paniculata   Baby's breath   Caryophyllaceae

The trusty standby of florists, *Gypsophila* looks equally pretty in the border but is not an easy plant to grow. It has a deep tap root and can be difficult to establish, even more difficult to move, is intolerant of wet, cold soil and even in good conditions is quite liable to die without warning.

OBTAIN AS: plants.

PEST, DISEASE OR OTHER PROBLEMS: none.

RECOMMENDED VARIETIES: 'Bristol Fairy' (90 cm (3 ft), double white), 'Compacta Plena' (45 cm (18 in), double white), 'Flamingo' (90 cm (3 ft), double pink).

Helenium hybrids   Compositae

Rich autumn colours for rich autumn-flowering daisies. I rate heleniums among the most valuable of all medium-sized perennials (they will attain around 90–100 cm/36–39 in) for late summer. They are undemanding in their requirements, remain compact for many years and, in a well-furnished border, may not even require staking but obtain their support from the surrounding plants.

OBTAIN AS: plants.

PEST, DISEASE OR OTHER PROBLEMS: none.

RECOMMENDED VARIETIES: 'Butterpat' (deep yellow), 'Chipperfield Orange' (taller, about 1.5 m (5 ft), orange-yellow with reddish markings), 'Crimson Beauty' (red-bronze), 'Moorheim Beauty' (red-bronze), 'Pumilum Magnificum' (shorter, about 60 cm (2 ft), deep yellow).

Helleborus spp. and hybrids   Ranunculaceae

The best known of the bowl-flowered species of *Helleborus* is the white Christmas rose, *H. niger*, but unaccountably it does not thrive in all gardens, including mine. Fortunately, there are other important species too, among which *H. orientalis* is the most significant. Sadly, most of the inumerable beautiful varieties are obtainable only from one or two specialist nurseries. There are also valuable species in this most amenable genus, with other types of flower, for shaded and otherwise difficult places.

OBTAIN AS: plants; some forms will self-seed readily but the best and most reliable stock plants are not raised from seedlings.

PEST, DISEASE OR OTHER PROBLEMS: stem rot, leaf spot.

RECOMMENDED VARIETIES: *H. argutifolius* (long called *H. corsicus*) (60 cm (24 in), coarsely toothed leaves, pale-green,

nodding flowers in spring); *H. foetidus* (60 cm (24 in), pale-green flowers in late winter and well into spring, invaluable for shade, almost evergreen); *H. niger* (Christmas rose) (30 cm (12 in), white, the best form is the large-flowered 'Potter's Wheel'); *H. orientalis* (Lenten rose) (30–45 cm (12–18 in), colour range from white through pink, pale purple, mauve to deep purple with many variegated forms; always buy plants in flower so that you are sure what you are obtaining).

Hemerocallis hybrids   Day lilies   Liliaceae

The day lilies are so-called because their flowers last only for about twenty-four hours; a pretty useless attribute for a border perennial, you may think. But in reality, the short-lived blossoms are merely sacrificed towards a greater good, for the plant as a whole continues to bloom for weeks. The foliage is strap-like, rather in the manner of a very large daffodil, while the more or less trumpet-shaped lily-like flowers arise in loose groups atop 60–90 cm (2–3 ft) tall stems from mid-summer onwards. I love to see the flowers on the slender but firm stems as they appear to hang above the remainder of the plants in the border. One word of caution; day lilies can be a little invasive and should be lifted and divided every two or three years.

OBTAIN AS: plants.

PEST, DISEASE OR OTHER PROBLEMS: none.

RECOMMENDED VARIETIES: 'Anzac' (red), 'Black Magic' (deep red), 'Bonanza' (orange with darker centre), 'Burning Daylight' (deep orange), 'Catherine Woodbury' (pink with green centre), 'George Cunningham' (pink), 'Hyperion' (yellow), 'Pink Damask' (pink), 'Stafford' (deep red with yellow centre).

Heuchera spp. and hybrids   Saxifragaceae

I am never really sure if I like heucheras. They are pretty enough with dainty, rather loose flower spikes up to about 75 cm (30 in) tall and slightly coarse leaves but neither flowers nor foliage seem positive enough to make a good display. They prefer moist conditions and slight shade.

OBTAIN AS: plants.

PEST, DISEASE OR OTHER PROBLEMS: none.

RECOMMENDED VARIETIES: *H. cylindrica* 'Greenfinch' (green-white); *H. micrantha* 'Palace Purple' (white flowers, purple leaves).

Hosta spp. and hybrids   Liliaceae

The hosta has become one of *the* border plants of our time, largely because of the enormous range of new varieties raised in the United States. They are adaptable plants and should by no means be confined to their traditional home in moist soil. Although grown primarily for their foliage, hosta flowers in tall spikes of white or shades of mauve add to the appeal for many people.

OBTAIN AS: plants.

PEST, DISEASE OR OTHER PROBLEMS: slugs – if these prove insurmountable, grow the plants in containers.

RECOMMENDED VARIETIES: *H.* 'August Moon' (60 cm (2 ft), yellow, slightly anaemic); *H. decorata* (45 cm (18 in), ribbed leaves with cream-white margins); *H. fortunei* (75 cm (30 in), steel blue), *albopicta* (60 cm (2 ft), yellow and green streaks), 'Francee' (60 cm (2 ft), green with white edge); *H.* 'Gingko Craig' (20 cm (8 in), green with white margin); *H.* 'Krossa Regal' (90 cm (3 ft), steel blue with wavy leaf edge); *H. lancifolia* (45 cm (18 in), elongated leaves, green); *H. sieboldiana elegans* (90 cm (3 ft), blue-green), 'Frances Williams' (1 m (39 in), steel blue); *H. undulata albomarginata* (often called 'Thomas Hogg') (60 cm (2 ft), green with cream edge).

Iris spp. and hybrids   Iridaceae

The genus *Iris* is one of the most familiar and largest of all garden plants. I have described bulbous and aquatic species elsewhere (pp. 233, 249). Here I shall concentrate on the taller species and on those usually called bearded irises. The border hybrids are usually grouped into Dwarf and Tall irises, a division that reflects their order of flowering as well as their size. (There is also a small group of Intermediate varieties, although I am not separating them here.) To succeed, irises must have well drained, preferably slightly alkaline or neutral soil and be divided every three years. It is also essential that their large, fleshy rhizomes be planted with their tops exposed at the soil surface and only their roots buried. I have never been able to convince myself that orientating them so that the rhizomes receive maximum exposure to the sun, as often recommended, makes any difference.

OBTAIN AS: plants.

PEST, DISEASE OR OTHER PROBLEMS: slugs and a leaf-spotting and tattering problem of which I am unsure of the cause, although a spray with a copper-containing fungicide seems to control it.

RECOMMENDED VARIETIES: **Tall bearded** (90–120 cm/ 3–4 ft): 'Amethyst Flame' (pale violet and reddish), 'Berkeley Gold' (deep yellow), 'Black Swan' (very deep purple), 'Dancer's Veil' (white with violet markings), 'Firecracker' (red-brown with yellow markings), 'Frost and Flame' (white with orange beard), 'Jane Phillips' (pale blue), 'Queechee' (maroon with orange beard), 'Saint Crispin' (yellow). **Dwarf bearded** (25–70 cm/10–28 in): 'Blue Denim' (25 cm (10 in), mid-blue), 'Cherry Gardens' (30 cm (12 in), dark maroon, deep-purple beard), 'Lilli-White' (30 cm (12 in), white), 'Pogo' (30 cm (12 in) yellow with brown-red marking). *I. foetidissima* (60 cm/2 ft, flowers brownish and insignificant but the scarlet seed pods are very attractive, ideal in dry shade). *I. pallida* 'Variegata' (60 cm (2 ft), blue flowers, cream and blue-green striped leaves). *I. sibirica* (90 cm/3 ft): 'Flight of Butterflies' (blue with white veins), 'Lime Heart' (white with greenish centres), 'Papillon' (pale blue), 'Snow Queen' (white).

Kniphofia spp. and hybrids   Liliaceae

Kniphofia 'Little Maid'

It comes as a surprise to many gardeners to discover that red hot pokers are not all red, and, indeed, none of them are hot. Their general appearance is well known, with a club-shaped flower head arising on a stout stalk from a rosette of strap-like leaves. They are rather exacting in their site requirements, however, needing a rich but fairly free-draining soil and, in many areas, some protection during the winter, which is best achieved by tying up the evergreen foliage over the crown.

OBTAIN AS: plants.

PEST, DISEASE OR OTHER PROBLEMS: none.

RECOMMENDED VARIETIES: *K.* 'Candlelight' (50 cm (20 in), yellow); *K.* 'Little Maid' (60 cm (2 ft), cream with yellow tip); *K.* 'Royal Standard' (60 cm (2 ft), yellow, scarlet tip), *K. uvaria* (2 m (6½ ft), red).

Lamium spp.   Dead-nettles   Labiatae

The dead nettles, with their white, yellow or pink flowers, nettle-like but non-stinging leaves and angled stems are among the more familiar garden weeds. Perhaps because of these, too many gardeners dismiss them as ornamental plants but whilst they will never be the gems of the border, there are some most attractive, low-growing forms that provide excellent ground-cover, especially in dry and slightly shaded places where little else will grow.

OBTAIN AS: plants.

PEST, DISEASE OR OTHER PROBLEMS: mildew, leaf-feeding beetles.

209

RECOMMENDED VARIETIES: *L. galeobdolon* 'Florentinum' (also called 'Variegatum') (silver-splashed leaves, pale-yellow flowers); *L. maculatum* 'Aureum' (golden foliage), 'Beacon Silver' (silver-white foliage, pink flowers), 'White Nancy' (silver-grey foliage, white flowers).

Lavatera spp.   Tree mallow   Malvaceae

The lavateras are very similar to their close relatives malvas, with cup-shaped, rich pink flowers. They require sun and a light, free-draining soil – they almost always thrive well in coastal areas. Although a range of species is offered from time to time, only one species and one variety is worth going out of your way to obtain.

OBTAIN AS: plants.

PEST, DISEASE OR OTHER PROBLEMS: aphids.

RECOMMENDED VARIETIES: *L. olbia* 'Barnsley' (2 m (6½ ft), deep pink, very floriferous).

Ligularia spp.   Compositae

Among my favourite perennials for providing yellow flowers in summer. The flower heads are all composed of individual daisy-like flowers but the overall form varies from tall, slender spikes to more robust forms in which the individual blooms are considerably larger. They thrive best in a moisture retentive soil (and are good waterside plants) but given mulch, will be suitable for most borders.

OBTAIN AS: plants.

PEST, DISEASE OR OTHER PROBLEMS: none.

RECOMMENDED VARIETIES: *L. dentata* (also called *L. clivorum*) (1.2 m (4 ft), large heart-shaped leaves, large daisy flowers) – 'Desdemona' (purple leaves, yellow-orange flowers), 'Greygnog Gold' (green leaves, more yellowish flowers); *L. przewalskii* (1.5 m (5 ft), dissected leaves, black stems, narrow spikes of delicate yellow flowers) (a variety called 'The Rocket' is very similar and is sometimes placed in this species and sometimes in *L. stenocephala*).

Lupinus spp. and hybrids   Lupin   Leguminosae

Lupins must be among the most familiar plants of the summer border. They evoke the old cottage garden feel, although most of the varieties grown are in fact of twentieth-century origin. They are pretty enough if a little sculptured and will grow in most soils, but unfortunately their 1 m (39 in) tall flower spikes do not die gracefully and once the blooms have faded, mildew and dereliction take over.

OBTAIN AS: seed (some varieties only) or plants.

PEST, DISEASE OR OTHER PROBLEMS: mildew, slugs.

RECOMMENDED VARIETIES: 'Chandelier' (shades of yellow), 'My Castle' (shades of red), 'Noble Maiden' (cream and white), 'The Governor' (blue and white). The 'Russell Hybrids' offer an extensive colour range, mainly of bicoloured flowers on strong plants while the 'New Generation Hybrids' (usually only obtainable as seed) are recently bred, robust plants in a range of single colours.

Lychnis spp. and hybrids   Catchfly   Caryophyllaceae

Lychnis is a genus of mostly medium-sized perennials, probably better known to wildflower lovers than to gardeners, for the native species are invariable components of many meadow-flower mixtures. The alpine enthusiast will be familiar with dwarf species too, but the mainly red-flowered border species are useful for contributing to the hot and fiery shades often needed towards the centre. They are sun-loving plants and thrive best in fairly light soils.

OBTAIN AS: seed or plants.

PEST, DISEASE OR OTHER PROBLEMS: Aphids.

RECOMMENDED VARIETIES: *L. × arkwrightii* (30 cm (12 in), individual vivid orange-red flowers, purple leaves); *L. chalcedonica* (1 m (39 in), rounded heads of scarlet flowers); *L. coronaria* (60 cm (2 ft), almost luminous red flowers and silver-grey woolly foliage, 'Alba' is a white form); *L. viscaria* (40 cm (16 in), spikes of double, intensely magenta flowers).

Lysimachia spp.   Loosestrife   Primulaceae

Lysimachias are often dismissed as the poor relations of the primula family, having nothing special to offer, but I find them very useful, easy-to-grow plants for the centre of the border, and they have the virtue of being tolerant of moderate shade too. There are yellow- and white-flowered varieties and the group also includes one excellent creeping ground-cover species.

OBTAIN AS: plants.

PEST, DISEASE OR OTHER PROBLEMS: none.

RECOMMENDED VARIETIES: *L. clethroides* (1 m (39 in), arching white flower spikes); *L. ephemerum* (1.2 m (4 ft), strong, erect white flower spikes); *L. nummularia* 'Aurea' (creeping jenny, 15 cm (6 in), yellow flowers, golden foliage, excellent ground-cover for damp shady places); *L. punctata* (90 cm (3 ft), stiff spikes of yellow flowers).

Lythrum salicaria   Purple loosestrife   Lythraceae

Quite unrelated, except in name, to the previous plant, the native purple loosestrife with its 90 cm (3 ft) tall dense spikes of rich-purple flowers is a beautiful waterside plant, suitable for any border with moisture-retentive soil. There are also some fine cultivated selections however.

OBTAIN AS: seed (true species) or plants.

PEST, DISEASE OR OTHER PROBLEMS: none.

RECOMMENDED VARIETIES: the normal species is probably the finest plant but selections include 'Firecandle' (deep rose-red) and the lower growing 'Robert' with pink flowers.

Malva spp.   Mallow   Malvaceae

Mallows are plants for big borders. Their cup-shaped pink flowers are borne rather sparsely on loose, untidy branches; and in due course, many of them can become very big plants indeed. They are closely related to *Lavatera*. If this type of flower appeals to you, but you have little space, grow the excellent annual forms of *Lavatera* instead.

OBTAIN AS: plants.

PEST, DISEASE OR OTHER PROBLEMS: none.

RECOMMENDED VARIETIES: *M. alcea fastigiata* (1.2 m/4 ft), *M. moschata* (1 m/39 in).

Meconopsis spp. and hybrids   Poppies   Papaveraceae

Anyone who has seen *Meconopsis* in flower will understand why, when stories first filtered back from the Far East of blue poppies, the gardening world lost its head. For these are plants of classic poppy form but with, in many instances, blooms of the most stunning, electric blue. Unfortunately, they are not easy plants to grow. They require a rich, moisture-retentive soil and partial shade. Most of the best forms tend also to be monocarpic: that is, they flower once and then die. With those species that come true from seed, starting again is relatively simple; with the others, you can sometimes avoid the necessity of constantly buying new plants by removing the very young flower buds from some of the off-sets of each clump. In this way, whilst parts of the plant will die, others should continue.

OBTAIN AS: seed or plants.

PEST, DISEASE OR OTHER PROBLEMS: none.

RECOMMENDED VARIETIES: *M. betonicifolia* (also called *M. baileyi*) (seed or plants, although flower colour is very variable and to be certain of obtaining the best coloured, least monocarpic forms, buy plants; 90 cm (3 ft), colours in the best selections range from sky blue (preferably the 'Harlow Carr' strain) to purple or white, in the form *alba*); *M. cambrica* (45 cm (18 in), an exception in being a yellow native species but very useful if allowed to self-seed); *M. grandis* (plants, 1 m (39 in), usually monocarpic, large flowers in a range of rich colours from white to deep purple); *M.* × *sheldonii* (a group of crosses between *M. betonicifolia* and *M. grandis*, 1.3 m (4½ ft), monocarpic-perennial, the best blue flowers are in the forms 'Branklyn' and 'Slieve Donard'.)

Nepeta spp.   Catmint   Labiatae

Catmints are among the plants too often disregarded by gardening snobs as common and boring, but in fact a clump occupies one of the most important positions in my own garden and contrasts beautifully with deep-pink blooms close by. They are somewhat straggly but, because of this, contribute very usefully to that informal cottage feel that so many gardeners hanker for. They are vigorous too and should be divided annually or biennially, although those that I have recommended are the least likely to become invasive. Like most of their family, they are at their best on light soil in a sunny position and the front of the border suits them admirably.

OBTAIN AS: seed or plants.

PEST, DISEASE OR OTHER PROBLEMS: none.

RECOMMENDED VARIETIES: *N. mussinii* (30 cm (12 in), mauve, greyish foliage); *N.* 'Six Hills Giant' (60 cm (2 ft), robust).

Omphalodes spp.   Boraginaceae

Imagine a 20 cm (8 in) tall, evergreen, shade tolerant forget-me-not but with flowers of the most intense electric blue, and no mildew, and you will gain an impression of one of the loveliest ground-cover herbaceous perennials. There are two species of which *O. cappadocica* is the best; and a white form too but I find

Omphalodes cappadocica

it inferior and more straggly.

OBTAIN AS: seed or plants.

PEST, DISEASE OR OTHER PROBLEMS: none.

RECOMMENDED VARIETIES: *O. cappadocica*; *O. verna* (blue-eyed Mary), white in form *alba*.

Paeonia spp.   Paeony   Paeoniaceae

Paeonies have their supporters and their detractors; the former adore their sumptuous form, colours and perfume and the latter object that they bloom for so short a period, are prone to being ruined by rain and take ages before young plants flower. I can't argue with any of the detractors' arguments and for these reasons I would never have many paeonies in a small garden, preferring to tuck one or two amongst other herbaceous plants; but I would always have some. Paeonies thrive best in a rich, organic soil, although in saying this I always remember that in the wild, many forms grow on more or less barren hillsides, with their tuberous roots close to the surface. It is because these tubers are somewhat resentful of disturbance that paeonies have gained a reputation for ceasing to flower after being transplanted. This is, however, a myth, and if you move them carefully, just after the shoots have emerged in spring, they should lose only one season's flowering, if any. Because the buds can be damaged by late spring frosts, it is sensible not to place them facing east, where frozen tissues thaw out very rapidly. Most of the herbaceous paeonies are derived from *P. lactiflora* and *P. officinalis* but I have also included here for convenience those usually called tree paeonies – beautiful, taller growing (although not tree-sized) shrubs that retain an above-ground framework throughout the winter. They are more tender than the herbaceous types and must be grown in sheltered positions.

OBTAIN AS: plants.

PEST, DISEASE OR OTHER PROBLEMS: bud drop, bud and stem rot.

RECOMMENDED VARIETIES: **Herbaceous species**: *P. mlokosewitschii* (75 cm (30 in), single yellow. Herbaceous forms of *P. lactiflora* (90 cm/3 ft) – 'Bowl of Beauty' (semi-double, deep pink, cream centre), 'Duchesse de Nemours' (double white), 'Felix Crousse' (double, deep pink, red centres), 'Festiva Maxima' (double, white, red flecks), 'President Franklin Roosevelt' (double, dark red), 'Sarah Bernhardt' (double, shell pink), 'White Wings' (single, white). Herbaceous forms of *P. officinalis* (75 cm (30 in), 'cottage garden paeony') – 'Alba Plena' (double, white), 'Anemoniflora Rosea' (semi-double, deep pink), 'Rubra Plena' (double, reddish pink). **Tree paeonies**: true species –

211

Paeonia mlokosewitschii

P. delavayi (1.5 m/5 ft) *lutea* (single yellow), *ludlowii* (more golden colour and deeply dissected leaves); Japanese varieties of *P. suffruticosa* (2 m/6½ ft) – a fairly large number of varieties in a range of rich red and pink colours as well as white is offered from time to time by various nurseries; they are attractive enough but are grafted onto herbaceous paeony stocks and have none of the appeal of the true tree paeonies.

Papaver orientale spp.   Poppies   Papaveraceae

Poppies need little introduction. The native red field poppy is one of the best-loved annual wild plants but it has many cultivated perennial relatives. Almost all have large, shaggy but short-lived flowers, each with a dark blotch at the base of the petals. They are of little use for cutting but delightful *en masse* amongst other, more durable border plants. They have little place in the formal garden, for their appearance is straggly, no matter how carefully they are staked. They flower in early summer but a second flush may be obtained if they are cut back promptly.

OBTAIN AS: seed or plants.
PEST, DISEASE OR OTHER PROBLEMS: aphids.
RECOMMENDED VARIETIES: 'Black and White' (70 cm (28 in), white), 'Curlilocks' (75 cm (30 in), fringed, orange-red), 'Mrs Perry' (90 cm (3 ft), salmon pink), 'Perry's White' (90 cm (3 ft), white), 'Turkish Delight' (75 cm (30 in), pink).

Phlox spp.   Polemoniaceae

I consider the border phlox to be one of the most valuable perennials for the second half of the summer. Their colour range is limited, although usually of fairly soft colours, they thrive well in slight shade, are long lasting and, most importantly, they require very little staking. The drawbacks are their susceptibility to eelworm attack, especially on soils where they have been grown extensively in previous years, and also to mildew, although this is not usually manifest until the flowers are fading.

OBTAIN AS: plants.
PEST, DISEASE OR OTHER PROBLEMS: eelworm, mildew.
RECOMMENDED VARIETIES: **Forms of *P. maculata*** (45 cm (18 in), tall, almost cylindrical flower spikes): 'Alpha' (rose pink), 'Omega' (white with pinkish eye). **Forms of *P. paniculata*** (60 cm/2 ft): 'Border Gem' (violet), 'Brigadier' (reddish pink), 'Eva Cullum' (pink with red eye), 'Franz Schubert' (lilac), 'Fujiyama' (white), 'Prince of Orange' (salmon orange), 'Prospero' (pale lilac), 'Sandringham' (deep shell pink), 'Starfire' (deep red), 'White Admiral' (white).

Polygonatum spp.   Solomon's Seal   Liliaceae

Arching stems of broad, rather fleshy leaves and pendulous, bell-like flowers make the Solomon's seals among the loveliest of plants for shaded positions on rich moist soils. Some are fairly feeble, spindly things and in consequence I recommend only one, a truly majestic plant, its only drawback being that shared with all its relatives, a susceptibility to attack by a voracious leaf-stripping sawfly.

OBTAIN AS: plants.
PEST, DISEASE OR OTHER PROBLEMS: sawfly.
RECOMMENDED VARIETIES: *P. biflorum* (more commonly called *P. giganteum*) (1 m/39 in).

Polygonum spp.   Polygonaceae

An undistinguished but useful genus of plants that includes the familiar knotweeds and also some invasive cultivated forms. They are characterised by stout, angular stems and compact, cylindrical flower heads. I recommend most strongly the none-too-invasive ground-cover species, although there are some taller growing forms suitable for the wild areas of the garden, and especially for informal water-garden plantings. Many of the species are now listed in the genus *Persicaria*.

OBTAIN AS: plants.
PEST, DISEASE OR OTHER PROBLEMS: none.
RECOMMENDED VARIETIES: *P. affine* – 'Darjeeling Red' (15 cm (6 in), red, with red autumn leaf colour), 'Dimity' (15 cm (6 in), pink, good autumn leaf colour); *P. bistorta* 'Superbum' (90 cm (3 ft), pink); *P. campanulatum* (75 cm (30 in), pale pink).

Primula spp.   Primulaceae

I have described several primulas in the section on alpines and that account includes many of those suitable for odd spaces at the front of borders. There are a few tall and more robust species, however, appropriate for further back in the border, and almost all thriving best on rich, moist soil. Indeed, they make excellent plants for the bog garden. Many have stems of candelabra form, that is with the upward-facing flowers arranged in discrete tiered whorls. As with the smaller forms, success is best achieved by dividing them every two or three years.

OBTAIN AS: seed or plants.

RECOMMENDED VARIETIES: *P. florindae* (Himalayan cowslip) (75 cm (30 in), aptly named, with tall, cowslip-like flowers on very robust stems around mid-summer); *P. helodoxa* (60 cm–1 m/24–39 in), candelabra form with yellow flowers); *P.* 'Inverewe' (75 cm/30 in, candelabra form, orange red); *P. japonica* (60 cm (2 ft), tall, candelabra form) – 'Miller's Crimson' (vivid red), 'Postford White' (white with orange-pink eye).

Pulmonaria spp.   Lungwort   Boraginaceae

The lungworts are low-growing, ground-cover perennials providing vivid blue, pink or white flowers and mottled foliage early in the year. They make an excellent accompaniment to spring bulbs. Provided they are given fertiliser whilst in flower, they seem not to suffer when overgrown with taller plants for the remainder of the season.

OBTAIN AS: plants.

PEST, DISEASE OR OTHER PROBLEMS: none.

RECOMMENDED VARIETIES: *P. angustifolia* (30 cm/12 in) – 'Mawson's Blue' (the most vivid of all of the blues), 'Munstead Blue' (not quite as intense as the former but an acceptable substitute and more widely available); *P. rubra* (30 cm/12 in) 'Redstart' (rich rose-red), 'Sissinghurst White' (pure white); *P. saccharata* (25 cm/10 in) 'Margery Fish' (also called *P. vallarsae*) (pink and blue with markedly mottled leaves).

Rudbeckia spp.   Black-eyed Susan   Compositae

Among the most valuable of the tall, summer-flowering daisies, the traditional *Rudbeckia* has yellow or golden flowers with dark centres, although the impact of the darker colouring vanishes with some of the double-flowered forms. The singles are, to my eye, more attractive. I have also included here the species now usually placed in a separate genus, *Echinacea*.

OBTAIN AS: plants.

PEST, DISEASE OR OTHER PROBLEMS: none.

RECOMMENDED VARIETIES: *R. echinacea purpurea* (now usually called *Echinacea purpurea*) 'White Lustre' (45 cm (18 in), white with orange-brown central cone); *R. fulgida* (90 cm/3 ft) – *deamii* (yellow, single with black central cone), *sullivantii* 'Goldsturm' (golden yellow, single, black centres); *R. nitida* 'Goldquelle' (90 cm (3 ft), double deep yellow).

Schizostylis coccinea   Kaffir lily   Iridaceae

Not to everyone's liking but these somewhat invasive, rhizomatous plants do have a useful place in a mixed border provided they can be divided frequently. The flower heads are rather gladiolus-like but there always seems to be a great deal of foliage in proportion to the number of blooms.

OBTAIN AS: plants.

PEST, DISEASE OR OTHER PROBLEMS: none.

RECOMMENDED VARIETIES: 'Major' (large, red), 'Mrs Hegarty' (pale pink), 'Viscountess Byng' (pink).

Thalictrum spp.   Meadow Rue   Ranunculaceae

Most of the meadow rues are tall plants for the rear of the border, with characteristically divided, sometimes almost fern-like foliage and tiny flowers in rather loose heads. Although the flowers are almost invariably seen from afar, they are very beautiful on close examination. A moist soil suits them best and some are tolerant of partial shade. I am also including with the more familiar tall species a dwarf native plant that I find one of the prettiest ground-cover species for shade.

OBTAIN AS: seed (true species) or plants.

PEST, DISEASE OR OTHER PROBLEMS: none.

RECOMMENDED VARIETIES: *T. aquilegiifolium* 'Album' (1.2 m (4 ft), white); *T. dipterocarpum* (also called *T. delavayi*) 'Hewitt's Double' (90 cm (3 ft), double mauve); *T. minus* (45 cm (18 in), yellow, ground cover).

Trollius hybrids   Globe Flower   Ranunculaceae

Trollius hybrid

Large-flowered, early summer buttercups for moist soils would be a fair description of the globe flowers. They are rather similar to calthas and can be planted very successfully in similar situations in bog or other water-side gardens.

OBTAIN AS: plants.

PEST, DISEASE OR OTHER PROBLEMS: none.

RECOMMENDED VARIETIES: *T.* × *cultorum* 'Alabaster' (pale yellow), 'Earliest of All' (yellow), 'Fireglobe' (deep orange), 'Orange Princess' (orange gold).

Verbascum spp.   Mulleins   Scrophulariaceae

There is no mistaking the tall, sometimes branched flower spikes of verbascums, rising above woolly grey foliage. They really are plants of the sunshine and light, free-draining soils. Several of the species self-seed but unfortunately many of the most attractive hybrids are very short lived and do not set seed readily and for this reason I do not recommend them. There are pink-flowered forms but, for me, a verbascum should be yellow or orange.

OBTAIN AS: seeds or plants.

PEST, DISEASE OR OTHER PROBLEMS: none.

RECOMMENDED VARIETIES: *V. chaixii* (1 m/39 in, yellow or white); *V. elegantissimum* 'Gainsborough' (1.2 m (4 ft), yellow, branched spikes); *V. nigrum* (1 m (39 in), yellow, purple centres); *V. olympicum* (2 m (6½ ft), yellow, branched spikes).

Annuals and biennials

THE plants described in this section include those sometimes referred to as bedding plants, which have the singular merit of providing colour quickly. The term bedding plant really relates, however, only to one role for them, for bedding is the use of annual ornamental plants to provide colour and appeal during the summer. Typically, the bed is exclusively devoted to this type of plant and the individuals are massed together to provide colour patterns of varying complexity. Many municipal parks departments still plant large areas of beds in public gardens in this way every year and these are the places to go to obtain ideas that you can adapt for your own garden, if this style of planting appeals to you. At their most complex, and using a specialised range of foliage species, such planting schemes are known as carpet bedding, for their patterns mimic those on Indian and other complex carpets.

But it is important to realise that the bed of annuals is a thing of beauty and a joy for a few months only. In the winter it is only as exciting as any other area of bare soil and many gardeners find that growing annuals to the exclusion of other types of plant is somewhat unrewarding. Other possibilities, therefore, include using them as edging around a mixed border or interspersed between perennials. I find that, used in moderation, they can add a great deal of interest to the kitchen garden – the combination of dark-blue lobelia and fresh green parsley, for instance, is particularly appealing. But perhaps the greatest value of annuals comes with their use in containers, for they are the stock-in-trade of the hanging basket, window box and tub. They are planted in the spring and early summer to replace biennials or bulbs and they are removed in the autumn when the new biennials and bulbs go in.

Although I refer to these plants as annuals, many of them in reality are perennials that we happen to grow as annuals; and whilst some of them are hardy, many (especially the potential perennials) are not. Thus, whilst some can be raised by the hardy annual technique, most cannot. I have included the relatively few ornamental biennials in this section because they complement annuals in providing colour at other times of the year.

It will be apparent from my comments in the individual descriptions that many types of annual are offered by seed companies only as mixtures; and it will be apparent that, in most cases, such mixtures are my second choice. To my mind there is no doubt that the best plantings, of whatever type, can only be made with individually coloured varieties. Only when you can predict which colours will appear in which place can the most attractive planting schemes be made.

As with vegetables, you will see varieties of some annuals designated as F_1 hybrids. But in the formal bedding scheme at least, unlike the vegetable garden, there is considerable merit in the uniformity that the F_1 hybrid offers, although the almost disgustingly large size of the blooms on some of the hybrid African marigolds takes some adjusting to.

Although I have indicated the ways in which the various types of annual should be raised from seed, it is well worth remembering two other options. Plants may be purchased from garden centres or nurseries almost ready for planting in the garden. But if you do choose to obtain your stock in this way, always ensure that you have fully hardened it off before planting; and if you want to be sure of obtaining your preferred varieties in your chosen quantities, ordering in advance is a sound insurance. For those gardeners who prefer to undertake at least part of the plant raising themselves (or for various reasons cannot or do not want to be bothered with seed sowing), the major

Opposite: Helichrysum 'Bright Bikini' mixed.

215

seed companies now have ways to help you. They offer young seedlings or 'plantlets' at various stages of growth from newly germinated onwards, for you to continue to raise yourself. Understandably, supplies are limited by their production capacity, so ordering well in advance is essential.

When planting an entire bed with annuals, the soil should be prepared in much the same way that it would be for vegetables (p. 114). Where they are simply to be slotted in amongst other types of plant this is more difficult, but always prepare the soil as thoroughly as possible and incorporate a dressing of general purpose fertiliser. Once growth is under way in the summer, annuals will require constant attention to watering, and will not give of their best unless they are provided with liquid fertiliser at least once every fortnight. Dead-heading too will help ensure an attractive appearance and the continuing production of new blooms. Pests and diseases are seldom serious problems, although mildew can take its toll in dry summers, encouraged by the almost inevitable close planting.

Ageratum hybrids   Floss Flower   Compositae

Soft powder-blue mounds (although there are now some pink and white forms that are best left in the catalogue) up to 30 cm (12 in) tall for the edges of beds. For some curious photographic reason, most seed catalogues contain an apology that their pictures of ageratum do not display the correct shades of blue, which undeniably they don't. They are useful plants that contrast well with the harder colour and form of blue lobelias.

SOW BY: half-hardy annual technique at medium-high temperature.

RECOMMENDED VARIETIES: 'Blue Mink' is a modern version of the taller old types of ageratum but there are also several lower growing varieties and among the best are 'Blue Danube' and several named after seas and oceans – 'Adriatic' is, I think, my favourite.

Alyssum   *Lobularia maritima*   Cruciferae

Still the best white edging plant; the white forms of ageratum and lobelia just don't come close to it in quality. Many of the forms will readily self-sow and, although they never become troublesome, they will crop up most attractively and unexpectedly between paving stones.

SOW BY: hardy annual technique.

PEST, DISEASE OR OTHER PROBLEMS: mildew.

RECOMMENDED VARIETIES: 'Carpet of Snow' or 'Snow Carpet' (15 cm (6 in), but choose 'selected strains' for this variety can be very variable); 'Little Dorrit' (10 cm/4 in).

Antirrhinum hybrids   Snapdragon   Scrophulariaceae

The snapdragon has made a comeback after years in the wilderness caused by rust disease. The modern forms (including those recommended below) have at least some resistance to the problem and, in most areas, a perfectly good display can be achieved. It is often forgotten that with their stems up to 50 cm (20 in) tall, they make excellent cut flowers.

SOW BY: half-hardy annual technique at medium temperature; leave seed uncovered until germinated and then sprinkle compost lightly over them.

PEST, DISEASE OR OTHER PROBLEMS: rust.

RECOMMENDED VARIETIES: 'Leonard Sutton' (rose pink); 'Orange Glow' (orange with pink throat); 'Scarlet Monarch' (scarlet); 'Yellow Monarch' (yellow); 'White Monarch' (white).

Aster   *Callistephus chinensis*   Compositae

Asters, with their shaggy flowers in a range of strong, rich colours, are old garden favourites, undeniably attractive and lovely as cut flowers but they are not easy. The problem is a wilt disease that persists for many years in the soil where asters have been grown. For this reason, it is sensible always to raise them individually (see below).

SOW/PLANT BY: half-hardy annual technique at medium temperature; raise the plants individually in 9 cm (3½ in) pots of fresh compost. Once they are well established, move them to 12.5 cm (5 in) pots and plant them out in the compost ball, taking care not to expose any of the roots.

PEST, DISEASE OR OTHER PROBLEMS: wilt.

RECOMMENDED VARIETIES: (all with a good range of colours including white, purples, reds and pinks): **Double flowers**: 'Duchess' (60 cm (24 in), incurved chrysanthemum-like petals, the best types for cutting); 'Dwarf Queen' (25 cm (10 in), one of the best dwarf bedding varieties); 'Ostrich Plume' (45 cm (18 in), long, feathery petals). **Single flowers**: you will generally find mixtures under a wide variety of names; some are more resistant than others to wilt but should be so indicated in catalogues.

Begonia spp. and hybrids   Begoniaceae

There are two principle types of begonia to grow from seed; the fibrous-rooted varieties of *B. semperflorens* and the (ultimately) tuberous-rooted types. They are very different in flower form; the fibrous-rooted types bear masses of small flowers in white and shades of pink and red, often associated with dark green or purplish foliage. The tuberous types have large, fully double flowers in all colours of the rainbow, and some quite hideous additional ones besides. Both are used for bedding, but it is the more compact, fibrous-rooted types that really are most suitable for this purpose (even in partial shade), the flowers of tuberous begonias being too large and their colours too assertive to look right with anything other than more tuberous begonias. They are fairly effective in containers.

SOW BY: half-hardy annual technique at medium temperature; do not cover the seed and sow thinly – the seeds are very tiny. Fibrous-rooted types require a longer growing season and should be sown a month or six weeks before tuberous forms. Neither are easy and you should carefully follow the directions on the seed packets. In practice, if tuberous begonias are your delight, you will probably find it worthwhile to buy tubers rather than raising them from seed at all.

RECOMMENDED VARIETIES: **Fibrous-rooted**: new varieties are appearing with great rapidity but among the best of the mixtures that I have grown (representing the range of flower and leaf colour) are those sold under the names 'New Generation' or 'Lucia', although you will find individually named varieties with the different flower and leaf colour combinations too. There are also some long-stemmed trailing types suitable for hanging baskets and among these 'Pink Avalanche' is especially attractive. **Tuberous**: the best known and most satisfactory are the so-called 'Non Stop' mixtures which have the full range of (generally revolting) colours.

Bells of Ireland *Molucella laevis* Labiatae

Molucella laevis

Uniquely distinct, with dead-nettle-like leaves and tiny white flowers hidden within an enveloping green ruff of sepals on a stem up to 1 m (39 in) tall. Adored by flower arrangers (and dries satisfactorily too) but also useful for the back of an annual border.

SOW BY: half-hardy annual technique at low-medium temperature.

RECOMMENDED VARIETIES: normal species only available.

Brachycome iberidifolia Swan River daisy Compositae

A plant with a very slowly increasing return to popularity. The flowers are of the classic single daisy form borne on plants about 20 cm (8 in) tall. The foliage is delicate and ferny and, a rather

unusual bonus from this family, there is perfume too.

SOW BY: half-hardy annual technique at low-medium temperature.

AFTER-CARE: pinch out the shoot tips to encourage the attractive bushy habit.

RECOMMENDED VARIETIES: the prettiest flowers are the whites but these no longer seem available as individual colours. A deep purple still exists, called 'Purple Splendour', but the remainder, including shades of pink and lilac, only occur in variously named mixtures.

Calendula officinalis Pot marigold Compositae

This is the old cottage garden marigold, not under any circumstances to be confused with the more recent French and African types (p. 221). The colours are vibrant and exciting and I think the plants always look their best in their traditional setting of the herb garden. The only real problem is how to prevent them from taking over, for they self-seed with promiscuous abandon. It is worthwhile resowing in early summer, nonetheless, for the individual plants are short-lived and succumb to mildew in most seasons. They must also have relatively poor soil (such as is found in most herb gardens) if they are not merely to produce foliage.

SOW BY: hardy annual technique.

PEST, DISEASE OR OTHER PROBLEMS: mildew.

RECOMMENDED VARIETIES: mixtures and individual colours are available; 'Orange King' (60 cm/24 in) and 'Radio' are fairly similar to the tall old cottage garden types but more appropriate to the small modern garden is the compact (30 cm/12 in) 'Gitana' range in individual yellows and oranges as well as mixtures.

Campanula isophylla Bell flower Campanulaceae

The recent development of being able to raise these 20 cm (8 in) tall campanulas from seed has made them increasingly popular for summer bedding and especially in hanging baskets and other containers. The flowers are actually more star- than bell-like.

SOW BY: half-hardy annual technique at low to medium temperature; the seed is very fine and should be surface sown.

RECOMMENDED VARIETIES: the only varieties available are 'Krystal Blue', 'Krystal White' and the more compact 'Stella Blue' and 'Stella White'. Most enterprisingly, some seed companies offer double packs with the two colour forms separate.

Candytuft *Iberis* spp. Cruciferae

Candytufts have the reputation of being the easiest of all plants to grow from seed; and apart from hairy bittercress or dandelions, this is probably true. They will grow almost anywhere, and most types will self-seed for several years, but this is not to be held against them for they have an undeniable old-world appeal.

SOW BY: hardy annual technique.

RECOMMENDED VARIETIES: there are two main types of candytuft; *I. umbellata* has given rise to the familiar mixture of white and shades of pink usually called 'Fairy Mixture' which has flat flower heads and reaches about 20–25 cm (8–10in).

I. amara has given us the so-called hyacinth-flowered types, in which the flower head elongates to about 30 cm (12 in). These too are available as mixtures, although pure white forms such as 'White Empress' are offered too. All are lovely.

Chrysanthemum spp.   Compositae

To those used to thinking of the chrysanthemum only in florists' terms, read on. For there are also lovely types suitable for raising as bedding plants from seed. They are derived from a number of wild species, and in some the single flowers are much better than the doubles (see below).

SOW BY: hardy annual technique (although some of those suggested below are listed in catalogues as half-hardy, I have sown them all directly outside with no problems whatever).

RECOMMENDED VARIETIES: forms of *C. carinatum* (45 cm/ 18 in) – 'Court Jesters' (mixture of large single flowers in red, orange, yellow, pink, mauve and white with contrasting rings of colour); forms of *C. coronarium* (45 cm/18 in) – 'Golden Gem' (small, semi-double, yellow); forms of *C. multicaule* – (20 cm/18 in, wide spreading) 'Gold Plate' (small, double or semi-double).

Clarkia spp. and hybrids   Onagraceae

The bedding clarkias fall into main two groups. Those derived from *C. elegans* are around 60 cm (24 in) tall (or even more in some selections) and with double or semi-double flowers rather like crumpled masses of tissue paper in a wide range of colours – orange, white, red, pink and purple. But reaching only half this height are forms of *C. pulchella* which tend to have rather more delicate and pastel-shaded blooms. They are all useful as cut flowers but not easy to blend with other colours in the border.

SOW BY: hardy annual technique.

RECOMMENDED VARIETIES: several mixtures are offered by seed companies but it is worth seeking out the single colours if you can find them – 'Purple King' is a dark, particularly attractive flower of *C. elegans* type.

Cornflower   *Centaurea cyanus*   Compositae

The blooms of the annual cornflowers are rather like a cross between a thistle and a scabious and are lovely, especially if small groups of the single colours are scattered among other plants in an informal border; they are certainly not plants for formal bedding for they can reach as high as 60 cm (24 in). Then they may need staking, but are excellent for cutting.

SOW BY: hardy annual technique; best sown in early autumn for the following year.

RECOMMENDED VARIETIES: as ever, most seed companies offer mixtures – blues, pinks, reds and purples. 'Frosty' is a mixture in which the petals have white tips but my preference lies emphatically with the solid colours. Among individual shades, look out for the compact deep-blue 'Jubilee Gem', the taller 'Blue Diadem' and also 'Red Boy' (rich, rose red).

Cosmos spp.   (sometimes called *Cosmea*)   Compositae

I have had a soft spot for the single daisy flowers of cosmos on their 1 m (39 in) tall stems adorned with feathery foliage ever since I saw them sown along every roadside verge in Korea, of all places. These fairly tall plants are derived from *C. bipinnatus*; semi-doubles also exist but have none of the singles' charm. They are a real riot of shades of pink, purple and red with white. Some forms include bicolours, most of them slightly revolting. Yellows exist too, in plants derived from a shorter, related species, *C. sulphureus*, although recently a tall yellow has become available too.

SOW BY: half-hardy annual technique at medium temperature or, probably better, sow directly outdoors shortly before the danger of frost has passed.

RECOMMENDED VARIETIES: several mixtures are available of which 'Sensation' is probably the best known but the single colours are hard to find. The dwarf yellow is 'Sunny Gold'; the new, taller one, 'Yellow Garden'.

Dahlia hybrids   Compositae

Forget about the tall, tuber-raised dahlias in the mixed border (but read p. 205 if you are really interested) and think of the seed-raised plant simply as another half-hardy bedding annual. They occur in the full range of dahlia colours and although the oldest (and I think some of the best) varieties are singles, there are doubles and quills too. They have the merit of reaching between about 35 and 60 cm (14 and 24 in) but have stout stems, good for cutting, and do not need stakes. You will also see tall varieties offered for raising from seed but these are a quite different matter and really not worthwhile for any purpose.

SOW BY: half-hardy annual technique at medium temperature.

PEST, DISEASE OR OTHER PROBLEMS: slugs.

RECOMMENDED VARIETIES: the best of the mixtures are 'Rigoletto' (45 cm (18 in), double), 'Unwins Dwarf Hybrids' (45–60 cm (18–24 in), semi-double) and 'Coltness Hybrids' (45–60 cm (18–24 in), single). 'Dandy' (60 cm/24 in) is a mixture of singles of collarette type where the flowers have an inner petal-like frill. 'Redskin' (40 cm/16 in) has double flowers and deep copper-red foliage.

Dianthus spp. and hybrids   Pinks, carnations   Caryophyllaceae

Several *Dianthus* species have contributed to the 20–30 cm (8–12 in) tall annual garden carnations, most importantly *D. chinensis*, often listed as *D. heddewigii*. It produces single flowers of classic dianthus form in a wide range of colours, some exquisite, some positively bilious. The best are delightful for the front of the border, especially on slightly chalky soils, and are very pretty when cut and displayed in a small glass.

SOW BY: half-hardy annual technique at medium temperature.

RECOMMENDED VARIETIES: most seed companies only offer mixtures among which 'Baby Doll', 'Magic Charms' and 'Princess' are the best known. Some single colours are available, however, most notably 'Princess Scarlet'. 'Snow Fire' is an award-winning variety of quite positive repellence, having white flowers with scarlet centres.

Dimorphotheca spp. and hybrids   Star of the veld
Compositae

Yet another South African daisy but rather different from many, having markedly shiny flowers in white and shades of orange, yellow, pink and red. They reach about 30 cm (12 in) but only really look at their best in bright sun on light soils. Dimorphothecas can be dried successfully and are sometimes grouped with the everlasting flowers.

SOW BY: half-hardy annual technique or hardy annual technique, sowing shortly before the danger of the last frost.

Dimorphotheca 'Glistening white'

RECOMMENDED VARIETIES: 'Glistening White' (particularly good and one of the best of all low-growing white annuals); 'Sunshine Hybrids' or 'Aurantiaca Hybrids' (yellows and oranges).

Eschscholzia spp. and hybrids   Californian Poppy
Papaveraceae

Few annuals have flowers with the colour range and vibrancy of eschscholzias but it is the yellows and oranges that are most characteristic of the genus. Unlike many poppies, they are relatively low growing (about 30 cm/12 in) but share the group's preference for light, sandy, even poor soils. There are singles, semi-doubles and doubles but the singles tend to be most striking.

SOW BY: hardy annual technique.

RECOMMENDED VARIETIES: most frequently you will find 'Monarch Art Shades', a mixture of semi-doubles in the full colour range, but if you can obtain it, try 'Orange King', the really vibrant single colour. Other individual colours still sometimes seen are 'Cherry Ripe', 'Milky White' and 'Purple-Violet', names that are nothing if not descriptive.

Everlasting flowers   *Acroclinium* (or *Helipterum*), *Helichrysum* and *Rhodanthe* (or *Helipterum*) spp.
Compositae

This is a group of fairly hardy or half hardy members of the daisy family in a wide range of colours that are generally grown solely for drying to use in flower arrangements. As may be imagined, their flowers tend to be rather tough and fibrous – helichrysums in fact are sometimes called straw flowers. The height ranges from around 30 cm (12 in) up to 1.2 m (4 ft) so

there are types to suit every type of arrangement. If you intend to use them as part of a garden display before cutting and drying the blooms, choose the single colours. But it may be simpler to grow mixtures in the vegetable garden solely for use as cut flowers.

SOW BY: half-hardy annual technique or hardy annual technique sowing shortly before the danger of the last frost.

RECOMMENDED VARIETIES: *Acroclinium* – 'Bonnie' (or 'Bonny') mixture (one of the few mixtures that include some reds); 'Tetrared' (red). *Helichrysum* – 'Hot Bikini' (gold and scarlet but only 30 cm (12 in) so less useful for arrangements); 'Double Mixed' (1 m (39 in), much better as a cut flower). *Rhodanthe* – 'Mixed' (a less than enterprising name for an attractive blend of pinks and white, although only 30 cm (12 in) tall).

Fuchsia   spp. and hybrids   Onagraceae

The bedding plant section might seem an odd place to find shrubs described, but in fact hundreds of varieties of non-hardy fuchsia are grown purely as bedding plants, or at least as annuals in tubs and containers. Stock plants or rooted cuttings are then protected over winter in much the same manner as pelargoniums. These named varieties cannot be raised from seed. Fuchsias, with their pendulous, bell-like flowers, are too well known to justify detailed description. Provided they are fed regularly they will give great rewards throughout the summer.

RECOMMENDED VARIETIES: from the vast numbers of both old and new varieties, many virtually indistinguishable from each other, it is almost impossible to know where to begin. Perhaps it is simplest, therefore, if I give a few of my own personal favourites among the two main groups of bedding fuchsias (with a low-growing upright form) and the so-called basket fuchsias which have a pendulous, cascading habit, especially useful for hanging baskets. **Bedding fuchsias**: 'Celebration' (double, pale orange), 'Countess of Aberdeen' (single, white), 'Dollar Princess' (double, tubes and sepals red, corolla purple), 'Fascination' (double, tubes and sepals red, corolla pink with red veins), 'Royal Velvet' (double, tubes and sepals crimson, corolla purple), 'Thalia' (single, terminal flowering, elongated flowers, tubes, sepals and corolla scarlet-orange, my favourite fuchsia). **Basket fuchsias**: 'Dusky Rose' (double, tubes and sepals dark pink, corollas red-pink with pink flecks), 'Marinka' (single, tubes and sepals red, corolla darker red), 'Pink Galore' (double, tubes, sepals and corolla pink), 'Tom West' (single, tubes and sepals red, corolla purple).

Gaillardia spp. and hybrids   Compositae

Gaillardias are useful as cut flowers, although *en masse* in the border they can be very assertive. They have the characteristic daisy flower in shades of red, yellow and orange and, yet again, the best are the singles. There are, in fact, two types of gaillardia grown as annuals, one being a true annual and the other a half-hardy perennial, but both have forms ranging from about 30 to 60 cm (12–24 in).

SOW BY: half-hardy annual technique at medium temperature or directly outside after the danger of frost has passed.

RECOMMENDED VARIETIES: 'Goblin' (35 cm (14 in), single,

golden-yellow with crimson centres); the doubles are usually sold as mixtures with enterprising names such as 'Double Mixed'.

Gazania spp. and hybrids   Compositae

Gazania 'Orange Beauty'

Yet more orange, white, red and yellow daisies, although gazanias suffer from the drawback that they only open fully in bright, warm sun. Nonetheless, they make very good cut flowers. They range in height from about 20 up to around 30 cm (8 to 12 in), and all have some degree of blotching at the base of the petals.

SOW BY: half-hardy annual technique at medium temperature.

RECOMMENDED VARIETIES: easily the best gazanis are the dwarf forms of the 'Mini-Star' range which are available as mixtures or as 'Mini-Star Tangerine' and 'Mini-Star White'. If you prefer taller types, then try the 'Sundance' range which also has considerably larger flowers, although there are no whites or pinks.

Godetia spp. and hybrids   Onagraceae

Godetias are related to clarkias but with flowers that look like azaleas. They are easy and they are good as cut flowers provided, as with so many modern annuals, you steer clear of the most assertive colours which really blend with nothing. With godetias, the assertive colours are some of the pinks,

which look no better on their 30–40 cm (12–16 in) tall stems than they do on real azaleas.

SOW BY: hardy annual technique. There are singles, semi-doubles and doubles in all of the colours.

RECOMMENDED VARIETIES: among the single colours, I suggest 'Crimson Fire' (crimson) and 'Duchess of Albany' (white). The most popular is 'Sybil Sherwood' which is one of those pinks that I loathe. There are, of course, mixtures also, both of colours and degree of doubling.

Grasses   Gramineae

There are several ornamental annual grasses that are well worth growing and useful in two ways. First for adding variation in colour and shape to garden borders and second for their value in dried-flower arrangements. Although some will self-seed, none in my experience do so invasively.

SOW BY: hardy annual technique.

RECOMMENDED VARIETIES: mixtures of grasses are of little value, inevitably resulting in a hotch-potch of plants with no resemblance to each other. I cannot understand why they are sold in this way – no one would sell mixed annual flowers. Among those sold individually, the best and most frequently seen are – *Avena sterilis*, animated oats (90 cm (36 in), loose, oat-like heads); *Briza media*, quaking grass (45 cm (18 in), loose pendant heads like tiny fir cones); *Lagurus ovatus*, hare's tail (45 cm (18 in), upright heads, woolly, more like rabbits' paws than hares' tails, my favourite although it tends to do less well in wet cool summers); *Pennisetum longistylum* (60 cm (24 in), feathery, arching heads).

Gypsophila elegans   Baby's Breath   Caryophyllaceae

Related to the perennial border gypsophila (p. 208), the annual has a very similar form, with masses of very tiny flowers that from a distance look almost cloud-like but arise on a plant that only reaches 45 cm (18 in). Their main value nonetheless is for use in cut-flower arrangements. Gypsophila for me, however, is a one-colour plant – the only one to grow is white; the pinks and reds have absolutely nothing to commend them.

SOW BY: hardy annual technique.

RECOMMENDED VARIETIES: 'Covent Garden White'.

Impatiens hybrids   Busy Lizzie   Balsaminaceae

One of the revolutions in modern bedding plant production has been the rise and rise of the busy lizzie. I confess to having mixed feelings about them for they embrace some of the colours that I love least but they have the undeniable merit of flowering in greater shade than any other summer bedding plant. They are also versatile plants and are at home in formal or informal bedding schemes and in containers of all types. Although half-hardy, their usefulness can be extended beyond the end of the season by bringing a few indoors as pot plants. Despite the proliferation of varieties in recent years, the modern busy lizzies fall into three main groups – the 'Blitz' range which have large flowers on fairly tall plants (30–35 cm/12–14 in), the 'Multi-flora' types, with smaller flowers and a more compact habit (15–20 cm/6–8 in), and various forms with double flowers.

SOW BY: half-hardy annual technique at high temperature; the seeds should be barely covered and the seedlings given plenty of ventilation as soon as they have emerged.

RECOMMENDED VARIETIES: There are numerous mixtures with corresponding single colours available for many of them. I have personal experience only of a limited number but the following have proved the best of those that I have tried. 'Blitz' types – 'Blitz Orange'. 'Multiflora' types – 'Accent' series in single colours; 'Super Elfin Mixed' (eleven different colours are claimed but I haven't counted; some are available as individually coloured 'Elfin' varieties). Doubles – 'Confection Mixed' (some companies now claim that the plants will all have either double or semi-double flowers but in my experience most strains still give rise to some singles). Gradually, more of the so-called 'New Guinea Hybrids' are becoming available for raising from seed. They have the advantage of combining masses of large flowers with coloured or patterned foliage; 'Tango', with tangerine flowers and dark green-bronze leaves, is among the most recent of them.

Larkspur *Delphinium* spp. Rancunculaceae

Yet again, an annual that really is better as a cut or dried flower than it is in the border. There are double (sometimes called hyacinth-flowered) and single flowered types, the taller varieties of the former especially betraying their relationship to perennial delphiniums. The range of colours includes those familiar from real delphiniums – white, blue and purple but with reds and pinks also, although many tend to be slightly softer than those of their giant relatives.

SOW BY: hardy annual technique.

RECOMMENDED VARIETIES: **Tall types** (often called annual delphiniums): 'Giant Imperial Mixed' (1.2 m/4 ft). **Shorter types**: 'Dwarf Hyacinth Mixed' (30 cm/12 in); 'Blue Cloud' (soft sky-blue, the only single colour widely available).

Lavatera spp. Malvaceae

Lavatera 'Silver Cup'

This really is a one-variety plant as far as most gardeners are concerned. Its flowers are reminiscent of petunias (or of the wild mallow if you know it), it reaches about 60 cm (24 in) in height and is an absolute mass of rich pink bloom right through the summer. One seed company describes it as 'the most stunning annual we know'.

SOW BY: hardy annual technique.

RECOMMENDED VARIETIES: 'Silver Cup'.

Limnanthes douglasii Poached egg plant Limnanthaceae

For some extraordinary reason, *Limnanthes*, which has been known as the poached egg plant for years, is now listed by one seed company under the name fried eggs. This must say more about the catalogue compiler than the plant but its rather daisy-like white flowers with yellow centres borne on 15 cm (6 in) stems certainly have a resemblance to some sort of egg. It requires fairly moist conditions and is one of the few annuals that looks at all effective in a rock garden.

SOW BY: hardy annual technique.

RECOMMENDED VARIETIES: normal species only available.

Linaria spp. Toadflax Scrophulariaceae

There are two common types of toadflax which have the appearance of midget snapdragons. They are almost invariably sold in mixtures containing almost every imaginable colour; some forms will self-sow with welcome ease.

SOW BY: hardy annual technique.

RECOMMENDED VARIETIES: *L. maroccana* (15 cm (6 in), 'Fairy Bouquet', 'Fairy Lights', 'Northern Lights' mixtures); *L. reticulata* (22 cm (9 in), 'Crown Jewels' mixture; 'Aureo-Purpurea', deep reddish purple with golden throats).

Lobelia spp. Campanulaceae

Lobelias are, I think, the most useful of all half-hardy bedding plants, being at home as edging around borders (I even use them around my salad garden) or in baskets, tubs, window boxes and other containers. The best are undoubtedly the blues (red just doesn't seem right for bedding lobelias), while the whites invariably have some contaminating blues among them and are not as effective as the best white alyssum.

SOW BY: half-hardy annual technique at medium temperature; surface sow very thinly and, to obtain the bushiest plants, collect a small clump of seedlings when pricking on rather than try to separate individuals.

RECOMMENDED VARIETIES: **Edging forms**: 'Cambridge Blue (powder-blue); 'Crystal Palace' (deep-blue flowers with bronze foliage, superb, the forms called 'Compacta' are the neatest of all); 'Mrs Clibran' (deep blue with white eye). **Trailing forms**: 'Blue Basket' or 'Blue Cascade' (powder blue).

Marigolds and Tagetes *Tagetes* spp. Compositae

This section of the book must begin with a statement. I don't like marigolds. At least, I don't find they look right in my own garden but I really cannot exclude them on these grounds for they play an undeniably important part in bedding schemes in many other gardens. Unlike the hardy pot marigolds or calendulas, all are half-hardy and all originate with species native to Mexico. Despite this origin, they are generally divided into those derived from *T. erecta*, which are called African marigolds, and those derived from *T. patula*, which are called French marigolds. The African varieties are generally tall, bushy and with double flowers, the more appealing French are lower growing, less bushy and with single, semi-double or double flowers. There are now hybrids between the two groups, so almost every combination of flower and plant is available. The new Afro-French hybrids also tend to be quicker into bloom. The colour range is limited – orange predominates with yellows and reds for good measure. The plants traditionally called tagetes are forms of *T. tenuifolia* and are low-growing with feathery foliage and masses of single flowers in colours similar to those of the marigolds.

SOW BY: half-hardy annual technique at medium to high temperature.

RECOMMENDED VARIETIES: the range of marigold varieties is now so enormous and increases so rapidly every season that it is almost impossible to be selective. Rather than give meaningless lists, therefore, that will soon be out of date, I shall indicate the features of the various subdivisions that you will generally see used in catalogues. In most groups, single-coloured varieties predominate and these should always be selected – there is nothing worse than a hotch-potch mixture of marigold colours. Dwarf French Carnation Flowered (up to 30 cm (12 in), fully double, compact, free flowering); Dwarf French Crested (up to 30 cm (12 in), single or double with the central petals rolled upwards in a crest); Dwarf French Single (not always very dwarfed, up to 30 cm (12 in), fairly compact, early and free flowering); Dwarf African Double (up to 35 cm/14 in); Tall African Double (over 45 cm (18 in), although valuable in vast municipal bedding schemes, these are really only of use in gardens as dot plants among smaller varieties); Afro-French F₁ hybrids (up to 40 cm (16 in), single or double); Tagetes (up to 25 cm (10 in), single).

Matricaria eximia   Compositae

Matricarias are related to chrysanthemums and look very like dwarf, fully double chrysanthemum flowers. There are two common forms, among which the whites tend to be prettier than the yellows.

SOW BY: half-hardy annual technique at medium temperature.

RECOMMENDED VARIETIES: 'Golden Ball' (30 cm (12 in), yellow); 'Snow Dwarf' (23 cm (9 in), white); 'Snow Puffs' (30 cm (12 in), white); 'White Gem' (20 cm (8 in), white).

Mesembryanthemum criniflorum   Livingstone Daisy   Aizoaceae

The Livingstone daisies are classic bedding plants for mild, seaside areas and although they will thrive in sunny situations on other gardens too, nowhere else are they as successful or do they look as appropriate. They are compact, their leaves fleshy and their flowers daisy-like (although, for once, not of the daisy family). Traditionally in shades of pink, red, and orange, yellows have now appeared too.

SOW BY: half-hardy annual technique at medium-high temperature.

RECOMMENDED VARIETIES: the normal species is often listed as 'Criniflorum' or sometimes given a proprietary mixture name and includes the pinks, reds and oranges; 'Lunette' (also called 'Yellow Ice') is yellow with deep red centre.

Mignonette   *Reseda odorata*   Resedaceae

Mignonette is one of those few bedding plants grown almost entirely for its perfume – significantly, most seed catalogues do not even illustrate it, for its small, dingy white flowers having nothing to commend them. But drop a pinch of mignonette seed amongst showier things in the border and its presence will be evident right through the summer and into the autumn.

SOW BY: hardy annual technique.

RECOMMENDED VARIETIES: the normal species is generally sold, somewhat unnecessarily, under the name 'Sweet Scented', although sometimes named forms are offered too.

Nemesia spp. and hybrids   Scrophulariaceae

The masses of irregularly shaped little flowers of nemesias in their dazzling arrays of colours on 20–30 cm (8–12 in) tall stems are invaluable for the early part of the summer. But therein lies a problem, for as summer progresses the nemesias fade away and I have found nothing, not fertiliser nor dead-heading nor late planting, that will keep them going. For this reason, you will either need to replace them with something else in the beds or try growing them in containers which are more readily swapped around.

SOW BY: half-hard annual technique at medium temperature.

RECOMMENDED VARIETIES: most mixtures contain the full range of colours – blue, pink, red, orange, lilac, yellow and white – but there are some more specific selections – 'Blue Gem' (sky-blue with white eye, rather like a lobelia); 'Funfair' (gold, orange, pink and reds); 'Mello White' (white); ('Mello Red and White' is a disgusting raspberry-red and white bicolour).

Nicotiana spp. and hybrids   Tobacco plant   Solanaceae

For a genus that gives rise to the revolting addictive weed, *Nicotiana* also includes some of the most exquisitely perfumed of all bedding plants. Although there are tall forms reaching well over 1 m (39 in), it is the newer dwarf hybrids that have special merit, with flowers in shades of red, pink and yellow as well as the loveliest virginal white.

SOW BY: half-hardy annual technique at medium temperature.

RECOMMENDED VARIETIES: 'Domino White' and 'Domino Purple' (30 cm (12 in), other 'Domino' coloured varieties are available, separately or in mixtures, but these two are the finest); 'Lime Green' (60 cm (24 in), pale-green flowers).

Nigella damascena   Love-in-a-mist   Ranunculaceae

One of the loveliest and easiest of all hardy annuals; and one to stay with you, too, for they self-seed fairly easily and pop up quite unexpectedly but never invasively. Nigella reach about 45 cm (18 in) and will thrive in most soils, although they are invariably happiest in a light soil and a sunny position.

SOW BY: hardy annual technique.

RECOMMENDED VARIETIES: 'Miss Jekyll' (deep blue, the loveliest of all); 'Persian Jewels' (a mixture with light and dark blue, deep and pale pink and white).

Pansies and violas *Viola* spp. Violaceae

The technical differences between pansies and violas relate to the wild species from which they originated but need not concern us here. Among modern varieties, it is most sensible to divide the group into those that will flower through the winter and into early spring, and those that flower in late spring and summer. There is some overlap between the varieties chosen for these roles but for flowers in winter and early spring, the seeds are sown and the plants planted in summer (they are therefore in the garden through the winter), while for essentially summer flowering, the seed is sown in the spring. The winter-flowering pansy has suddenly leapt into recognition as a winter colour plant, thanks in part to some very mild recent winters. How effective some of them will be in persistently very hard weather remains to be seen. There are now dozens of varieties, especially of pansies, but many, sadly, are mixtures, some being of remarkably unpredictable content. My preferred choices are of varieties with single colours or defined colour combinations.

SOW BY: biennial technique (winter and spring flowering) or hardy annual technique (summer flowering).

RECOMMENDED VARIETIES: **Winter-flowering**: choose individual colours of 'Winter flowering' or 'Universal' pansies (I have seen about twelve distinct types) under whatever names seed companies offer them; if you really cannot find these individual colours, then choose 'Universal Mixture' in preference to 'Floral Dance'. **Spring/summer flowering**: 'Universal' types will suffice for early spring but for late spring and early summer, try 'Azure Blue' (light blue with yellow eye); 'Blue Laser' (dark-blue lower petals with pale-blue upper petals); 'Coronation Gold' (deep yellow-gold); 'Crimson Queen' (deep velvet red with darker blotch); 'Forerunner Tangerine' (orange); 'Joker' (pale blue with dark-blue centre and white surround – also called 'Joker Light Blue' but should not be confused with 'Joker Mixed' nor 'Jolly Joker' which is more or less revolting); 'Oxford Blue' (deep blue-violet); 'Ullswater' (deep blue with very dark blue blotch). **Smaller-flowered viola types for summer**: 'Baby Lucia' (bright sky blue, exquisite); 'Prince Henry' (purple with gold markings); 'Prince John' (golden yellow – I think this is the same as a variety called 'Yellow Prince').

Pelargonium hybrids Half-hardy geranium
Geraniaceae

Pelargonium 'Multibloom' series: 'Bright Rose'

There have been two consequences to the development of seed-raised F$_1$ hybrid pelargoniums in recent years. First, many more gardeners now grow them and they have taken on an even more important role in public bedding displays. But second, and sadly, many of the old forms with very attractively patterned foliage have disappeared. The lovely old types are now so few in number and in many instances have become so reduced in vigour through virus contamination that I shall not consider them in detail – although I hope that gardeners who love them will take the trouble to seek out specialist nurseries and then perpetuate the stock by softwood cuttings. I must confess that I like pelargoniums, but with several provisos. Some of the colours, especially among the reds, are very assertive; some of the flowers are fairly feeble so you must choose carefully; they always look their best, I think, in containers rather than in garden beds (municipal parks and traffic islands are a different matter); and they must have heat from very early in the season to make raising them from seed worthwhile – they are, indeed, among those bedding plants where the availability of young plantlets from seed companies has been a real boon. There are two main types of pelargonium to raise from seed – the ivy-leaved trailing type, of which only one can be raised in this way, and the zonal types (although many of the modern zonals do not have the traditional zonally patterned leaves). But within the zonals, there are also some important subdivisions, sometimes given different names by different companies – 'Standards' with single flowers in a few fairly large heads, 'Breakaways' which are half way to trailing in that the branches bearing the small individual flowers tend to arch outwards, and, most recently, the 'Multibloom' types with ten or more compact rounded heads of flowers in bloom simultaneously. All of these I am sure there are others as good that I have not tried; and of course, new ones are appearing each season – 'Appleblossom Orbit' (30 cm (12 in), rich pink), 'Sprinter' (not 'Sprinter Mixture') (30 cm (12 in), red), 'Sundance' (40 cm (16 in), more or less orange); **Breakaways**: 'Breakaway Red', 'Breakaway Salmon'. **Multiblooms**: these are too recent for me to have given them a thorough trial but the most interesting range includes lavender, pink, salmon, scarlet and white.

Petunia spp. and hybrids Solanaceae

Petunias are the mainstays of window boxes and containers for many gardeners every summer. Undeniably, they have much to commend them – a wide range of colours (although some of the bicolours are utterly disgusting), weather resistance (if you choose your varieties carefully) but they have two drawbacks. They are not particularly easy to raise from seed and they must be dead-headed constantly if they are to continue blooming. They fall into two main groups, the 'Multiflora' types, with masses of fairly small blooms, and the 'Grandiflora' types, with few but much larger blooms (and with a need for some protection from the weather in most cases). There are some doubles too, if these are to your taste, although few of them are really satisfactory, and many mixtures within which are some truly disturbing colour and petal form combinations – such names as 'Plum Pudding Mixed', 'Fluffy Ruffles', and 'Razzle Dazzle' say it all. My preference, with very few exceptions, is for single-coloured single flowers.

SOW BY: half-hardy annual technique at medium to high temperature; surface sow, reduce the temperature as soon as the seed has germinated and then scatter sieved compost very thinly over the surface.

RECOMMENDED VARIETIES: **'Multiflora' types**: any of the 'Resisto' series which are highly tolerant of rain, 'Blue Danube' (double pale lilac-blue with darker veins). **'Grandiflora' types**: only available as mixtures among which 'Daddy' contains less of the objectionable colours. Rather recently, the so-called 'Floribunda' types have appeared, more or less intermediate in flower size and form between 'Multiflora' and 'Grandiflora' – most are mixtures but 'Mirage Sugar', which is a pale pink with darker veining, caught my eye.

are available as single colours and often in mixtures too, although if it is mixtures that you desire, you will find the F_2 types much cheaper – but with the lottery that you will not know exactly what colour the flowers will turn out, and they flower much later.

SOW BY: half-hardy annual technique at high temperature; sow before the end of January or, if you can obtain the seed early enough, in October. This will then enable you to overwinter the plants at around 7°C (44.6°F).

RECOMMENDED VARIETIES: **Ivy-leaved**: 'Summer Showers' mixture; **Standard zonals**: 'Video' series in pink, salmon, scarlet and white (20 cm/8 in), 'Diamond' series in cherry red, pink and scarlet (30 cm (12 in) with a fairly spreading habit and low branching), 'Gala' series in pink, reds, salmon and white ('Gala White' is the best white standard I have grown) (30 cm/12 in); among individually named standard varieties, I have been pleased with the following, although

Phlox drummondii   Polemoniaceae

Phlox only grow about 20 cm (8 in) tall, they have no perfume and not many colours and they are not easy to persuade to flower for very long. But many gardeners still love them and, given a fairly rich soil, they will undoubtedly provide a bright splash of pinks and blue with some white flowers and a rather dingy yellow.

SOW BY: half-hardy annual technique at medium temperature.

RECOMMENDED VARIETIES: **Large-flowered types**: various named mixtures which contain most of the colour range – 'Beauty' (the only mixture with the yellow); 'Brilliancy' and the lower growing 'Cecily'. **Small-flowered types**: 'Twinkle', 'Twinkle Mix' or 'Twinkle Stars' (I think these are all the same); 'Petticoat' (which includes several bicolours).

Poppy   Papaver spp.   Papaveraceae

The native annual red field poppy (or as it is now sometimes known, the Flanders poppy), *P. rhoeas*, is as familiar as any plant can be. And it has its place in the garden too, although never in the formality of the annual bed. Its correct home is the rather more haphazard plantings of the cottage garden. There are now many differently coloured forms, although none to my mind rival the real red. 'Shirley' poppies, in both single and double forms, are derived from the wild red poppy but should have no mauve and no black in them. The opium poppy, *P. somniferum*, in its wild state is purple but it too has given rise to various other colours and forms.

SOW BY: hardy annual technique.

RECOMMENDED VARIETIES: **Derived from** *P. rhoeas*: the normal species or vigorous selections of it are often offered as 'Cornfield' or 'Flanders' poppies; the 'Shirley' poppy strains vary widely and some are called 'Reverend Wilkes' Strain'; others specify single or double flowers but many are complete mixtures and almost impossible to blend with anything else. **Derived from** *P. somniferum*: various 'Paeony flowered' mixtures with large double flowers; 'Danebrog' (large red singles with a white cross on each petal).

Rudbeckia spp. and hybrids   Cone flower   Compositae

Rudbeckia 'Goldilocks'

The annual forms of the popular perennial cone flowers (p. 213) are quite obviously members of the daisy family – the singles are very like orange daisies and the doubles very like orange bedding dahlias. Their real merit is their height (up to 1 m/ 39 in), their relatively late blooming and their value as cut flowers.

SOW BY: half-hardy annual technique at medium temperature or, as they require a long growing season, try treating them as hardy annuals, sowing in summer and planting out in the autumn.

RECOMMENDED VARIETIES: 'Goldilocks' (semi-double, golden-yellow with black centre); 'Marmalade' (golden-orange with black centre); 'Rustic Dwarfs' (single, large flowers on stems only 60 cm (24 in) tall, golden-orange with dark centre).

Salpiglossis spp. and hybrids   Solanaceae

Salpiglossis are related to petunias and look a little like them, although to my mind are prettier; but they are even more prone than petunias to the vagaries of a wet climate. I prefer them to petunias because they have rather classic dark-coloured veins instead of garish candy stripes. I usually grow them in pots where I can place them in the warmest, most sheltered parts of the garden (they do, incidentally, make lovely subjects for a conservatory when grown in this way). All are sold as mixtures of blue, gold, pink, reds and/or yellow; and all those I suggest are relatively dwarf.

SOW BY: half-hardy annual technique at medium to high temperature.

RECOMMENDED VARIETIES: 'Diablo' (45 cm/18 in); 'Flamenco' (30 cm/12 in); 'Kew Blue' (30 cm/12 in, blue only); 'Splash' (45 cm/18 in).

Salvia spp. and hybrids   Labiatae

If you must have rows of upright scarlet soldiers in your garden beds, then you must have salvias. They are individual and they are very assertive. But they are also difficult – at least they are difficult to raise from seed. Several different salvia species have given rise to varieties used as garden annuals but I shall limit myself to the traditional salvias, derived from a small Brazilian shrub called *S. splendens*. There are now two main groups of scarlet garden varieties derived from this species – one with upright flowers and rather dark coloured leaves and the other, older type, with paler leaves and rather shorter and more spreading flower heads. Other colours also exist but only one colour and one variety among them is at all attractive. The mixtures are especially unpleasant.

Sow by: half-hardy annual technique at low to medium temperature; the compost must be moist but the propagator well ventilated. Sow in late winter to obtain large plants for dot planting or for use in tubs; but leave sowing until April for smaller plants for bedding out.

Recommended varieties: **Dark upright**: 'Red Riches' (also called 'Ryco'); 'Red River'; 'Torpedo'. **Pale spreading**: 'Blaze of Fire'. **Purple flowered**: 'Laser Purple'.

Scabious Scabiosa spp. Dipsacaceae

Quite inexplicably, scabious are among the unsung of the hardy annual world. Inexplicably, because I find the globular flower heads of the forms of S. atropurpurea, especially the mauves, to be quite enchanting. Their stems are tall and stiff – meaning that they require no staking and are excellent as cut flowers too. There is also a commonly seen species called S. stellata which complements these roles by providing most attractive seed heads for winter decoration.

Sow by: hardy annual technique.

Recommended varieties: **Forms of S. atropurpurea**: 'Cockade Mixed' (1 m/39 in), 'Double Mixed' (1 m/39 in) – I think these two are the same; 'Dwarf Double Mixed' (45 cm/18 in). **Forms of S. stellata**: 'Drumstick'; 'Paper Moon'.

Schizanthus spp. and hybrids Butterfly flower, Poor man's orchid Solanaceae

The name 'poor man's orchid' is an odd one for schizanthus, for whilst they certainly have an exotic look, they are scarcely orchid-like. They bear masses of flowers that I can only describe as rather like large lobelias, but in shades of red, purple and pink, with white also, although they belong, improbably, in the potato family. The throats are characteristically yellow with vein patterns. I am very fond of schizanthus but they only succeed well in warmth and sun and for this reason I much prefer to grow them in pots, where the dwarf varieties especially look very pretty. They are only available as mixtures.

Sow by: half-hardy annual technique in late spring.

Recommended varieties: 'Hit Parade' (30 cm/12 in); 'Star Parade' (20 cm/8 in).

Stock Matthiola and Malcomia spp. Cruciferae

The name stock covers rather a large range of rather dissimilar although related plants. They are most familiar as richly perfumed cut flowers, although there in fact are two principal groups, the annuals and the biennials. The annuals in turn are divided into 'Ten Week' stocks, which flower ten weeks after sowing, the 'Trysomic Seven Week' stocks which flower after seven weeks, 'Beauty of Nice' types which are slightly taller (reaching 60 cm/24 in) and later flowering than the ten week types, and the 'Column' stocks, which are taller still (reaching 80 cm/32 in) and excellent for cutting, but less successful outside than in a cool greenhouse. The biennials are divided into 'Brompton' stocks and the similar but shorter 'East Lothian'

stocks. But to complicate matters further, there are also the plants derived from M. bicornis, the 'Night Scented' stock, a 30 cm (12 in) tall plant grown exclusively for its heavy night-time perfume. And finally, there is the Virginia Stock, a 20 cm (12 in) tall stock with a faint perfume that is useful for filling odd sunny corners.

Sow by: hardy annual technique at low temperature (except for 'Virginia Stock' for which you should use the biennial technique). The desire among gardeners who grow stocks is to obtain all double flowers. With 'Ten Week' and 'Brompton' stocks this is done by choosing 'selectable' varieties and reducing the temperature to about 7°C (44.6°F) after germination. The potentially double flowering plants will then develop pale yellowish, not dark-green, leaves. With 'Seven Week' stocks, simply keep the stronger seedlings which will produce the double flowers. Recently, a variety called 'Stockpot' has appeared in which selection for double flowers is achieved simply by choosing those seedlings with a small notch in their cotyledons or seed leaves.

Recommended varieties: apart from 'Stockpot', there appear to be few unambiguous individual variety names so it will simply be a matter of choosing mixtures of the groups that appeal to you; but do remember to choose 'selectable' strains where appropriate.

Sunflower Helianthus annuus Compositae

The sunflower is like nothing else in the garden and it is ridiculous even to think of it as part of a bedding or planting scheme. They are there to amuse and little else. They are available in a very limited range of colours and also a range of sizes, although it seems to me that if you want to grow a sunflower, you will want it big.

Sow by: hardy annual technique.

Recommended varieties: 'Autumn Beauty' (1.8 m/6 ft); 'Autumn Sunshine' (1.2 m/4 ft); 'Russian Giant' (3 m/10 ft); 'Tall Single' (1.2 m/4 ft – and there's a name to conjure with); 'Teddy Bear' (60 cm/24 in).

Sweet William Dianthus barbatus Caryophyllaceae

Closely related to carnations and pinks, but outdoing them all, sweet williams have fallen from favour. Mainly this is because of the drawbacks associated with growing any biennial (p. 215). Unfortunately, the new varieties that I have seen are pure red and so lack the lovely contrasting eyes and rings that make these flowers so appealing. My plea is for more of the old style sweet williams to be grown again; and for once, I wouldn't object to mixtures.

Sow by: biennial technique.

Recommended varieties: 'Auricula Eyed Mixed'; 'Indian Carpet' (if you prefer plants less than 30 cm (12 in) tall); 'Roundabout Mixed'.

Tithonia sp. Mexican sunflower Compositae

I have been conducting a one-man campaign for years on behalf of this plant which is one of the most underrated of annuals. It is a bushy thing, about 1 m (39 in) tall and bearing masses of fairly small, calendula-like flowers; I plant it among the greens in my kitchen garden.

Sow by: hardy annual technique at medium temperatures.
Recommended varieties: choose the normal species if you can still find it; failing this, 'Torch' and then failing this, 'Goldfinger' (also called 'Torch Improved', although it is in fact not as good).

Verbena spp. and hybrids   Verbenaceae

Verbena 'Sandy Scarlet'

Verbenas will never set the world alight but if you want something low growing, compact (mostly around 20 cm (8 in) although there are some more upright forms too) and garish (and are prepared for some disappointments in germination), then they will satisfy you. Although in fact there are pinks, blues, whites and purples, it is really the reds that are the most valuable.
Sow by: half-hardy annual technique at medium to high temperature but do not allow the compost to become too wet.
Recommended varieties: **Upright**: 'Derby Mixed' (pinks and red); 'Showtime Belle' (magenta); 'Tropic' (deep cerise red). **Compact or low spreading**: 'Sandy Scarlet' (scarlet, very neat); 'Sparkle Mixed' (reds, pinks and purples).

Wallflowers   *Cheiranthus* spp.   Cruciferae

After a mild winter, wallflowers are wonderful, their rich evocative perfume filling the spring garden. After a very hard winter, they are as useless as dead twigs. And to compound the problem, they are large plants and they are biennials. Thus, they take up a large amount of garden space before they even think about flowering and so gardeners are tempted into buying plants in the autumn. If you are so tempted, always try to obtain them freshly lifted from a nursery and do not trust to plants that have spent weeks in a cold store. But bear in mind also that wallflowers are highly prone to clubroot disease and can introduce it into a garden. Ask for assurance that the nursery from

where you obtain your plants is clubroot-free, therefore. Sadly, some of the named varieties have gone but most seed companies offer at least a small range of single colours which are very much better than the mixtures. The standard varieties reach about 45 cm (18 in), the so-called bedders only about 30 cm (12 in).
Sow by: biennial technique.
Recommended varieties: **Standard**: 'Blood Red' (dark, velvet red); 'Cloth of Gold' (rich gold); 'Fire King' (scarlet); 'Golden Monarch' (gold); 'Ivory White' (rather creamier than its name suggests); 'Primrose Monarch' (yellow); 'Purple Queen' (dark purple); 'Vulcan' (dark crimson). **Bedders**: 'Orange Bedder' (the Siberian wallflower, actually a species of *Erysimum*); 'Primrose Bedder'; 'Scarlet Bedder'.

Zinnia hybrids   Compositae

Zinnia 'Persian Carpet'

It takes only a couple of warm summers for the zinnia to return to favour; and only a couple of wet ones for gardeners not to bother again. They are classic warm-climate daisies, prone to damping off and to being damaged by rain (and also, incidentally, to sulking unless transplanted very carefully without root disturbance). They are available in three main groups of varieties – the tall (60–70 cm/24–28 in), large-flowered forms, especially valuable for cutting, the intermediates (35–60 cm/14–24 in) and the low-growing types (15–30 cm/6–12 in). There are singles, semi-doubles and doubles in reds, pinks, oranges, yellows and white.
Sow by: half-hardy annual technique at medium temperature.
Recommended varieties: **Tall types**: 'Dahlia Flowered Mixed' (the name says it all); 'Envy' (green flowers, said to be appreciated by flower arrangers); 'Ruffles' (double mixture in yellows, reds and oranges and claimed to be especially weather-resistant, although I have only seen it in a warm summer). **Intermediate types**: 'Persian Carpet' (semi-double and double mixture with bicoloured flowers in many colour combinations). **Low growing types**: 'Thumbelina' (double mixture with most colours).

I N MANY respects, the plants that fall into this group have little connection with each other. And in numerous instances, the appearance of their flowers and above-ground growth generally reflect this. What they do have in common lies out of sight below ground – a swollen and modified part of the root or stem that serves as a food store when the top growth has died down (usually, although not invariably, during the winter). Most are monocotyledons and have the narrow, strap-like leaves characteristic of this group, but for gardening purposes it is simplest to think of them all as herbaceous perennials of a rather special type. The difference between a bulb, a corm, a rhizome and a tuber is more of botanical than horticultural interest and, indeed, some structures once known by one name have recently been reclassified under another – the underground bodies formed by cyclamen, for instance, were formerly called corms; botanists now call them tubers, but we still grow them in precisely the same way. In common with general practice, I shall refer to all of these plants as bulbous.

Bulbous plants vary enormously in size from tiny species suitable for the rock garden or for growing in containers, to giants that can only really be found a home at the back of a large border. There are types that require rich moist soil and others that need hot, impoverished conditions. Most are hardy and can be allowed to grow unmolested for years (this is generally referred to as naturalising them), although a few are tender and must be lifted when their above-ground growth has been killed back by frost. A very few, although in reality perennial, tend to decline in vigour and flower sparsely after the first season and are better treated as annuals.

Almost all bulbous plants, however, share one feature. Their swollen underground storage organ is liable to be damaged by pests and is also prone

Bulb, corm, rhizome and tuber-forming plants in the garden

to attack by decay fungi in moist conditions, especially while it is dormant. Thus, although many species can tolerate wet soil whilst they are in leaf or bloom, they will rapidly succumb if these conditions persist all year round. A heavy clay soil is seldom ideal for them, therefore, although even here, some localised improvement can be made when planting (see below). Growing bulbs in established areas of grass is popular but should be done with some circumspection. Relatively few types can compete sufficiently well with the grass to thrive – even among the daffodils and narcissi, some varieties grow very vigorously among grass whilst others soon fade away. But even those bulbs suitable for growing in this way should never be planted in lawns or other grass that is constantly mown. A sound general maxim is to leave the foliage of bulbous plants undisturbed for six weeks after the last flowers fade before cutting it down, something that clearly is quite impossible in mown turf.

The majority of bulbous plants thrive best in full sun and relatively few are tolerant of deep shade; among the significant exceptions suitable for these conditions being those woodland plants like bluebells that produce leaves and flowers early in the year before the tree canopy comes into leaf. Bluebells, incidentally, are also among the few bulbous plants that can become invasive and must therefore be positioned with caution.

In general, bulbous plants are probably fed less than almost any other type of garden ornamental – and this is one of the main reasons why gardeners so often complain that their plants have failed to bloom after the first year. In that first season, of course, the food reserves in the bulb itself are sufficient to produce a good display of blooms. But to give of their best, bulbs require fertiliser when they are planted, in order to help them establish a strong and supportive root system, and then require feeding annually (preferably with a quick-acting liquid fertiliser) during the six-week period after flowering. Only in this way can they build up again the food reserves that enable flowering to take place. Unless I have indicated otherwise, this is the only after-care normally needed.

Most reputable bulb suppliers now give full planting directions but there is still considerable confusion in gardeners' mind regarding planting depth. A good general rule is to place the bulb with its base at a depth in the soil equal to three times its diameter. And even in a light soil, it is wise to lay in the bottom of the planting hole approximately 3–4 cm (1½–1¾ in) depth of sand to which a little bone meal has been added. This will minimise the likelihood of rotting. Cylindrical hand tools called bulb planters are available at garden centres and work on the principle of removing a plug of soil or turf to produce a hole into which the bulb or bulbs can be placed. In practice, however, I have never found these easy to use and a trowel or spade, depending on the area involved, is much easier. Although some types are readily raised from seed using the hardy annual technique, or occasionally by other means, as I have indicated in the individual descriptions, most plants will be bought as dormant bulbs or other storage bodies. After a few years, most will then produce smaller or daughter bulbs which take anything from two to about seven years to attain flowering size.

In the following listings, I have excluded those few plants such as dahlias, paeonies and the large bearded and similar irises that, although strictly falling within my definition, have more in common with conventional herbaceous perennials (p. 200).

Agapanthus spp. and hybrids   African lilies   Liliaceae

If you have a mild, preferably maritime, climate you must grow these magnificent plants. If not, then they are not worth the expense and effort. Agapanthus are large plants, making huge clumps up to 1.5 m (5 ft) tall so they will require plenty of room and well drained but fertile soil; they do, however, look superb in very large containers. The flowers are borne in very large loose, rather allium-like heads.

RECOMMENDED VARIETIES: there are several species but the plants most frequently available are the 'Headbourne Hybrids' with blue or white flowers derived from *A. campanulatus*.

Allium spp.   Ornamental onions   Liliaceae

Among the more neglected garden bulbs, largely because of a belief that all will smell like onions or garlic. In practice, few do, even when the foliage is bruised. An increasing number of species is becoming available in a wide size range from tiny rockery species to large plants suitable for the middle of the border. All have a more or less spherical terminal inflorescence, although this can sometimes be of rather loose form. The commonest colours are pinks, blues, mauves and white, although there is at least one common yellow species.

RECOMMENDED VARIETIES: **Dwarf forms**: *A. karataviense* (20 cm (8 in), pink, leaves broad, strap-like); *A. oreophilum* (sometimes still called *A. ostrowskianum*, 15 cm (6 in), deep pink, multiplies rapidly); *A. moly* (25 cm (10 in), yellow, can be invasive, tolerant of partial shade). **Taller forms**: *A. aflatunense* (75 cm, (30 in), lilac-purple); *A. caeruleum* (sometimes called *A. azureum*, 45 cm (18 in), deep blue); *A. sphaerocephalon* (60 cm (24 in), purple); *A. giganteum* (1.2 m (4 ft), rose-violet).

Anemone spp. and hybrids   Rananculaceae

The genus *Anemone* includes a very wide range of rather different plants, some of which are included in the account of herbaceous perennials (p. 203). Among the bulbous species, there are two main groups – first, the 30 cm (12 in) tall 'De Caen' forms of *Anemone coronaria*, which are not reliably perennial and in all except very mild areas are best treated as annuals; and the dwarf spring-flowering species allied to the native wood anemone, *A. nemorosa*. The 'De Caen' anemones make excellent cut flowers while the dwarf types are invaluable for spring display alongside crocuses, scillas and early flowering cyclamen.

RECOMMENDED VARIETIES: *A. coronaria*: 'De Caen' (sometimes called 'Giant French') usually sold as mixed colours of single-flowered types, but named individual colour strains are well worth looking for, especially 'His Excellency' (vivid red), 'Mr Fokker' (blue), 'Sylphide' (violet) and 'The Bride' (white); 'St Brigid' is a mixture of doubles, but choose strains from reputable suppliers as they vary enormously; that called 'Creagh Castle' is particularly reliable. **Dwarf spring-flowering types**: *A. apennina* (sky-blue); *A. blanda* (blue), which occurs as named varieties among which the best are 'Blue' (various shades of blue); 'Charmer' (various shades of pink); 'Radar' (vivid magenta). *A. nemorosa* (white) and the best of its named forms 'Alba Plena' (double white); 'Allenii' (pale-blue); 'Royal Blue' (rich-blue, large flowers); *A. ranunculoides* (yellow).

Arum italicum   Arum lily   Araceae

Arum italicum 'Pictum'

Arums in flower are readily recognisable, having an unusual structure in which a large hare's-ear-like spathe encloses a narrow club-like spike on which the individual flowers are borne in summer. These flowers are followed by attractive, brightly coloured fruits. Many species, especially the warmer-climate types, are large and foul-smelling, and the family as a whole is an extensive one. There is one species, however, approximately 50 cm (20 in) tall, closely related to the native cuckoo pint (*A. maculatum*) and thriving in moist, shaded situation, that is well worth growing for its attractive white-patterned leaves.

RECOMMENDED VARIETIES: *A. italicum marmoratum* (also commonly called *A. italicum pictum*).

Bulbocodium vernum   Red crocus   Liliaceae

Closely related to colchicums, and very like a small colchicum that has been pushed into the ground to leave a 3–4 cm (1½–1¾ in) tall, rather star-like reddish purple flower in spring. Leaves appear around the base of the flowers but do not emerge fully until after the flowers have faded. Bulbocodiums are useful, partly for the flower colour which is slightly different from that of the crocuses, and also for more unusual flower shape.

RECOMMENDED VARIETIES: normal species only available.

Cardiocrinum giganteum   Giant lily   Liliaceae

A really spectacular relative of the true lily, reaching 3–4 m (10–13 ft) in good, moist soil in partial shade. The flowers are typical lily-like trumpets, up to 15 cm (6 in) long, slightly drooping and a rich cream with reddish streaks inside. This is a magnificent plant but it must be given good growing conditions to develop its full potential.
PLANT: with top of bulb just below soil surface.
RECOMMENDED VARIETIES: the normal species is the one almost always offered but the variety *yunnanense*, although shorter, has lovely purple stems.

Chionodoxa spp.   Glory of the snow   Liliaceae

Spring-flowering blue or occasionally pink-flowered bulbs, ranging from about 5 to 25 cm (2 to 10 in). The flowers are prettily star-shaped with white centres but the great merit of chionodoxas is their flowering time which in my garden very closely follows that of the snowdrops.
RECOMMENDED VARIETIES: *C. luciliae* (blue flowers, a particularly robust form is often called *C. gigantea*).

Colchicum spp. and hybrids   Naked ladies, Meadow saffron   Liliaceae

Colchicum 'The Giant'

Colchicum flowers on their characteristic naked stems, which give them the shape of a goblet, range in height from 5 to about 20 cm (2 to 8 in). Most appear in autumn, the large lush leaves developing subsequently in the spring. Most species are pink or white and some have rather attractive foliage. The appeal of colchicums is elusive, for their weak stems are usually inadequate to support them and they fall over with the first heavy rain. My only real success has come from planting them in deep, rarely mown grass which gives them the physical and visual support that they need.
PLANT: at least 15 cm (6 in) deep.
RECOMMENDED VARIETIES: *C. autumnale* (20 cm (8 in), pink-purple); var. *album*, white; var. *pleniforum* (also called *roseum plenum*, double pink); *C. speciosum* var. *album* (20 cm (8 in), white); *C. luteum* (10 cm (4 in), spring, yellow). *C.* 'The Giant', (deep lilac); *C.* 'Water lily' (deep lilac, double).

Corydalis spp.   Papaveraceae

Low growing (mostly up to 20 cm/8 in) relatives of poppies but with small rather pea-like tubular, lipped flowers. There are several species available but some can become invasive. Those recommended are generally well behaved and thrive best in rich, moist soil in full sun or slight shade. They are useful plants for relatively out-of-the-way places, but are not really worthy of centre stage.
RECOMMENDED VARIETIES: *C. cashmeriana*, the prettiest species with vivid blue summer flowers, really needs acid conditions; *C. cheilanthifolia*, yellow, late spring, the species most frequently seen but with rather too much leaf in relation to the flowers; *C. solida*, rather dark purple-red flowers, spring.

Crinum powellii   Liliaceae

Substantial late summer- or autumn-blooming plants with heads of trumpet-shaped flowers and large, strap-like leaves, reaching 1 m (39 in) when in full sun and rich, well drained soil. There are several species but the pink-flowered hybrid *C. powellii* is the most widely available.
RECOMMENDED VARIETIES: the normal hybrid is pink-flowered but there is a lovely white-flowered form 'Album'.

Crocosmia hybrids   Montbretia   Iridaceae

The traditional summer-flowering garden montbretia with orange flowers and reaching a height of 1 m (39 in) can become invasive. There are, however, more recent varieties with a better colour range and more compact habit. I have always believed them to need very well drained soil and good sun to succeed but recently saw a magnificent planting on a boggy stream-side.
RECOMMENDED VARIETIES: 'Canary Bird' (60 cm (24 in), golden yellow, late summer); 'Emily McKenzie' (60 cm (24 in), deep orange with dark-red throat, late summer); 'Lucifer' (1 m (39 in), flame red, early summer).

Crocus spp. and hybrids   Iridaceae

Crocuses are too well known in some respects but not well enough known in others. Most gardeners are familiar with the 10 cm (4 in) tall, large-flowered Dutch hybrids which are lovely enough, and invaluable for massed planting in grass, even in light shade beneath trees, provided the grass will not be mown too closely. But there are many other smaller-flowered hybrids and species for the rock garden, the front of borders or odd corners of well-drained soil where they will receive plenty of sun; and many of these flower at other times of the year. Specialist nurseries list dozens of them but my experience has been that many, especially of the so-called winter-flowering types, bloom reluctantly, are damaged by rain and are not truly perennial, fading away after a few seasons. The following recommendations are essentially of those with which I have succeeded well.
RECOMMENDED VARIETIES: **Large-flowered 'Dutch'**: *C.* 'Large Yellow' (golden yellow); *C.* 'Queen of the Blues' (pale blue); *C. vernus* 'Jeanne d'Arc' (white); 'Purpureus Grandiflorus' (blue-purple). **Small-flowered late autumn/**

winter: *C. ancyrensis* (orange yellow); *C. laevigatus fontewayi* (blue violet with brown outer markings, the most reliable for Christmas flowering). **Small-flowered early spring**: *C. sieberi* 'Bowles' White' (white), 'Violet Queen' (blue-violet, excellent); *C. tommasinianus* 'Albus' (white), 'Whitwell Purple' (purple-red). **Small-flowered autumn**: *C. sativus* (lilac with violet veins); *C. speciosus* (lilac), 'Albus' (white).

Cyclamen   Primulaceae

Despite what you may read or be told, there are very, very few types of cyclamen that are reliable for naturalising outdoors. Most of the many species offered are really suitable only for the protection of an alpine greenhouse or, at best, the very well drained situation of an alpine trough. Specialists will seek out sources of these and will also want to assure themselves that the plants have been raised in Western Europe and not collected in the wild where natural populations have been seriously depleted. Cyclamen of all types always look their loveliest in light shade beneath trees.

PROPAGATE BY: seed or tubers.

PLANT: only half buried at the soil surface, if possible while in leaf, but this is rarely practicable, so plant dormant tubers in 11 cm (4½ in) pots of soil-based seedling compost in a cold frame or other sheltered spot and then transplant them into the garden after the leaves form. Ideally, they should be grown on in pots for a year.

AFTER-CARE: mulch with leaf mould and a light dressing of bone meal while the tubers are dormant to encourage further root development and facilitate the establishment of seedling plants.

RECOMMENDED VARIETIES: *C. hederifolium* (still sometimes called *C. neapolitanum*), easily the best autumn-flowering species, followed by its white form 'Album'; for spring, choose *C. coum atkinsii* which is often offered as variously patterned foliage types.

Endymion   Bluebell   Liliaceae

I am using the fairly familiar scientific name *Endymion*, although strictly bluebells are now called *Hyacinthoides*. They are tolerant of most types of soil and are unusual among bulbs in thriving even on fairly heavy clay. Bluebells are invaluable for carpeting the ground in shaded, wilder parts of the garden or in larger areas under trees because they come into flower and leaf well before most deciduous species; they will often survive even beneath beech. It is always a mistake, however, to plant them anywhere that you plan to keep neat and tidy for they are notoriously invasive and will spread rapidly through beds and borders. For the same reason, they are not suitable bulbs for small gardens.

RECOMMENDED VARIETIES: the native English bluebell is *E. non-scriptus* (*Hyacinthoides non-scripta*) which also occurs in pink- and white-flowered forms (usually called simply pink bells and white bells). A rather broader leaved species is the Spanish bluebell (*E. hispanicus* or *H. hispanica*) which has more erect scentless flowers; it also exists in pink and white forms (sometimes given fancy names) but many of the bulbs listed by nurseries as Spanish bluebells are in fact hybrids between this and the English species. There seems to have been little effort made at selecting the best strains so my advice must be simply that you obtain your stock from a reputable supplier.

Eranthis hyemalis   Winter aconite   Ranunculaceae

Aconites look like low-growing buttercups, to which they are closely related. In some gardens, they can be almost as invasive too, whilst in others they are unaccountably difficult to establish. The bright-yellow flowers are very welcome early signs of spring. Because of the possibility of their becoming somewhat rampant, aconites, like bluebells, are best kept out of beds and borders; they may be grown around trees in short grass, or among large shrubs, for they are fairly shade tolerant.

PLANT: the best way to establish aconites is to plant them whilst in leaf. They may be difficult to buy in this condition, however, so the simplest solution is to find a friend or neighbour who will part with a small clump from an established colony.

RECOMMENDED VARIETIES: normal species only is available.

Eremurus spp.   Foxtail lily   Liliaceae

Eremurus lilies are the giants of the bulb world, reaching up to 2–3 m (6½–10 ft) in good conditions, with a massive upright inflorescence composed of many tiny flowers. Obviously, a plant of this height is at home at the back of a border but they must have shelter and adequate staking. They also require a warm position and well-drained soil.

PLANT: carefully to avoid damage to the brittle, star-like tuberous roots – the operation is rather like planting a dead octopus.

AFTER-CARE: cover the crowns with compost, straw or bracken mulch in winter to prevent damage by early frosts.

RECOMMENDED VARIETIES: *E. himalaiacus* (2m (6½ ft), white); *E. robustus* (3 m (10 ft), pink). There are other species and also several hybrids frequently offered, but they are lower growing and have nothing of the drama of the two giant species.

Erythronium spp. and hybrids   Dog's tooth violet   Liliaceae

Erythroniums are among the most beautiful but under-appreciated tuber-forming garden plants. They produce two rather broad, sometimes almost strap-like leaves from the base of which slender stems arise in spring, approximately 25 cm (10 in) tall and bearing star-like flowers with characteristically recurved or swept back petals. They require moist, partially shaded conditions.

PROPAGATE BY: seed or tubers; raising from seed is worthwhile for erythroniums, for the tubers are rather expensive.

RECOMMENDED VARIETIES: *E. dens-canis* (very broad, dark-green leaves with purple-brown spots and deep-pink flowers, although there are also forms with white and purple flowers that are sometimes given appropriately descriptive names); *E.* 'Pagoda' (very slightly mottled leaves, yellow flowers); *E.* 'White Beauty' (mottled leaves, white flowers).

Fritillaria spp.   Fritillary, crown imperials   Liliaceae

Although this is a very large genus, the common spring-flowering garden forms of fritillary fall into two groups. The snake's head fritillary, *F. meleagris*, is a 30 cm (12 in) tall plant with very graceful, nodding bell-like flowers. Its natural home is water meadows and it is always most successful when growing among moist grass. Very different are the crown imperials, *F. imperialis*, which have stiff stems 1–1.5 m (3–5 ft) tall, bearing whorls of leaves and surmounted by a group of bell-like flowers. The crown imperials are useful for the centre of the border and have the advantage of requiring no additional supports but they take time to settle down and resent disturbances. The bulbs have a characteristic fox-like smell.

PLANT: the bulbs should be placed on their sides to prevent moisture accumulating around the stem base and leading to decay.

RECOMMENDED VARIETIES: *F. imperialis* 'Lutea Maxima' (yellow flowers), 'Rubra' (orange flowers); *F. meleagris*: the species only is normally available, although a white-flowered form 'Alba' and other coloured selections and hybrids are sometimes offered.

Gagea lutea   Liliaceae

Gageas are valuable for their bright-yellow colour, which few if any common spring-flowering bulbous plants with star-like flowers possess. They provide an excellent complement to crocuses, reach around 15 cm (6 in) in height and require well-drained conditions. Unfortunately, the bulbs do not seem to be widely available but they are well worth searching for.

RECOMMENDED VARIETIES: normal species only is available.

Galanthus spp. and hybrids   Snowdrops   Liliaceae

There are few more welcome signs of spring than snowdrops, but many gardeners are unaware of the wide range of forms available. All have the familiar white, nodding flowers but the degree of green colour on the petals varies (and a few forms actually have some yellow), as do the numbers of petals. But perhaps the greatest range arises in height, some being barely 3 cm (1¼ in) tall whereas others reach almost ten times this. Partially shaded, or at least sheltered, conditions and a fairly rich soil suit snowdrops best, although some forms will grow in surprisingly poor soil.

PLANT: the best way to establish snowdrops is to plant them whilst in leaf, for they are sometimes reluctant to flower if moved as dry bulbs. Many nurseries now supply them in active growth for this reason.

RECOMMENDED VARIETIES: *G. nivalis* (12 cm (5 in), native snowdrop), 'Flore Pleno' (12 cm (5 in), double flowers), 'Viridapicis' (23 cm (9 in), pronounced green petal markings); *G.* 'Sam Arnott' (20 cm (8 in), particularly strong with markedly rounded flowers); *G. atkinsii* (23 cm (9 in), graceful and probably the easiest to naturalise of the tall forms).

Galtonia candicans   Summer hyacinth   Liliaceae

White, rather loose hyacinth- or hosta-like flowers for later summer or early autumn, on tall stems that reach 1–1.2 m (3–4 ft). Once established they should, if possible, be left undisturbed and are therefore ideal subjects for the centre of the border.

RECOMMENDED VARIETIES: normal species only is available.

Gladiolus hybrids   Iridaceae

Gladioli are at the same time familiar and unique, for no other common garden bulbous plant requires similar treatment. Apart from the somewhat specialised cultivation of the small species, which I shall not consider here, and with the exception of the rather small-flowered and low-growing butterfly hybrids (see below), gladioli do not make ideal subjects for a mixed planting. They are much better treated as a cut flower crop and grown away from established ornamental plants in the vegetable or kitchen garden. The soil must be light, free draining but fertile, and the position in full sun.

PLANT: corms in succession from about ten to six weeks before the likelihood of the last frost. In this way, you will obtain a succession of blooms throughout the summer for, on average, gladioli take around one hundred days from planting to flowering.

AFTER-CARE: lift the corms around the time of the first autumn frosts. Ideally, as with other bulbs, you should allow six weeks after the flowers have faded and the old flower spike has been cut off, before lifting, so if fairly mild weather returns after one or two frosts, leave the corms in the ground until the full six weeks is completed.

RECOMMENDED VARIETIES: because gladiolus varieties seem to come and go considerably faster than those of most plants, and because individual varieties are generally only available from one or two suppliers, I see no merit in merely listing the names of those that I have found successful in the past. So for the larger-flowered hybrids, it is a matter of seeing what is available in the colours of your choice. But for border planting, do look out for the butterfly hybrids (small flowered, 60–120 cm/2–4 ft), especially the greenish-flowered 'Greenland' and, among other small flowered hybrids, 'The Bride' (45 cm (18 in), white).

Hyacinthus hybrids   Hyacinths   Liliaceae

Although hyacinths are most usually thought of in terms of the treated bulbs that are planted indoors for winter flowering, some varieties make fine spring-flowering subjects for the garden too. They are hardy, so do not require lifting, although the flower quality will be inferior to that of the selected indoor bulbs. But waste not, want not is a sound maxim in gardening, and bulbs purchased for indoor use can be planted outdoors in the following autumn, having been carefully stored dry after the foliage has died down. Remember, however, that the hyacinth is a fairly robust plant with a stout stem that does not blend readily with most of the other, rather more delicately formed spring-flowering bulbs.

RECOMMENDED VARIETIES: when planting out bulbs purchased primarily for indoor use, you will of course use what is on offer. But specifically for outdoor planting, I have found the following widely available types to be especially good – 'Carnegie' (white), 'City of Haarlem' (yellow), 'Delft Blue' (pale blue), 'Ostara' (deep blue), 'Pink Pearl' (deep pink).

Ipheion uniflorum   Liliaceae

With flowers rather like miniature campanulas but only 15 cm (6 in) tall and with grassy leaves, ipheions are among the more neglected spring-flowering bulbs. They will tolerate full sun but in my experience are much better in light shade.

RECOMMENDED VARIETIES: although there is a white variety, the best forms are undoubtedly 'Wisley Blue' (sky-blue) and 'Froyle Mill' (violet), both great improvements on the normal species.

Iris spp. and hybrids   Iridaceae

I have mixed feelings about the small bulbous irises, sold in large numbers for their spring (or in one instance, winter) flowers. They are assuredly very lovely but in many gardens some of them are little more than annuals, the bulbs forming masses of daughter bulbs after one season which take a very long time to reach flowering size again. The rhizome-forming Pacific hybrids, which are quite exquisite when in flower and reliably perennial, have the different disadvantage of taking several years to establish. The winter-flowering *I. unguicularis* thrives best in a very sunny position in poor soil and generally succeeds well in containers. All the other forms require rich but very well drained soil and full sun or the very lightest shade. They generally succeed best in slightly alkaline conditions, although this is not essential.

RECOMMENDED VARIETIES: *I.* Californian or Pacific Hybrids (35–45 cm/14–18 in) – many named forms and also mixtures are available, all are lovely and display complex mixtures of colours including pinks, yellows, oranges, purples and deep reds; *I. histrioides* (10 cm (4 in), blue violet/dark blue, white flecks, yellow streaks); *I. reticulata* (15 cm (6 in), deep purple with gold streaks), 'Harmony' (sky blue with yellow streaks), 'Clairette' (sky blue, dark blue, white flecks), 'Joyce' (sky blue, orange streaks), 'Pauline' (pink-mauve, white spot), 'Violet Beauty' (deep violet, orange streaks); *I. unguicularis* (20 cm (8 in), winter-flowering, 'Mary Barnard' with deep blue-purple flowers is much the best form).

Leucojum spp. and hybrids   Snowflakes   Amaryllidaceae

Snowflakes take over when snowdrops leave off, and continue the theme of lovely nodding white bells right through the season. For me, they are indispensible. They require very similar conditions to snowdrops – a moist, rich soil and light shade.

RECOMMENDED VARIETIES: *L. aestivum* (80 cm (32 in), spring, 'Gravetye Giant' is the tall, elegant form to choose); *L. vernum* (15 cm (6 in), spring); *L. autumnale* (15 cm (6 in), autumn).

Lilium spp. and hybrids   Lilies   Liliaceae

Every gardener knows of lilies, but most also know of their reputation for being difficult to grow. Undoubtedly, this is true of some species, and was true in the past of many hybrids which succumbed to virus or other problems. Nonetheless, I have grown a good selection in my garden for many years with little difficulty, and recommend below those that have proved must reliable. Although many lilies make good subjects for the centre or back of a mixed border, they are also very successful in pots, and by choosing varieties with a range of flowering times, it is possible to have a fine display in containers right through the summer. And of course, if you grow the scented forms close to

Lilium regale

the house, there is an additional bonus. A rich, moist but freely draining soil (or potting compost) is essential.

PROPAGATE BY: bulbs, bulbils or scale cuttings. Good quality lily bulbs are very expensive and although raising them from seed is a laborious and lengthy process, that only then repays the effort after many seasons, it is well worthwhile making use of two other methods of propagation. Some types, especially the tiger lilies, form tiny bulb-like bulbils in the axils of the leaves. Pot these up in a gritty compost, apply liquid fertiliser whilst the plants are in growth, and they should attain flowering size within three years. Additionally, remove up to six of the fleshy scales from around a dormant lily bulb, place them in a plastic bag or peat-based potting compost and place it in a warm place such as an airing cupboard. Within a few weeks, roots should form and the rooted scales should then be potted up and treated in much the same manner as bulbils; they should flower in two to three years.

AFTER-CARE: more than any other bulbous plants, lilies respond to a top dressing mulch early in the spring, before growth has commenced. Use well rotted leaf mould to which a dusting of bone meal has been added.

PEST, DISEASE OR OTHER PROBLEMS: aphids, grey mould, viruses.

RECOMMENDED VARIETIES: **Species**: *L. candidum* (Madonna lily, 1.2 m (4 ft), early summer, white, the only lily to plant with the bulb just below the soil surface); *L. hansonii* (1.2 m (4 ft), early summer, golden yellow with darker spots); *L. henryi* (2 m (6½ ft), late summer, orange-yellow with darker spots); *L. martagon* (Turk's cap, 1.2 m (4 ft), summer, pale purple with darker spots); *L. monadelphum* (1.5 m (5 ft), early summer, yellow with spotted throat); *L. regale* (1 m (39 in), summer, white with darker streaked outsides, exquisite perfume, the finest of all lilies, especially in the form 'Album'); *L. speciosum* (1.2 m (4 ft), late summer, white with brown stamens, the best forms are the beautifully scented 'Album' and 'Ellabee'). **Hybrids**: there are numerous hybrids and undoubtedly many of them make excellent garden plants but the following are those that I would not be without: 'Bright Star' (1 m (39 in), summer, silver white with pale orange centre); 'Citronella' (1.2 m (4 ft), summer, lemon yellow); 'Green Dragon' (1.5 m (5 ft), summer, white with faint green outside, beautiful perfume); 'Orange Sensation' (a form of tiger lily, 1 m (39 in), late summer, orange); 'Stargazer' (1.2 m (4 ft), late summer, red with pale margins).

Muscari spp.   Grape hyacinths   Liliaceae

Muscaris, with their bright-blue spring flowers, 15 to 20 cm (6 to 8 in) tall, are both familiar and notorious. The notoriety arises from the invasiveness of some species, but given an area in full sun where they may be allowed free rein, these certainly provide a useful function as ground cover. With the exception of the distinctly dignified *M. comosum*, they are not plants that I would choose for a small garden, however; they can be a menace between paving slabs.

RECOMMENDED VARIETIES: *M. armeniacum* 'Blue Spike' (double, sky blue with white margins); *M. botryoides* 'Album' (white); *M. neglectum* (deep blue, the most invasive form, for wild places only); *M. comosum* (tassel hyacinth, feathery violet flowers, graceful).

Narcissus spp. and hybrids   Daffodils and narcissi   Amaryllidaceae

Daffodils need no introduction for they are the most popular, familiar and, in many instances, most easy of bulbs to grow. Nonetheless, there are points about them that are worth making. Not all varieties are equally suitable for naturalising in the garden, some being much more appropriate for growing in containers or other situations where they can readily be lifted each year. There is a wide range in their flowering times and by careful choice of varieties, daffodil flowers can be in bloom from early March to May, or longer still if some of the dwarf narcissus species are chosen also. It is especially important, however, to bear in mind my remarks about planting mixtures – few sights are more depressing than late flowering daffodils attempting to present an attractive show when they are intermingled with the dead heads of their earlier companions.

RECOMMENDED VARIETIES: **Daffodils** with small or large trumpets: 'Arkle' (golden yellow), 'Carlton' (yellow), 'Dutch Master' (golden yellow), 'Empress of Ireland' (white), 'Golden Aura' (golden yellow), 'Golden Harvest' (golden yellow), 'Ice Follies' (white with yellow interior to trumpet), 'King Alfred' (golden yellow), 'Mount Hood' (white), 'Professor Einstein' (white with orange trumpet), 'Salmon Trout' (white with buff-yellow trumpet), 'St Keverne' (yellow with darker trumpet), 'W.P. Milner' (pale-yellow). **Small cupped narcissi**: 'Barrett Browning' (white with flame-orange trumpet), 'Merlin' (white with yellow red-rimmed trumpet). **Double daffodils and narcissi**: 'Acropolis' (white with red centre), 'Cheerfulness' (small, white with yellow centre), 'Double Event' (white with yellow centre), 'Golden Ducat' (yellow), 'Irene Copeland' (white intermingled with pale orange), 'Petit Four' (white with apricot centre), 'Unique' (white with yellow centre), 'Yellow Cheerfulness' (yellow). **Triandrus and cyclamineus narcissi** (with recurved or swept back petals): 'April Tears' (golden yellow with paler cup), 'Beryl' (yellow with orange cup), 'Charity May' (yellow), 'Dove Wings' (white with yellow trumpet), 'February Gold' (golden yellow with darker cup), 'Hawera' (yellow), 'Jack Snipe' (white with yellow cup), 'Jenny' (white with pale-yellow cup), 'Liberty Bells' (lemon yellow), 'Little Witch' (golden yellow), 'Peeping Tom' (golden yellow), 'Rippling Waters' (white), 'Tête à tête' (yellow with golden-yellow trumpets), 'Thalia' (white). **Jonquils** (two or more small, scented flowers per stem): 'Baby Moon' (yellow), 'Bobbysoxer' (yellow with darker cup), 'Suzy' (yellow with orange centre), 'Sweetness' (yellow), 'Trevithian' (yellow). **Tazettas** (clusters of usually small, scented flowers): 'Geranium' (white with red-orange cup), 'Minnow' (cream with yellow cup). **Poeticus** (small, flat coloured cup with white petals): 'Cantabile' (white with greenish, red-edged cup). **Split corolla** (orchid flowered): 'Cassata' (white with yellow centre), 'Dolly Mollinger' (white with orange centre). **Species and other hybrids**: *N. asturiensis* (golden yellow, a true miniature daffodil); *N. bulbocodium conspicuus* (golden yellow, a hoop-petticoat daffodil); *N. canaliculatus* (white with tiny yellow cup); *N. poeticus recurvus* (old pheasant's eye) (white with yellow, red-edge cup); *N. pseudonarcissus* (The Lent lily, yellow with darker cup); *N.* 'Rip van Winkle' (tiny double, yellow with greenish edges).

Nerine bowdenii   Amaryllidaceae

Rich pink, rather loose flowers on 45–60 cm (18–24 in) tall stems in early autumn make nerines unique among common garden bulbs. They must have a light, well-drained soil and a very sunny situation but are unaccountably difficult to establish in some gardens (such as mine) that seem to offer the correct conditions.

PLANT: with tip of bulb just breaking the soil surface.

RECOMMENDED VARIETIES: there are several named forms including a white but I prefer the normal species.

Ornithogalum spp.   Star of Bethlehem   Liliaceae

Useful if rather unexciting would sum up these plants with their star-shaped white flowers with characteristic green reverses to the petals. They will grow almost anywhere but are most successful in light shade. One species, *O. umbellatum*, not recommended, can become an invasive weed.

RECOMMENDED VARIETIES: *O. narbonense* (spring, 30–40 cm/12–16 in); *O. nutans* (spring, 30 cm/12 in).

Puschkinia scilloides   Liliaceae

Puschkinias look very much like scillas and are successful in similar situations. They can usefully find a place, therefore, among the other blue-flowered bulbs of spring.

RECOMMENDED VARIETIES: the normal species has bright-blue flowers but there is also a white form 'Alba'.

Scilla spp.   Squills   Liliaceae

Scillas are my most valuable spring-flowering bulbs. Although only 15 cm (6 in) tall, the colour of the best forms is electric-blue and in mild seasons they will be pushing through the soil before the end of January. They prefer well-drained soil and sun, although they will thrive in partial shade and look particularly attractive when forming a carpet beneath dormant deciduous shrubs.

RECOMMENDED VARIETIES: *S. mischtschenkoana* (also called *S. tubergeniana*) (pale blue); *S. siberica* 'Spring Beauty' (rich sky blue, easily the finest of all scillas), 'Alba' (white, a few intermingled with the blues form a pleasing pattern).

Sternbergia lutea   Amaryllidaceae

Although there are spring-flowering species, the autumn-flowering *S. lutea* is the really valuable member of this genus. It is at first sight an out-of-season, large (15 cm (6 in) tall), bright-yellow crocus, although I do not find them as hardy as crocuses and they must have a sunny, sheltered and well-drained site.
RECOMMENDED VARIETIES: choose the normal species.

Trillium grandiflorum   Wood lilies   Liliaceae

Perhaps because many gardens do not have the appropriate shaded, woodland conditions, trilliums are little known. But in the right situation, with moist, preferably slightly acid soil, they are splendid. The stems, with their characteristic whorls of leaves, reach 40 cm (16 in) and are topped by delightful, large, white three-petalled flowers in spring.
RECOMMENDED VARIETIES: although there are several species of *Trillium*, *T. grandiflorum* is the most widely available and easiest. It has an attractive double form *flore pleno*.

Triteleia laxa   Liliaceae

Triteleias are related to the ornamental onions, *Allium*, and their blue-purple flowers are similar, although the heads are much more open and loosely formed. They will thrive in similar, well-drained and sunny situations and produce their 50 cm tall flower stems in early summer.
RECOMMENDED VARIETIES: the normal species is sometimes called *Brodiaea laxa*; there is a rather more robust form called 'Queen Fabiola'. You will also sometimes see *Ipheion uniflorum* (p. 232) listed as *Triteleia*.

Tritonia rubrolucens   Iridaceae

Rather iris-like leaves and rather freesia-like pink flowers on 50 cm (20 in) tall stems in late summer would describe tritonias. Although not hardy in cold areas, they will generally succeed where nerines (p. 234) succeed and require similar sunny, well-drained situations.
RECOMMENDED VARIETIES: normal species only is available.

Tulipa spp. and hybrids   Tulips   Liliaceae

Tulips follow daffodils, both in flowering time and in popularity. They differ significantly, however, in the very large number of fairly small-flowered species available in addition to the more familiar, large-flowered hybrids. Tulips require free-draining soil and almost all, species and hybrids, thrive best in full sun. The hybrids are usually lifted after flowering (see below) and for this reason are particularly appropriate for planting in tubs or other large containers.
AFTER-CARE: the foliage on large hybrid tulips dies down in a particularly miserable manner, and yet must not be cut off before the bulb has been built up for the following season. If you have garden room, therefore, it is sensible to lift the plants carefully after flowering and then heel them in temporarily elsewhere in the garden.
RECOMMENDED SPECIES: **Species**: *T. acuminata* (45 cm (18 in), twisted green and red flowers); *T. batalinii* 'Bronze Charm' (12 cm (5 in), apricot and bronze, exquisite); *T. biflora* (15 cm (6 in), two tiny white flowers per stem); *T. clusiana* 15 cm (6 in), cream white with pale-red streak); *T. greigii* 'Red Riding Hood' (20 cm (8 in), red with black base and mottled leaves); *T. humilis* (also called *T. pulchella*) 'Violacea' (8 cm (3¼ in), violet purple with black centres); *T. kaufmanniana* (20 cm (8 in), white, yellow and pink); *T. kolpakowskiana* (30 cm (12 in), yellow inside, red outside); *T. maximowiczii* (15 cm (6 in), scarlet); *T. praestans* 'Fusilier' (20 cm (8 in), three to five orange-red flowers per stem); *T. saxatilis* (30 cm (12 in), pink); *T. sprengeri* (35 cm (14 in), scarlet with bronze outside); *T. sylvestris* (40 cm (16 in), yellow); *T. tarda* (15 cm (6 in), white with yellow centre, the easiest to naturalise); *T. turkestanica* (20 cm (8 in), up to nine white, orange-centred flowers per stem); *T. urumiensis* (15 cm (6 in), golden yellow and bronze); *T. whittallii* (30 cm (12 in), bronze with deep-orange outside).
Large-flowered hybrids: Early single – 'Bellona' (gold), 'Keizerskroon' (red with golden edges), 'Pink Beauty' (pink with white stripe); Early double – 'Peach Blossom' (rose pink), 'Scarlet Cardinal' (scarlet), 'Snow Queen' (white and cream); 'Triumph' (rounded single flowers, late spring), 'Attila' (deep purple), 'Fidelio' (pink and pale orange), 'Garden Party' (pink with white streak), 'White Dream' (white). **Darwin hybrids** (variably shaped single flowers, mid to late spring): 'Apeldoorn' (scarlet), 'Daydream' (shades of orange), 'Elizabeth Arden' (shades of pink), 'Golden Apeldoorn' (golden yellow); Single late – 'Bleu Aimable' (pale mauve), 'Clara Butt' (pink), 'Queen of Night' (dark purple, close to black). **Lily-flowered** (narrow, waisted flowers): 'China Pink' (pink), 'Marilyn' (white with red streaks), 'White Triumphator' (white). **Viridiflora** (some green colour in the petals): 'Artist' (green, deep pink and pale apricot), 'Groenland' (green, cream and pink), 'Hollywood' (green and crimson), 'Spring Green' (shades of green, white and yellow). **Parrot** (single flowers with frilled petals): 'Black Parrot' (very dark purple, close to black), 'Blue Parrot' (pale mauve), 'Flaming Parrot' (golden yellow with red streaks), 'White Parrot' (white). **Late Double** (paeony-flowered): 'Angélique' (pink and yellow), 'Gold Medal' (golden yellow), 'Mount Tacoma' (white).

Zantedeschia aethiopica   Arum Lily   Araceae

The characteristic white aroid flowers of zantedeschias, reaching 1 m (39 in) in good conditions, are familiar as florists' cut flowers but they can be grown outside in fairly mild areas. Nonetheless, they are more successful when grown in pots and taken indoors over winter or, alternatively, grown as marginal water plants where they will be protected by the mud in the pool base.
RECOMMENDED VARIETIES: the normal species is attractive enough but the variety 'Crowborough' is more robust.

Alpine and Rock Garden Plants

THERE is something innately fascinating about the plants that gardeners generally lump together under the name of alpines. I suppose it is their dwarfness that is so appealing, all of their components being perfectly scaled down, but quite commonly still reminiscent of their larger relatives. The name alpine is in fact a fairly vague term, for relatively few of the group actually originate in the Alps and a fair number indeed do not even hail from mountain regions at all, but from lowland habitats close to the Poles. The unifying feature, apart from their smallness, is that the plants originate in habitats with climatic extremes; but not necessarily, despite the popular belief, constantly cold ones. In the heat of the mid-day sun, the rocks of a mountain top or exposed Arctic landscape can become very hot indeed. And so a plant growing close by must be able to tolerate this, whilst at the same time be equipped to withstand the grim cold of an alpine night. From a gardener's standpoint, therefore, these are difficult conditions to reproduce. But equally difficult are the other characteristics of the alpine habitat – a very free-draining almost grit-like soil, very high rainfall and very strong and sometimes almost constant winds. Even within the general term alpine, there are individual sites that are more exacting than others, and you will be a specialist gardener indeed to adopt the challenge of cultivating plants that grow on continually moving screes or beneath the edges of melting glaciers.

For the more general gardener, I prefer to select carefully from the numerous alpine genera and suggest only those that are most readily adapted to a normal garden. In my recommendations, therefore, I have omitted those plants that will thrive only in very special conditions or even that require the shelter of an alpine greenhouse. Provided you can supply them with a gritty, free-draining soil and take care to minimise the likelihood of damage caused

Some types of alpines require moist conditions such as they find in my peat garden.

by clinging damp, these little ornamental gems will beautify your garden. In general, the alpines most prone to damage from damp are those with hairy, moisture-retaining foliage, and it may be worth placing a simple open-ended cloche over them for protection during the winter, or at least in the early spring when their flower buds are swelling. And always remove any dead leaves that become trapped among alpines in the autumn.

But where in the garden should alpines be grown? Traditionally, they have occupied a feature called a rock garden, some sort of attempt to reproduce on a small scale a part of their natural environment. Sadly, an artificial rock garden constructed in a modern home garden almost invariably looks both out of place and quite frankly ridiculous. If an artificial rock garden is not to look stupid, it must be constructed from stone that is appropriate to the geology of the area, the stones must be laid in a manner that simulates a natural outcrop (sedimentary or layered rocks being laid with their bedding planes parallel, for instance) and it really must be fairly large. All in all, this calls for expense, expertise and labour that are beyond the scope or inclination of most gardeners. Even some of our best known and most visited public gardens have not managed to create satisfactory rock features; I can think of one that bears more resemblance to the side of a Greek temple than anything geological. I shall not therefore be giving you instructions on rock gardening. My advice is to grow alpines in conventional containers, in troughs, in table beds or in hollow wall or raised beds. All of these offer you several advantages. They can be filled with a soil that has been deliberately amended with grit to improve drainage, without damaging your bank balance; and they enable the plants to be grown in a slightly elevated place so that their diminutive features are closer to eye level. For convenience, however, and because there is nowhere else logically to place them, I have included in this section a number of small, compact plants for the peat garden. Although their conditions must be damp and often rather shaded, they seem to me to have much in common with alpines in their overall appeal, and some very important genera such as *Primula* and *Gentiana* span both habitats. I have, however, omitted a few that, although fairly small, are essentially plants for the front of the mixed or herbaceous border, and I have also excluded dwarf bulbs which I have described elsewhere (p. 227).

A peat bed may be constructed successfully on any soil that does not actually contain lumps of limestone or chalk – 'free lime' as this is known. For a representative range of small, peat-loving species, an area of about 10 square metres (10 sq yds) will be adequate. It is easiest to raise the bed slightly above the surrounding garden; although this may be done with peat blocks, these are fairly expensive and I have constructed mine with stout lengths of hardwood tree trunk. These retaining walls should be about 20–30 cm (8–12 in) high. Within the bed, double dig the soil, but incorporate only plant remains (garden compost is ideal) rather than animal manures, which many peat garden plants do not appear to relish. Then add the peat itself and fork this thoroughly into the underlying soil. You will need to import further soil as you fill and a ratio of about three parts by volume of peat to one part of soil is ideal. I have always used sedge peat, finding it much cheaper than moss, and although it is usually undeniably less acidic, I have found this no disadvantage. The bed needs to be topped up with a few centimetres of peat each year and I also use a mulch of pine or other conifer needles.

Alpines should be planted much as other perennials are – in a carefully prepared planting position, in soil to which a small amount of peat or compost has been added, together with a few handfuls of grit and a light dusting of bone meal. During dry weather, do take care to water the plants regularly and then, early each spring, give them a top dressing of bonemeal. I prefer not to use a general-purpose fertiliser as this tends to give them too much nitrogen and encourages soft, disease-prone foliage. Apart from damp-induced moulds, alpines are fairly free from pest and disease problems, as much as anything because they are in active growth and flower early in the season before most harmful organisms are abroad.

Many alpines can be grown successfully from seed. Autumn is my preferred sowing time and I leave the seed pans or trays outdoors over the winter for the natural cold and frost to play its part in breaking dormancy. Subsequently, they may be divided or rooted from softwood cuttings (p. 106) in order to multiply the stock. Most alpines are spring or early summer-flowering and only where particular genera or species are conspicuously flowers of the autumn have I mentioned flowering times.

Acaena spp.   Rosaceae

Fairly vigorous but always containable ground-cover plants reaching about 10 cm (4 in) in height but 75–90 cm (30–36 in) in spread, with tiny leaves and wiry stems. The leaves turn attractive reddish shades in autumn but usually remain on the plants over the winter. Because of their wiry growth, acaenas do not usually form a completely compact mat and are useful therefore in areas where other plants such as bulbs can grow through them. The flowers are attractive and unusual, forming more or less rounded spiky heads.
OBTAIN AS: seed or plants.
AFTER-CARE: cut back the more straggly growths in early spring.
RECOMMENDED VARIETIES: *A. anserinifolia* (reddish flower heads), *A. buchananii* (greenish flower heads), *A.* 'Blue Haze' (steely-blue leaves), *A. microphylla* (red flower heads).

Adiantum spp.   Maidenhair ferns   Polypodiaceae

These are among the most useful ferns for the alpine garden, being more or less evergreen, small and relative compact in habitat. Unfortunately, many species are barely hardy and will be killed in hard winters. The appearance is familiar and attractive, with thin wiry stems bearing tiny, more or less rounded green fronds. I find they succeed best in moist, peaty pockets within an overall alpine bed.
OBTAIN AS: plants.
AFTER-CARE: cut back dead growths in spring.
RECOMMENDED VARIETIES: *A. capillus-veneris* (light-green fronds, black stems), *A. pedatum subpumilum* (very tightly congested overlapping fronds on black stems, often said to need alkaline soils, but flourishes in my peat bed).

Alyssum saxatile   Cruciferae

There is a perennial relative of the white bedding alyssum that is quite invaluable in the alpine garden, or anywhere else where a wall or path edge is to be clothed with spring colour. The vivid golden-yellow of *A. saxatile* is one of the joys of my garden.

OBTAIN AS: plants; I have never yet found a seed-raised form to be as neat and compact.
AFTER-CARE: trim hard after flowering.
RECOMMENDED VARIETIES: 'Compactum' – all others tend to be straggly and unkempt.

Androsace spp.   Primulaceae

Neat, cushion-forming evergreens, most with very soft hairy foliage and heads of small, pink, white or yellowish primula-like flowers. These are among the most useful of alpines but their soft leaves must be given protection from winter damp.
OBTAIN AS: seed or plants.
AFTER-CARE: give protection in winter and early spring.
RECOMMENDED VARIETIES: *A. carnea* (at least two named forms are commonly available) (heads of single pink flowers), *A. cylindrica* (white flowers with yellow-green eye), *A. lanuginosa* (lilac-pink flowers with darker pink or yellowish eyes), *A. sarmentosa* (pink flowers with yellow eyes).

Antennaria dioica   Cat's ears   Compositae

A good compact ground-cover plant for a very well-drained situation. The densely woolly mats of foliage can be damaged by winter damp but this is nonetheless a plant to persevere with, for the appeal of its rather fluffy white or pale-pink flower heads.
OBTAIN AS: seed (normal species) or plants (named varieties).
AFTER-CARE: be careful to remove dead leaves or other traps for winter moisture.
RECOMMENDED VARIETIES: the normal species is attractive but 'Nyewoods Variety' has particularly deep pink flowers.

Aquilegia   Ranunculaceae

There are several dwarf aquilegias not immediately recognisable to those gardeners only familiar with the tall border species. Nonetheless, on inspection, all will be seen to have the typical spurred, bell-like flowers. Those that I have recommended have

proved particularly easy to raise from seed and to grow.
OBTAIN AS: seed or plants.
AFTER-CARE: none.
RECOMMENDED VARIETIES: *A. alpina* (violet-blue flowers, 45 cm (18 in) tall; *A. discolor* (white and blue flowers, 5 cm (2 in) tall.

Armeria spp.   Plumbaginaceae

Armeria maritima

The most familiar *Armeria* species is *A. maritima*, the sea thrift, which makes an attractive rock-garden plant although there are other suitable species too. They have wiry, rather grass-like leaves and compact rounded flower heads of pink, red or white.
OBTAIN AS: seed or plants (named varieties).
AFTER-CARE: none.
RECOMMENDED VARIETIES: *A. juniperifolia* (fairly open, rose-pink flower heads), 'Bevan's Variety' has the best colour; *A. maritima*, the normal species, has pink flowers but 'Alba' is white and there are others such as 'Laucheana' with particularly deep colours or robust habit.

Artemisia spp.   Wormwoods   Compositae

This is an interesting genus with fern-like or feathery foliage that includes some familiar border plants and tall herbs such as lad's love, but there are some lower-growing alpine species too. Don't expect dramatic or even interesting flowers, for these are essentially plants to be grown for the appeal of their glaucous or silvery foliage.
OBTAIN AS: seed or plants.
AFTER-CARE: trim lightly with shears in spring.
RECOMMENDED VARIETIES: *A. schmidtiana* 'Nana'.

Asplenium trichomanes   Maidenhair spleenwort fern
Polypodiaceae

This is one of the most useful dwarf, semi-evergreen ferns, superficially very much like a true maidenhair (p. 206) and thriving in similar situations. Although it tolerates lime in the soil and considerable dryness, I find it is always better planted in a moist, peaty pocket.
OBTAIN AS: plants.
AFTER-CARE: trim off dead stems in spring, especially after hard winters.

RECOMMENDED VARIETIES: the normal species is the only type usually available although, as with many ferns, foliage variants do occur.

Aster alpinus   Alpine aster   Compositae

The dwarf alpine species of Michaelmas daisy is all that you would expect it to be – a scaled down version of the familiar border perennial. It has rich, purple, daisy flowers with yellowish centres.
OBTAIN AS: seed or plants.
AFTER-CARE: cut off dead heads after flowering.
RECOMMENDED VARIETIES: the normal species is the one frequently seen, although there are several named forms with larger flowers or deeper colour; *albus* is a white-flowered variant but not as attractive to my eye.

Aubrieta   Cruciferae

Aubrietas are very familiar as edging to garden borders of all types but far too frequently gardeners are content with the seed-raised plants in mixed colours. It is very much better to seek out the named colour forms, of which some of the more widely available are listed below.
OBTAIN AS: plants.
AFTER-CARE: trim back with shears after flowering.
RECOMMENDED VARIETIES: 'Dr Mules' (blue-purple), 'Greencourt Purple' (purple), 'Gurgedyke' (deep purple), 'Lodge Crave' (semi-double, violet), 'Red Carpet' (red), 'Wanda' (double red).

Campanula spp. and hybrids   Bell flowers
Campanulaceae

Campanulas are further examples of those flowers that have good representatives in both the border and the alpine garden. Their blue, purple or white bell-shaped flowers are very familiar but in choosing forms for a rock planting, choose carefully. The two forms with tongue-twisting names, *C. portenschlagiana* and *C. poscharskyana*, are extremely invasive and are best used only for such situations as extensive dry stone walls, where they can be allowed free rein.
OBTAIN AS: seed (species) or plants (named varieties).
AFTER-CARE: trim lightly after flowering.
RECOMMENDED VARIETIES: *C. barbata* (one-sided spikes of pale blue-mauve flowers); *C.* 'Birch Hybrid' (prostrate, deep-purple flowers); *C. betulifolia* (prostrate, white/pink flowers); *C. carpatica* (clump-forming, 'Bressingham White' is white, 'Jewel' is deep purple); *C. cochlearifolia* (spreading clumps with mauve-blue flowers, one of the best alpines for light shade; there are many named forms of which 'Blue Tit' and 'Elizabeth Oliver' are among the best); *C. garganica* (spreading clumps, lavender flowers, 'Blue Diamond' is a fine form); *C. haylodgensis* (spreading clumps, lavender-blue flowers).

Cassiope spp. and hybrids   Ericaceae

Dwarf shrubs, related to heaths and heathers and with similar bell-like white flowers and tightly congested, almost cypress like leaves. They are highly suitable for slightly shaded, moist peaty corners and look particularly effective when dwarf bulbs are allowed to grow up through them.

OBTAIN AS: plants.

AFTER-CARE: trim back lightly with shears after flowering.

RECOMMENDED VARIETIES: C. 'Edinburgh'; C. lyco-podioides; C. 'Muirhead'; C. selaginoides.

Delphinium tatsienense   Ranunculaceae

Delphiniums of course are familiar as giant herbaceous plants for the back of the border, but there are low-growing species too, including this one that is easily raised from seed and is well worth a place in an alpine garden. It will reach about 30 cm (12 in) and has very obvious delphinium spikes of bright-blue flowers.

OBTAIN AS: seed or plants.

AFTER-CARE: cut down dead spikes after flowering; a fairly short-lived perennial.

RECOMMENDED VARIETIES: the normal species is widely available, although there is a white form 'Alba' that as far as I know does not come true from seed.

Dianthus spp. and hybrids   Caryophyllaceae

How much more dainty and lovely are the dwarf dianthus species and varieties than their tall, large-flowered border or greenhouse carnation relatives. There are indeed so many now available that is hard to know which among the true species to recommend, for I love them all. I have also included here the old-fashioned (and a few good modern) pinks which, although slightly straggly, are as at home in an alpine garden as anywhere and will pervade all around with their heady perfume. Ideally, dianthus require a slightly alkaline soil to give of their best.

OBTAIN AS: seed (species) or plants (named varieties).

AFTER-CARE: cut back dead heads after flowering; renew plants every three or four years.

RECOMMENDED VARIETIES: **Dwarf species and hybrids**: D. alpinus (clump forming, compact, rose-pink); D. 'Bomba-dier' (double scarlet); D. deltoides (maiden pink), the best forms are 'Albus' (white) and 'Flashing Light' (deep red pink); D. gratianopolitanus (Cheddar pink) (pale pink); D. 'La Bourboule' (also called 'La Boubille') (pink, strong perfume); D. 'Little Jock' (semi-double pink with darker eye); D. 'Pike's Pink' (semi-double pink). **Old Garden Pinks** (all strongly fragrant): 'Dad's Favourite' (semi-double white with brown lacing); D. 'London' series (a range of modern laced pinks in the old-fashioned style); D. 'Mrs Sinkins' (double white); D. 'Sam Barlow' (double white with brown centres).

Diascia rigescens   Scrophulariaceae

Mat-forming plants with narrow, evergreen leaves and erect spikes of deep pink, characteristically lipped flowers. Although often described as rare or unusual, this is in fact a widely available and very easy to grow plant.

OBTAIN AS: plants.

AFTER-CARE: cut down heads after flowering.

RECOMMENDED VARIETIES: 'Ruby Field'.

Draba spp.   Whitlow grass   Cruciferae

These are certainly not classical plants but they are nonetheless pretty and useful mat-forming species with typical cruciferous yellow flowers. Their major disadvantage is that most types appear all but dead and decidedly dismal in winter.

OBTAIN AS: seed or plants.

AFTER-CARE: none.

RECOMMENDED VARIETIES: D. aizoides; D. longisiliqua; D. polytricha.

Dryas spp.   Mountain avens   Rosaceae

Finding the native mat-forming Dryas octopetala, with its lovely little white, yellow-centred flowers and characteristically oak-like leaves, is one of the great delights of mountain walking. In the alpine garden, it can be very attractively joined by two related forms with white or cream flowers.

OBTAIN AS: seed or plants.

AFTER-CARE: none.

RECOMMENDED VARIETIES: D. drummondii; D. octopetala; D. suendermannii.

Erinus alpinus   Scrophulariaceae

I have seen this plant called the hairy foxglove. Certainly it belongs to the same family as the true foxglove but it is a midget, with rather open pink flowers, not like the real fox-glove's tubes.

OBTAIN AS: seed or plants.

AFTER-CARE: none.

RECOMMENDED VARIETIES: the normal species occurs in a range of colours from white through pink to red but 'Dr Hanelle' is a particularly fine deep-pink form.

Erodium spp.   Stork's bill   Geraniaceae

The erodiums have never achieved the popularity of their close relatives, the geraniums, which is a shame, for although many fewer in numbers of species, they make extremely pretty plants for the alpine garden. All form more or less compact mounds.

OBTAIN AS: seed or plants.

AFTER-CARE: none.

RECOMMENDED VARIETIES: E. chrysanthum (white flowers, fern-like silvery leaves); E. reichardii (also called E. chamae-dryoides) (small, oak-like leaves and pink or white flowers, 'Roseum' is a good deep-pink form).

Gentiana spp. and hybrids   Gentianaceae

Gentians are among the best known and most beautiful of all alpine plants, instantly recognisable with their vivid blue trumpet-shaped flowers. Yet they have a reputation for being fickle to grow. I am sure that this impression derives from a few species such as G. acaulis, which is certainly a difficult species to induce to flower in many gardens. A few species have clearly defined preferences for acid or alkaline conditions and these must be adhered to if flowers are to result.

Gentiana asclepiadea

OBTAIN AS: seed (species) or plants (named varieties).

AFTER-CARE: none.

RECOMMENDED VARIETIES: *G. asclepiadea* (willow gentian, arching stems of mid-blue flowers in autumn, 'Alba' is a lovely white form; both revel in the partial shade of my peat bed); *G. septemfida* (lime tolerant, mid-blue); *G. sino-ornata* (prostrate, vivid blue flowers in autumn on acid soil; 'Brin's Form' is the best and most reliable variety).

Geranium spp. and hybrids   Geraniaceae

Although many of the most familiar species of hardy geranium are tall-growing types suitable only for the herbaceous border, a number of small ground-cover or clump-forming forms are perfectly at home in the alpine bed. I find all of them particularly rewarding plants, for they flower over a long period of time and grow substantially even within the first season after planting. Some of the more vigorous low-growing forms are described on p. 207.

OBTAIN AS: seed (species) or plants (named varieties).

AFTER-CARE: cut back fairly hard after flowering.

RECOMMENDED VARIETIES: *G. cinereum subcaulescens* (deep-red flowers with black centres, 'Giuseppii' is a particularly fine red form while 'Ballerina' and 'Apple Blossom' have rich pink flowers); *G. dalmaticum* (pink flowers, or white in the variety 'Alba'); *G. sanguineum splendens* (often called *G. lancastriense*) (rich pink flowers, the best form is 'Shepherd's Warning'); *G. pylzowianum* (one of my favourites, with pink flowers and very attractive variegated foliage).

Helianthemum hybrids   Rock roses   Cistaceae

The rock roses are among those relatively few plants that I don't like but have included in the book out of a sense of duty, for I know that many others appreciate them. They are familiar enough, with their elongated glaucous evergreen leaves and single flowers in most shades of shocking pink and related colours. Although some form relatively large straggly sub-shrubs, I have included them here because they are more usually grown with alpines in sunny conditions on light soils than anywhere else.

OBTAIN AS: seed (species) or plants (named varieties).

AFTER-CARE: trim lightly after flowering.

RECOMMENDED VARIETIES: 'Ben Nevis' (gold-orange); 'Cerise Queen' (double rose-red); 'Henfield Brilliant' (deep orange); 'Jubilee' (double yellow); 'Mrs C.W. Earle' (also known as 'Fireball') (double red); 'Wisley Pink' (pink); 'Wisley Primrose' (yellow).

Leontopodium alpinum   Edelweiss   Compositae

If it hadn't been for the wretched song, perhaps the edelweiss would have been left on the mountains where it belongs, for it really is not a very suitable nor pretty plant for the alpine garden. It is so woolly that it is almost bound to attract dampness and decay, and as a garden plant almost always becomes straggly and unkempt. But some people evidently love it.

OBTAIN AS: seed or plants.

AFTER-CARE: trim back carefully after flowering.

RECOMMENDED VARIETIES: only the normal species is usually available.

Lewisia hybrids   Portulacaceae

I am afraid that this is the third genus in a row that seems to be admired by everyone except me. My objection to lewisias is not that they can be very difficult to grow, for a challenge is always welcome (and in this case, the problem is usually overcome by planting them on almost vertical slopes so that water does not collect in their flowers); it is the colours of some which are so lurid as to be almost luminous. There are some deciduous species which can be very troublesome, but all of those recommended are evergreen, clump-forming types.

OBTAIN AS: seed or plants (hybrid forms may sometimes come true from seed).

AFTER-CARE: none, provided careful attention is given to initial planting positions.

RECOMMENDED VARIETIES: 'Cotyledon Hybrids' (a range of hybrids derived from *L. cotyledon* in various orange, yellow, pink and purple shades); 'George Henley' (deep-pink flowers with darker veining).

Lychnis alpina   Alpine catchfly   Caryophyllaceae

The tall-growing pink-flowered native catchfly or ragged robin is a familiar meadow plant, but it has some low-growing relatives too, and one particularly neat form for the alpine garden. Its only drawback, in my experience, is that it tends to live up to its name and is unusual among alpine plants in attracting not flies but aphids.

OBTAIN AS: seed or plants.

AFTER-CARE: none.

RECOMMENDED VARIETIES: 'Rosea' is a selected deep-pink form.

Oxalis spp.   Oxalidaceae

I have a soft spot for *Oxalis* for one of their number was the first alpine that I ever bought. Their most characteristic feature is the three-lobed clover-like leaf. A few species have gained extreme notoriety through becoming almost ineradicable weeds. Those that I recommend, however, are extremely well behaved clump-forming or very slowly spreading plants with delicate nodding flowers. They have an especial value in being among the very few alpines that are shade-tolerant.

OBTAIN AS: seed or plants.

AFTER-CARE: none.

RECOMMENDED VARIETIES: *O. acetosella* (wood sorrel) (white flowers, fresh green leaves); *O. adenophylla* (pink flowers, glaucous leaves); *O. laciniata* (blue flowers, glaucous leaves).

Phlox spp.   Polemoniaceae

Phlox douglasii

Although most alpines are readily identifiable with taller growing herbaceous-border relatives, the alpine phlox are exceptions. They are prostrate, mat-forming plants and in a few instances can become decidedly invasive. There are two important alpine species, *P. douglasii* and *P. subulata*, each with a number of fine varieties.

OBTAIN AS: seed (species) or plants (named varieties).

AFTER-CARE: trim back with shears after flowering.

RECOMMENDED VARIETIES: **Forms of *P. douglasii*:** 'Boothman's Variety' (lavender blue with violet eyes, delightful), 'Crackerjack' (crimson), 'Red Admiral' (red), 'Waterloo' (crimson). **Forms of *P. subulata*:** 'Beauty of Ronsdorf' (pink), 'May Snow' (white), 'McDaniel's Cushion' (pink, very compact), 'Scarlet Flame' (scarlet).

Potentilla spp. and hybrids   Rosaceae

The dwarf potentillas are much neater plants than their larger shrub-garden relatives. The flowers, leaves and entire plant are

all scaled down and, although they do not flower for as long a period, I find them indispensable alpine garden plants.

OBTAIN AS: plants.

AFTER-CARE: none.

RECOMMENDED VARIETIES: *P. aurea* (yellow); *P. crantzii* (yellow, orange centres); *P. nitida rubra* (red); *P. tonguei* (orange yellow, red centres).

Primula spp. and hybrids   Primulaceae

The genus is a huge and invaluable one. The very tall and robust species are described elsewhere, but this still leaves a great many that are superb members of the alpine or peat garden flora, and I have included here the plants of primrose size and form that can be used in a wide range of garden situations. Although many exotic primulas are readily recognisable as having affinities with the common primrose, the relationship of those which bear many flowers massed together is betrayed most readily by their foliage. The secret of success with almost all is to divide them every two or three years.

OBTAIN AS: seed or plants.

AFTER-CARE: divide frequently.

RECOMMENDED VARIETIES: *P. alpicola* (moisture loving, a wide range of colours ranging from white to purple with massed tiny flowers at the tops of short stems); *P. auricula* (must have very good drainage, be sure to choose only the normal species or border varieties; the show auriculas are only for indoor culture) – 'Dusty Miller' (yellow), 'Old Red Dusty Miller' (dark red); *P. bulleyana* (moisture loving, purple flowers on tall spikes): *P. cockburniana* (vivid orange nodding flowers on short spikes); *P. denticulata* (pink and purple 'drumstick' flower heads on tall spikes, 'Alba' is a white form); *P. elatior* (oxlip) (yellow nodding flowers on tall spikes); *P. sikkimensis* (moisture loving, nodding yellow flowers on tall spikes): *P. veris* (cowslip, more or less nodding yellow or orange flowers on short spikes); *P. viallii* (tiny purple flowers in dense spikes, most uncharacteristic of the genus); *P. vulgaris* (primrose, the normal yellow-flowered species is delightful but look out for any of the named double-flowered forms among which the golden yellow 'Sunshine Susie' is especially lovely. There are also many named single flowered forms in various colours of which the best known is the deep red-purple 'Wanda').

Raoulia spp.   Compositae

The raoulias have very dense, close-textured mats of growth with flowers so small as to be barely visible. They are extremely useful for the edges of trough or other alpine gardens where they form a carpet of glaucous, often woolly foliage.

OBTAIN AS: plants (they are extremely slow growing to raise from seed).

AFTER-CARE: none.

RECOMMENDED VARIETIES: *R. australis* (silver-grey foliage); *R. hookerii* (green foliage).

Sagina spp.   Caryophyllaceae

The mat-forming saginas are similar in many ways to raoulias in forming a dense mat and in having almost invisible flowers. They are in fact often mistaken for moss growth and for this reason I find them less suitable for planting where bulbs are to grow through them, for the entire mat becomes lifted by the bulb shoots.

OBTAIN AS: seed or plants.
AFTER-CARE: none.
RECOMMENDED VARIETIES: *S. boydii*, *S. subulata*.

Saponaria ocymoides   Caryophyllaceae

The trailing alpine soapwort is such a delightful pink-flowered plant for the edge of a trough or other alpine garden that I am astonished it is not grown more widely. It makes a refreshing change from aubretia in similar situations.

OBTAIN AS: seed or plants.
AFTER-CARE: trim back after flowering if growth becomes straggly.
RECOMMENDED VARIETIES: only the normal species is usually available but there is a white form 'Alba' and a red form 'Rubra Compacta' that may not come true from seed.

Saxifraga spp. and hybrids   Saxifrages   Saxifragaceae

Saxifraga urbium (London Pride)

There cannot be an alpine garden anywhere without a fair sprinkling of saxifrages but whilst the devoted alpine gardener will have hundreds, it is possible to select a relatively small number that are both easy to grow and rewarding. The genus is both large and botanically complex but it is simplest to sub-

divide it into four groups. First there are the encrusted saxifrages which have a very low growing habit and an encrusted appearance brought about by lime deposits on the leaves; they require a well-drained soil and sunny situation. Second are the mossy saxifrages in which the foliage is moss-like; they require slightly more moist conditions and preferably light shade. Third is the Kabschia group which must have good drainage but also some shade. And fourth is a group often described in catalogues as 'various'; it includes species not in the other three groups.

OBTAIN AS: seed (species) or plants (named varieties).
AFTER-CARE: generally none, although the more vigorous species, especially among the mossy group, benefit from trimming back after flowering and certain types may require individual care – in a few, for instance, the main rosette dies after flowering and the off-sets must be replanted. It is worth checking with the nursery from which you obtain the plants or refer to specialist alpine gardening books regarding the needs of individual types.
RECOMMENDED VARIETIES: **Encrusted types**: *S. cochlearis* 'Minor' (white flowers with red spots); *S. cotyledon* 'Southside Seedling' (white flowers with pink spots); *S. paniculata* (often called *S. aizoon*) 'Lutea' (pale yellow), 'Rosea' (deep pink); *S.* 'Tumbling Waters' (white). **Mossy types**: *S.* 'Dartington Double' (double pink); *S.* 'Gaiety' (rose pink); *S.* 'Golden Falls' (white flowers, cream and green leaf variegation); *S.* 'Knapton Pink' (pink); *S. moschata* 'Cloth of Gold' (gold flowers); *S.* 'White Pixie' (white). **Kabschia types**: *S. apiculata* 'Alba' (white), 'Gregor Mendel' (yellow); *S. elisabethae* 'Boston Spa' (yellow), 'Carmen' (yellow); *S. irvingii* 'Jenkinsae' (pink). **Various**: *S. cortusifolia* (also called *S. fortunei*) (white flowers, autumn), *fortunei* 'Wada' (white flowers, purple leaves, autumn); *S. oppositifolia* 'Ruth Draper' (pink-purple); *S. urbium* (London Pride) (pink and white flowers with red spots).

Sedum spp. and hybrids   Crassulaceae

Sedum kamtschaticum 'Variegatum'

Sedums are perhaps best known as succulent house plants, although there are numerous species hardy enough to grow outdoors. Many are subjects for specialist collectors and a few are notoriously invasive. All are characterised by fleshy foliage and small, rather star-like flowers in a wide range of colours. The limited selection given here is of those that I have found to be the most attractive and best behaved.

OBTAIN AS: seed or plants.
AFTER-CARE: usually none but the more straggly, trailing species should be trimmed back after flowering.
RECOMMENDED VARIETIES: *S. cauticolum* (trailing, flat heads

of pink-purple flowers); *S. ewersii* (trailing, rounded heads of pink-purple flowers); *S. floriferum* 'Weihenstephaner Gold' (golden yellow); *S. kamtschaticum* 'Variegatum' (yellow flowers, green leaves with cream margins); *S. rubrotinctum* 'Ruby Glow' (red flowers); *S. spathulifolium* 'Cape Blanco' (also called 'Capablanca'), yellow flowers, purple-green leaves with silver tinge), 'Purpureum' (yellow flowers, purple leaves); *S. spurium* 'Purple Carpet' (pink flowers, red-purple leaves).

Sempervivum spp. and hybrids   Houseleeks Crassulaceae

Sempervivum arachnoideum

Another genus of succulents, very closely related to *Sedum* but with quite characteristic fleshy rosettes of leaves from which upright flower spikes arise – although with many species this occurs infrequently and the main rosette dies thereafter, the plant being perpetuated by off-sets. It is indeed primarily for the foliage that most sempervivums are grown and some types are used for this purpose in carpet bedding schemes. Some species long known as *Sempervivum* have now been placed in the genus *Jovibarba* but I have listed one of these here for convenience.

OBTAIN AS: seed or plants.

AFTER-CARE: replant off-sets after flowering.

RECOMMENDED VARIETIES: *S. arachnoideum* (green leaves with red tips and cobweb-like covering of white hair); *S. (Jovibarba) sobolifera* (grey-green leaves with reddish tips); *S. tectorum* (dark-green or purple leaves).

Silene spp.   Campion   Caryophyllaceae

The campions are close relatives of the catchflies (*Lychnis*) and are also best known for their fairly tall meadow species, but they also have a few rather lovely dwarf alpines. They have characteristic pink or red flowers with rather deeply divided petals.

OBTAIN AS: seed or plants.

AFTER-CARE: cut back dead heads after flowering.

RECOMMENDED VARIETIES: *S. alpestris* (fairly compact, white flowers); *S. hookeri* (trailing, prostrate, pink or orange flowers); *S. schafta* (rose-red flowers).

Thymus spp. and hybrids   Labiatae

I have described a number of thymes in the account of herbs (p. 133) but there are many species in this useful genus that have little culinary merit but are worth growing for their aesthetic appeal. The span in habit among thymes is large and they range from almost rampant straggling forms to exceedingly neat and compact little clumps. The latter are much to be preferred.

OBTAIN AS: plants, few if any of the best forms come true from seed.

AFTER-CARE: trim very lightly after flowering.

RECOMMENDED VARIETIES: *T. citriodorus* 'Bertram Anderson' (often called 'Anderson's Gold') (vivid golden leaves, carpeting); *T.* 'Doone Valley' (green leaves with gold flecks, carpeting); *T. praecox* 'Porlock' (greyish foliage, dwarf bush); *T. serpyllum* 'Annie Hall' (green foliage, pink flowers); *coccineus* (red flowers, carpeting); 'Elfin' (green foliage, tiny clumps), *lanuginosus* (woolly foliage, carpeting).

Veronica spp. and hybrids   Speedwells Scrophulariaceae

Gardeners will be most familiar with the genus *Veronica* as the group which contains some of the most notorious garden weeds – the dreaded blue lawn syndrome is due to one of its species. But the tiny flowers are in fact quite delightful and fortunately there are some non-invasive little forms suitable for the alpine garden.

OBTAIN AS: seed or plants.

AFTER-CARE: none.

RECOMMENDED VARIETIES: *V. armena* (neat mounds, blue flowers); *V. pectinata* (blue or violet-blue flowers, carpeting, 'Rosea' is a red-flowered form but I believe that speedwells, like gentians, should always be blue); *V. prostrata* (carpeting, blue flowers, 'Loddon Blue' has deeper blue flowers and 'Mrs Holt' pink but 'Trehane' with deep violet-blue flowers is perhaps the loveliest).

Viola spp. and hybrids   Violaceae

I have described the familiar bedding pansies and violas elsewhere (p. 223) but there are numerous small-flowered perennial species well worth including in the alpine garden. Some can be rather invasive and spread or self-seed with somewhat carefree abandon; but who can bring themselves to uproot flowers with such pretty little faces? Many have the advantage of tolerating light shade.

OBTAIN AS: seed or plants.

AFTER-CARE: none.

RECOMMENDED VARIETIES: *V.* 'Ardross Gem' (dark-blue flowers with gold throats), *V. cornuta* 'Alba' (white), 'Boughton Blue' (light blue); *V. hederacea* (white or purple); 'Irish Molly' (gold and brown, not shade tolerant); *V. labradorica* (purple flowers, green/purple leaves, highly shade tolerant); *V. odorata* (sweet violet) (purple flowers, or white in the variety 'Alba', can be invasive so not to be grown in limited space); *V. septentrionalis* (violet or white, creeping).

Water and
water plants

MY OWN experience tells me that the gardener who has once had a
pool or other water feature in his or her garden is unlikely ever to be
without one again. The value of water in the garden is a hard one to define
but when you have appreciated it for yourself, you will know exactly what
I mean. Visually, it has a very special quality that catches the light and catches
the eye. Audibly it is uplifting too, the merest, gentlest sound of water
movement being sufficient to bring life to any garden landscape. And it has
the indefinable appeal that can only be summarised crudely by that bland
word 'interest'. Once again, anyone who has ever sat by a pool and watched
the constantly changing pattern of life within will know precisely what I have
in mind. Time seems to fly by, for a good, well-planned pool contains not
only plants, fish and snails but also myriads of other creatures, attracted as
magnetically to the presence of the water as we are. Insect life abounds
below, on and above the water surface and can range from beetles, pond
skaters and caddis larvae to, if you are lucky, the stunningly beautiful large
dragonflies. Amphibians will almost inevitably arrive as if by magic – frogs,

toads and, if you are very fortunate, newts will lay their spawn there. With the contamination of farm ponds and other waterways so widespread, I now much prefer to leave all of the spawn in my own pool (or share it with less fortunate neighbours) rather than transfer it elsewhere as once I did. Bird life too will seek out the water of your pool, especially if you can keep a small area free from ice in the winter (see below) – although one always hopes that the local heron population will not discover your stock of fresh fish.

But before describing anything further on the subject of water gardening, one point must be made. Garden pools and young children should not co-exist. A child can drown in very few centimetres of water and simply to stay your impatience for aquatic horticulture for a few years is a small price to pay to avert possible tragedy. If your garden already has a pool, you have two main options – either to cover the whole with a robust net which will be functionally effective although aesthetically dreadful, or to fill in the pool and convert the area to some other purpose – a bog garden perhaps.

The forms that your water garden can take are varied. A pool can be small or large, formal or semi-natural. Water movement can be limited to a fountain or small waterfall or as ambitious as an artificial stream. And indeed, the water feature can just as readily be a bog garden with no open water at all. But there are certain planning considerations that apply to them all.

If you are one of the fortunate few who has a natural watercourse running through your garden, there may be restrictions imposed by your local water authority concerning the extent to which you can divert its course, abstract any of the water or remove or add to the plant life of the banks. Individual situations vary, so do check first before you embark on any changes to be sure that you remain on the right side of the regulations.

Pools should be positioned on level ground, away from shade and, most importantly, away from deciduous trees. For whilst any pool will catch windfall leaves in the autumn, the fewer of these that you have to pull out the better, for any left in the water over the winter will sink, decay, use up oxygen and bring about the build up of gases poisonous to plant and fish life. It is when pools freeze in winter that the greatest harm to fish life ensues because the gases then have little chance to escape. Moreover, the proximity of trees means tree roots that can undermine a pool and cause disturbance to the structure and consequent leaks.

Perhaps the most important single requirement for the correct functioning of a pool is sunlight – almost no pool plants are shade tolerant, and water lilies, the most important of all water plants, really need six or more hours of direct sunlight each day. This then is a further reason to position your pool away from trees or, indeed, from any other shelter. But aesthetically, the major decision at this stage relates to the choice between a formal and a not so formal structure. By a formal pool, I mean one with hard edges of stone or concrete slabs, brick or similar material. Such a pool sits most appealingly within an overall area of similar structure such as a patio or a small courtyard. An informal or semi-natural pool has soft edges – the water margin grades gradually into a zone of soil, mud or possibly of irregular stones or rocks, much as is found with a natural pool. Thus plants grow right up to the water's edge. Such a feature certainly should be placed in appropriate surroundings – close to a rock garden or other informally planted area.

Constructing a pool is no longer the major piece of civil engineering that once it was. Whilst the need to dig a hole of appropriate size remains, the traditional ways of sealing the base with puddled clay or even, more recently,

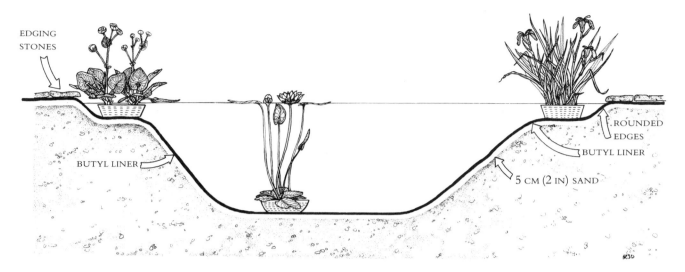

EDGING
STONES

BUTYL LINER

ROUNDED
EDGES

BUTYL LINER

5 CM (2 IN) SAND

Cross section through a garden pool showing the important constructional features. The plastic liner is bedded on sand, the hole has been excavated to form ledges of different depth, the plants have been planted in special baskets and care has been taken to place different species in the appropriate depth of water.

with concrete, have now gone. The modern pool is lined with plastic. Whilst it is possible to purchase ready-shaped (or 'pre-formed') rigid liners, much the most versatile method is with a sheet of butyl rubber. Excavate the hole for your pool, ensuring that you leave rounded corners and sloping sides – and leave some shelves or ledges for shallower planting. Remove any stones from the base and then add a layer of fine sand, about 2 cm (¾ in) thick on which the rubber will be bedded. Drape the sheeting over the hole and carefully fill in with sand around the sides, under the sheet. Leave a generous overlap of sheeting at the edges – of twice as much width as the pool is deep – and anchor this with stones. Then carefully fill the pool with water (the weight of the water will stretch the rubber) and cover the edges with your chosen edging material – slabs, rocks or soil.

Allow a minimum of two weeks for the pool to settle down before you introduce first plants and then, about three weeks later still, fish and snails. The time intervals between setting up the pool and planting will inevitably be longer if you build it in autumn, for it is unwise to introduce plants to any pool before the beginning of May. Apart from the few floating species, water plants should be planted in soil in proprietary planting baskets lined with coarse plastic or nylon mesh to prevent the soil from spilling out. Never use soil containing organic matter or fertiliser (specially prepared sachets of slow release aquatic plant fertiliser are, however, perfectly safe) – vegetable garden soil is, for these reasons, best avoided. Always place a layer of coarse gravel over the soil in the planting basket as fish will inevitably let their curiosity get the better of them and stir it up. Be sure to position the planted basket at the appropriate depth for each plant species (details are given within the individual descriptions).

Pool maintenance is relatively easy, and although gardeners often ask me how frequently their pools should be cleaned out, the general answer is never. Provided plants and fish are thriving, the pool will largely look after itself. There are certain routine tasks that will help it nonetheless. Feed the fish with a proprietary fish food every week during the summer and occasionally during mild weather in winter. Pull out excessive growths of green cotton-wool-like blanket weed in the summer; this algal growth is impossible to avoid, but resist the temptation to kill it with chemicals for these merely result in masses of dead blanket weed that then begin to decompose. The surface spread of the tiny flowering plant duckweed is also impossible to stop, and whilst it too can be pulled out, it will continue to spread very rapidly over the surface where its presence stops light from entering the pool. It is very important, therefore, to check all new plant purchases carefully for any duckweed contamination and so prevent its initial introduction.

Pests and diseases do not normally cause problems in pools, although water lilies and water irises especially can become infested with aphids. These should merely be hosed away, however, no chemical pesticides should be used near any pool or water garden. Dead leaves and dead flower heads should be cut away as necessary – and as feasible; do not be tempted to reach too far over the water in the cause of dead heading.

Ice must not be allowed to form a complete cover to the pool in winter, for fish beneath it will asphyxiate. In relatively severe frost, a continuously running fountain will prevent total ice cover, but in really hard conditions, there is no substitute for a small pool heater. Modern ones operate through a mains transformer and so only a low voltage cable need be laid through the garden. Modern fountain pumps too work from similarly transformed voltage (although not through the same transformer as the pool heater) and with magnetic couplings and other sealing devices, submersible models are perfectly safe. Be sure to select a fountain appropriate to the size of your pool, however. Not only does a large fountain in a small pool look ridiculous, but it can lead to over-cooling of the water, to the detriment of both plants and fish. The larger fountain pumps have adaptors to enable them to form a waterfall rather than a fountain and also to provide the continuously circulating water of an artificial stream. Such a stream may be constructed very readily using butyl rubber liner in much the same manner as it is used for a pool.

A bog garden is simply an area where plants are grown in constantly wet soil. Such a feature can form the marginal zone of a pool or be an entity in itself. In the latter case, it may be constructed in a similar manner to a pool, using butyl rubber, except that the whole is filled with a mixture of soil and water instead of water alone. But remember that if there is no natural water source nearby, an artificial bog garden will need constantly to be topped up with water during the summer – no easy matter if you live in an area of low rainfall where hosepipe bans are to be expected.

In the following listing, I have divided plants into oxygenators (those types that grow submerged and have the essential function of supplying oxygen to the pool), marginal plants (those that grow in damp soil at the edge of a pool or in a bog garden), floating plants, whose roots dangle freely in the water, and true water plants that are rooted in soil at the bottom of the pool in water of varying depths but whose leaves and/or flowers rise to the surface. In suggesting the sizes of pool suitable for each species, I have considered a large pool to measure at least 4.25 × 3 m (14 × 10 ft) with a depth of at least 55 cm (22 in), a medium pool to be approximately 3 × 1.75 m (10 × 6 ft), depth 45 cm (18 in) and a small pool to be approximately 1.75 × 1.25 m (6 × 4 ft), depth 30 cm (12 in).

With the exception of a few marginal species, it is not practicable to raise water plants from seed and so, unless I have stated otherwise, I advise you to buy plants from a garden centre or specialist aquatic plant nursery. Sadly, expertise in water gardening is rather thinly spread among the horticultural trade and to obtain the best selection of varieties, a specialist supplier is essential. Without exception, lifting and division should always be performed in late spring or early summer; after autumn disturbance, water plants usually have insufficient time to re-establish before the falling water temperature in autumn brings growth to a halt for the season. Dead leaves should be pulled or cut away in autumn, however, to prevent them falling to the bottom of the pool and fouling the water.

Arrowhead   *Sagittaria sagittifolia*
Alismataceae [Marginal]

Few plants have more descriptive names than the arrowheads, whose vivid green aerial leaves are very much in the form of barbed arrow heads. They reach 45–50 cm (18–20 in) above water, although strap-like submerged leaves and oval floating leaves form also. In summer, the plants bear tall angular spikes of white flowers with pronounced purple and black centres.
POOL SIZE: medium or large.
PREFERRED WATER DEPTH: margin to 25 cm (10 in).
RECOMMENDED VARIETIES: the normal species is most usually seen, although there is an attractive double-flowered form 'Flore Pleno'.

Bog arum   *Calla palustris*   Araceae [Marginal]

This is a typical aroid with rounded, dark-green shiny leaves and small spikes of orange flowers surrounded by a white spathe in summer. Sometimes masses of red fruits form towards the end of the season, a process facilitated by snail pollination.
POOL SIZE: small to large.
PREFERRED WATER DEPTH: margin to 10 cm (4 in).
RECOMMENDED VARIETIES: normal species only is available.

Bogbean   *Menyanthes trifoliata*
Menyanthaceae [Marginal]

A spreading, almost scrambling but none too invasive plant reaching about 25 cm (10 in) with large, three-lobed, broad-bean-like leaves and small white, star-like flowers in spring. Bogbeans, despite their unattractive name, are very good plants for concealing the margins of the pool.
POOL SIZE: medium or large.
PREFERRED WATER DEPTH: 5–10 cm (2–4 in).
RECOMMENDED VARIETIES: normal species only is available.

Bog iris   *Iris* spp.   Iridaceae [Marginal]

The relatively few species and varieties of rhizome-forming aquatic iris are as useful in the water garden as their dry-land relatives are in other places. All are fairly tall growing (reaching between 75 cm and 1 m/30 and 39 in) and with characteristic iris flowers in a wide range of colours. The relatively short flowering season is nonetheless no real disadvantage, for the fresh green sword-like leaves add an attractive dimension to pool-edge plantings from spring right through to autumn. The three principal species are *I. kaempferi*, which has large flowers with widespread wing-like petals and a midrib on the leaves, *I. laevigata*, which has no marked leaf midrib but is otherwise

Iris kaempferi 'Hokkaido'

similar to *I. kaempferi*, and *I. pseudacorus*.
POOL SIZE: small to large (*I. pseudacorus* large only).
PREFERRED WATER DEPTH: margin to 10 cm (4 in).
RECOMMENDED VARIETIES: **Forms of *I. kaempferi*** (now usually called *I. ensata*): the normal species and varieties such as 'Hokkaido' have lilac-blue flowers with golden throats but other notable variants that are fairly widely available are 'Alba' (white), 'Higo' (abnormally large flowers) and 'Variegata' (cream and green leaf stripes). **Forms of *I. laevigata*:** the normal species is almost identical to *I. kaempferi* but rather more varieties of this species are commonly found, among which some of the best are 'Alba' (white), 'Atropurpurea' (deep violet), 'Rose Queen' (a hybrid with *I. kaempferi* – rose pink), 'Snowdrift' (white with yellow bases to the petals) and 'Variegata' (pale-blue flowers, cream and green leaf stripes and a characteristic fan formation to the foliage). **Forms of *I. pseudacorus*:** the normal species is the one almost invariably seen, with rich golden-yellow flowers, but it is well worth looking for the form *bastardii* (pale cream) and the varieties 'Golden Queen' (larger leaves and flowers) and 'Variegata' (cream and green leaf stripes).

Brooklime *Veronica beccabunga*
Scrophulariaceae [Marginal]

A native British species, closely related to the many familiar veronica weeds, but rather more disciplined in its behaviour, although it will require cutting back and thinning. It has slightly succulent creeping stems and, unusually for water plants, is almost evergreen. The flowers are neat, small, blue and reminiscent of forget-me-nots.

POOL SIZE: Small to large.

PREFERRED WATER DEPTH: margin to 5 cm (2 in).

RECOMMENDED VARIETIES: normal species only is available.

Canadian pondweed *Elodea canadensis*
Hydrocharidaceae [Oxygenator]

The most familiar and best known oxygenating plant, well established in natural waterways in Europe. It has thin, narrow leaves in dense whorls around markedly brittle stems. Although said to be invasive and rampant, it can readily be kept in check simply by pulling out handfuls every season. It is not, however, my preferred choice as an oxygenator; as much as anything because in my experience it seems to provide an ideal support for the growth of blanket weed.

POOL SIZE: small to large.

RECOMMENDED VARIETIES: normal species only is available. The naming of this and related plants by suppliers may be confusing, however. The correct name for *Elodea canadensis* is now *Anacharis canadensis* but a related species with more curled leaves is sometimes offered, either as *E. crispa* or as *Lagerosiphon major*. Yet a third species, *E. densa*, is sometimes seen, also with an alternative name, *Egeria densa*.

Cardinal flower *Lobelia cardinalis*
Campanulaceae [Marginal]

Although not reliably hardy other than in mild areas, this is a striking plant (up to 1.5 m (5 ft) tall in good conditions), well worth growing in terracotta pots at the pool's edge and taking indoors in winter, for it is uniquely lovely. It has tall spikes of deep-red flowers, rather reminiscent of salvias (but with much more class) and shiny green leaves, although related hybrids have reddish foliage.

POOL SIZE: small to large.

PREFERRED WATER DEPTH: margin to 10 cm (4 in).

RECOMMENDED VARIETIES: the normal species is widely available but a hybrid called 'Queen Victoria' is lovelier, having rich red-purple leaves.

Fairy fern *Azolla caroliniana* Azollaceae [Floating]

Azollas look like moss or even surface scum but in fact are a species of fern. They are extremely pretty with their bright-green irregular fronds which turn most attractive shades of red in autumn. But they are frightfully invasive and, once established in a pool, will be there for the duration. Nonetheless, excessive growth may easily be removed by netting, and on balance, it is a plant that I would willingly have in a medium-sized pool – in a small one, they too rapidly take over; in a very large one, you will be unable to reach far enough to net them.

Azolla caroliniana (Fairy fern)

POOL SIZE: medium.

AFTER-CARE: keep a few plants indoors in shallow dishes of water over the winter to ensure their survival – the survival 'buds' which fall to the bottom of the pool in autumn may be killed in a very hard winter.

RECOMMENDED VARIETIES: normal species only is available.

Frogbit *Hydrocharis morsus-ranae*
Hydrocharitaceae [Floating]

This plant is best likened to a midget water-lily with thin leaves barely 2 cm (¾ in) in diameter. It produces tiny white, star-like flowers with yellow centres and should be kept in check much like azolla, although it normally only becomes troublesome in very shallow water.

POOL SIZE: small to large.

AFTER-CARE: keep a few plants indoors in shallow dishes of water over the winter to ensure their survival – the survival 'buds' which fall to the bottom of the pool in autumn may be killed in a very hard winter.

RECOMMENDED VARIETIES: normal species only is available.

Golden club *Orontium aquaticum* Araceae [Marginal]

I am very fond of this rather curious member of the arum family and cannot understand why it is not grown more widely. It has rather typically aroid, large, dark-green, shiny foliage, although in deep water it forms very large, paler green, floating leaves also. The flowers are fascinating – rather like very slender white candles with golden tips.

POOL SIZE: small to large.

PREFERRED WATER DEPTH: margin to 30 cm (12 in).

RECOMMENDED VARIETIES: normal species only available.

Hornwort   *Ceratophyllum demersum*   Ceratophyllaceae [Oxygenator]

Hornwort is not only the most attractive but, I think, almost the best oxygenating plant. Its stems bear masses of whorls of rather brittle, horny leaves which provide a huge surface area for gas release. It is also much appreciated as shelter by all forms of sub-aquatic life.

POOL SIZE: small to large.

RECOMMENDED VARIETIES: normal species only is available.

Marsh marigold, kingcup   *Caltha palustris*   Ranunculaceae [Marginal]

One of the most familiar and best loved of all marginal plants, the marsh marigold is like a giant form of celandine with large, shiny, kidney-shaped leaves reaching 30 cm (12 in) in diameter, and lovely cup-shaped flowers in spring.

POOL SIZE: medium to large.

PREFERRED WATER DEPTH: margin to 8 cm (3 in).

RECOMMENDED VARIETIES: the normal species is widely available but two interesting forms are 'Plena' (sometimes called 'Flore Pleno') with double flowers and 'Alba' which is white.

Pickerel weed   *Pontederia cordata*   Pontederiaceae [Marginal]

This is an elegant species with elongated heart-shaped leaves on rounded 60 cm (24 in) tall stems with 15 cm (6 in) long spikes of very soft blue flowers, rather like those of a soft, blue plantain. The flowers are especially useful in lasting well into the autumn.

POOL SIZE: medium to large.

PREFERRED WATER DEPTH: margin to 10 cm (4 in).

RECOMMENDED VARIETIES: normal species only is available.

Skunk cabbage   *Lysichitum* spp.   Araceae [Marginal]

An appalling name for some of the most attractive of the aroids for pool-side planting. They are quite typical of the family in their erect, hare's-ear-like spathe surrounding a club-shaped spike of minute flowers but the two species are particularly large and dramatic with leaves up to 1 m (39 in) in length, an unusual size indeed for a hardy aroid of any sort.

POOL SIZE: medium to large.

PREFERRED WATER DEPTH: margin to 5 cm (2 in).

RECOMMENDED VARIETIES: *L. americanum* (deep-yellow spathe); *L. camschatcense* (white spathes).

Sweet flag   *Acorus calamus*   Araceae [Marginal]

Superficially this plant resembles a large iris but the resemblance stops with the foliage, for the flowers betray its relationship to arums. They are small, green-brown and produced in spikes towards the tops of the stems. It is a useful plant for the more wild style of water garden but has little place in smaller, more formal plantings.

POOL SIZE: medium to large.

PREFERRED WATER DEPTH: margin to 15 cm (6 in).

RECOMMENDED VARIETIES: the normal species is most commonly seen but 'Variegatus' has cream and white leaf stripes.

Umbrella sedge   *Cyperus involucratus*   Cyperaceae [Marginal]

Although barely hardy in cooler areas (and often grown in fact as a house plant), this most attractive sedge is well worth trying. For in its form it is rather unusual and different from other marginal plants, having 1 m (39 in) tall stems topped with a fan-like array of spikelets within which the greenish flowers are borne.

POOL SIZE: small to large.

PREFERRED WATER DEPTH: margin to 15 cm (6 in).

RECOMMENDED VARIETIES: normal species only is available.

Water forget-me-not   *Myosotis palustris*   Boraginaceae [Marginal]

This plant is just as its name suggests, a forget-me-not to grow by the water's edge. It is very easy to establish and although it spreads quickly and readily, it seldom becomes mischievous.

POOL SIZE: small to large.

PREFERRED WATER DEPTH: margin to 8 cm (3 in).

RECOMMENDED VARIETIES: normal species only is available.

Water hawthorn   *Aponogeton distachyum*   Aponogetonaceae [Water plant]

A lovely and rather choice species with ovoid to strap-like floating leaves and forked spikes of perfumed waxy white flowers with black anthers – a most striking sight in summer.

POOL SIZE: large.

PREFERRED WATER DEPTH: 15–60 cm (6–24 in) (young plants should only be planted in shallow water).

RECOMMENDED VARIETIES: normal species only is available.

Water lily   *Nymphaea* spp. and hybrids   Nymphaeaceae [Water plant]

Unquestionably, the water lily is the queen of the garden pool. All have the same recognisable star-shaped flower but variety comes with colour (yellow, white, red, pink and shades between), with degree of doubling, hardiness, perfume and, most importantly, with vigour and tolerance of particular water depths. Sadly, most garden centres stock a pitifully small range of water lilies so I would urge you to buy from specialist suppliers. After all, the average-sized garden pool is only likely to contain two or three plants; it is important to have the right ones.

POOL SIZE: small to large, depending on variety.

PREFERRED WATER DEPTH: 10 cm to 1.2 m (4 in to 4 ft), depending on variety.

RECOMMENDED VARIETIES: **Vigorous** (water depth 30 cm to 1.2 m (1 to 4 ft); surface spread up to 1.5 m/5 ft): *N. alba* (white, yellow stamens), 'Colossea' (pale pink, yellow stamens, fragrant), 'Conqueror' (red with white flecks, yellow stamens), 'Colonel A. Welch' (yellow, yellow stamens). **Moderately vigorous** (water depth 20–60 cm (8–24 in); surface spread up to 1 m/39 in): 'Marliacea Albida' (white with pink tinge, yellow stamens), 'Marliacea Carnea' (white with pink tinge, yellow stamens), 'Escarboucle' (rich flame red, red stamens with gold tips, fragrant), 'Marliacea Chromatella' (yellow, golden-yellow stamens). **Small** (water depth 15–45 cm (6–18 in), surface spread up to 60 cm/24 in): 'Odorata Alba' (white, golden-yellow stamens, fragrant), 'Pink Opal' (pink, yellow stamens), 'James Brydon' (deep pink-red, orange stamens with gold tips, fragrant), 'Sunrise' (golden-yellow, golden-yellow stamens, fragrant). **Tiny** (water depth 10–30 cm (4–12 in), surface spread up to 30 cm/12 in): 'Pygmaea Alba' (white, golden-yellow stamens), 'Laydekeri Rosea' (deep rose pink, golden stamens, fragrant), 'Ellisiana' (red, yellow stamens), 'Pygmaea Helvola' (yellow, orange stamens).

Water milfoil *Myriophyllum verticillatum*
Haloragidaceae [Oxygenator]

Jointly with hornwort, this is my choice for the best oxygenating plant. It bears whorls of slightly flattened vivid-green leaves which have a very large surface area. Like hornwort, milfoil is also a very valuable plant in offering shelter and egg-laying sites for fish and other pool animals.

POOL SIZE: small to large.

RECOMMENDED VARIETIES: normal species only is available.

Water mint *Mentha aquatica* Labiatae [Marginal]

This plant has exactly the characteristics of other mints – it has beautifully perfumed foliage, flowers that attract bees and other insects, and it is very invasive. It is best planted in a solid container such as a large plastic pot rather than a normal planting basket therefore.

POOL SIZE: small to large.

PREFERRED WATER DEPTH: margin to 5 cm (2 in).

RECOMMENDED VARIETIES: normal species only is available.

Water plantain *Alisma plantago-aquatica*
Alismataceae [Marginal]

The common name for this plant derives from its plantain-like foliage that protrudes well clear of the water surface. Its flowers

are certainly very different, however – superficially more like those of gypsophila, on 1 m (39 in) tall, rather straggly stems.

POOL SIZE: medium to large.

PREFERRED WATER DEPTH: margin to 15 cm (6 in).

AFTER-CARE: remove flower heads before seed is shed to limit the otherwise invasive progression.

RECOMMENDED VARIETIES: normal species only is available.

Water soldier *Stratiotes aloides*
Hydrocharitaceae [Floating plant]

Stratiotes aloides (water soldier)

The most striking of the hardy floating plants, looking very much like the leafy tops of pineapples, with rosettes of spiny foliage. The plant floats and sinks at regular intervals during the year – in spring it lies just below the surface, in summer it rises up to display small white flowers. Thereafter it sinks and produces side shoots with large buds. The whole then rises once more, the shoots break away and grow into new plants which then, believe it or not, sink again until the spring.

POOL SIZE: medium to large.

RECOMMENDED VARIETIES: normal species only is available.

Water violet *Hottonia palustris*
Primulaceae [Water plant]

A real misnomer is this one, for the water violet is a member of the primula family, although you rarely see enough of it to know. For much of the year, it is wholly submerged, its finely divided fern-like leaves visible only through clear water where their large surface area provides an excellent oxygen supply. But its presence is revealed by spikes of white or pale-mauve flowers which are thrust above the surface during the summer.

POOL SIZE: medium to large.

PREFERRED WATER DEPTH: 10–45 cm (4–18 in).

RECOMMENDED VARIETIES: normal species only is available.

INDEX

General subjects such as fertilisers, pests and diseases have been indexed where they are discussed in the main text but not where they are mentioned in descriptions of individual plants. For advice on these subjects as they affect a particular plant, the reader should consult the detailed description of it as well as the index.

Acacia dealbata, silver wattle, mimosa, 163
Acaena, 238
Acanthus mollis, bear's breeches, 202
Acer, maples, 163
Achillea, 202
acidity, of soil, 58–9
aconite, winter, *see Eranthis hyemalis*
Aconitum, monkshood, 202–3
Acorus calamus, see sweet flag
Acroclinium, 219
Actinidia kolomikta, 183
Adiantum, maidenhair ferns, 238
African lilies, *see Agapanthus*
African marigolds, 221–2
Agapanthus, African lilies, 229
Ageratum, floss flower, 94, 216
Akebia quinata, 183
Alchemilla mollis, lady's mantle, 203
Alisma plantago-aquatica, see water plantain
alkalinity, of soil, 58–60, 64
Allium, ornamental onions, 229
alpine aster, 239
alpine catchfly, *Lychnis alpina*, 241–2
alpine plants, 236–44
alpine soapwort, *see Saponaria ocymoides*
Alstroemeria, 103
Althaea officinalis, hollyhock, 203
Alyssum, *Lobularia maritima*, 93, 216; *Alyssum saxatile*, 238
Amelanchier lamarckii, snowy mespil, 163
Androsace, 238
Anemone, anemones, 229; *A. hybrida*, 203
annuals, 50, 105, 215–26; in children's gardens, 28; half-hardy, seed sowing, 93–8; hardy, seed sowing, 99–101
Antennaria dioica, cat's ears, 238
anthocyanins, 16
Antirrhinum, snapdragon, 216
apical dominance, 70
Aponogeton distachyum, see water hawthorn
apple, 142, 143–4; crab, 166
apricot, 144–5
Aquilegia, columbine, 203–4, 238–9
archways, 190
Aristolochia macrophylla, Dutchman's pipe, 183
Armeria, 239
arrowhead, *Sagittaria sagittifolia*, 249
Artemisia, wormwooods, 204, 239

artichoke, *see* globe artichoke; Jerusalem artichoke
arum lily, *Arum italicum*, *Zantedeschia aethiopica*, 229, 235
asparagus, 115
Asplenium trichomanes, maidenhair spleenwort fern, 239
Aster, 204, 216; alpine, 239; *see also Callistephus chinensis*
Astilbe, 204
Astrantia, 204
aubergine, 96, 115
Aubrieta, 239
Aucuba japonica, spotted laurel, 170
Azolla caroliniana, see fairy fern

baby's breath, *see Gypsophila*
bacteria, 75
barbecues, 11
bark: as compost or mulch, 45, 90; for paths and surfacing, 25; for winter colour, 18
barrels, *see* tubs and barrels
basil, 130
bay, 131
beans: seeds of, 96, 102, 103; *see also* broad bean; French bean; runner bean
bear's breeches, *see Acanthus mollis*
bedding plants, 50, 105, 215–26
beds and borders, 14; carpet bedding, 215; formal bedding, 17; herbaceous border, 17–18, 201; mixed border, 201; peat bed, 237
bee balm, *see* bergamot
beech, 155, 156
beetroot, 115
Begonia, begonias, 216–17; seeds, 96, 103
bell flowers, *see Campanula*
Bells of Ireland, *Molucella laevis*, 217
Berberis, 156–7, 170
bergamot, bee balm, Oswego tea, 134
Bergenia, elephant's era, 204
Betula, birches, 163–4
biennials, 99, 215
biological control, 80, 87
birches, *see Betula*
black-eyed Susan, *see Rudbeckia*, *Thunbergia*
blackberry, 138, 139–40
blackcurrants, 140
blackthorn, 157
blood, fish and bone, 63, 64, 65, 114, 138, 142, 156, 162, 202
bluebell, *Endymion*, *Hyacinthoides*, 228, 231
blueberry, 140
bog arum, *Calla palustris*, 249
bog gardens, 248
bog iris, 249
bogbean, *Menyanthes trifoliata*, 249
bonemeal, 64, 65
borage, 134
borders, *see* beds and borders
boundaries, 19–21, 154; *see also* hedges
box, 157

Brachycome iberidifolia, Swan River daisy, 217
brambles, flowering, *see Rubus*
brassicas, 99, 103, 105; *see also* individual species
bricks, for paths and surfacing, 23
broad bean, 115–16
broccoli, 116
brooklime, *Veronica beccabunga*, 250
brooms, *see Cytisus*; *Genista*
Brussels sprouts, 116
Buddleia, 170
bugbane, *see Cimicifuga*
bulbils, 89
Bulbocodium vernum, red crocus, 229
bulbs, bulbous plants, 76, 227–35
busy lizzie, *see Impatiens*
butterflies, 41
butterfly bush, *see Buddleia*
butterfly flower, *see Schizanthus*

cabbage, 114, 116–17
Calamintha, 204
Calendula officinalis, pot marigold, 134, 217, 221–2; African and French marigolds, 221–2
Californian poppy, *see Eschscholzia*
Calla palustris, see bog arum
Callistephus chinensis, 216
Calluna vulgaris, heather, 170
Caltha palustris, see marsh marigold
Camellia, 170–1
camomile, 134, 149
Campanula, bell flowers, 204–5, 239; *C. isophylla*, 217
campion, *see Silene*
Campsis radicans, trumpet vine, 183
Canadian pondweed, *Elodea canadensis*, 250
Canary creeper, *see Tropaeolum*
candytuft, *Iberis*, 217–18
canna, 103
capillary matting, 34
capsicum, sweet papper, 117
Caragana arborescens, pea tree, 164
cardinal flower, *Lobelia cardinalis*, 250
Cardiocrinum giganteum, giant lily, 230
carnations, *see Dianthus*
carotenoids, 16
carrot, 99, 117
Carson, Rachel, 39
Cassiope, 239–40
Catalpa bignonioides, Indian bean tree, 164
catchfly, *see Lychnis*
caterpillars, 82, 87
catmint, *see Nepeta*
cat's ears, *see Antennaria dioica*
cauliflower, 93, 96, 101, 117–18
Ceanothus, 171
celeriac, turnip-rooted celery, 118
celery, 118
Centaurea cyanus, see cornflower
Centranthus ruber, valerian, 205

Ceratophyllum demersum, see hornwort
Ceratostigma, 171
Cercis siliquastrum, Judas tree, 164
Chaenomeles, ornamental quince, 171
chain saws, 71
Cheiranthus, see wallflowers
cherry, 145; ornamental, 166–7
chervil, 131
children: gardening by, 27–9; pool danger, 291, 246
Chilean bell flower, *see Lapageria rosea*
Chinese cabbage, 117
Chinese gooseberry, *see* kiwi fruit
Chinese rain tree, *see Koelreuteria paniculata*
Chionodoxa, glory of the snow, 230
chives, 131
Choisya ternata, Mexican orange blossom, 171
Christmas rose (*Helleborus niger*), 208
Chrysanthemum, 205, 218
Cimicifuga, bugbane, 205
cinquefoils, shrubby, *see Potentilla*
Clarkia, 218
clay, 57
Clematis, 108, 182, 184, 205
climbing plants, 11, 182–8; fruit, 147; pests and diseases, 182; roses, 195–6; supports for, 182–3, 189–91
cloches, 100, 115
clubroot, 105
Cobaea scandens, cup and saucer vine, 184
cobbles, for paths and surfacing, 24
cobnuts, 145
Colchicum, naked ladies, meadow saffron, 230
cold frames, 97–8
colours, colour combinations, 15–18
columbine, *see Aquilegia*
compost, 44–8; compost heap/bin, 45–7, 92; for containers, 37–8, 65; for cuttings, 107; for half-hardy annuals, 94, 96; shredder, 56; weight of, 35
concrete paving, 23
cone flower, *see Rudbeckia*
conifers, dwarf, 171–2
containers, 35–8, 50, 65
coriander, 131
corms, 227; *see also* bulbs
cornflower, *Centaurea cyanus*, 218
Cornus, dogwoods, 164
Corydalis, 230
Cosmos, 218
Cotinus coggygria, smoke bush, 172
Cotoneaster, 157, 172
cotton lavender, 135
couch grass, 89, 92, 149–50
courgette, 119
crab apple, *Malus*, 166
cranesbills, *see Geranium*
Crataegus, thorns, 164; *see also* blackthorn; hawthorn
Crinum powellii, 230

253

SELECT BIBLIOGRAPHY

This brief list is of a few encyclopaedic works which will amplify, if need be, any parts of this book that especially attract your interest. The publication dates are those of the first editions although some have been reprinted at least once.

BRICKELL, C. (editor), *The Royal Horticultural Society Gardeners' Encyclopedia of Plants and Flowers*, Dorling Kindersley, 1989.

BROOKES, J., *The New Small Garden Book*, Dorling Kindersley, 1989.

BUCZACKI, S. T., *Understanding your garden*, C.U.P., 1990.

Food from your garden, Reader's Digest, 1977.

BUCZACKI, S. T., & HARRIS, K. M., *Collins Guide to the Pests, Diseases and Disorders of Garden Plants*, Collins, 1981.

HAMILTON, G., *Successful Organic Gardening*, Dorling Kindersley, 1987.

Hillier's Manual of Trees and Shrubs, David & Charles, 1972.

LORD, T. (editor), *The Plant Finder*, Headmain, annual publication.

Reader's Digest Guide to Creative Gardening, Reader's Digest, 1984.